AF345295

Publication, Volume 82

PUBLICATIONS

OF THE

NAVY RECORDS SOCIETY

Vol. LXXXII

CAPTAIN BOTELER'S RECOLLECTIONS

RECOLLECTIONS OF
MY SEA LIFE
FROM 1808 TO 1830

BY

CAPTAIN JOHN HARVEY BOTELER, R.N.

EDITED BY

DAVID BONNER-SMITH

PRINTED FOR THE NAVY RECORDS SOCIETY
MDCCCCXLII

CONTENTS

INTRODUCTION

CAPTAIN JOHN HARVEY BOTELER, R.N., died at Grand Parade, St Leonards-on-Sea, on April 19th, 1885, in his ninetieth year (*The Times*, April 22nd, 1885).

He published his Recollections in 1883, for private circulation. For the purpose of the present reprint, the narrative has been divided into chapters and chapter headings have been introduced. So much as is appropriate of Captain Boteler's title page has been retained ; the original reads :

> Recollections / of / my Sea Life. / By / Captain John Harvey Boteler, R.N. / From 1808 to 1830. / For private circulation. / London : / Diprose and Bateman, Sheffield Street, / Lincoln's Inn Fields. / 1883.

The family of Boteler of Eastry is set out in Burke's *Landed Gentry*, and other information is given in *Liber Estriae ; or Memorials of the Royal Ville and Parish of Eastry, in the County of Kent*, by the Rev. William Francis Shaw, Vicar of Eastry (London, 1870). In view of Captain Boteler's own references to his family, it will be useful to state here that his father was Mr William Boteler, F.S.A., of Brook Street in Eastry, Sandwich, Kent. Mr William Boteler, who died on September 4th, 1818, was twice married. ' We were a very extensive family, nineteen ', writes Captain Boteler. Not all of them concern us, and it is only necessary to say that, by his first wife, Mr Boteler had one son, William Fuller Boteler, Q.C., who was of sufficient eminence to be accorded a place in the *Dictionary of National Biography*.

Mr Boteler's second wife, whom he married on March 15th, 1785, was Mary, daughter of Captain John Harvey, R.N., who had purchased Harnden House, Eastry, in 1784. She died on October 24th, 1853, aged eighty-nine. Of their family, six sons and five daughters survived childhood. The sons were

(2) Lieutenant-Colonel Richard Boteler, R.E., who was lost in H.M. Packet *Calypso* in 1833 whilst on passage to England from Halifax, N.S.

(3) Captain Henry Boteler, R.N., who died August 22nd, 1861. He was born February 15th, 1793; and obtained the rank of Lieutenant September 18th, 1812, Commander August 12th, 1819, and Captain April 1st, 1856.

(4) Captain John Harvey Boteler, R.N., author of these Recollections. He was born February 11th, 1796; and obtained the rank of Lieutenant September 19th, 1815, Commander September 14th, 1830, and Captain April 1st, 1856.

(5) Commander Thomas Boteler, R.N., who died in command of H.M.S. *Hecla* on November 28th, 1829, whilst surveying the West Coast of Africa. He was born May 1st, 1797; and obtained the rank of Lieutenant October 5th, 1816, and Commander September 30th, 1826.

(6) Rev. Edward Boteler, Vicar of St Clement, Sandwich.

(7) Captain Robert Boteler, R.E.

Of the daughters, Eliza married on July 5th, 1819, the Rev. C. J. Burton, Vicar of Lydd; and Julia married on January 18th, 1820, the Rev. Thomas Stephen Hodges, Vicar of Little Waltham, Essex.

John Harvey Boteler was the first son born to the Botelers after the battle of ' The Glorious First of June ', at which Mrs Boteler's father, Captain John Harvey, commanded the *Brunswick* and died of wounds. Captain Harvey's brother Henry commanded the *Ramillies* in the same battle, and was promoted Rear Admiral July 4th, 1794; Admiral Sir Henry Harvey, K.B., died in 1810, and was the father of Vice Admiral Sir Thomas Harvey, K.C.B. (who obtained the rank of Lieutenant October 8th, 1794, Commander July 3rd, 1796, Captain March 27th, 1797, Rear Admiral July 19th, 1821, and Vice Admiral January 10th, 1837, and who died whilst Commander-in-Chief on the North America and West Indies station in 1841).

Mrs Boteler's brothers, sons of Captain John Harvey, were

(1) Mr Henry Wise Harvey, who inherited Harnden and died in 1852; he was father of Captain John Harvey, R.N. (who died in 1882), Lieutenant Henry Wise Harvey, R.N. (who died in 1861), and Elizabeth, wife of Captain George Hilton, R.N. John Harvey entered the service in 1804, nearly four years ahead of Boteler, and obtained

the rank of Lieutenant on November 13th, 1813 ; Henry Wise Harvey entered the service in 1811, three years after Boteler, and obtained the rank of Lieutenant in 1819.

(2) Vice Admiral Sir John Harvey, K.C.B. (who obtained the rank of Lieutenant November 3rd, 1790, Commander September 5th, 1794, Captain December 16th, 1794, Rear Admiral December 4th, 1813, and Vice Admiral May 27th, 1825, and died in 1837).

And (3) Admiral Sir Edward Harvey, K.C.B. (who obtained the rank of Lieutenant July 24th, 1801, Commander January 7th, 1808, Captain April 18th, 1811, Rear Admiral December 17th, 1847, Vice Admiral September 11th, 1854, and Admiral June 9th, 1860, and died in 1865).

It is clear that in writing his Reminiscences, Captain Boteler's object was not to write the life story of the many persons with whom his service brought him into contact ; so, in editing the book, no attempt has been made to convert them into something he never intended. For details about very many of the officers named, the reader is referred to William R. O'Byrne's *Naval Biographical Dictionary* (1849). The editor has contented himself, for the most part, with altering Boteler's spelling of proper names to conform with that in the contemporary Navy List ; for Boteler spelt names as he remembered them, and is as often wrong as right. In all probability, his service colleagues spelt Boteler's own name as Butler.

PREFACE

I HAVE taken a sudden fancy to write some of the principal events of my sea life. It is rather late in the day to think of this. Friends have often wondered, after being entertained with my numerous yarns, that I did not write them. Had a shorthand writer taken down my words, the said yarns would be well worth reading ; but there is a vast difference between talking and writing. My memory is exceedingly acute and accurate, and I am quite satisfied I have never varied from facts or in any way exaggerated them. Although sixty or seventy years have gone by since the events I now describe took place, yet as they cross my mind they are as plainly before my eyes as if happening only yesterday. When I joined my third ship in 1810, I began a list of the officers, with their after fate, promotion, death, &c., and continued it till the close of my sea life, and this book has helped me in all material dates. My great regret is, that I did not enter upon this narrative full thirty years back ; I should then have better remembered names of persons, ships, &c. Having so far broken the ice, I think I will extend my views and run over a short history of my very early life.

J. H. BOTELER,
Capt. R.N.

September, 1883.

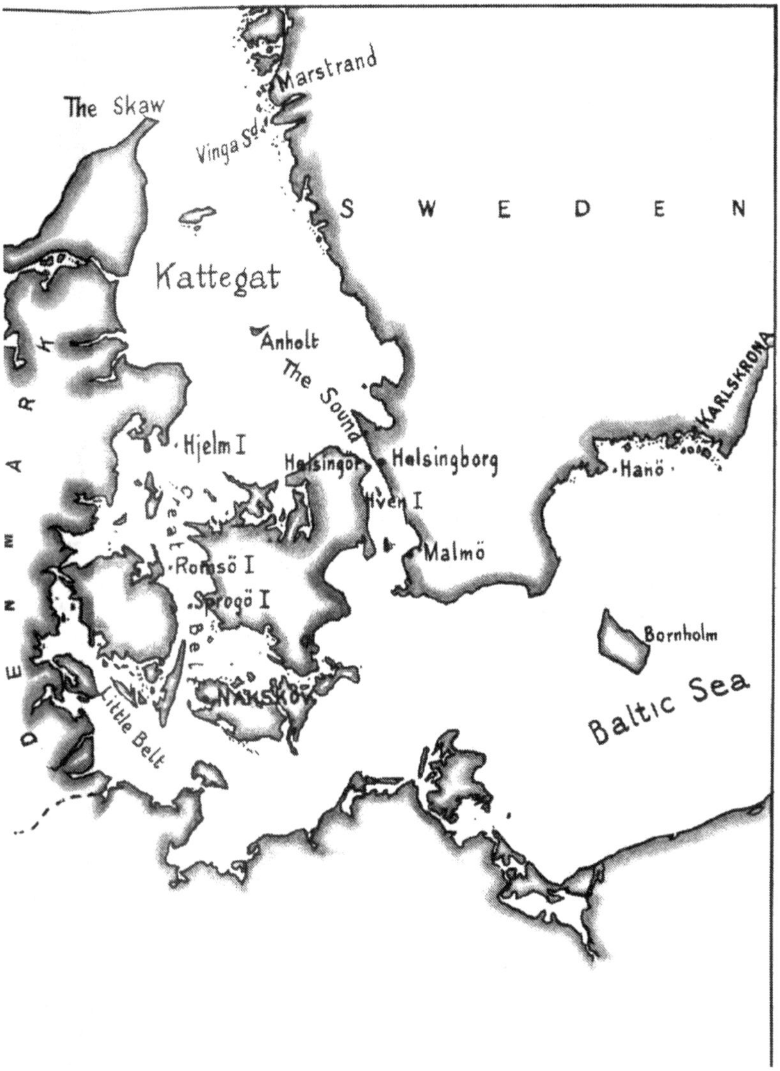

The Skaw
Marstrand
Vinga Sd.
SWEDEN
Kattegat
Anholt
The Sound
KARLSKRONA
DENMARK
Hjelm I
Helsingör
Helsingborg
Hven I
Hanö
Great Belt
Malmö
Romsö I
Sprogö I
Bornholm
Little Belt
Nakskov
Baltic Sea

CHAPTER I

I WAS born at Eastry, 11th of February, 1796, and may almost say I was born a sailor, that is to say, my relations on my mother's side were all sailors. Her father, John, with his brother Henry, both commanded ships of the line in Lord Howe's battle of the 1st June; my grandfather lost an arm and was otherwise so wounded that he died after reaching Spithead with his shattered ship, the *Brunswick*, and Parliament voted a monument to his and Captain Hutt's memory in Westminster Abbey; as a curious circumstance it may be here related that he and Captain Hutt went down to Portsmouth together in a post-chaise to command their ships, both lost a limb in the action, and both died within a day or two of each other. The sons of John Harvey and Henry Harvey were both Post-Captains, and a younger son shortly after.

We were a very extensive family, nineteen; and my earliest recollection is the walking out with my father and mother to see a *new* brother or sister at nurse in the village—for we were all like fox-hound puppies sent out to be nursed—and they tell the story of my father meeting a woman with a child in her arms, and my father, in his love for babies, saying: ' What a nice little fellow you have got there,' chucking the atom in the cheek. ' Lord, sir ! why he's your own boy.' My father laughed and told me I was the baby.

At a very early age when asked my name, I always answered, ' Captain John Harvey Boteler ; ' and when very young, I remember a gentleman dining with us who was with Captain Cook in his last voyage. His hair was all drawn back, the sides braided in three strands and so carried into his long tail. He had me on his knee and drew different scenes, when through Behring's Straits, of the ship fastened with hawsers to the ice and there shooting the walrus.

Before I was *breeched* I remember going up a ladder and picking my pin-cloth full of pears ; one step was gone and coming down I missed that, fell through, and awfully stung myself among the large rank nettles at the foot of the tree.

At about six years of age I was taken to my aunt, Elizabeth Boteler, at Shepherdswell. I had had an attack of influenza and my father came over to see me, and while in with his sister, left me in charge of his horse and gig tied to the railings. I had the whip in my hand and I said I was dusting the flies off, but I suppose now it was rather different, and the new and spirited beast broke his bridle and started off at a gallop, going between two elm trees and smashing the gig to pieces, the horse with one shaft dangling behind him. Out rushed my father, and I only remember his saying, ' I will hang you.' It was quite enough to utterly confound me ; I ran to my cousin to protect me, and she shut me up in my small bedroom till my father had gone. The two elm trees we called our turnpike, was where Frederick De Chair (the grandfather of the young midshipman De Chair,[1] the hero of Cairo) and I drew our little waggon of fir cones through.

At another time, Henry Sankey, afterwards a lieutenant in the Navy, was throwing a rotten cucumber at me, and I said I would blow him up, seizing for that purpose a powder-horn, kept over the kitchen chimney, and taking the hot poker began to pour some of the powder on it. Of course there was an explosion, the bottom of the horn blew out and my wrist was much scorched ; fortunately, my whole hand escaped ; the kitchen windows were clean blown out but no other damage.

In 1803, my uncle Harvey, of Harnden, who had a pollard ash tree and steps to it from which he could see the Downs and all that was going on there with the men-of-war at least, rode over to tell us the *Agamemnon*, Captain John Harvey, was in the Gull Stream ; so my father took as many of us boys with him as the carriage would hold to Deal, and in a shore boat we were all launched from the beach and went right down to the Gull and on board, my father and uncle going up the ship's side, but we boys were put through the lower-deck ports. What a strange sight to me ! The ship was at anchor, but weighed and beat up to the Downs and anchored. I recollect well, a marine every now and then firing over any merchant

---

[1] On July 29th, 1882, ' Midshipman Dudley Rawson De Chair of the *Alexandra*, while carrying dispatches between Ras et Tin and Ramleh, lost his way and fell into the hands of the rebels, near Siouf. He was well treated by Arabi Pasha, but liberated only upon the occupation of Cairo by the British Army ' (Laird Clowes : *The Royal Navy, A History*, VII, 339).

vessel who should pass a man-of-war without lowering her top-gallant-sails. Such was then the custom of the service! No vessel was permitted to pass a man-of-war without this respectful salute.[1] One thing made a great impression on me, and that was a marine, with a drawn cutlass, as sentry over some water that any man might take a drink from. This was my first initiation of a man-of-war, and I never shall forget it.

The next year (1804) I was sent to school, being then eight years old. I rode on my father's horse, Dancer, to Dover. The schoolmaster was named Lancaster, a clergyman, and the school a small house in Woolcombe Street. Here I at once received a lesson that I never forgot. I began to inquire of my school-mates: ' Who is your father ? ' Says one, ' My father is captain of a ship,' a collier. Another, ' My father is a King's pilot ' ; and yawns a third, ' Mine is a contractor, and supplies beef to men-of-war.' He was simply a butcher ; and when, in reply to the question as to what my father was I announced, ' My father is a gentleman,'—at this was an outcry, and I was fain to retire into the yard, and have a good cry.

I believe I was the only one with any pretence to good rearing in the whole school.

When I knew Dover at that time, no parade, lawns, Liverpool Terrace, not a house near the sea ; the only constructions were two or three red tarred herring-drying houses, and the harbour had merely for its protection one pier with a light on it. The packets were sloops only, and there was a harbour outside of the jetty formed by the shingle in which the sloop packets anchored,—it was called Providence Harbour, a sort of large pond only.

At the end of twelve months Mr Lancaster moved to the free school at Folkestone. My father could never have known the nature of the school, or he would not have permitted his son to remain. The living was abominable. A piece of tainted meat was kept on table a whole week. I was fain to get a penny bun for my dinner. I managed to ' play with gunpowder,' made a hole—a sort of mine, put powder in, and with a sloping way to it, a sort of touch-hole, attempted to explode it ; it would not ignite, when another boy, with a lighted stick, began poking it about, when the charge went off, striking him in the face, blowing off his eyebrows, and singeing off all his hair. I well remember him in his agony, running and lying down in the asparagus bed.

---

[1] For the International Law about this ' respectful salute ' see ' The Salute in the Narrow Seas and the Vienna Conference of 1815 ' in *The Naval Miscellany*, Vol. III (Navy Records Society, 1928).

The garden was our only play-ground, and this reminds me. Over the hedge, with a gap or two, and a descent of three or four feet, was an orchard, with trees full of delicious-looking apples. We tossed up who should go in and take. It came upon me, and in I went. The owner was a wheelwright, and caught me, giving me a thrashing with his horsewhip. Not knowing what I was about, I began scrambling through the hedge, holding on to the apples. ' Oh, you young villain, that's it, is it ? ' and he began again to thrash me. I dropped the fruit, and made my escape. In a few weeks after, this man, Hodgson, to our delight, was detected in an attempt at forging at Halford's Bank, Canterbury. As he gave the cheque the clerk noticed the butt of a pistol in his breast-coat pocket, and on some pretence went in to Mr Halford ; a constable was sent for, the man secured and confined in West Gate. By some means he procured files and a small saw made from a watch-spring, cut through the bars of an arrow slip and escaped to Holland ; from thence he wrote a saucy letter to Halford, that he might catch him if he could. So we had not the pleasure of having him hanged.

At the foot of Cæsar's Hill, where the remains of a Roman station are still plainly visible, was a splendid cherry orchard, and for twopence we were allowed to get into the trees, and cram ourselves,—but carry none away. Our way to these gardens was through some low marshy grounds and a running stream, and we found a number of small frogs, not quite as large as a hazel nut. We thought it incumbent to swallow them to kill the animalculæ in our stomachs. I swallowed a couple, but never repeated the experiment.

Whilst at this school the *Victory*, with the body of Lord Nelson on board, came past Folkestone. Knowing something of a man-of-war, I was considered a great authority ; and I explained to the boys the *iron bars !* still sticking in the ship's sides were fired by the Frenchmen. These bars in reality being the chain-plates of the lower rigging, but at that time I firmly believed them as I said.

In December, 1805, I left the Folkestone school, and was sent to the King's School, Rochester, in the following January.

During the holidays our next door neighbour, a Mrs, or, as we called her, Betty Rammell, exceedingly eccentric, occasionally attempted to make acquaintance with us, would give us a peach, which we snatched from her, and ran for it, half frightened. She never went to bed till the servants began to move, and this was

4

very early. One morning the servants awaked, not hearing their mistress's bell, remained quiet for a time ; then on getting up found the house had been broken in and robbed, Mrs Rammell tied to her bedposts, and gagged. The thieves had got in at the drawing-room window by a ladder, and had stolen a lot of guineas stowed in old tea-pots, and sample bags. My brother in London was written to, and a Bow Street officer sent down. After a little examination, he pronounced the thieves to be London men, and looking round, he noticed a gap in a hedge between Mrs Rammell's and our property, and tracing certain marks through two of our orchards to a ploughed field, he observed the clods of earth thrown aside by the action of a string-halt horse, and then came to Butshole Pond, and this he dragged and found two tea-pots. He said it was quite sufficient, and left for London ; enquiring at every public-house on the road if they had noticed a horse with a string-halt ; at last, at the Bull Inn, Rochester, a hostler said, ' Don't you remember, that horse I said would kick the doorpost down ? ' and when asked how the man was dressed, said, ' The man had a Belcher necktie.' The officer was satisfied, and this led to the man's detection, and in the course of time he was hanged on Pininden Heath. Mrs Rammell declined to prosecute further, said they had treated her well.

My father was exceedingly tickled at learning how to kill rats. A beggar boy came to the door, and he would not go, saying he was so hungry, and that if my father would give him something to eat, he would tell him how to kill rats ; and my father did order him some bread and cheese and some ale, when the boy, looking first to his retreat, said, ' You'll take them by the tail, and knock their heads against the waa-all ' ; and away he ran, my father after him for a time, shaking with laughter.

We had a carriage of the same sort as the present mourning coaches, and a pair of long-tailed black horses. About this time the old coach was disposed of, and a handsome chariot got instead, and a pair of strong bay horses. One, the best looking, was used as my father's charger, he being Lieutenant of the Walmer Troop of Yeomanry. It was most strange, the way Prince behaved when in saddle, he would prance about, shewing his pleasure, till my father was mounted, and then was steady as a rock. It was our delight when the trumpeter came to the door to call my father, to take out a glass of ale, and get a blow at the trumpet.

The second year my father used the carriage, he took it two days' journey, to Maidstone Assizes. By some mismanagement, in the grooming or otherwise, both horses got inflammation in the feet,—

so much so that the hoofs came off, and the horses were destroyed ;
a great loss, for they were valuable.

Well, I went to Rochester School. The master, Mr Griffiths,
was very strict, and an awful disciplinarian. I was never flogged,
but had it often over the hand. Mr Griffiths would have me in
his study, and preached till I cried; and at one time begged to be
flogged instead. When I came to the school there were but eighteen
boys, and when I left the number was eighty. The Backhouses,
our neighbours at Deal, had eight sons there ; and there were boys
from the principal families in Kent.

In the first half of my school-days, I was struck in the neck by
a steel port-crayon, leaving an ugly scar to this day. So, when I
came home for the holidays, I was sent on board the *Canada*, 74,
Captain Harvey, then in the Downs, to be under Dr Booth's care.
I don't know how or what arrangement was made, but I messed with
the lieutenants, and was very happy. I saw some strange sights.
The first lieutenant flogged two midshipmen—one had a dry dozen,
i.e., with his nankeen trowsers pulled tight. I saw the ship cross
her topsail yards like top-gallant yards ; two or three attempts,
till they ran them up,—the boatswain's mates, with a rope's end,
thrashing the men all round. I returned to the school cured ; but
I was afterwards taken very ill with fever ; and I remember Mr
Griffiths, in carrying me into the sick room, hitting my head against
the doorpost, and his crying over me after.

One of my school-fellows, Henry Brook, had a remarkable attach-
ment to me ; spent his pocket-money in oranges ; and Mr Griffiths
could not drive him away from my bedroom door. I have this day
a little copper box, enamelled on it, ' This box I intend a gift for my
friend.'

I may as well finish this boy's history ; when I was first appointed
to a ship, without leaving the school, this boy ran away, that he
might by chance come across me in some ship. He was caught,
not far from Rochester, and brought back but not punished. He
afterwards went to sea under Captain Dick, his cousin, and at
Barbadoes attempted to desert ; he became incurably mad, and was
sent to an asylum. I never heard more of him.

It was about this time, I think, that we pummelled a boy for
telling lies ; he said that a number of iron posts were put up in
Piccadilly, and that a man went up, put a light to them, and that a
flame came out and lighted the street. It was the first experiment
in gas. And I think this was the year of the Jubilee—the fiftieth
year of the reign of George the Third, and Mr Griffiths gave us a

dinner, roast beef and plum pudding ; our usual dinner was pudding
before the meat ; but, as he said, ' The King always had his meat
first, so on this day should we ' ; and he gave us each a glass of wine
to drink the King's health.   One of the boys said, ' Here is a health
to King George, and long may he reign ; and may this Jubilee
come round again and again.'   On which Mr Griffiths gave him
another glass.

To show the contrast between the living of this school and my
last.   One day the meat proved to be tainted.   The dinner was put
off, and different cook-shops were sent to, and we had a magnificent
dinner of cold turkey, and chicken, and ham.   Verily it turned out
a grand day for us.

In May, 1808, I entered the service as a volunteer of the first
class, on board the *Rochester*, a ship for French prisoners, at
Gillingham, in the Medway, two and a-half or three miles from the
school.   A memorable day to me !   There was a landing place
abreast of the ship, and I was told to watch for a boat with an ' R '
on her bows.   One came, and I went on board ; the lieutenant in
command had notice, and I was duly entered, and put to mess with
the gunner—who benefited largely by the transaction, as he drew
my provisions—giving me a piece of roast beef and pudding on
Thursdays, my day of going on board to muster.

The *Rochester* was a 74 gun ship ; the orlop deck was pierced
with ports, which, like those of the main and lower deck, were all
grated ; we had stages outside the ship, on which a sentry walked,
and by the ship's side a large floating stage, with another sentry.   I
don't know the number of prisoners on board, but suppose six or
seven hundred.   They were most ingenious with bones, making
boxes of dominoes, ships marvellously turned out in build and
rigging, with guns and everything requisite, and so minutely finished.
I bought a little frigate, eight inches long, for £1. 8s.—a perfect
treasure, complete in all her fittings ; and my eldest son has it now.

There was a fleet of prison ships here.   The *Queen, Sandwich,
Irresistible, Rochester,* and a hospital ship.   With all the strict
watch kept, there were occasional escapes.   It was very difficult,
though ; the dress of the prisoners was yellow cloth, stamped over
with black broad-arrows.   In one ship, the prisoners contrived to
cut out, with their knives only, an orlop-port, cutting round the
whole iron grating,—a work of months—and on a dark night fifteen
escaped, and none of the party were ever recaptured.

I had on this, my first visit to my ship, so much to see, that my
time slipped away, and returning to the school by a different road,

was very late. Mr Griffiths became alarmed, and set off in a post-chaise to look after me. He gave me a lecture on the occasion, and it never happened after.

In June the same year I was moved into the *Irresistible*, 74, Commodore Fowke, who had charge of all the prison ships. In 1809 I was made very proud in receiving my first year's pay—over £9—*well-earned*. In the *Irresistible* I again messed with the gunner, Mr Gallant, who took great care of me.

I don't know that anything in particular occurred in this year at school, excepting, indeed, Mr Griffiths sending for me to his study, to my great discomfort, expecting a lecture, which I abominated ; but it was to tell me, after some opening, that I was now an officer in His Majesty's Service ; that he should never think of lifting his hand against me ; ' but mind me, nevertheless, if you should offend sufficiently to incur punishment, I shall think it right to send you home. Now, after this, I think I may trust to your honour not to misbehave.' I was considerably relieved ; felt quite an affection for Mr Griffiths ; and I may say that from this time I never did anything wrong. And I came down from him as proud as Lucifer. He completely overpowered me. But, otherwise, I was not a bad boy ; on the contrary, as a reward, was one day sent into the mulberry tree, and the consequence was that I loathed a mulberry for some years after.

By the way, as a method of treating a culprit. On our way to the river side for bathing, we had, two and two, to go through the garden. A fine, large, tempting pear overhung the walk, which one of the boys could not pass, but put up his hand and grappled. Mr Griffiths saw him and kept his eye on him, giving him no opportunity of eating it. On our return to school, the boy was called up, with ' Take that pear out of your pocket.' The boy, John Latham, coloured and hesitated. Mr G. called to a little boy, ' Take that pear out of L.'s pocket,' which was done. ' Now, sir, had that pear been the property of any other person, I should have punished you ; but as it is, you will eat it now in the face of the school.' I never saw a boy more distressed ; he cried, he sobbed, he gulped ; the pear went against him, but eat it he must, and did. Then the Master said, ' Now you may go, and you will remember this as long as you live.'

As a good boy, I had the daily office of taking the newspaper to Mrs Griffiths' father, Mr Jones, a Minor Canon of Rochester Cathedral,—of which, by the bye, my younger brother, Edward, was a King's Scholar.

Our school broke up 20th December, 1809, and I got leave from my ship for the holidays ; but my name was kept on the *Irresistible's* books till the 19th of January, 1810, when I was sent on board the *Majestic*, 74, Captain Thomas Harvey, then in the Downs ; so that I had a fortnight or three weeks time in fitting out ; and I remember my pride on the box of my father's carriage, turning my head, that the Eastry folks might admire the gold lace of my cockade.

I went off to the ship, and in two days sailed for the Nore, Sheerness, and halfway up the river to get out our guns, preparatory to paying off. I was put under the care of John Parker, a mate. In two or three days I met with the misfortune of having my fine white watch-coat stolen. The *Majestic* was a long-legged ship, drawing more water than any ship of the line afloat, and when we got to Chatham, she took the ground, and heeled over very much indeed. After being docked, she proved so much out of order, that she was paid off ; and I, on the 1st February, 1810, was transferred to the *Ruby*, 64, Captain Robert Williams,[1] fitting for the Baltic. We were hulked on board the *Formidable* ; she, I remember, was full of large Bandicote rats ; we caught several with a fish-hook.

As we were nearly ready for sea, we went down the river to Salt Pan Reach for our guns ; and here I was sent away on my first duty, to go to Chatham, and the best way I could, to pick up stray seamen, and a terrible job I had. In a public-house, the King's Arms, near the Marine Barracks, Brompton, I found half-a-dozen men with their women, who began to pet me, trying to make me drink, till I nearly cried with vexation ; when one of the men said, ' Oh, come along ; we shall get the young gentleman into a scrape,' and so they all came down to the boat, and I brought them on board.

From the *Majestic*, we took Hooper, Paine, and Lucas, midshipmen, so that I was not quite alone. We went to the Nore for final orders, and there I recollect taking the ground and the commotion in the ship ; we soon got her off. And here was the Duke of Clarence on board a frigate. It was always said and understood among the mids. that if ever the Duke got into power, he would put us all in red cuffs and collars and red breeches ; and how nearly true it turned out, for when he became Lord High Admiral in 1826–7, he changed the uniform to red cuffs and collars, but he did not disturb the breeches.[2]

---

[1] Rear Admiral Robert Williams died March 1st, 1827 (see notice in the *Dictionary of National Biography*).

[2] The Admiralty Circular beginning ' His Majesty has been pleased to command that the Collars and Cuffs of the Uniform Coats of the Commissioned Officers of the Navy shall in future be scarlet instead of white,' is dated July 10th, 1830. The Duke of Clarence had by then become King William IV.

From the Nore we went on to Yarmouth roads, where we hoisted
the flag of Manley Dixon.[1] Here at anchor in the launch on the
booms, loaded with hay, I remember being very sea-sick ; a very
little motion, only pitching. I have no remembrance of anything
in particular in this ship. One of the lieutenants, Manley Dixon,
I remember, had a very squeaky voice, and in hailing the top, the
Admiral saying, ' Manley, my dear, you will spoil your voice ' ; and
it was quite a saying among the youngsters, of ' Manley, my dear,
you'll spoil your voice.'

On the 5th June we fell in with the *Dictator*, 64, Captain [2] * * *,
with whom Captain Williams exchanged ships, bringing with him
five midshipmen ; myself, Hooper, Lucas, Paine and Denby, his
coxswain and barge's crew. We were mostly employed convoying
large bodies of merchant vessels through the Great Belt, an arduous
service ; the passage was so swarming with privateers and row-
boats. We were supplied with two extra twenty-oared barges,
which were stowed on skids outside the waist hammock nettings,
just above the main-deck guns.

At one time, with over 400 vessels, under charge of the *Hero*,
ourselves, two frigates and a bomb, we never saw the head of the
convoy from the time of leaving Wingoe Sound. We had charge
of the rear. No sooner was the night set in, when there would
be a tar-barrel on fire, or a rocket, or lights shewn at different parts
of the convoy ; then the exciting pipe was ' Away there, all boats'
crews.' Barges and pinnaces and two cutters would be sent in
various directions. Lieutenant Parker took a barge, and me with
him,—I was always his midshipman. We pulled for a large ship
on the outskirts of the convoy, on the chance that an enemy might
be induced to pounce on her. The crew were called on board, and
it was great *nuts to me*, the Master asking us into the cabin, and
giving us a first-rate supper. While below, the coxswain came to
the door, and reported a suspicious boat. We all went on deck,
and sure enough there was a large boat, hesitating whether to board
us or not. At last she dashed at us. Our men, fully armed with a
cutlass and pistol, were snugly ensconced under the waist, Mr
Parker and I on the quarter-deck ; when up came a Danish
lieutenant. He stood astonished ; then bowed, and said, ' Me
your prisoner, sir.' It was no use to shew any fight. We had
the rest of her crew up, secured them,—they were eighteen or

---

[1] Admiral Sir Manley Dixon, K.C.B. (died in 1837), father of Admiral Manley
Hall Dixon (died 1864).
[2] Captain R. H. Pearson, invalided June 5th, 1810.

10

twenty-four. I felt so proud on returning on board with our prize.

We were all delighted with the change of ships. Everything was so smartly done; no man on duty ever walked up or down the rigging, it was always a run; and so in hoisting the topsails or with the capstan at up-anchor. So different in the *Ruby*. And we young mids. were wonderfully enchanted. ' This is something like a man-of-war ! ' But alas ! the crew began to find out the difference in the two captains; things began to be slovenly done. The skulkers lagged behind; and the good men did the work. At last the men said, ' I wish Captain * * * was back; then all would have to do their duty. I would sooner sail with a rogue than a fool.'

One of the lieutenants, a Mr Bailey, an Orkney man, who had his ' blubber knife ' mounted and worn by him as a dirk, chose to be down on me. I was midshipman of his watch. If I was a minute late, ' To the mast-head, sir ! ' and there I was kept, night or day, for two or three hours. At another time, I was put in the weather quarter-deck netting (at night), so that I had difficulty in walking, the shrouds of the lower rigging preventing me standing upright; and this treatment continued for three or four months, till I was fairly worn out, and only solaced myself thinking if ever I mounted the white lapel, wouldn't I serve someone else out. At last Mr Bailey sent me to walk on the splinter netting—a net spread over the quarter-deck, the meshes about six inches square; and when I turned rusty, he had the captain of the afterguard with a boat-hook progging my legs; and I called out he had better throw me overboard at once. Well, this was the last of it. The next day he sent for me to his cabin, shook me by the hand, said he had made me a smart officer, told me to make use of his cabin to read; that there was a cask of American crackers and reindeer tongues and some loaf-sugar, to do what I pleased with them,—and from that time he was my best friend. But he might have broken my spirit in the meanwhile.

A great character in the ship was the second-master, Jack Woodthorpe; a very jolly, fat man; full of fun; his delight and our delight also was after dinner to roll him; he and all of us laughing; he grunting, ready to split. He was very stout—it was a wonder he did not burst !

When in Wingoe Sound we heard of a privateer (Danish) being harboured in Maestroom, one of the numerous fiords on the Norway coast; and although in a neutral port, she took the advantage,

dashing out and capturing our ships. So we determined to cut her
out.[1] A barge of twenty men was manned, and Lieutenant Parker
and Mr Ireland were told off for the purpose. Poor Ireland! He
had a presentiment that he would be killed; and in case it turned
out so, he gave away all his kit,—his linen to one (who was to pay
a washing bill). Well, it turned out that they found the privateer,
who, not dreaming of an attack, was easily captured; and when
coming away with the prize and Lieutenant Parker telling Ireland
that he was all right,—in fact, while almost speaking, a shot from
a battery passed right through Ireland's head. We were all greatly
disturbed at this mishap.

In the middle of the Belt was an uninhabited island, Sproe;
no great size, chiefly of fine turf, a pond or two, and myriads of
frogs. Many of the ships had gardens on it; running the chance of
reaping the produce, for it was the anchoring place of most ships;
we used to land there for leap-frog and other games.

The *Sultan*, 74, anchored too close in and grounded. Three
other ships were at hand; but it took us three days to get her off;
we had to almost clear her of guns, water, and heavy stores. I
remember firing three guns and giving three cheers when she floated.

From the *Sultan* we received six supernumeraries; one of them,
a great hulking fellow, who was the terror of our berth. They
absolutely turned six of us youngsters out, to make room for them,
and we had our dinners in the wing.

And here I may relate our game of able whackets, a sort of
commerce. The cards called ' good books ': the hand, ' flipper ';
a handkerchief tightly braided up, ' Good money.' At the loss of
the game he that was the winner would say, ' I demand the good
money,' and to the loser, ' Hold out your flipper: this is for the
loss of the good game called Able Whackets, and a precious hard
thump '; another would say, ' This is for the same,' and so on all
round. The last saying, ' Who demands the good money? ' no one
speaks, and he keeps it ' warm,' *i.e.*, putting it into his breast;
a man unwarily says ' *Cards* '; someone calls out ' Watch,' and
' I demand the good money,' and in his eagerness takes the ' good
money ' before it is relinquished, at which the call is again ' watch,'
and the first one says, ' Hold out your flipper; this is for calling
the good books out of the proper name,' and whack he has it all
round. Then the other man says to this one, ' Hold out your

<hr>

[1] *Naval Chronicle*, November 1810 (vol. 24, p. 439), Obituary. ' Mr James
Ireland, of Lancaster, midshipman of H.M.S. *Dictator*. He was killed by a musket-
ball in an attack, by the boats of that ship, on a Danish vessel under Carlsrand
Castle, at Marstrand, in the Kattegat.

flipper ; this is for taking the good money before it was relinquished.'
Then in the game one might be 27, and stands able ; another, sure
of being first, would stand able at 31. On comparing notes this
one would say ' Watch,' and when in possession of the good money
would demand the other able's ' flipper,' and ' this is for your
standing able and my standing able, and my able being better than
yours by one, two, three, and four whacks.' Now, this big brute
from the *Sultan* was an awful customer ; he used to punish us most
severely.

At another time, while at anchor not far from Sproe we saw
two gunboats pulling round a point in the Island of Romsoe. Boats
were directly manned, under charge of our first lieutenant in the
launch, and Lieutenant Parker, with whom I was in a cutter, besides
four barges, and away we pulled, when in about an hour the enemy
were joined by four more gunboats, and we were evidently in the
wrong box. Our ship was not slow in seeing our scrape, and made
the recall with a gun, and there was no more to be done than turn
tail, and at this the enemy opened fire—one, two, three—shot in
quick succession. They came in a good direction, but flying over us.
I could not help exclaiming they looked like cricket balls. I had no
idea they could be so plainly seen. Then the firing was kept up
more rapidly. At last a shot hit the launch, throwing two oars
into the air and wounding two men, one very badly, nearly taking
his thigh away. Our ship got under way, standing towards the
gunboats, making them skedaddle in no time.

We had another second master, Dickey Strauhan, a dirty fellow.
He never seemed to unfold his necktie, so one evening we opened it
out and rolled up a fresh herring into it instead of the stiffener.
The following day the fish began to give out an unpleasant odour.
Strauhan began to swear, saying ' wherever he went there was a
strong scent of stinking fish.' At last it was so bad no one could
go near him, except by holding the nose. In the end the stench
was dreadful, and yet he never divined the cause, till the fish began
to ooze through the silk necktie. Then was he not in a passion,
and we all so innocent ! He tried hard to find the culprit.

Somewhere at this time the *Africa*, 64, got a terrible mauling
at the hands of the Danish gunboats, who caught her in a calm.
There was a whole fleet of boats, she unable to get a shot at them,
for though anchored with springs to her cables, yet they both were
shot away, and their men were obliged to be sent below to be out
of the way of the enemy's shot, and in this condition the ship was
fired at for two or three hours, the ensign shot away more than

once ; in fact, it was down so long that the Danes declared she had struck, and claimed her as a prize. The breeze fortunately sprung up, and the ship got her anchor up, and then the fight soon ended, and the Danes rowed away well satisfied with their work. Had the Danes come to closer quarters while the *Africa* was in that crippled state they might have taken her.

All the Baltic squadron at the close of the year returned to England, and in November we were ordered to Sheerness, bringing home Captain Toker, who was promoted from some brig. We did not remain at Sheerness, but were ordered to Chatham to refit. I went home on leave for a month.

On rejoining my ship at Chatham there was a great row between the mids. of the squadron and the dockyard mates, which generally began at the theatre when ' God save the King ' was called for, and all the actors would appear on the stage to sing it. Then it was. ' Off hats,' and if anyone refused, the mids.. would storm the gallery, and there was a free fight. I remember a mid. of the *Poictiers* going up and throwing a dockyard young fellow right over into the pit. The thing was to get safe to our ships. We had horns and whistles to call for aid if required, and scenes of this description were carried on night after night.

When ready for sea we were in the hands of workmen putting up a strong boarding on the orlop deck. Our lower deck guns were taken out, and we proceeded down the river, and at Sheerness embarked 400 or 500 French prisoners for Edinburgh Castle, and landed them safely, then returned to Portsmouth for another cargo. I recollect poor fellows, for want of air, being drawn up from below in a fainting state, notwithstanding a studding-sail was sewed up into a large wind-sail. After this about a hundred men were allowed on deck, and the rest were more comfortable.

On the way to Scotland, in company of the *Glatton,* she let us know there was a mutiny among the prisoners, and to keep a sharp look out. One of our prisoners, an American, disclosed the plot, so that we were prepared, and had a strong party of our men properly armed, and all went off quietly enough.

In beating into Inchkeith we got close in on a lee shore, Kirkcaldy ; and I saw an evolution performed, that may be the luck of one sailor's lifetime to witness, *i.e.,* to ' club-haul ' the ship. We were so close in, that the chance was, the ship might not go about, with the little sail she could shew, and there decidedly was no room to wear. So that when all was ready and good way put on the ship, ' down with the helm,' when head to wind ' let go the anchor '

14

and so check her on the other tack, then cut the cable and the ship
was safe round—we made two or three tacks after, then safely
anchored in Leith Roads and got rid of our human cargo ; we never
recovered our anchor ; the Scotchmen had cut away and stolen the
copper buoy.

At this date, 1811, there were no houses between Leith and
Edinburgh.

We got six assistant-surgeons at Leith. It was said by us,
' Only veer a raft on shore baited with burgo, and you would catch
an assistant-surgeon.' However, we returned to Sheerness, got our
lower deck guns in, did away with the prison fittings, and were once
more ready for sea. We had our larks on shore, at the only inn,
Fountain. We were strong in midshipmen, and in the evening at
tea there was a great outcry for more toast. ' Tom—Tom, more
toast and be hanged to you.' Tom was deaf or affected deafness,
for when I said quietly ' Tom, when at leisure, let us have more
toast,' Tom would look knowing and toast was brought. At last
we pressed Tom ; he only laughed, taking it for a joke, but when at
the end of three days he was kept on board, he began to cry out,
then Tom was released and thought himself very lucky.

As the spring came on in 1811, we again sailed for the Baltic
and were joined by a large squadron, the *Victory*, Admiral Sir James
Saumarez ; *St George*, Admiral Reynolds ; *Dreadnought*, *Hero*,
Cressy, *Defence*, *Vanguard*, *Glatton*, &c. I never knew why so
large a force was sent to the Baltic, for there were many other
vessels, frigates, bombs and brigs.[1] We first went to Anholt,[2] a
small sandy island with a lighthouse, there being a long dangerous
reef extending one and a-half or two miles from it. There was a
garrison of marines (under a Colonel Nicholls) and a number of
bluejackets with a lieutenant and two midshipmen. An eighteen-
pounder carronade was mounted in one of the ports of the lighthouse, and there was a battery of three guns as well. The peculiarity
of this sandy island was, that pure fresh water was to be had at any
part, even within twenty yards of the sea, we had only to sink an
empty flour cask in the sand and it would instantly be filled, and
with this contrivance ships would complete their water.

[1] For the situation of affairs in the Baltic in 1811, see *Memoirs and Correspondence
of Admiral Lord de Saumarez*, by Captain Sir John Ross, C.B., R.N. (2 vols., London,
1838).

[2] Anholt was occupied on May 18th, 1809, by a force under Captain William
Selby, commanding H.M.S. *Owen Glendower*, and Captain Edward Nicholls, Royal
Marines. ' The acquisition of this island is stated to be of importance in furnishing
supplies of water to H.M. Fleet, and affording a good anchorage to the Trade in going
to or coming from the Baltic ' (*London Gazette*, May 27th, 1809).

I knew Captain Nicholls very well, he was with my uncle Captain
Thomas Harvey in the *Standard* on the Mediterranean station two
or three years, and was in every brush with the enemy in that ship's
boats. While here, I remember Captain Glynn of the *Venerable*,
coming on shore wet, and giving me his necktie to dry, and which
I burned, and his shaking his finger at me with his stuttering speech,
'You shall never be my valet again,' all in good humour.

There were about a dozen horses in the stables, and two or three
of us used to get in and pull the hair from their tails, with which
we manufactured fishing lines, by using three quills and three pegs,
and by renewing, by a hair, the different strands, contrived to make
a very excellent line. I have mine still, many yards in length.

One morning the island was attacked by three Danish gunboats
(they were a trifle late), and the gunner who went to the battery to
fire the morning gun caught sight of them and gave the alarm just
in time. The garrison was aroused and all three of the enemy were
captured. I saw these gunboats hauled upon the sand. The consequence of this attack was, that the garrison was increased, and a
post captain appointed governor, a Captain Morris, a very different
command to his last, the Bell Rock, at the entrance of Fort Royal,
Martinique. This rock, or rather small island, perpendicular on all
sides, was captured by one of our line of battle ships, and heavy
guns sent to the top by a stout hawser and a traveller, it was considered quite a feat. Captain Morris held the command for a length
of time and at last was starved out, after great privations, and
retaken.[1]

While going through the Great Belt in company with the *Hero*,
we noticed three luggers in shore by Naskoe, and we directly hauled
off as if to sail away, and when nearly dark made all sail in shore,
piped the boats away, and as we closed in with muffled oars, pulled
towards them. Besides the *Hero's* boats we had our launch ; with
a carronade, a pinnace and cutter, with Lieutenant Parker and
myself ; we could see nothing and thought we had missed them or
that they had gone into some harbour. We paddled silently alongshore, when we came upon them and, without hesitation, firing the
carronade close to one, dashed at them. My boat was the second
one, and I with my little dirk was about to scramble up. One of
the men caught hold of me with 'Not yet, sir,' and then directly

---

[1] See the notice of Rear Admiral James Wilkes Maurice in the *Dictionary of
National Biography*. The Bell Rock off Martinique is, of course, a mistake for
Diamond Rock. The Danish attempt on March 27th, 1811, to recapture Anholt
was a very different affair from what is here related (see *London Gazette*, April 9th,
1811).

16

after, ' Now, sir, come along ' ; but it was all over as to resistance, they were in no respect ready ; their crews in general were on shore, not dreaming of our being near. One man, waking up from sleep, made resistance and was cut down, there were five killed, at least that was the number in our lugger, the other two luggers fell to the *Hero's* boats. But we brought them out to our ships in great triumph. It made me quite sick next morning going on board our lugger, the mainsail soaked with blood and the dead men on her deck. One shot right through the lungs by a grape shot, and yet he lived till the evening.

We one day captured a large ship laden with wheat and we sent her to England in charge of Mr Buchanan, a tall, powerful Scotch master's mate. He was caterer of the mess and, for fear of any accident, before he left us he took up all provisions due to us— flour, raisins, suet, bread, and several gallons of rum—all of which he left to our discretion, excepting the rum, and that he wished to be reserved against the time of being in England when we should have a lot of delightful rum shrub ! Well, he was off and we hoped he might never come back, he was very tyrannical and thrashed us on any pretence.

We had the usual employment of taking large convoys through the Belt, when, night after night, there were the same alarms from different parts of the convoy—blue lights, rockets, tar barrels, &c.— and, of course, on our part of ' all boats away.' In one instance Jack Broad, in a twenty-oared barge, with marines, pulled to the assistance of a small galliot which had a Danish row boat alongside, and as our barge dashed in she was in the act of shoving off, the bow of the barge running between her and the galliot, the master of which had just come up and was about to fire into our boat. ' Fire into the other boat,' said Jack. ' Oh, all the same,' said the fellow. In the meantime, ' Hold on with your boat-hook ' to our men. One got hold of the row boat, the other boat-hook was entangled on the galliot's channel. ' Fire low, marines,' but up went the sail of the row boat, and notwithstanding all attempts to hold him he got off, but not before, by the cries, several were wounded, and when our boat did get clear it was the cow after the hare. We captured two other boats in the same night.

When close in to Reef-ness, a long reef running from a point of the main island of Zealand, six or eight gunboats sallied out upon the convoy, it being, too, a calm. There were three men-of-war— *Cressy*, *Defence*, and ourselves. We all out boats and sent them in a body to the attack, but the odds were against us. The gunboats

fired with great precision, one shot struck and swamped a barge of
the *Cressy* and her lieutenant called out ' The *Cressy's* boats will
follow me,' and they did ; another boat was also hit. Our first
lieutenant, standing on the launch's gun-slide, waved his sword for
us to follow him and would have led to the attack had not the recall
been made. We then turned our attention to an unfortunate ten
gun brig which got into the line of fire and was being well peppered.
We took her in tow, keeping a good line ahead of her, for what shot
missed her would ricochet by our oars , then a breeze sprung up and
the big ships shewed their teeth, when it was time for the gunboats
to retreat in their turn.[1]

Before this I was taken aback and made very uncomfortable by
the first lieutenant saying ' How is it, Mr Boteler, you have not
enrolled yourself among the list of heroes ? ' I felt so ashamed and
stammered some excuse of not thinking myself big enough , indeed
I knew nothing of the other mids volunteering their services.

In one of our convoys the quartermaster came down. ' It's up
anchor, young gentlemen, the gunboats are out.' ' Gunboats ? '
we said. ' Yes, don't you hear them ? ' and then thud, thud, and
out we jumped The cutter was piped away and in her Mr Parker
and I went, shoved off, and with oars and sails pushed away after
a Danish row boat, who, however, had the best of us ; and who
should be in the boat but young Lucas, a daring boy, something of
a scamp and whom we called Billy Hell Flames He was determined to see what was going on and so stowed himself in the boat.
We gave up the chase and on looking round observed a large vessel
of the convoy with her ensign, stars downwards, as a signal of
distress. It seemed that the gunboats had attacked her, wrongly
supposing her to be a man-of-war They fired carcasses, *i.e.*, loaded
shot, and twice set fire to her, she being loaded with hemp. We
were welcomed on board, our boat's crew was of great help in shifting his topmasts and in other repairs. The captain had Mr Parker
and us two mids. into the cabin to a splendid breakfast, and a breakfast was also given the boat's crew. A signal with two guns was
made from the man-of-war The Yankee had no convoy instructions, in fact, he had no business with us, so I borrowed a small
boat and pulled to a galliot, to look at his instructions, and there

---

[1] This may be the incident mentioned in the *London Gazette*, July 23rd, 1811,
where it is stated that Captain Pater of H.M S. *Cressy* had reported an attack made
off Hjalm Island, on July 5th, 1811, by a Danish flotilla of 17 gunboats and 10 heavy
row-boats, on a convoy under the protection of H M Ships *Cressy*, *Defence* and
Dictator, the *Sheldrake* sloop and the *Bruizer* gun-vessel. The attack was repulsed
without loss to the convoy, and four Danish gunboats were captured

18

it was, the signal to anchor, which suited us well. Young Lucas
who was in the foretop called out 'Three gunboats just ahead of
us.' The wind had dropped and a fog set in and it was rolling past
us in clouds, our ship had two guns aboard, but no powder, all had
been thrown overboard when she caught fire, but we opened our
magazine, got out powder, made a cartridge and loaded one of his
guns with a bag of bullets, all this time watching the gunboat which
seemed all abroad; presently we saw one of our ships' barges
pulling for her, and her crew, instead of shewing fight, with their
bags on their backs. It turned out this was the Commodore's boat,
a sailing one, and in the fog had gone wrong and found herself in
the convoy. The Commodore flung his sword into the sea after
cutting through the heads of his big drum, for he had a regular
band on board, and to account for the hurry the men were in to
leave her, a crowbar had been rammed through her bottom, which
one of our men stopped with his jacket. However, the boat was
towed away to our ship. In a short time another boat was sent to
relieve us.

On going on board to report myself to the first lieutenant, there
sat at the rudder head a Danish lieutenant, Bull, with his jacket off
and his shirt bloody. It seems we had captured three gunboats,
all sailing ones, and strange to say, all taken from us two years back.
They were fine handsome vessels, sloop rigged, rowed with thirty
oars with cleats on the looms, to enable two men to row them; they
had each a long thirty-two pounder gun forward and a carronade
abaft.

When the Danish Commodore stepped on board the *Dictator*
there was a great uproar between our Captain and him. Said old
Williams: 'What do you mean, sir, by throwing your sword overboard instead of giving it up to the lieutenant?' 'I did not know
what I did, I would sooner go to the devil than be taken by the
English.' 'I have a great mind to put you in irons, sir.' He only
shrugged his shoulders; at last after two or three more words the
Commodore said, 'Bless me, sir, were you not at the Free School
at Rochester?' 'Yes,' said Williams, 'and you are then Count
Rosenberg'; and so it proved; they shook hands and went into the
captain's cabin, laughing, a most strange meeting.

The prisoner, Lieutenant Bull, was an amusing fellow, very
shrewd, I caught him looking over my shoulder at the signal book.
By the way, he was taken in one of the gunboats that attacked
Anholt, and had there lost his arm. I forgot to say that he was
then taken by Captain Stewart who came in, just in time, in command

of an eighteen gun brig, and who told Bull when he saw him in our wardroom, that the next time he crossed him it would be his last, and so it proved, for some months after this, when Captain Stewart was posted and had command of the *Dictator* he got intimation of a Danish frigate, the *Daphnæ* or *Danæ*, and two eighteen gun brigs being harboured in one of the fiords of Norway, and he determined to cut her out.[1] He went on a long way among the rocks; at times there seemed to be no opening whatever; the water was very clear alongside and very deep, they could see the bottom, and they ran so close to the shore that a topman went down by a rope from the yard-arm into a farmhouse, and got back again. They went so far that they began to suspect the ships had got away, when on rounding a high point of the shore the enemy's ships suddenly shewed themselves, and the *Dictator* opened fire; by some unaccountable chance the frigate blew up with all her crew, and Lieutenant Bull was one of her officers. Captain Stewart then secured and brought out one of the two brigs, the other one contriving to make her escape, and here the big brute Buchanan was suspected of shewing the ' white feather '; he stayed in the shot locker under the pretence of hastening them in handing up the shot. Well, he was turned out of the ship into a ten gun brig, when the lieutenant and master being on shore and he had the grog-serving, he contrived to help himself to a gallon of rum, and he was dismissed the brig, drummed on shore, towed on a grating.

While in Wingoe Sound with convoy signal up, our two young captain's clerks made a very lucrative thing of it, by placing some small Swedish coin in a saucer on their desk; many captains came on board for their instructions, a sheet or two of printed paper sewn together, with day, night and fog signals. They looked at the saucer, hesitated, but generally put some coin in.

Once in the Baltic there was a remarkable mirage or deception; we noticed a whole fleet of ships coming towards us, their top-gallant masts touching the water, and as they continued to near us, the royals and top-gallant sails of another fleet would show themselves, eating up, as they approached, the feigned squadrons.

There was a bomb vessel the *Meteor* in our squadron, she was a merchant ship converted, with a half-deck that took off in gratings and a fifteen inch mortar below; she was made as little like a vessel of war as possible—a main top-gallant and royal mast, a fore-top gallant mast only and no mizen. The ropes were sixes and sevens,

---

[1] The Danish frigate was the *Nayaden*. Stewart's despatch was published in the *London Gazette*, July 18th, 1812.

none kept taut, and her hull was painted with a sheer. Her own
broadside carronades were hidden, and four quaker guns secured to
the ship's sides, and she captured more privateers and row boats
than all the squadron. They were taken in, all boarding her making
sure she was a prize.

We anchored off the island Romsoe, where ships usually went
for wood and water; and for two days I was on duty with a strong
party of seamen and carpenters, watering, cutting down timber,
sawing it up for firewood (much to the purser's satisfaction, as it
saved his pocket), as also small brushwood stuff for brooms. Three
or four other midshipmen went for a ramble, and the surgeon hearing
that there was an abundance of leeches in the large stagnant ponds
asked us to get some, supplying us with large-mouthed pickle bottles.
I could in no way have done this in after-life; but we off shoes and
stockings, tucked our trowsers over the knees, and so walked into
the ponds. In an instant the leeches were crawling on our legs.
We dashed them off and into bottles before they had time to fix.
I even then shuddered when they attacked me.

All at once, with a report and whiz, a bullet passed over our
heads, and then another, and we retreated. Two of the lieutenants
were firing across the ponds, which were in a hollow, at some mark.
I well remember ducking on hearing the shot, and one of our party,
young Lucas, saying, ' What a fool you are, Boteler, what is the
use of ducking; the shot had passed before you bobbed your head ! '

I also well remember, after some refreshment in the lieutenants'
tent, we lay down for a nap. After a time, Payne jumped up,
saying water was in his boot. It was blood. The bunting covering
of a bottle had got loose, and the leeches were out crawling about
the grass, and so three of them into his boot.

The cottage of the owner or his gardener had been carelessly
burned the year before by some sailors. The gardens and orchards
uninjured; small fruit, gooseberries and currants had gone by; but
to the intense delight of us mids., there were quantities of apples,
though only half-grown, still a grand prize for us. We half filled
a purser's bread bag, and for a week were baking and boiling
dumplings and tarts, in saucers, tins and dishes, morning, noon and
night, and for this we had to use all back flour due to us.

Well, Mr Buckannon came back from England, was well pleased
with the state of provisions left and was satisfied with us for not
touching the rum. But that very evening and indeed the following
one as well, he invited Dicky Strahan and another to a drinking
bout, and they all got drunk together. Then we mids. caballed, and

attacked the rum, each of us taking two half-gallon bottles (the surgeon's lime juice bottles) into our keeping. The fool complained to the first lieutenant, and he carried it to the captain, and we were all sent for : on hearing our story Captain Williams turned on Mr Buckannon, saying ' Rum in the wing, sir, rum in the wing ; set the ship on fire,' and took our parts in all the work, so that we came off with flying colours, much too, to the disgust of the first lieutenant. Buckannon was of course down on us, and shortly afterwards his watch and station bill was found cut to pieces. He was furious and tried for several days to discover the offender, fixing his eyes on me, whom he seemed most to suspect. I naturally coloured, which made him more sure. In the end he said, he had an unerring method of discovering the culprit. He produced a Bible in which were a number of pieces of string which we were to draw, he letting us know that the longest string would prove the guilty person, that we were not to show the strings to each other, but that they would be compared in the evening. To my utter horror my string was of great length, and I feared I had drawn the longest. However, in the evening all were proved of the same length but Lucas's, and he had cut his ; he of course being the criminal ; well, as he daringly said, ' I was not going to be proved guilty by a stupid piece of string, so I cut it ' ; this was the only clever thing I knew of Master Buckannon.

In this ship I met with an accident that might have proved fatal. I had been fishing, and returning in the cutter was called by the mids. on the gangway, saying they had got a boat of fish. I had a mackerel on my finger and was obliged to hitch along the guess-warp-boom into the lower deck, then up the ladder, and crossing the main-deck hatch, the grating tilted and I fell into the hold, full twenty to twenty-two feet, for the hold was cleared to the very dunnage of wood. Directly I fell it was as if in a dream, my father, mother, and sisters were about me. I felt no pain, in fact I was totally insensible. Men were quickly down and got me up with a rope and it was not till the doctor was in the act of bleeding me that I came to. I only broke a finger, but it was some days before I was about.

While with the usual convoys in the Belt, and on fine days, the mids. would ask for a boat and row among the different ships to see what they could pick up, generally asking if they had anything to sell, but it mostly ended by our being offered a bottle of schnapps, a chicken, a dried goose (split and smoked), a tongue, ham, sausage, &c., and one large ship gave us a whole bolt of duck-cloth. Towards the autumn we sailed through the Belt, past Bornholm to off Riga, right away to the Swedish large naval arsenal at Carlscrona. I visited the dockyard and saw the model room, where was the whole Swedish navy in miniature, a very fine display.

One of our line of battle ships was here docked. She had been ashore, and a large piece of rock was sticking in her bottom. Had it fallen out the chance is the ship would have foundered.

From Carlscrona we hied back and sailed for another port, Hano, and there met the *St George* 98 three-decker, bearing the flag of Admiral Reynolds. We sent a boat under Lucas with a party of hands to cut small stuff for brooms. In the evening young Lucas appeared in the berth with a bucket, out of which he poured on the table a leg and shoulder of pig, all bloody and wretchedly killed. ' Here, my boys, what do you think of my catering ? ' We all stared with astonishment. ' Why, Billy, how did you manage this ? ' He said : ' While wandering in the woods a drove of pigs came by ; one looked as if he wanted to be killed, and I chased and knocked him down, and then and there cut off his head and dragged the carcase to the men, and they had half and I the other, as you see ; but,' added Billy, ' to-morrow I will be more particular.' The next day he again went, singled out a young pig, knocked it down, tied it to a tree till it was cool, then he killed it, cut it up, and brought three quarters on board, so that we had pork morning, noon, and night, chiefly boiled, or in pies, for we were afraid to dress it more openly. On the following day Lucas got leave to be of the brooming party, which was very large, killed a third pig, and had a grand supper with all the men, so that their tongues were tied. But by this time the Swedes had partially discovered their loss, and had complained to the admiral, who issued a flaming order saying if he detected the thief he would hang him, if it was his own brother. We all began to quake in our shoes, and were right glad when we got under weigh for the Belt, in company of the *St George* and a small convoy.

One ugly-looking night,[1] the wind bristling up in squalls, we all anchored on a lee shore, so close to the rocks apparently, that in the middle of the night, on an increase of wind, we feared to give her cable, when, just as I was relieved at midnight, and got snug into my hammock, the ship parted, and it was, ' Stand clear of the cable below.' I never jumped out of my bed more smartly. The cable tore round, taking our hammocks with it, and the ship brought up without touching the rocks astern. About eight o'clock, as day-

---

[1] November 15th, 1811. For Rear Admiral Reynolds's official report see Ross's *Life of Saumarez*, II, 252–4.

light shewed itself, we distinguished, as we supposed, a large farm-house. It was the *St George*, totally dismasted. A merchant ship had drifted athwart her hawse, carried away the bowsprit and the lower masts ; all went over the side one after the other. The *St George* also tailed on to the rocks, and carried away her rudder. The gale had moderated, and with our help she was soon in deep water again. It took us three or four days to get her ready for sea. We made her a temporary rudder from a plan of Tommy Paken-ham's, and it answered admirably.

As soon as we weighed, as we had always beaten her with all her masts in, we sent our stream cable to her and took her in tow. Strange to say, under jury rig we stood no chance with her, and before we had time to get our stream cable in and cast her off, she ran her bowsprit into our ward-room windows, and she continued to beat us all the way to Wingoe Sound.

While here I got leave to visit a friend, and did not return till just as dinner was over ; it was rather sharp practice, nothing was reserved for me, I being on pleasure. However, I contrived to open the cupboard and helped myself. Two days after I was away on duty, and again nothing was kept for me ; as I had helped myself before, although a new lock was put on the cupboard, I made use of my carpentering knowledge, opened it and helped myself. This was too much for Buchanan, he laid a trap for me, into which I fell. I again was late for dinner and pitched into the remains of a cold beef pie. In a few days my mouth became sore, the gums inflamed and I was aware of a fetid breath. At last I spoke to Lucas and asked him if my breath was not bad. He turned from me with a grimace, saying ' Pheugh ! you are rotten, Boteler, it is time you were buried.' I did not find it out till long after, but the pie was drugged with calomel.

Well, we went to England and arrived safely at Sheerness, and were ordered to Chatham to be refitted. It would have been better, had the *St George* started with us while the weather was fine, but she delayed till later and then sailed with the *Defence*, David Atkins, and *Cressy*, and on the coast of Norway encountered heavy weather. Jury masts were very well in fine weather, but they were not of sufficient weight in a gale. The squadron got on a lee shore, and the admiral, finding little probability of saving his ship, made the signal to part company. The *Cressy* made sail away, and old David Atkins could have done the same, but he heroically stood by the admiral and both these ships went ashore on the rocks, and only fifteen souls saved out of about 1,400. It was a most disastrous

24

autumn; two other line of battle ships, the *Hero* and another, went on shore on the Haik sands by the Texel, on the coast of Holland, as also an eighteen gun brig, losing nearly all hands, and on the coast of Ireland by Loch Swilly, the *Saldanha*, Sir Thomas Pakenham. I remember subscribing a week's pay for the widows and orphans.[1]

While the ship was refitting, I went home on a month's leave. My father was greatly disturbed at the state of my mouth, and he questioned me rather closely as to calomel having been prescribed for me, and he had a medical man to consult on it. It was agreed, on my assuring them I had not knowingly taken calomel, that it was an attack of scurvy, and I was treated accordingly. All my clothes were looked to, shirts, sheets, stockings, &c. and renovated; and I returned to my ship, and was astonished to find a great to-do. One day Lucas was half-drunk and boasted to Buckannon of his ability to get a glass of port whenever he chose, and the next day he was in the same state, and being led on to explain himself, he took down a board separating the lieutenants' store room from the midshipmen's berth, for he had cut round a nail or two, and removed the plank so that he could put in his hand and take what he chose. There was a great uproar, Lucas was flogged and turned out of the ship; and another mid., Denby, was also flogged.

And here I became acquainted with the calomel affair as Buckanon's handiwork. It was not over brave of me, but to serve him out, I cut a hole in the lid of his chest and poured into it the contents of the midshipmen's slop pail. It was a large chest and filled with the plunder he had extracted from the different mids. whose money he was entrusted with, for their fit out in various ways.

Before I leave the *Dictator* I must name a little affair in the Baltic. In our berth in the cockpit away from any daylight, we were lighted by miserable dips (twelve to the pound), and they constantly required snuffing, and we had no snuffers, so when the snuff came to a large toad-stool head, the cry would be ' Top—top,' and the last to answer had to snuff the candle with his fingers. I had to do this and dropped the snuff on Giddings' head, he being asleep with his head on the table. The piece of snuff began to fizz and burn down till Giddings started up, and seizing a ruler, made for me. To escape his fury I ran for the door, but I was not

[1] See *The Naval Chronicle*, 1812 (Vol. 27), for the loss of the *St George* and *Defence* on the coast of Jutland (pp. 44–6); the *Hero* and *Grasshopper*, sloop, on the Haak Sand off the Texel (pp. 43–4); and the *Saldanha* frigate (Captain the Hon. William Pakenham) off Lough Swilly (pp. 42–3).

clear of the berth door when his boot gave me a ' precious whack
where the tail joins on to the small of the back.'   I was in no absolute pain, but a deadly sickness came over me, and I fainted right
away.   When I came to, all the midshipmen were about me, some
of them fancying I was really gone ; Giddings more frightened than
any.

My great friend in the ship was young John Jones, midshipman,
a young Welsh lad, very good-humoured.   He had nothing but his
pay, and yet he was the neatest dressed midshipman in the ship,
his ' weekly account ' kept so white with pipe-clay.   He used to
tell of his living in the wild regions of Tan-y-Bwlch, in North Wales.
Another mid. I remember, T. L. Crooke, who in one of our rows at
the theatre at Rochester jumped on the stage, and, amidst a shower
of oranges and ginger-beer bottles, sang ' So neatly he handled the
turf-cutting trade,' this in full uniform, cocked hat, and sword.

I left out a remarkable circumstance in the *Dictator*.   On our
way to England we became bewildered in the middle of the North
Sea and the captain determined to anchor, which we did in twenty-
eight fathoms water.   We veered to three cables on end and rode
very pleasantly, but pitching tremendously at times bowsprit under,
and the water coming over the forecastle poured into the main-
deck.   We remained at anchor three days and were visited by two
fishermen, who gave us our bearings.   We weighed very easily and
we found our way to the Swin and into Sheerness.

CHAPTER II

Channel—North Sea—Baltic

In February, 1812, four of us were discharged into the *Sceptre*, Captain Thomas Harvey, at Plymouth—John Harvey, Hooper, Paine, and myself—and we were joined in London by another—G. Thomas. Our heavy baggage was sent by road waggon and we four went to London, putting up at Jack's Coffee House, Dean Street, Soho. We secured our places, five insides in a six-inside coach for Plymouth, and three of us went for a stroll ; seeing a great crowd in the street, we joined it to find out what was going on, when Hooper said, ' A crowd was only created for the sake of plunder—we had better cut away,' and we hustled out ; directly the cry was ' That's him,' and Hooper took to his heels. I got away in a different direction. Hooper ran at speed and fancying they were going to cut him off, turned back, and by that way baffled them. Had either of us been taken we might have been locked up for the night, no excuse would be taken and our passage to Plymouth interrupted. I was soon lost, could not find my way back, indeed, when asking for Dean Street was directed wrong, and I had, in the end, to get back in a hackney coach.

The next morning we all started and had the coach to ourselves ; the roads were very bad and we had generally six horses, and at every stage the postboys would apply for a tip ; at first this was given, but latterly refused, or we pretended to be asleep. I forget where we halted to dine, but as it seemed, we were barely seated when the horn was blown for starting, and we got no dinner. There was a laugh at our expense. The second day we were not done, but when the horn was heard one snatched up a whole fowl, another potatoes, beef and bread, and took them into the coach with us, and we had a jolly dinner and a good amount of laughing. The second night we halted for about three hours at the Crescent or Half-moon, Exeter. A miserable stoppage, no fire, no waiter, empty coffee-room, and I recollect strolling into the cathedral yard by moon-light. When we were about to start two gentlemen got inside and wanted to turn us out : they had taken inside places at Exeter and they would not move till a gentleman interfered, saying we had places all the way from London and were therefore entitled to keep them ; eventually the two men had to go outside. Our friend turned out to be a Plymouth outfitter and we promised him our custom. On the way he fell asleep and we stowed away his wig, which he seemed to enjoy as much as ourselves. We reached Plymouth Dock (as it was called in those days) in the afternoon—three days' and two nights' journey—and we all went on board in a pinnace that was in waiting at Mount Wise and here it was, as I said in another place, my chest was so well taken care of by a man who afterwards proved to be James Butler.

In two or three days the captain sent for us, saying that he heard from Mr Foote, our quondám fellow-traveller, something of a promise to employ him, and that he thought we were bound to do so, considering, too, how he had protected us. There was nothing more to be said but to him we went, I for a hat, others for shoes or what not and he asked us in for a cup of tea.

We went into Cawsand Bay and after a little delay hoisted the flag of Sir H. B. Neale, and together with the *Dreadnought*, 98, and two 74's, sailed to watch the enemy's fleet in Brest Harbour. We kept the sea, having a frigate inshore to observe the French-men's movements. We had a hard gale from the south-west with a very heavy sea on from the poop at times, although as clear as possible, every now and then we could not see the masthead vanes of either of the squadrons—the sea as it came foaming above seemed as if it must break right over us, instead of which all at once it rolled beneath us. As we heavily rolled, our spare topsail yard, stowed outside the chains, was completely under water. At last, in one of these lurches, we carried away the foretopmast and it took a long while to shift it.

From information of the movements of the French squadron we were recalled, and returned to Cawsand Bay. We had three or four trips on shore and enjoyed our tea-drinking at Mrs Elliot's, the mother of Captain Elliot, C.B.[1] From Cawsand Bay we were ordered to join the North Sea fleet, Admiral Sir William Young, then at anchor on the eighteen fathom bank off the Texel, but far out of sight of land. On our passage through the Downs, one of

---

[1] Possibly Captain William Elliott, C.B., K.C.H. (knighted in 1837), whose sister married William Frederick Lapidge, subsequently mentioned.

our mids., John Paine, outside by the mizen chains catching a bird, missed his footing, fell overboard and was drowned ; it is supposed he struck against a lower deck port, for he never appeared above water ; he was a very superior young fellow. His death was much regretted by us all.

Our first lieutenant had a spaniel on board, the animal was well aware of the standing and authority of his master, and it was ridiculous to notice the difference of the dog's behaviour when his master was on or off deck. When on, the dog would strut about the midshipmen, now and then showing his teeth at them, very different when off deck, then it was to get away from the mids. for fear of a kick, and to make himself scarce.

We had also a long-tailed monkey, I don't know if anyone owned him, but he was a general favourite, especially with the ship's company. His tail was prehensile, and he could hang by it. The dog and he were at drawn daggers ; the dog would fly at him whenever he shewed himself on the quarter-deck. One day the dog was asleep by the topsail haulyard rack, when the monkey was coming up the companion hatch ; as soon as he spied the dog, he dodged below, but apparently considering the matter, he had another look, chuckled to himself, disappeared, ran along the main deck, and came up again by a waist ladder. The men saw him— ' What's Jacko up to now, I wonder ? ' The monkey soon solved the doubt, he mounted the main rigging, till from rope to rope he reached the topsail haulyards, and by this he descended till just over and within reach of the dog, then hanging by his tail and his hind legs he caught the dog by both ears, lifting him up and shaking him soundly, chattering and apparently laughing the whole time, the dog howling all the while ; when well shaken the monkey ceased, hauled himself up a little, well pleased. Strange, ever after this, the two were excellent friends, the dog would wag his tail whenever he saw his friend the monkey and they both would sleep together on the quarter-deck.

But Jacko came to grief once : on the foremast cabin bulkhead on the main deck was hung a salt-box, and in it a few cartridges for a signal gun : one, two, and three disappeared ; the gunner at first, supposing it the trick of a mid., said nothing ; but when the third went he named it to the first lieutenant, and when a fourth was taken, the complaint went to Captain Harvey, who said he would flog all three sentries, at the wardroom door, if another cartridge was stolen that night. The sentry from eight till twelve was determined to be on the look out ; so, when relieved, he lay down by the capstan under the half-deck, and in sight of the salt-box, and in the course of an hour Jacko appeared, and on seeing the marine (of course he was the culprit), hesitated, then examined the Jolly closely, and on finding him in a sound sleep, jumped on a gun then to the salt-box, whipped out the cartridge, and tucking it under his arm jumped through the port and from gun to gun to the fore part of the ship and then below to the lower deck, the marine after him like a shot, and then with lights they discovered four or five cartridges stowed away under the breast of the foremost gun. In the morning it was duly reported to the captain, who said he was ' quite sure with the threat of flogging the sentries, that the theft would be discovered.' Then the monkey was produced, perfectly aware he was in a scrape, hanging his head aside and looking very sheepish ; the master-at-arms here said he would teach him better manners, he would never touch powder again. The captain saying ' He would not have the monkey hurt, it was the nature of the creature to be mischievous,' &c., &c. But the monkey was taken below, a cartridge taken down before him, a match sent for, a little powder strewed on the deck, poor Jacko's nose held over it, and the powder fired, flashing up into his face. He set off screaming, rubbing his eyes, for his whiskers and eyebrows were singed, but he never went near the powder again.

Every fortnight four ships of the line were sent away to Hoseley Bay, on the Norfolk coast, to complete water and get about twenty bullocks for the fleet, then to go off the Texel, to be in sight of the large Dutch and French fleets at anchor in the Zuyder Zee, and there remain four or five days. Spring tides were the only time those ships could get out. We generally counted from twenty-three to thirty large ships. While backing and filling off the Texel, we would have our large trawl net over the side ; it was hung by a nine-inch hawser, rove through a block on the fore yardarms and hauled in by the two watches, as they were relieved, at twelve and four in the morning ; the take was very uncertain, at times so full that a boat was lowered for the produce, at other times only a few fish, but let the fishing be large or small, it was all the same to us mids. The take was usually put into large tubs abaft a carronade, under the poop awning and in charge of the sentry at the cabin door. Well, we mids. used to have three fish hooks lashed back to back, and as we innocently leant against the carronade, would throw the hooks over our shoulders into the tub and very sure in a short time to pull out some fish or other. Then if a windsail was down the companion into the cockpit, the fish would be sent flapping

30

below, and there would be somebody at hand to catch it. One night it so happened that I caught a large sole and there being no windsail, I put it under my great coat and walked forward, intending to carry it below by the waist ladder ; but I counted without my host : by ill luck I had the fish head downwards, and as I went across the quarter-deck, I felt it slipping lower and lower till flop it went on the deck, the lieutenant, Tom Chrystie, merely saying— ' Eh, Mr Boteler, take him bock again, mon.'

Occasionally there would be a successful haul of turbot, and one or two of the best were reserved for Sir William Young, the admiral ; unfortunately, once there was but a single turbot, and it came to the share of the mids. depredation. The loss was instantly discovered, and there was a tremendous row. The captain was very angry, no one knew anything about it. The master-at-arms, was sent to search our berths. At the first alarm fortunately, it was hidden away, at any rate the fish was never found, and the next haul of the trawl was successful, so all was soon forgotten.

These trips away from the fleet were always considered a great holiday to us all, at Hoseley Bay we had a game at cricket, and at any rate a nice stroll on shore.

We had an amusing little creature in the ship, a coati mundi. It had all the tricks and misfortunes of a monkey ; for instance, he took into his head to rub out all the chalkings of the log board, and at the same time to pinch off one of his claws with the fall of it. He enjoyed eau de cologne or lavender water ; if poured on the deck, he seemed half crazy over it, scratching, putting his tail between his legs and rubbing the scent into it, and then strutting off with the tail on end, every now and then taking a sniff at it.

The captain had two small hanging tables in his cabin, with water or what not on them, on one he had an egg, which disappeared no one knew how. At last the captain lounging on his sofa saw the coati eyeing the table, and the creature seeing him took himself off, then returned, went up to the captain and examined him, satisfied that he was asleep, leaped on the carronade and on to the hanging table, helped himself to the egg and cut away with it, taking it into the main chains, and discussed it. Captain Harvey, to be even with him, sent to the carpenter's mate and had a chalk egg made and put it on the shelf. The captain again took to the sofa, and in a short time the coati appeared, satisfied himself that the captain was asleep, got once more to the hanging table and set off with the egg, the captain running to the quarter galley, whence he saw the creature's movements. He first bit at it, eyed it wonderingly, then he tapped it on the chains, looked at it enquiringly, when the captain called out—' Ah—ah ! ' The coati looked round, dropped the sham egg, but never went near the hanging shelf again.

By way of recreation, the ship, being at sea and all sail set, it was agreed that eight mids. were to storm the main top, where was an oldster with a rope's end to defend it ; one of the mids., Carter, son of the ship's carpenter, was in the act of getting into the top with his hands on the top rim, when the oldster hit him over the knuckles, and Carter let go both hands and rattled down the rigging, rolling over and over; fortunately the mainsail was set and the foot rope taut on the lower rigging, and so caught poor Carter, who not knowing where he was, or indeed, where he came from, jumped out, disappearing down the Jacob's ladder and never stopped till he got into the berth in the cockpit. His father, hearing of his extraordinary tumble, called out to the first lieutenant ' Flog him, sir, flog him ! ' scarcely knowing what he was saying. It was a most wonderful fall and a miraculous escape from death.

Captain Harvey always sent the remains of his puddings to us midshipmen, and we regularly looked for them. The cook had a large table hung between two guns abreast of his fire-place, and one of the mids. passing saw a plum-pudding just taken up and put under a cover ; notwithstanding a sentry was on his post by the table, and the cook not far off, he seized the pudding and brought it down to us in our berth. ' Here, my boys, is a nice present ; attack it at once and don't lose time, it is a cut out,' and we all did attack it, and had just finished it when the master-at-arms came down to search and make enquiries, all to no purpose ; at the captain's dinner, when the time came for the pudding, there was delay. Fraser, his steward, was fidgety. ' Well, sir, where's the pudding ? ' At last it was reported the pudding was stolen. It was not believed, and a threat was thrown out that the cook would be punished for omitting to make one at all, and there was a great uproar ; the mids. were at once suspected, and search was made, to no purpose of course. It was a most silly trick and might have proved most serious. Some years after, when the truth was known, Captain Harvey laughed, saying ' he always knew it was the mids., but all the same he had played his father the same trick when with him as an admiral on the *Prince of Wales* in the West Indies.'

We had a midshipman named Worth, brother to a Captain Worth, a great bully, he carried a rope's end for the purpose of thrashing us, which he did on every and no occasion. We one day waylaid him, four or five of us, and gave him a great pummelling.

32

He again thrashed us and then we arranged an attacking party, waited for him at the foot of the cockpit ladder, and as he came down, half-blind from the light, we pitched into him. Young Pickford (Charlie) was our commodore of the gunboats : he would be the first to rush in and receive the knock-down blow, but he was well backed and we gave Worth such a decided thrashing as to completely cure him of molesting us. He never touched one of us afterwards. Among us was young Thomas at these two attacks ; he would put his hands to our backs : ' Come on, don't be afraid,' but taking good care to be out of the way of the two or three first blows.

Apropos of Charlie Pickford : after he got his promotion he went abroad to Blois or Tours. He was but a few days there when he was told there were two French gentlemen, and one in particular, who were the terror of the English residents, contriving to pick a quarrel and, as they were good swordsmen, managed to disfigure or kill those opposed to them. Charlie said nothing, but walking on the parade was jostled by the most conspicuous of the two, at which Charlie took no notice. On this, in passing a second time the French-man with an unmistakable sneer turned him off the pavement. This was too glaring, Charlie turned at him and spit in his face, to the astonishment of the Frenchman and his friends. A challenge ensued and as Charlie had the choice of weapons, he chose pistols. A large number of French were present as well as several English. When on the ground Charlie said ' I know you are a dead shot, and that I must be killed, but I will not fall alone, we shall fire across a hand-kerchief.' At this there was a great outcry : ' it was not in the annals of duelling.' Charlie then said ' he should proclaim his opponent a dastardly coward wherever he went, a man who would only fight where he knew he had the advantage.' There was a considerable discussion on the point, at last Charlie said ' I will give him another chance, I propose that one pistol shall alone be loaded, the two put into a hat, taken out, and God speed the victor.' After much talk this was agreed to, and Charlie by good luck drew the loaded weapon and shot his adversary ; no other Englishman was insulted after this. Charlie's end was melancholy : shortly after the duel his constitution gave way and he died of consumption.

Our purser, Mr Taylor, died, we were in the Downs, and the body in its coffin was sent on shore to be buried at the Naval Hospital. The surf was so great that it was found impossible to land it, and it had to be floated on shore, a party of hospital nurses and marines managed to get hold of it. A few days afterwards a survey was held on the remains of the purser's stores and among them the battered ends of lanterns ; for it was the custom of the mids. whenever they could get hold of a lantern to smash it in revenge for the miserable dips we were allowed for lighting the berth. While the survey was going on someone called out : ' Take care the purser's ghost don't appear,' and by some means this got among the crew and it was said the ghost was to appear on a particular night. The corporal relieving the sentry in the cockpit at midnight got out of the way as fast as possible. In the surgeon's cabin was a long case containing a full-sized skeleton, and it so chanced that a big cat jumping out of the cabin window, upset the case and the skeleton came prone into the cockpit, and at the same time a mid. (ever ready for mischief) threw his pillow at the sentry, who was in a great tremor in expectation, and being close to the purser's cabin, screamed out and fell into it in a dead faint. In an instant was heard the pattering of feet overhead of every man jumping from his hammock and racing forward, and then a dead silence, till the officer of the watch and first lieutenant were heard : ' Cockpit there, what is the row ? ' Master-at-arms, ship's corporal, sergeant of marines, &c., all called, at last down came the sergeant of marines, the first lieutenant and a whole posse comitatus to find the sentry still in a faint, and when brought to declaring that the purser's ghost had taken him by the shoulders and shoved him into the cabin, and this was all that could be got from the poor fellow. The ship's company were in a crowd forward, beginning to recover themselves, but for a long while none would go aft. So much for a ghost story.

At this time an alteration in naval uniform took place.[1] A lieutenant had one epaulette on the right shoulder, a commander who had an epaulette on the left shoulder before, had now two epaulettes ; and a post captain under three years who had one on his right shoulder, had now two with a silver anchor on the strap, and a post captain, over three years, had now two epaulettes with a silver crown and anchor, and the service was given till the following 1st January to wear out the old uniforms, but in the first two or three days some lieutenants began to mount the swab. The signal man would report a post captain coming and the guard turn out to receive him, when it proved to be *only* a lieutenant.

I must not forget our monkey's last exploit ; the young marine officer had his cabin abaft the after lower deck gun, and there was an opening for light, through this opening the monkey observed the marine shave himself and then powder his hair before going up to

---

[1] Uniform Regulations of March 23rd, 1812.

34

breakfast, giving his servant, who was in his mess between the after
guns, orders to clear away. He sat at his ease for a time. The
monkey in the meanwhile entered the cabin, sat himself before the
glass, took up the shaving brush and lathered his face, then seized
a razor, cut his finger, and threw it into the basin, he then took the
powder puff and began to daub his face (lather and all) ; and his
head and face with its lather, powder and blood was a sight worth
looking at. At this time the servant disturbed him, but not till the
powder puff and shaving brush were in the basin, and Jacko made
his escape, and as he danced along the lower deck, the men called
after him ' There goes the major.' When the marine officer was
acquainted with Jacko's doings, he took an opportunity to well
thrash the poor brute, but Jacko was his master after all, he took
the opportunity of the marine's absence, and made the cabin in such
a filthy mess that it took many days to sweeten it, for in that way
a monkey is far more offensive than a cat.

Well, at the close of the year 1812, the *Sceptre* was ordered
to Chatham, and it became rumoured that Captain Harvey would
be superseded and the ship ordered to the American station for the
flag of Sir George Cockburn ; while at Chatham the captain was
ordered to Sheerness to sit on a court-martial, and I went down in
the gig as gig midshipman. The Russian fleet was in Sheerness
Harbour to be out of the way of Napoleon's army. I don't know
now how it was, but I spent an hour or two on board one of their
frigates, and was asked by an officer, who spoke English, to lunch
with them. There was a capital looking beef steak, but oh, my
interior ! it was fried in rancid oil, enough to turn my stomach.
However, they were exceedingly obliging and a glass of good wine
set me quite to rights. I remember one person that took my
attention, a long-coated black-bearded priest.

A day or so after this, the captain again went to Sheerness, and
returning in the evening was upset in his gig, fortunately not far
from a frigate in Long Reach, which picked him up. But I heard
him complain of the injury to a splendid gold watch, part of a
present by one of the Leeward Islands to his father, Sir Henry
Harvey, in 1796.

While at Chatham, of course I paid frequent visits to my old
school, where I had still two brothers—Edward and Robert—the
last got into a scrape that deserved a flogging, but Mr Griffiths
when he came to the block threw down his birch, saying ' he had
never yet flogged a Boteler and could not do it now.'

In January, 1813, I was discharged into the *Zealous*, 74, Captain

Thomas Boys, then lying at the Nore—a miserable day for me, I was
so thoroughly happy in the *Sceptre*, on such good terms with all the
officers; one thing made it more palatable, Captain Harvey was
leaving the ship and I had my brother Thomas on the *Zealous*; still
it was hard lines. The *Zealous* was in miserable order, had been
turned out of the Mediterranean fleet for her untidiness.

Before I leave the *Sceptre* I must relate something of her early
history. There were forty of the same class vessels built by contract at different private yards, and they were termed the ' Forty
Thieves.'[1] From inattention, or worse, of the Government In-
spector of Works the most shameful frauds were committed, in the
case of two or three of them at any rate : a vast number of copper
bolts were stolen and devil's bolts used instead, *i.e.*, a short piece of
copper bolt driven in and another short piece at the end and *clinched*,
as was proved in the *Sceptre*. On her way home from India the ship's
sides gave out ; they had to throw overboard all the main-deck
guns and frap to the ship's sides by hawsers across the main deck
or the whole deck would have fallen. The ship did not make much
water and she was brought safely home.

It was on a Sunday, and while the ship's company was at prayers
I was wandering about the deck very miserable, thinking of my
change of ships, when old Butler, who had watched and seemed to
know all my feelings, came to comfort me, saying, ' Don't fret, sir,
it may be all for the best, depend on it,' and he kept with me for
some time. However, my time was up, and I was sent to Sheerness
and joined the *Zealous*.

For a time I was so much depressed with my change of ships
that I have no recollection of when and how we sailed, or of anything
till our arrival in Wingoe Sound. I remember my father giving me
ten guineas, for each of which in Sweden I got twenty-six shillings,
such was their value over silver. At Wingoe, Swedes came down
from Gottenburg, with plentiful supplies of bread, fish, vegetables,
and eggs, the latter eighteen and twenty for a shilling. From
Wingoe Sound three ships of the line, under an admiral—*Minotaur*,
Venerable, and ourselves—started with about thirty sail of convoy
to force the passage through the Sound, past Elsineur Castle. When
under some high land on the Swedish coast we were caught by a
sudden storm as we were in the act of stowing the jib. There was a

---

[1] ' Forty Thieves : A name given to forty line-of-battle ships ordered by the
Admiralty at one fell swoop, to be built by contract, towards the end of the
Napoleon[ic] war, and which turned out badly. . . . Many never went to sea as
ships of the line, but were converted into good frigates ' (*The Sailor's Word-Book.*
By Admiral W. H. Smyth. 1867).

tremendous loud thunder clap directly overhead, more like a volley
of big guns than anything else, accompanied by a blinding flash
of lightning which struck the jib-boom, throwing four men overboard, killing them outright ; four of the remaining five crawled
in, the fifth man remaining across the boom ; not answering to
his call two men went out to his assistance, but he, too, was stone
dead, so that five were killed out of the nine. The lightning ran
from gun to gun on the lower deck, but where it made its exit
nothing shewed. The next flash struck a brig and splintered her
topmast.

After this we went on through the Sound, keeping well over the
Swedish shore. Elsineur Castle opened fire on us, and many shot
passed over us, doing but little harm—hitting one ship only and
wounding two of the crew. It seemed inconceivable the fright some
of the convoy were in, two of them absolutely running on shore,
giving us almost a day's employment in getting them off again.
Once through, we let them run alone and ourselves anchored off
Helsinbourg ; here we all went on shore and I remember were
shewn a shot, fired by the Danes, sticking in the walls of a church.
We bought fish and eggs, twenty-four to thirty for a shilling. The
next morning we went on a little further, and anchored off Huen
Island and a party of us went on shore for a walk, visiting Tycho-
Brahe tower and getting ham and eggs for luncheon. I was started
off with a letter to our consul at Malmo, fourteen or sixteen miles
away. I remember sitting at dinner with the consul, his wife, and
white-headed children. I don't know the purport of my communication, but I brought back a written answer, getting on board
when nearly dark.

The ship returned to Wingoe Sound, and here the mids. got leave
to take a cutter and two seamen for a bathe among the rocks.
I did not go ; in the course of time the boat was seen pulling hard
for the ship and calling for the surgeon, for in her was apparently
the corpse or body of my brother. He was like a dead man and
was directly rolled in a blanket and taken to the galley fire, and for
a long while every means taken to revive him ; at last he gave signs
of life and was put into a cot in the captain's cabin, and eventually
perfectly restored. It seems that they all left the boat for a smooth
rock for a dip. The rock was very slippery and my brother, unable
to help himself, slid off at once into deep water ; he came up once,
but gradually sank and could be seen lying on his back at the
bottom, the water was so clear. Richards, a mid., dived but could
not reach him ; they ran to the boat at the other end of the rock for

a boat-hook which a mizen-topman, the boat-keeper, brought over and with it fished my brother out, to all intents quite dead. There was the pull also to the ship. It was marvellous his recovery after such a time inanimate. He described his coming-to as far more painful than his drowning. Then he only went off in a dream that his father and mother and others were about him, but in coming to he had all the horrors of struggling and tearing his nails against the rocks.

In the ship was the purser, George Thorn, whose escape from wreck was rather remarkable. He was purser of the *Athenian*, 64, which while in the Mediterranean was sailing towards Malta, having on board a general officer who, after dinner, said, ' Well, captain, where are the famous Quirk rocks you speak so much of ? ' The reply was, laughing, ' If anywhere we should be about on them,' and at that moment the ship struck hard and fast.[1] The rocks were well known to exist, but they occupied so small a space that ship after ship sent to survey them came away baffled. There was not the remotest chance of getting the ship off. She had a good deal of way on her when she struck, and she struck heavily. The object was to save the crew, and all attention was paid to getting the boats out and provisioning them. This was pretty well accomplished. The ship forged off a little and directly began to sink, when George Thorn appeared on the poop. He had gone to his cabin for a bag of money, so to reach the launch had to jump for it, and of course went down like a stone, till he let go of his money, when he rose and was taken in.

From Wingoe we sailed south, and when considerably beyond Anholt Island two barges were manned, in one Lieutenant Slade and I, in the other Mr Roberts as mate, the captain sending for me and giving me a written order to put myself under the orders of Lieutenant Slade, as he said, ' to ensure you the treatment of an officer in case of being made prisoner.' We had the necessary provisions, and were to cruise for a week. We started off, and were soon out of sight of the ship. The second day I remember an exciting wild-goose chase ; we met with a whole flight and winged one, and we were quite half-an-hour before we could get him. He was quick in diving away from our shot and evading us when we fancied we could pick him up, dodging us in every way. The lieutenant had a fowling piece, I a ship's musket, and sheet lead cut

<hr>

[1] For the wreck of H.M.S. *Athenienne* (64) on Skerki Bank, October 27th, 1806, see *The Naval Chronicle* (1806), Vol. 16, pp. 493-5, and (1807), Vol. 17, pp. 57-9. The general officer was Brigadier-General Campbell. Thorn is stated to have been taking passage in her ; he was not her Purser.

38

into squares for my shot. The third day we pulled for an island, of which Lieutenant Slade had some knowledge, the name of which has escaped my memory, but it was a small one, some distance from the mainland, and inhabited by a farmer, his wife, sons and daughters and a labourer. As we neared it the son came down to shew the best landing. He was dressed in sheep skins, and looked a veritable Robinson Crusoe. We landed our crews, who were immensely happy, and forming three parties started across the island, the lieutenant in the middle, and Roberts and I on either flank, and in this way chased a whole legion of hares down a bank at the end of the island on to a flat that ran to a point, finishing off in a long reef. A great many hares escaped on either side, but we managed to knock over three, and then returned to the farmhouse to dinner, for the old lady had cooked a fillet of veal for us, and we sat to it with great appetites. Our men at their dinner had grog and half a pail of milk, and were very jolly, and after some time we formed across the island for another hunt, and with more care, driving before us a larger quantity of hares. Poor things, when at the point they dashed through our closed ranks, the men hitting at them with sticks. One hare, bewildered, stood on his hind legs and I shot it. We killed four, but in the scrimmage I lost a case of green ivory-handled knife and fork, which shut into each other. It was a great loss to me ; I had had it three or four years. We left two hares with our hostess ; she was very thankful, and regretted the absence of her husband. We had another evening meal, with grog and milk and songs, and then launched our boats again. We had but one chance, and she eluded us at night. Nothing else took place, and we returned to the ship, which we easily found. I well remember the curious feeling in my legs on walking across the deck after a week's cramping in the boat.

A week after this we observed a brig, the *Hearty*, coming down. She had on board Count d'Artois, the Duke d'Angoulême, and two or three French nobles. Our captain had them all on board to dinner. The Duke d'Angoulême came down to our berth and sat awhile with us, and we sent for Sinclair, the ship's barber, whose father, Mayor of Marseilles, was hanged, à la lanterne, during the Reign of Terror. The duke took great notice of him, promised if his party came to the throne he would remember him, which no doubt he did. The French princes, in their small accommodation of a ten-gun brig, were on their way to Russia.

At Wingoe Sound we got half a dozen geese, which we were obliged to keep in the wing, by our berth. Watts, a mid., had the care of them, and it was strange how soon they appeared to know him. I recollect their cackling and following him into our berth, but they were not very long lived. This Watts was upset in a boat going off to Spithead, and was drowned, when I, a lieutenant of the *Antelope*, was on my way off at the same time, and narrowly escaped filling in the cross sea of the Spit.

We sailed through the Great Belt to the Island of Bornholm, and right away to Riga, in Prussian Pomerania, where we found a ten-gun brig, and for some purpose I was sent on board her, and how disgusted I was at the midshipmen's berth. It seemed such a dismal little place as compared to our nest, even though in a cockpit. I remember, too, feeling very qualmish in her, and was glad to get into our boat again.

It was getting rather late in the year when we returned to Wingoe Sound, and I well remember thrashing through the ice, occasionally brought up by it, and our having capstan bars over the bows to save the copper; all the fore part of the ship was covered with ice, the ropes so frozen as with difficulty to run through the blocks. However, we got into Wingoe, in perfect smooth water, and one morning there was a sort of film over it, and by the evening thick ice had formed, and next morning the ship was hard and fast in ice five or six inches thick. While in this condition the Swedes visited us in sleighs drawn by shaggy ponies; they brought down soft bread, fish, eggs, &c. One day my brother and I jumped into the sleigh and set off. The ice was very rough, and the Swedes were soon after us; I was jolted out and pretended to be hurt. The Swedes only shook their heads, and laughed at me, and they soon overtook the sleigh and turned my brother out, first giving him a good shaking, and there was a fine laugh at us when we returned to the ship.

I don't know how long we were frozen up, but I recollect the fun of clearing a transport of provisions with our boats on skids. In the end we were relieved by ice-saws, sent I believe from England. We set to work, and by cutting out squares of ice, which with capstan bars, handspikes, and hooks we shoved under the ice on either side, till we made a canal, and warped the ship to open water outside. No sooner out than a thaw set in, and we again anchored in company of other ships till time for going home.

We started with the *Venerable, Minotaur* and another. When some distance from Yarmouth we met two fishing boats which were on the look out for us with supplies, and what seemed to enchant us, had red herrings and ginger-bread, and it so took our fancy that the day before anchoring each of us got paper, heading it with ' Things

40

that I want most,' and all began the same—red herrings and ginger-bread, and then blacking, a brush, knife, writing paper, &c., for we all knew how treacherous our memory becomes when on shore. Well, we had our run, and all brought on board a stock of herrings and ginger-bread, and there seemed to be a general pull at them, Dan Knowles saying, ' Never mind, my boys, I have lots in my chest when these are all gone,' but lo, and behold ! when the time came, all his stock had disappeared. We had opened his chest and taken all.

I must not forget the *Venerable* coming through Smith's Gap and taking the ground. The tide was on the flood, and she did not remain long, but she made a great noise firing guns, &c.

While in the North Sea, blowing rather fresh, and a dark night, the signal was made ' to wear.' By some mismanagement the *Minotaur* put her helm up out of turn, and in coming to on the opposite tack, ran us on board, her bull's head close on upon one of our main deck ports. It was a serious time for both ships, and as her head ground against our side an Irishman called out, ' Where is Mr Gee ? send for Mr Gee to cut the tongue out,' Mr Gee, the second master, being noted for getting the tongues of all cattle killed on board. There was a general laugh throughout the ship at this exclamation of the Irishman. It ran like wildfire, and tended much to restore quiet among the crew. From Yarmouth Roads we set off for Sheerness, and arrived there in October.

CHAPTER III

West Indies—Passing for Lieutenant—Channel—Battle of Waterloo

On the 20th December, 1813, my brother Thomas and I, having served so far in ships of the line, both wished for a more active time in frigates and we speedily got appointed, my brother to the *Hamadryad* and I to the *Orontes*, Captain N. D. Cochrane, C.B., she being at Sheerness, and I was allowed to go home on leave for a month, at the end of which I joined my ship then at the Nore. The *Orontes* was a 38 gun frigate, built of fir entirely, every portion having been injected with coal tar, she had a square tuck and floated very light. There were four of this class—the *Euphrates, Tiber, Heber* (?) [1] and ourselves—but they soon wore out, none of them lasting over five years.

The *Orontes* was a very cosy, comfortable craft ; what made the greatest impression on my mind was the difference in my sleeping berth, in a liner it was in the cable tier, and in the frigate in the steerage next the pumps, being the last midshipman on board. We all messed in a good sized cabin on the larboard side of the steerage.

Our first freak I remember was with little Matthews, the Chatham tailor. There was little love between us, all of us, I may say. He sent my bill for a dress coat, a week old only, to my father and he now came on board dunning some other of the officers. We left the coal hole hatch off near the foot of the ladder and down he went, the hatch being instantly on, and there we kept him two or three hours, when we let him out, and over the ship's side he started quicker than he came.

Our captain was staying at the Mitre Hotel, Chatham, and to him Mr Lethbridge, of Sand Hill Park, Taunton, brought his son. It was ridiculous to hear young Lethbridge, the ' Squire ' as he was termed, describe the proceedings. ' Hold your head up, John,

---

[1] Probably *Hebrus*.

the captain is coming,' &c.   Lethbridge was intended for the army
and was some time at the Military Academy at Bagshot Heath, but,
while Queen Charlotte was giving new colours to the cadets, he
managed to run away to London.   He did not seem to take especial
care of himself there, but told us of passing through the Horse
Guards and lifting his hat, shewing his soldier's close crop, the
sentry remarked, ' I think I could get £3 by you, sir.'   He was
shortly after taken by Vickery, the Bow Street runner, and taken
down towards Taunton.   On the road he met his Uncle Rufford
who relieved Vickery of him, but the first thing Lethbridge did was,
hearing a coach would pass at three in the morning, to desire the
chambermaid to call him and he was in London again by it.   A
second time he was taken to his father, and here Lethbridge described
the interview with his parents, his mother sitting by the fire knitting
and his father with his back to the fire looking at him for some time,
at last saying, ' Are you my son John ? ' to which the ' Squire '
made no answer.   However he was sent to a private tutor, but got
into such scrapes, and having often talked of going to sea his father
determined to send him with Captain Cochrane.   Well, he joined,
and we were quite friends.   I told him he could not run away
now, as from the Military Academy ; that there was only the *stern
port*, &c.   The squire was in Mr Hodder's watch, an Irishman full
of fun, and he had the squire by his side, in general highly amused
with his stories.   As is usual in men-of-war, the carpenter's mate
reported the well every half-hour ; his first report, ' Three inches,
sir,' the next half-hour, three and a-half inches, and then to reach
four.   Lethbridge could stand it no longer.   ' What does the man
mean, Mr Hodder ? '   ' Oh, there's a man in the sick bay whose
nose is taking to growing and the carpenter's mate has orders to
measure it every half-hour.'   The squire was marvellously struck,
and directly he awoke next morning called out, ' How is the man
with the growing nose ? ' to the surprise of his messmates, when the
whole story came to light, to the confusion of Lethbridge.

It was a most severe winter, the Thames was frozen over, a large
fire lighted and a perfect fair held.   ' Hot-Pole ' for the benefit of the
colliers was at a premium.   We sailed for Portsmouth and afterwards
for Cork (the Cove of Cork) so-called in those days.   The officers who
went on shore after woodcock brought off a number, thin and half-
starved with the extreme cold ; so tame as to be knocked down.

We were considered a crack ship, and the midshipmen dressed
in cocked hats, tight white pantaloons and Hessian boots, with gilt
twist edging and a bullion tassel !

From Cork we were at sea for a few days and put into Crook
Haven, running up some distance in a narrow channel of rocks till
we came to an opening for anchoring, the Irish peasants running by
our side with their long coats and many coloured patches. That
night it blew hard and we drifted a trifle and found the rocks close
under our stern ; we hove her off, and in doing this the hawser parted,
broke a poor fellow's leg and hit me across the back. I was taken
below and bled till I fainted ; I was said to have called out ' Snubber,
Doctor Snubber,' to check him, as one would call in veering cable
blowing hard. However, I was none the worse. The Irish came
off and we had a dance ; two or three of the officers dined on shore,
where the little waiting maid attended without shoes or stockings.
We returned to Cork and were joined by a mate John Arthur Moore
and a raw Irish mid. Hodnèt.

I was here told off to attend a press gang : we had intimation of
a lot of seamen hid in a small public-house in the cove, and after
a scrimmage secured very prime hands, such a scene ; a wake was
got up, women howling over a coffin, where a corpse was said to be,
but our lieutenant would not believe them, and sure enough out
popped a seaman, who laughed himself, when all was over.

We hoisted signal for convoy to the West Indies and in due time
started with about thirty vessels under our charge and the *Con-
questador*, 74. We touched at Madeira, and I had a run on shore,
and a ride up the hill to the Convent St Clara. We met here with
the *Hotspur*, frigate, Captain the Honourable Jocelyn Percy, an
appropriate name for such a ship. She came in much damaged,
her quarter-deck bulwarks carried away by a sea.

In three days we were off again, and when close to the line, had
to tow a lame duck, and as we came up hand over hand, her master
called out that we were dragging her under water, and threatened
to cut the hawser ; at this time Neptune's gang had possession and
the master seeing this, said, when hailed by his majesty, asking if
any of his sons were on board, ' I think you have a top chain down
your throat, Mr Neptune,' on which Neptune got permission and
hauled the brig alongside, jumped on board and shaved all the crew
but the captain. I was not shaved, but was let off on paying half a
gallon of rum, for in those days, be it known, we each had half a pint
of spirits, or a pint of wine or a gallon of beer a day.

Love, the assistant surgeon, quite a character, came down from
the north to us and we persuaded him that the dirk was not his
proper uniform : we gave him a steel scabbarded sabre instead, and
with this he appeared in the streets of Sheerness. In a copy of

verses J. A. Moore wrote, he had Love at night walking down the
dockyard wall, and the sentry hailing, and on being answered
' Officer,' replied ' Officer, I cannot take your word.' ' D——n your
bleed, don't you see my sword ? ' drawing it and flourishing it in the
air. At another time he called, ' Bring me a pun, boy Day ' ; a
pen was brought. ' A pun, I say, bring me that whip fornent the
beam, and I will let you know a pun from pain.' At another time
looking and leaning over the gangway, one of the lieutenants with
a good smack ' en derrière,' ' Well, Doctor, what do you think of
it all ? ' Without moving he replied : ' When the wind blows fair
and the sea thus smooth, 'tis uncommon pleasurable.'

We reached Barbadoes, and directly Poll Smashum came on
board to bumboat the ship ; she was a light coloured mulatto, woolly
hair, nearly brown, her cheeks cracked with the sun, the skin hanging in flakes ; she was a most repulsive-looking creature. It was
supposed she had smuggled some spirits on board, and her rage at
the accusation ! ' I, sar, what you tink, where I carry the spirit ? '
and she off with an outer garment ; ' you tink, sar, I hab any,' and
off went another, and she was in the act of dispensing with the only
one left, when Captain Cochrane burst out with ' I believe you, Poll
——no more ! no more ! ' and she, spitting and blustering, walked off.

And here I first became acquainted with Betsy Austen who kept
a tavern, the best in Bridge Town. I was surprised at seeing the two
plates of my grandfather's battle of the 1st of June hanging up, as
also the portrait of himself. It was sufficient for me, I never went
to any other house. We took on board several boxes of specie, and
a commissariat officer, and started for English Harbour, Antigua,
where we waited a few days for the *Serapis*, a storeship, and when
she was ready, made sail for Jamaica, and as we neared Port Royal
we made a signal for a pilot, with a gun, and a dapper little negro
soon came on board. I shall never forget him, well dressed in a white
frock and trowsers and a straw hat ; after looking round, he desired
the frigate to be hove to, head to sea, and jamming his head under
a carronade slide, desired to be called at daylight, and as day broke,
and the scene became more distinct, first one breeze mill would
show itself, then another, then a team of oxen carrying off a hogshead
of rum, a stream of negroes with bundles of canes on their heads,
all was animation. We saluted the admiral, but who he was my
memory is at fault ; [1] we had hardly been at anchor two days when
the funeral of Captain Stackpoole of the *Statira* took place : he was

------

[1] Rear Admiral William Brown ; succeeded late in 1814 by Rear Admiral
Robert Rolles.

shot in a duel as I have related. I had a little money for a wonder,
and when my Lord Rodney, a hoary-headed negro with his laced
coat and cocked hat, came alongside with oranges, sour sop, Avocado
pears, pine-apples and spruce beer, I indulged in purchasing two
fine pines, one of which I gave to Squire Lethbridge, and the other
I eat myself! it was far too much for me, the consequence was I
had a surfeit, and from that time to this (1882), I have never touched
another.

While at Jamaica I walked on the Palisades, the burial place
of the squadron; it is an isthmus of sand connecting Port Royal
with the mainland and forming the splendid harbour. The whole
place is like a rabbit warren, pierced with holes, at the mouth of
which you see either the regular land crab or a species of a smaller
sort, one claw much larger than the other, and which the creature is
ever waving over his head, in a quiet monotonous way. The land
crab is most active, runs with great rapidity, and if nearing him off
he dodges at right angles and you miss him.

I got Lethbridge to accompany me to the dockyard and introduced him to the joiner's shop, desiring one of the men to measure
him. The negro grinned and did so, saying there were some of the
exact size aloft, and on going up to see what was meant, there was
a store of about forty coffins. The poor squire was awfully startled,
particularly as a large hole was left in the bottom of each to let in
the land crab! for in a gale the sands of the Palisades are for ever
shifting, so that coffins are often exposed.

Time was up and we were off to beat against the trades all the
way to Barbadoes, six weeks of it, when in running down we were
only a week. We kept well in with the St Domingo coast, to get
the land wind which spun us on our way merrily. We reached
Barbadoes, and after a time we were off again to Gros Islet Bay
and Dominique. I shall never forget Prince Rupert's Bay; I landed
there and picked Guava fruit, *ad libitum*, and I saw the Governor's
lady [1] mounted and dressed in a blue habit, braided across the chest
and a pair of epaulettes on her shoulders. From Dominique we
went to Les Saints, nothing much more than a nest of large rocks,
but with a convenient harbour and a hospital establishment; and
I remember while bathing, stepping on a sea urchin or sea egg, the
spikes of which ran into my heel and for a time were very painful.

When first in the country and going to English Harbour, Antigua,
where we were hauled in by a hawser fast to the stem of a cocoa

---

[1] The Governor of Dominica was Major-General G. R. Ainslie; the Lieutenant-
Governor was Lieutenant-General Sir John Stuart.

tree, for the sake of having our stern to the eastward and consequently getting the benefit of the sea breeze; I quite forgot to mention finding there, close to the dockyard, the *Dunira*, Captain Edward Boys, fitting for England. The capture of this frigate together with another, her consort, was very remarkable and must be told here.[1] About three weeks before, Sir Philip Durham, coming out as commander-in-chief in the *Venerable*, at daybreak found themselves close to the two Frenchmen, cleared for action in no time, giving the two ships an opportunity to communicate. They then directly bore round and made a determined attack on the *Venerable*; after some heavy firing, one of the frigates ran alongside the *Venerable* and was instantly taken, the other cut away and ran out of sight, while the *Venerable* was taking possession. Her captain told Sir Philip that both had agreed to board the *Venerable* together, and had she done so, instead of running away, the result of the fight might have been different. They probably would have been mistaken. Six or seven days had passed; in running down the trades a large ship was come upon, which soon proved to be the other Frenchman : all sail was made, and here the *Venerable* had much the best of it, and a chance shot cutting her main topmast, succeeded in closing and capturing her. She was on her way to Martinique. She was much surprised at being overtaken by the British admiral, as he imagined the admiral was before him. This frigate the admiral named the *Palma*, and gave her to his flag lieutenant.

I dined with Captain Boys and well remember having the toughest old cock chicken that ever was cooked : we both laughed over it. Captain Boys had a short time before escaped from Verdun, where he, with many others, was strictly confined and treated with great harshness; he published a narrative [2] of his exceedingly clever escape and which the Admiralty republished and supplied to the libraries of men-of-war. The whole, almost verbatim, is most cleverly introduced by Marryat in *Peter Simple*. The tale told with the only difference, the making Peter dance through France on stilts.

I was asked to dine in the gunroom. There was a beast of a monkey skipping about, making himself very obnoxious, asking for

---

[1] Official account in the *London Gazette*, February 26th, 1814. The French ships were the *Alcmene*, captured on January 16th, and the *Iphigenia*, captured two days later.

[2] *Narrative of a Captivity and Adventures in France and Flanders, between the years 1803 and 1809.* By Captain Edward Boys, R.N., late a Midshipman of His Majesty's Ship *Phoebe* (London, 1827).

biscuit. When near my legs, his master pinched his tail: the creature directly bit me sharply, and for which, when I had him in the
steerage, he got more kicks than halfpence.

Whilst at Barbadoes I had a very pleasing employment, *i.e.*,
with the ropemaker and a boat's crew at work in the dockyard,
making small rope from the yarn of old junk. I was a full week at
this work, and one day a rifle regiment came down to bathe, going
in and coming out by sound of the bugle. Two of the regiment,
good swimmers, swam a good way out. I knew what was likely to
happen and called to the boat's crew to run to the end of the long
pier shouting to the soldiers. They turned back, but all too late:
the outer man gave a piercing scream, being caught by a shark.
We saw the creature tugging and shaking his victim before he disappeared, and the other poor fellow, notwithstanding his exertions
and our near approach, was also attacked and taken away.

At the yard I had ample amusement in watching the tiny crabs,
which, like those on the Palisades of Port Royal, only much smaller,
with one claw larger than the other, but with the like monotonous
action of waving it over its head, for what object I could never
discover. There were countless other reptiles, and among them
numbers of lizards. I used to angle for them with the centre of
the long cocoa-nut leaf, pulling it before them with a noosed end,
till they walked through it, then catching them by the middle.
This often ended with a fight, as I held them up one in each hand.
It was strange how soon they bit each other's tails off; it seemed
nothing, the tails slipping off so easily.

I don't know what possessed the men, but they stuffed a jacket
and trousers with oakum and hung the effigy over the dock fence.
Directly it was seen, there was a race of soldiers from the barracks
to the spot, when our men hauled it in, well satisfied by the joke.

Our captain was a Tartar, severe in punishments. At night he
would call a man down from the yards and give him two dozen, and
he was hard upon the midshipmen. One, a Mr Smith, he declared
grinned at him looking up from the main deck. It was a natural
way he had of baring his teeth, and for this he disrated the poor
fellow, putting him in the foretop for three months; and another
mid. he served in the same way, disrating him and putting him in
th e maintop to do all duties with the men.

After a lengthy cruise we anchored in Carlisle Bay, and there
found the *Gloucester*, 74, commanded by my old captain, Robert
Williams. In those days a captain could take into another ship
almost any amount of officers he chose, and Captain Williams

availed himself of the privilege. He had his boatswain, a lieutenant, coxswain, and barge's crew, the master and five or six mids., all old messmates of mine. I was not long in getting leave to visit them, and while in the mids.' berth at grog and biscuits, a message came from the wardroom, 'glad of my company,' and it was 'Well, youngster, how are you? and the news of the station?' After a glass or two of wine I was delighted to make my salaam, and get among the mids. again.

I found there was a passing day the next morning, and I had served my time, but having no admiral's order thought it was no use to apply. It happened that in the morning, when old Williams shewed himself on deck, they said to him, 'Who do you think was on board yesterday, sir?' 'Who, who?', 'Why, young Boteler.' 'Bless my soul! not come on board to see his old captain?' 'Yes, sir, and he says he has completed his time, but thinks as he has no order from the admiral it was useless to apply.' 'Oh,' said old Williams, 'make his signal to come on board to pass.' While on deck there were our own pendant on board the *Gloucester*, followed by a telegraph of 772, 'Send Mr (spelling pendant) B O T E L E R on board to pass.' I was fairly taken aback; I never dreamed of an opportunity, had looked into no book of navigation, nor had I my logs written up. There was no help for it. I went down to the first lieutenant with the telegraph in my hand. 'Why this is you, sir.' 'Yes, sir.' 'Well, set off at once.' 'May I go down to clean myself?' 'Yes, but be sharp about it,' and in a few minutes I was off to the *Gloucester*, dived into the gunroom, and with John Hamilton Moore [1] and Robinson's *Elements* [2] before me, tried to look at some problem or other, but deuce a bit, they all swam before me, and what made it worse, the entry of a mid. who had missed stays, saying, 'if it were not for going to the devil he would jump overboard.' Then another came with 'Hurrah, steward, some grog, by return of packet there will be my promotion. A bottle of champagne for luck: I have passed,' in great glee. Then 'Mr Boteler,' and up I went. 'How do you do, Boteler; bless my soul, what a fine young man you are grown! great mind not to pass you, not to come and see your old captain,' shaking me by the hand all the time. 'How is my old friend John Harvey, and Tom Harvey too? Well, Captain Cochrane, what do you say as to his

<hr>

[1] *The new Practical Navigator.* By John Hamilton Moore. There were numerous editions of this text-book.

[2] *The Elements of Navigation.* By John Robertson (Headmaster of the Royal Academy at Portsmouth). This standard text-book, which was revised by William Wales, ran to several editions.

navigation ? '   ' Well, Captain Williams, his day's work is generally the best in the ship.'   ' Well, that will do ; if his captain says as much for him, there is no occasion to ask any question in navigation. And now as to seamanship ? '   ' Well, so good that I once gave him charge of a watch, and he acquitted himself entirely to my satisfaction.'   And it was merely thus, on a Sunday when the captain, as was usual, dined in the gunroom, he called the officer of watch down, leaving me, the mate, in charge.   Soon after, as we drew in shore, I reported it, and was told to put the ship about.   A mid. putting the frigate round !   Well, ' Hands about ship,' all the mids. in their places looking at me.   Then ' Down with the helm, rise tacks and sheets, mainsail haul,' and looking round, there was Captain Cochrane, with his little carroty whiskers, eyeing me from the companion hatchway.   However, the ship was round, and this was the only time I ever had charge of a watch.   ' Well, well,' said Captain Williams, shaking me cordially by the hand, ' that will do, a very creditable examination ;   I congratulate you on passing so well.'   As I turned to go out, the third captain, Henderson, who had not been present, showed himself, and directly said—' Stop, young gentleman,' and on Captain Williams saying I had been ex- amined he said, ' I wish to ask him a few questions ;   you, perhaps, are not aware of the late letter from the Admiralty on the importance of strictness,' &c.   ' Captain Henderson,' said old Williams, ' you have absented yourself from the examination, and I have made your signal with two guns :   I have a great mind to put you under arrest, sir, for inattention,' and, turning to me, said, ' *That* is not the way to pass, to linger there when you are told you will do.'   So out I bolted like a hunted rat, and had to send the sentry in for my hat and logs.   While making out our own passing certificates, Captain Henderson came on and no one offering him a pen, said— ' I won't sign a single paper then.'   We all tendered him a pen. Such was my passing, and I venture to say it stands alone in the service.

I am puzzled as to dates, the different events are very distinctly on my memory, but I forget their proper places ;   but it was at the close of the year, we were at Barbadoes one morning, overwhelmed with the arrival of a large squadron of men-of-war and transports full of troops for the attack of New Orleans.   There was the *Norge*, 74, *Bucephalus, Fox, Armide, Brune*, &c., all but the *Norge* ' armed en flute,' about twenty guns each and with reduced spars.   The 95th Rifles were in the *Fox* and I went on board her to see my schoolfellow, John Backhouse, a captain of that regiment.   Asking for him, had some difficulty in finding him : ' I dare say, sir, he is in the mizen-top, where he goes for a sleep,' and sure enough there he was. He was very glad to see me, and returned with me to the *Orontes* and spent the evening with us. He was shortly after killed at the disastrous attack on New Orleans.

The next day, while pulling on shore for a bathe in the jolly boat, we overtook a large flat-bottomed troop boat with several soldier officers, also going for a bathe. Lethbridge recognised three or four, his contemporaries at the military college, Duthy, Ormsby, &c. Hodder called ' B. 42, Ormsby, bread and water and blackhole 48 hours.' The officers jumped up staring, and we passed on. After landing, we foregathered and were great friends. This was a copy of the Squire's stories of the college when he was called ' C. 26, Lethbridge, blackhole 48 and bread and water 24 hours.' We used to make him relate the various scrapes he got into, and so worried him one day that he darted from Hodder's knee and rammed his head against the bulkhead.

Pulling on shore one evening, I came upon a man swimming away from the *Bucephalus*, and I took him on board. Captain Hughes (afterwards D'Aeth) was so pleased that, to the surprise of all on board that ship, he asked me down and gave me a capital supper.

The expedition after being reinforced by some other troopers and men-of-war left us. We were very fortunate, losing in the country but one man (the purser, Mr Goddard), and he died of consumption. We attributed our good health to the captain making every seaman wear a flannel shirt. The captain was considered an eccentric but clever doctor. A man was reported dying and given up ; the head of a cask was knocked out, a grating for a seat constructed, hot water put in, and then the man, a blanket round him, his head only through, and thus he was steamed, and I shall never forget the poor fellow's face, the water streaming down it and his agonising look ; but he recovered.

We youngsters had a schoolmaster, a clever seedy-looking creature, whose besetting sin was the love of grog ; with very little trouble it floored him and then, I don't much like to record it, we used to grease his head and flour it.

Towards the close of the year cruising a long way to the west-ward at night, we fell in with a large ship ; all was bustle clearing for action, it being the American war, but on showing the private signal with lights, she proved to be the *Leviathan*, 74 ; we communi-cated and she gave us the unwelcome news of peace and Buonaparte's expatriation to Elba. I am not quite sure how or exactly when we started for England, but we picked up a convoy of twenty-five vessels and set off, I think in January, 1815, and had a very fair passage till near the banks of Newfoundland, when we got a strong westerly gale. I well recollect that, with the foretop mast staysail alone, we headed all the convoy, and after running three or four days gradually and daily losing them, we made sail and anchored at Portsmouth, February or March 1815.

Here I met my brother Thomas, mid., and John Harvey a lieutenant of the *Astraea*. Tom and I went on shore to overhaul some baggage belonging to my brother Richard, which we were to forward on to him at Spike Island, Cove of Cork ; some articles we were to detain, some old clothes and a handsome French shawl, which I gave to my messmate Hodder, in exchange for a desk.

We were not very long at Portsmouth when we took on board the Duchesse D'Angoulême, the Marquise La Rochejaquelein, and some other dignitaries of the new school, and carried them over to Dieppe, a most desolate place, nothing but old men, women and children. The army conscriptions had carried off all the able hands. We could see on the houses ' Napoleon le Grand,' only washed out with a brush of whitewash. But the *lively* Frenchmen came off and danced on our quarter-deck, as happy, apparently, as if their country was over-prosperous.

Here I recollect going for oysters and getting two or three bread bags full for a mere trifle, and, coming alongside, handing a lot into the scuttle of our mids.' berth, they belonging to the lieutenants all the same. From Dieppe we were ordered to the Downs and there lay guardship for a considerable time, part of it with an admiral's flag flying.

Guinea smuggling was carried on with great daring. Eight-oared galleys were built for that purpose alone, and started off with their cargo according to the weather. We kept a sharp look out and used to slip our cable at a moment's notice, but it was like sending a cow after a hare. Notwithstanding our shot, they would pull in the wind's eye and easily escape.

Here young Lethbridge got into mischief and the captain threatened to flog him. The ' Squire ' bought a pocket pistol, which I persuaded him to give up. I am convinced had the captain sent for him in the cabin that he would have shot him.

While in the Downs I was sent with the launch full of empty casks for the Victualling Office at Dover, piled up beyond stowage ; fortunately the weather was fine and we got there safely, but I lost

two of the men. I waited some time but they did not return. All
that the captain said, ' Well, sir, you must go back to Dover and
pick them up.' I did go, stayed two days without effect, and
returned. Had it been any other mid. the chance was he would
have been disrated.

I recollect boarding a small brig from Cork with part of a regiment on board for the Netherlands. In a miserable cramped state
they were, a small cabin, which held about half the officers, and
there they were shaving. I thought of the contrast between their
accommodation and that of a man-of-war. While in the Downs I
had an opportunity of going to Canterbury to see my father &c.

The end of May we were ordered off Dunkirk to land despatches,
which we did by night, a person there on the look out to receive
them. Here we cruised off and on for a fortnight or three weeks,
till one day, the 18th, a low rumbling noise was heard, and the
wonder whence it came. The seamen, who have wonderful sharp
ears for guns, exclaimed among themselves, ' Hallo, what's up, I
wonder ? Something going on, I'm blowed if there isn't.' We were
all agog, the thing was going on so long. It was the Battle of
Waterloo, for some days after 300 poor fellows were marched down,
most of them slightly wounded in the arms and legs, to be taken by
us to Portsmouth. They were chiefly cavalry men of the Old Guard
Cuirassiers, and they gave us an exciting account of the battle.

I must not omit to name a curious circumstance : while off
Dunkirk, sweeping the horizon with my glass, I suddenly saw the
tower of Dover Castle. I could not be mistaken, for there was the
Union Jack also. I called another officer to look and then went and
reported it to the captain, who remarked that was all nonsense.
However, he came on deck and was satisfied himself. It was a
strange atmospheric disturbance, for the tower of Dover Castle was
far below the horizon.

Well, we, from Portsmouth, were ordered to Sheerness to be paid
off. Here Lethbridge again came to the fore. He told me he
should run away and had his box all ready on the forecastle ; some
of the men were on the look out—many of them from the west of
England and knew his family. A peter boat (a Thames fisherman)
dropped under our bows, I thought accidentally, but on looking at
her shortly afterwards there I saw Master Lethbridge, bare-headed,
looking out of the cabin. I burst out laughing : who should be by
my side but Captain Cochrane. ' What's up, Mr Boteler ? ' ' Oh,
sir,' I laughed, ' the wooden-leg fisherman tumbled over his fore-
sheet.' I may as well say that the Squire soon after joined the

Hebrus, but remained on her only a short time, when he left the
service.

When we were at Portsmouth a boat came alongside, and I
recognised little Matthews, the Chatham tailor, and reported him to
Lieutenant Bayly. ' Pray, sir, is Mr Bayly on board ? ' The
lieutenant made signs to be mute and said, ' Who are you wanting
to see, sir ? ' ' Mr Bayly.' ' Oh, we left him in the West Indies.'
' Very sorry to hear it, sir ; he owes my father £30.' ' I have all
Mr Bayly's papers, I will look among them.' And there he found
the receipt for the £30 ; little Matthews exclaiming, ' A forgery,
sir, a forgery, a forgery, sir.' ' What do you mean ? you vagabond, I am Mr Bayly, I knew I had paid you. Go along, sir, out
of the ship at once.' And off he went, and had a bucket of dirt
emptied over his shoulders as he went.

CHAPTER IV

LIEUTENANT—*Antelope*, FLAGSHIP ON THE LEEWARD ISLANDS
STATION

I GOT leave and went to Canterbury for a month. I don't know
that anything particular passed, but my father, who was getting in
years, employed himself with paste &c., smoothing out and collect-
ing the various documents in the Cathedral Registry Office, putting
in order sundry old deeds that were in a great state of confusion.
My younger brother Robert was at home and we were good companions, when one morning returning from a long walk I was greatly
gratified with my sister Julia calling out, ' Oh John, here is your
commission.' And there it was, the long looked-for commission,
dated 18th [1] September, 1815. I lost no time in getting all my
traps sent from the *Orontes* to Canterbury, and then went to London
to be sworn in at the Admiralty. Our full dress then consisted of
the white lapelled coat and epaulette on the right shoulder, white
kerseymere waistcoat and knee breeches, silk stockings and buckles
on the shoes. I put up in London at my brother William's in
Southampton Street, and at the first board day, appeared at the
Admiralty in full dress except the breeches, having on white jean
trousers instead, with silk stockings and buckled shoes. Sir J. Yorke [2]
took exception at this. ' What is the reason, sir, you are not in
proper uniform ? go away, sir, and come again next board day,'
sending me off for another week in my hackney two-horse coach.
Another officer had on an *undress* coat, but he had breeches : nothing
was said to him. Now Sir J. Yorke when captain of the *Venerable*
in the Baltic was said to be the finest man in his ship, and so he
was, barring his legs, and when he appeared at the companion
hatchway, there was no doubt of it while his legs were hidden, and
that was the joke. However, I had to get measured for my breeches

---

[1] Actually 19th.
[2] Vice Admiral Sir Joseph Sydney Yorke, Senior Naval Lord at the Admiralty.

by a tailor in Beaufort Buildings, Strand, and a second time was at the Admiralty accosted by Sir Joseph with—' Well, sir, upon my word you need not have been ashamed of your legs,' and then I was sworn ; the burden of the thing seemed to be, to be faithful to our King and to kick the Pope. By this time my uncle John Harvey was appointed Commander-in-Chief of the West Indies,[1] his nephew John Harvey, flag lieutenant, my brother Henry, first lieutenant, and I junior, and I made another journey to the Admiralty for my commission, and not finding it sent my card up to Sir Joseph, who, on enquiry, was told it was made out. ' That's my brother Henry's, Sir Joseph.' ' What, sir, uncle and two nephews, Father, Son and Holy Ghost, it must not be ' ; but after vapouring about for some time, my commission was made out, and I set off for Portsmouth with my brother Thomas, mid., and joined the *Antelope*, fitting in the harbour.

The *Antelope*, 50, was in the basin, with her lower masts only in, and we had an arduous job fitting her out. The complement of officers rapidly filled, but we found great difficulty in securing a tolerable crew. We obtained the use of the convicts for most of the heavy stores, such as cables, anchors, tanks, yards and spars in general, and I was sent off to get round Mr Craddock, the second master attendant, who had the care of these scamps, and I generally succeeded. It was weary work plodding about the dockyard, after stores of various sorts, but my brother kept us at it. Sundays, our day of rest, we usually had our walk. Two or three times my brother and I dined with Captain Searle, who had a son a mid. on board. This Captain Searle was a distinguished man : when commanding the *Sparrowhawk*,[2] he cut out and captured several small vessels of war and was presented with a sword of honour by the Patriotic Fund. However, we bent our sails and went out of harbour to Spithead in December, 1815. Here Horatio James rejoined from Tower Hill, London, where he had established a rendezvouz, hanging a large union flag from a public-house window. He brought but thirty men in all, a queer lot ; my brother paraded them on deck with the usual word, ' Toe the line, men,' *i.e.*, dressing them by the seam on the deck to which they put their toes. Enquiries were put as to their fitness for going aloft, &c., each man

[1] More accurately Leeward Islands station. The appointments of John Harvey as Flag Lieutenant and Henry Boteler as First Lieutenant of the *Antelope* were dated August 22nd, 1815. John Harvey Boteler's commission as Lieutenant was dated September 19th, and his commission (appointment) to the *Antelope* October 3rd, 1815.
[2] *Grasshopper* (see O'Byrne's *Naval Biographical Dictionary* and the *Dictionary of National Biography*).

being put in charge of a seaman to shew him the way. Among them was one, a most queer character, a countenance deeply marked with small-pox, bushy eyebrows, a tiny cocked-up nose, high cheek bones, in fact, more like a baboon than a human being. ' Well, what's your name ? ' ' John Martin, *alias* Owen Nulty, yer honour,' and he bared his arm with a large O. N. on it. ' Well, sir, what are you fit for ? ' ' Indeed sure, I am the best big drummer and captain of the sweepers in his Majesty's fleet.' ' The very man we want ' ; and John Martin was instantly installed in both these characters ; two days after a man came aft to complain of his watch being stolen. My brother was furious and determined that everyone leaving the ship should be searched. I was on my way in the launch to the dockyard for some heavy stores, and was overtaken by a cutter with the ship's corporal, the mid. telling me his orders were to search the crew. I had a trifling difficulty with the men, who at first felt it ' *infra dig.*' till I set them right on the point—the watch was not found. The Admiral's flag was hoisted and saluted, and we started on our voyage and had a very bad time of it, both in and beyond the Bay.

Young Searle, who was in my watch, was a constant thorn in my side ; he was never up in time, had lost his garters, or some paltry excuse. I threatened him, telling him to walk the deck, and not sculk under the poop awning. One night he objected, the ship rolled so ; I told him there were life lines fore and aft the decks ; he would not use them, and at a sudden heel over of the ship, he fetched away, and jammed his leg under the carronade slide. ' There, sir,' said he, ' had I broken my leg, what would you have to answer for ? ' I said, ' Be off ; it was your own stubbornness ! ' And he directly ran to the gangway, and if one of the men had not caught hold of him, I verily believe would have jumped overboard. I ordered him below, and not to appear on deck again in my watch ; and I had him moved to another watch by the first lieutenant.

We made the Isle of Madeira, and lay to for a large boat, which brought off forty-two different sized casks of Madeira. We had ordered them beforehand, and they were luckily all ready. I had two puncheons for Dr Griffiths, and I was horrified on seeing a stream running from one as it was hoisted in, when I remembered it was cased. In two or three days after the admiral said, ' So you have two casks to help lumber the hold ! ' and on my saying I had them cased, ' More fool you ! ' was his answer ; ' some one will stick a gimlet in, and not be able to stop the leak after.' True enough ; but fortunately the attempt was never made ; and at the

end of our time I had the satisfaction of giving the wine up at
Rochester Custom House with the loss only of six or eight gallons.
Many casks were not near so fortunate, the leakage or evaporation
of the wine reaching thirty or forty gallons. A pipe of the Duke
of York's lost over fifty gallons ; the wood seemed to be perforated
by some insect.

I must here digress. As soon as the weather permitted, we beat
to division ; mustering the men ; taking down the different stores
wanted ;—' Well, sir, twelve yards duck, thread and needles in
course, three or six lbs. tobacco, soap, and a black silk handkerchief.'
A brass nail at three or six yards driven into the deck, as a guide for
measuring ; and before the retreat was drummed, ' Hear the news,
fore and aft, by next muster day everyone will be expected to appear
in a frock and trowsers.' You would see fellows run to the galley
fire, burn a stick, down on the deck, spread out their duck, dot off
the shape, and commence the work at once. Others, unable to do
this, would give their grog to those more expert : and the consequence was, at the end only of a week, there were not above fifty,
or so many defaulters. The same thing with straw hats. Every
bumboat attending the ship was expected to bring off a bundle of
the peculiar grass used for that purpose, so much to each man at a
very moderate price, and soon you would see the men at work at
their sinnet and in a very short time with first-rate hats.

Well, we made the land and anchored in Carlisle Bay, Barbadoes,
in January, 1816. Found here the *Venerable*, Sir Philip Durham ;
and in the space of three days she sailed, leaving us ' cock of the
walk.' I well remember going on board the *Venerable*, and my
surprise at the black visages of all the crew, and no doubt they were
equally struck with our pale faces and rosy cheeks. Poll Smashum
came, and at my recommendation was installed bumboat woman,
and the very next morning came to the first lieutenant : ' I tink it
right, sar, to tell you a sailor bring um watch for sale ; I a'most tink
it not come to him honestly.' Enquiry soon detected the thief ; it
was John Martin ; the watch the same—stolen at Spithead. Martin
did not deny the theft ; and the following morning had three dozen
with the thieves' cat. On his shoulders being exposed, they showed
unmistakable marks of constant punishments, and they were so
hardened that the flesh did not creep, nor did Martin seem to care ;
but he must have done so,—the thieves' cat is a most awful weapon.

The next morning Mr Baron, the chaplain, came into the wardroom, holding up his hands and shaking his head. He was attacked
with fever, and instantly gave in. He was in the habit of asking
58

if such a fruit was wholesome, and if not dash it away with
repugnance ; and so, poor fellow ! at the end of three days he was
dead ! I can't tell how it was we were so taken by surprise. We
had arranged to have him buried in the grave-yard of the church.
I went, with others, to attend the funeral, landed the coffin, and
sent the boat off, and then waited, as we strangely expected, for
negro bearers. The clerk at last came to us, saying the clergyman
was waiting ; and we had to take the coffin ourselves, Betsey
Austin sending to us some towels, by which we carried it. It was
enough to have given the whole of us the fever.

Our squadron was very small. The *Antelope*, 50 ; *Scamander*,
38 ; *Tigris*, 38 ; *Hazard*, 'Donkey' frigates ; [1] *Mutine* and *Epervier*,
brigs. We ran through the various islands—St Lucie, St Vincent,
Tobago, Grenada, and Trinidad ; and were there in September
and October, 1816, to escape the hurricane months—' June, too
soon ; July, stand by ; August, look out you must ; September,
remember ; October, all over.' We began to lose several officers ;
in fact, during the first nine months we lost fifteen officers, mostly
young. In case of an attack we almost knew to a certainty who of
them would or would not succumb, and we judged according to
the dread they had of the fever. We were out in respect of Durre,
the captain of marines, who was getting well, but unluckily indulged his appetite too soon, and so got a relapse and went off.
Littlewort became very ill and thought dying, when one of the mids.
said to him, ' Johnny, what do you do in your hammock all this
time ? I am keeping double watch.' ' Well,' said Johnny, ' how
is Bannister and Mr Sparks, the carpenter and gunner ? ' ' Oh,
getting round nicely.' They were both dead. ' Well, I won't stay
here any longer,' and he stirred himself up and recovered. But
the surgeon's practice was an awful one ; excessive bleeding to the
extent of sixty or seventy ounces, and he never lost a patient after
this treatment. The *Epervier* was near us, and she had the fever
very bad. Her purser died, and Mr Baxter, our captain's clerk,
had an acting order to supply his place. On going on board they
were in the act of burying the corpse. He had to step over the
coffin, and it had such an effect on him that on the fourth day he
was himself dead. · Another clerk, Gregory, got the vacancy. She
entered a few seamen at Trinidad ; one man was so horrified with
the state of fever that he took refuge in the foretop, and would not

---

[1] 'Donkey Frigates : Those of 28 guns, frigate-built ; that is, having guns protected by an upper deck, with guns on the quarter-deck and forecastle ; ship-sloops
in contradistinction to corvettes and sloops' (Smyth, *Sailor's Word-Book*, 1867).

come down till the brig went to Barbadoes, where her captain and all the sick were landed, when the poor fellow was induced to descend, and was instantly attacked and was dead on the third day. It seemed singular, but it was general that death took place on the third or fifth day. The brig went down to Antigua, where she was cleared out and sunk for a whole week. The negroes who cleared her, dockyard labourers, could not stand the peculiar effluvia which arose from her hold, and two absolutely fainted. She had lately completed with wood, which, being green, fermented, and so, it was said, caused the mischief.

I must go back to Barbadoes. Young Searle's conduct was so bad that the first lieutenant threatened him. The fellow went below and mixed up a cake of white lead and one of red, wishing success to everyone, deliberately drank the whole. The doctor administered a strong emetic, and tickled his throat with a feather till he threw it all up. However, it was a settler for him. In a few days he had his discharge, and was sent off.

I brought a letter of introduction to a Mr Pinder, of 'Hogsty,' and did not deliver it till I received a reminder from Mr Pinder, and then, looking small, delivered it. I also brought out a letter together with a cheese and other good things from Captain Boys for a Mr ——, the purser of the Naval Hospital at Barbadoes. Captain Boys came down himself to Portsmouth to see them off, and I shall not forget his saying ' You are lucky fellows ; you will all come home post captains,' instead of which not a single vacancy occurred, and we each returned as we went out, lieutenants. I dined with Mr ——, and had a challenge for a throw from his daughter, a stout handsome girl with red hair, and she very nearly got the better of me. In one thing she certainly beat me—in shooting at a mark with her father's rifle. She handled it well. I recollect her turning very faint, and in pulling off her glove, there was a large centipede in it. Fortunately it did not bite her.

· Paddy Martin got drunk and was severely punished. Drunk again ! and my brother gave him twelve-watered grog, then he stood with two or three more for half an hour at a stretch drinking it. Again he got drunk, and then salt water was added to his grog, and he drank it apparently with a relish. He said to me : ' Mr John, tell your brother there was only one first lieutenant in the service that kept me sober, and he gave half-a-pint of raw rum a day, and for fear of losing that I kept sober.' He was incorrigible, but he never told a lie. ' Martin, the band is wanted to-night at St Lucie ; do you intend to be drunk or sober ? ' ' I can't answer

for myself, sir,' and it was no use to send him, whereas, if he had
said the contrary, he was safe not in any way to exceed. This
fellow, apart from his besetting sin of drunkenness, was a most
amusing character. In evading an onslaught of my brother he
stumbled over the combings of the gangway and tipped over into
the waist. ' Oh, Mr Boteler, you have broken my shoulder ; won't
ye give me my grog now ? see, Mr John, put your hand here ; don't
you feel and hear it crackling ? ' and it did so. We had him tied
to the galley funnel for a time, and he kept it polished perfectly.
In going forward to the forecastle he jumped out to the extent of
his tether, and on my shying on one side he said, ' Oh, Mr John,
don't be frightened, sir, I wouldn't hurt you.' At last, to keep him
out of the way of getting grog, we confined him to the poop, allowing him to go to the copper for his allowance of beef. Returning
one day he leered at the admiral, patting his beef with a long knife.
He did this in such a comical way that the admiral said, ' Get along,
you ugly scoundrel.' The fellow instantly replied, ' Eh, your
honour, had you seen my brother ; my mother fainted when she
first saw him,' and this with such an air. While on the poop he
contrived one day to get very drunk. We had a tub with a high
stave at each end and four or five bottles of wine hung across a
piece of wood in bags, and in the sun the evaporation was so great
that the wine became perfectly cool. I need not say how Martin
got drunk. He contrived to finish two bottles. In his tantrums
he smashed in the end of his drum, and it was curious to see him
with a sheepskin pinned on the deck, he on his hands and knees
dressing it, till at the end of a week he had contrived an excellent
drumhead, and it was then he made the witty reply to Mr Littlewort, who was chaffing him on breaking his drum, ' Indeed, sur,
the sham commission they sent you would have helped me.' One
day we were at St Kitts and all invited to a ball. Martin went, as
he promised to keep sober. During the ball the president, Colonel
Thomson, said he understood we had a character in the balcony,
our big drummer. ' Introduce me, will you ? ' He was taken up
and introduced, the colonel saying, ' Well, Martin,' to which the
other answered, ' Well, colonel ' without hesitation, and on the
colonel asking him to take some porter, ' Thank ye, colonel, I have
told this gentleman's brother that I would keep sober, and if I taste
porter it will be all up with me,' and the colonel then asked him
to get leave and come and see him. Marching down to the boat
through the streets to the tunes of ' God save the King ' and ' Nancy
Dawson,' it being broad daylight, we went on board. My brother

was on deck, and on Martin asking to go on shore, my brother said,
' Why, you have just come off.' ' Yes, yer honour, but Colonel
Thomson asked me to his house,' and on my corroborating this, he
was allowed to go, and he came off at the end of three days in a
dreadful pickle. He had rolled down a cactus bank, and was
covered with prickles. The worst was that they were suckers,
barbed the wrong way, and he was half the forenoon at the galley
fire, rubbed in with grease, and two or three marines over him with
tweezers, &c., pulling them out. One Sunday the admiral was
dining in the wardroom and only I on deck. I went aft; there
was Martin lounging on the taffrail. ' Well, Martin.' ' Well, Mr
John, you are very smart to-day with your new epaulette.' ' Well,
Martin, if you were to meet me in London, for old shipmate sake,
you would not rob me ? ' ' Rob you, sir, you would not be worth
my while, a half-pay lieutenant.' This a little nettled me, and I
said I did not believe half the stories he told of robbing people,
' and I will give you a bottle of rum if you rob me in a week.' ' I'm
robbing you now, Mr John, and you looking at me so ; I'm robbing
you, sir, and you don't know it.' Of course I knew he was not,
but to make sure I went forward with the intention of emptying
my pockets, telling what had happened to the captain of marines,
as the wardroom dinner was over and he had come up. He agreed
with me to empty my pockets, and as I turned to go down the poop
ladder Martin called, ' Mr John, you have left something behind
you, sir,' and there he had my handkerchief and knife. The marines
were laughing. It seemed the fellow had followed me on his feet
and one hand, and with the other deliberately picked my pockets.
I gave a quarter dollar instead of the rum. It came to the admiral's
ears, who told me I ought to have given him the promised rum.
Soon after this, the captain made application for the man's discharge as a rogue and vagabond. The admiral fired out at him,
saying, ' This ought to have been done a twelve-month earlier,'
and he was instantly discharged. When ordered some punishment,
in anger he had said to the first lieutenant, ' I shall see you furl
sails at Spithead yet,' meaning that he would never be promoted,
and when released he came into the wardroom to wish all good-
bye, and my brother said to him, ' You will not see me furl sails
after all, Mr Martin.' ' Indeed, but I will, sir, unless I am in limbo.'
Martin went on shore, and stayed six or seven days at Government
House for the amusement of Cotton, Colonel Finch, &c., and then
was sent home. Almost by return of packet there was, ' For
petty larceny, John Martin, late a seaman in one of His Majesty's

ships in the West Indies,' and when we anchored at Spithead no Martin shewed himself to see the first lieutenant furl sails, but at Sheerness, in passing through, a letter from him dated 'H.M. Convict hulk ship *Bellerophon*,' asking for a few coppers to purchase tobacco, and desiring to be remembered to Mr John and the admiral.

While at Trinidad the ship went off a little distance to Shagaremus [1] Bay for the purpose of wooding and watering. The Bay was famous for the destruction of the Spanish squadron by fire by Sir Henry Harvey in 1796. Mr Harvey and I were rowed over the spot in a canoe, and there the negro shewed us a frigate, the hull only, but very perfect, almost seemingly a thing of life: the trembling of the water gave her an appearance of moving; it was indeed a singular sight, though twenty years since her wreck. The water was so transparent that she shewed most distinctly though in six or seven fathoms.

We called on a little Frenchman, who exhibited two grey parrots with great glee; it was on a waxed floor, and he merely lifted the edge of a plate, till the birds began to wheel about with their crooked beaks to the floor, one wing a little raised, waltzing round and round with most amusing stolidity.

When at Trinidad we made an excursion to the Pitch Lake, a most wonderful production of nature. When we landed, the first thing that struck us were the roads all made by blocks of a hardened sort of asphalt, and over this we walked, a large party of lieutenants and mids., to the lake, covering many acres of ground, consisting of patches of bitumen, in islands with water between, shallow from one inch and never deeper than one foot, but at times having a crack in the middle of about three to four feet wide. The whole lake, by the excessive heat of the sun, was sufficiently softened to take the impression of the feet. So we all off shoes and stockings which we put under our coat tails, buttoned up and so ran from water to water as the only means of keeping cool, with one or two poles to feel our way over the cracks, into which we occasionally floundered; and in this way, amidst great fun we came to a few stumps of shrubs, and at last reached what we called the kettle, the lake in fact in a bubble; we could go no nearer, the whole was too soft. We caught, I remember, a hammer-headed shark, a curious but spiteful-looking fellow.

I dined with the governor, Sir Ralph Woodford, and there read

---

[1] Sir Henry Harvey spelt it Shagaramus in his despatch of 1797 (*not* 1796). The current *West Indies Pilot* spells it Chaguaramas.

the first [1] of Scott's novels, *Rob Roy*, which I thought delightful, although I was obliged to read it standing, moving my legs up and down and all my fingers in motion to keep off the mosquitoes. Before we came to Trinidad we inspected the purser's accounts, and on investigation found he had made dead men chaw tobacco, take up slops and otherwise, besides altering the account to the satisfaction of his own pocket. We tried him by court-martial and dismissed him the service.

Before coming to Trinidad the yellow fever was making awful havoc, among our young midshipmen in particular. Our captain's two sons [2] were attacked; the eldest died, the youngest one got through and was sent home. It was singular how he grew, from his long illness—two or three inches. We lost Messrs Preston, Amrink, Lloyd, Carter, Ainsworth, Osborne, G. Smith, Baxter and Gregory, besides Captain Durre of the marines, Sparke the gunner and Bannister the carpenter. We did not lose more than ten seamen in all.

From Trinidad we went to Antigua, English Harbour, where the admiral went on shore and stayed with Judge Athole. Thomas, a fine young rosy-cheeked fellow, one of our mids., was made lieutenant of the *Scamander* and died a few months after, and my brother Thomas,[3] who had just passed, got his vacancy, the first piece of luck for the family. The *Tigris* frigate was here as well as the *Epervier* brig; she had been sunk for fever, and was just raised again. The admiral ordered Captain Sayer, myself and the master to go on board and survey her. John Harvey came with us to keep us company. The captain thought it risky and did not half like the job; when looking round we came to the purser's cabin, in which three pursers had died, John Harvey said, ' Here, sir, you must look in here, the admiral will never be satisfied unless you look in.' ' John, John, you are too venturesome '—the old boy was not to be persuaded. However, the report was made, the brig refitted and the fever was completely eradicated. Lieutenant Shortland of the *Tigris* was moved to the hospital with fever. I went there to call on him; he received me with ' Well, John, how are stocks on board the flagship? '—alluding to the occasional stock jobbing going on there. He looked very bad indeed, and in three days was dead. I attended the funeral, arm in arm with Lieutenant Thurgood; our

---

[1] He presumably means *Rob Roy* was the first of the Waverley Novels that he read. It was not the first of Scott's novels.

[2] Sons of Captain George Sayer, commanding H.M.S. *Antelope*.

[3] Thomas Boteler, appointed Acting Lieutenant of the *Scamander*, October 5th, 1816.

band followed playing the 'Dead March in Saul,' 'Adeste Fideles,' &c., wailing most melancholy airs ; we had a long uphill walk to the burying ground, and poor Thurgood was very low. I told him to brush up : if he gave way thus he would be next to go. I little thought how true it was likely to be. He was taken ill that night and dead in three days, and I followed him as I did Shortland. Johnny Littlewort was here made supremely happy by having the vacancy. He would not credit the good news till he had seen the admiral. ' No, no, I will believe what he says, and no one else,' so on shore he went and was satisfied.

We went in a party though not half the size expected to dine with the Registrar of the Admiralty, Mr John Pye Molloy. A terrible road : the master, driving the carriage, knocked the bottom out, driving against a large rock on one side of the road ; for his satisfaction it was stated that other sailors had fared worse at the same place. We kept it up till late and had a most jolly drive home. Here I was asked to a Mr Nihill, living two or three miles up the country ; I stayed two days with him. In going out I had to pass close to a manganeel shrub,[1] and the leaves touching my cheek, left at first a red mark then turning to quite black. The virulence of the poison is so searching till one knows the shrub ; you may be tempted to take shelter during a storm of rain : if you do, woe betide you, every drop of rain from the leaves to your hands or face raises a blister. After dinner on the second day I had a stirrup cup in the shape of noyeau, which got into my head, and away I started over a road I was almost afraid to walk coming out. I had wit enough to stop at a commissary's at Falmouth and dismount, and there Mr Nihill found me and we walked from this to the dock-yard, and were instantly admitted ; found a boat waiting which took us off. Mr Nihill I had given a passage to Trinidad, where we were to go shortly. I introduced him to my brother and that was all, for to tell the truth I was a little in the wind.

And a very strange occurrence took place just as I was about to leave the ship ; a half dispute was going on relative to the capture of one of our frigates, the *Guerrière*, Captain Porter,[2] by an American, and it was said the captain was to blame—I do not know that it was in direct terms, as showing a want of courage. I was not sufficiently attending, but the captain of marines, Durre, combatted the story, saying that Captain Porter was his relative. Paddy

[1] Possibly Boteler's ' manganeel shrub ' is the manchineel tree.
[2] The *Guerrière* (Captain J. R. Dacres) was captured by the *Constitution* (Captain Isaac Hull). Captain David Porter, U.S.N., attained celebrity in command of the *Essex*.

Boyle, who was relating the fact, said, ' That's nothing to do with it,' and so they seemed to wrangle. However, as I was stepping into my boat, Boyle said, ' Boteler, I will take a passage with you,' and then as we cleared the dock gates he turned and asked me to walk aside with him. Not dreaming what was up, to my surprise, on turning round two or three rocks, there was Captain Durre and an assistant-surgeon, his second, and both he and Boyle out with their swords and began playing away. I instantly stopped it, saying to Boyle, ' What do you mean, taking me as your second without a syllable to me beforehand, or acquainting me with the nature of your dispute ? ' and I called on the doctor, as his superior officer, ' to withhold his hand at once.' Boyle ignored any intention of wounding Captain Durre, holding at the same time his opinion of Captain Porter, so ' If was your only peace maker,' and they parted, I am happy to say, as good friends as ever ; though not for long after all—Durre was attacked by fever and died.

Now something of Boyle.[1] He came out to us without any notice from the Admiralty, without an appointment or anything ; the admiral put him on the ship's books as a supernumerary, and he was eventually confirmed. He was the most ignorant man I ever encountered, unable to write two or three consecutive words properly spelled ; he used to get the midshipmen to write his letters, but, strange to say, was in the first ranks of society in London. As officer of the guard his written reports were marvellous. He had letters from the first of the nobility. He told us a strange story of his becoming acquainted with Miss Hamlet, daughter of the famous jeweller and goldsmith at the top of the Haymarket. He was a handsome, fine-looking fellow, and it appeared very evident that Miss Hamlet highly favoured him, when, by chance, he let out something to one of the Lord C——l's, who got Boyle to introduce him ; the consequence was that Boyle was speedily cut out. Mr Hamlet presented the lord with a rich diamond ring, or rather to his daughter for Lord C——. A very few days passed when, in the Strand, Mr Hamlet was called in by a jeweller, to look at a ring offered him for sale and to ask his advice as to its value, when, lo and behold, the ring proved to be Hamlet's one. There was a great uproar ; the lord was dismissed, the lady losing both her lovers, and Boyle swearing he would take care for the future how he confided again in a lord. Boyle was a great martyr to rheumatism ; I used

---

[1] Lieutenant Robert Boyle (seniority December 18th, 1809), appointed Acting Lieutenant of the *Antelope*, September 21st, 1816, and Lieutenant of the *Scamander*, July 25th, 1817. Promoted Commander December 7th, 1818. He died in 1825.

to hear him groaning in his cabin under the quarter-deck. The only respite he seemed to have was after dinner and his full whack of wine, then he cheered up and was very amusing ; at last he got his promotion from England. The effect was wonderful, his back instantly straightened, his rheumatism left him and he was altogether a different man. I may as well dismiss him, giving his last letter recommending a bumboat man at Spithead.

Dear Doctor,

The Bearer of this is an old shipmet of mayn, is name is drinkwater and worthy flough. He knew Archdeacon and Olivir a littel, will you speak to Botler for him, I am going to the Custmhous.

We went down to Trinidad and remained some time in the Gulf of Paria. From this we went to Tortola and Tobago. While in St George's Bay I noticed a shoal of fish agitating the water, and, as if by magic, a large flock of pelicans came and dashed in among them, and the singular thing was that they were attended by a number of tern, who hung over them, flapping their wings, and occasionally resting even on the pelicans' heads, snapping at the fish from their bills. I thought this such a strange sight that I went down and reported it to the admiral, who thanked me and came on deck to see the sport.

Early in 1817, our new purser, Archdeacon, joined us. He came out in one of the regular packets. In the same ship was Von Sholton, the governor of the Danish Island of St Croix ; talking one day of different dishes the purser named a ham boiled in champagne : this seemed to tickle the governor vastly, for he exclaimed, ' Oh, mein Got ! and what did they do wid de soup ? ' and he declared that the first English ship that came to his island they should have one, and it so chanced that the *Scamander* went, and my brother, who was one of her lieutenants, told me they had one.

Captain Philips [1] also joined us from England. He was both an epicure and a gourmand, eyeing every dish that came on the table, giving his servant his *un*finished soup that he might strike in for the first help, also parading his glass to the light, telling the steward it was not clean, and this he would do till by chance a larger one was brought and then all was right. This caught my attention ; one day I was seated on the left of the president, Captain Philips my *vis-à-vis* on the opposite side ; it was blowing hard and the ship was rolling very much, sending over with great violence. We had a leg of boiled pork before the president, who had quite a job in the

---

[1] Robert Philips, Captain, Royal Marines.

carving. The leg was tied by a string round the knuckle, each end
fastened to the leg of the table. The ship gave a lurch over to my
side and I slily cut the string ; and, of course, as she again sent over
to starboard the leg went right into Captain Philips' lap : he jumped
up to save his red coat and went bang through the canvas panelling
into the first lieutenant's cabin. Such a scene and outcry, and to
make it worse, there was a genuine shout of laughter. It was not
even suspected to be the work of my hands.

We were not idle, but always on the move, running down the
islands,—Guadaloupe, Port Royal, Martinique, St Kitts, and Barbadoes. At another time at Guadaloupe, where we gave up the
island again to the French, embarking ourselves the 25th regiment
(Borderers). We had difficulty in making room for so large a party.[1]
We put the officers to sleep in the cockpit, and each took two or
three in his cabin to tidy themselves. They were in three watches
with us, and one-third of the men on deck at night,—so that there
was a constant move. We made it out very well on the whole,
and passed a pleasant time. In my watch there was a young Irish
lieutenant, Pat Wolseley, and in a night-watch we caught a booby
asleep on the quarter-deck hammock nettings. I had it put into
the Irishman's cot between the sheets. My emissaries reported that
on putting his feet into bed, the uproar was tremendous. ' Oh,
Jasus, what's this ! the divil sure is in the bed ! '—for the bird
began to peck at his legs. ' What's the matter, Pat ? ' ' Oh sure,
there is something alive in my bed ! ' and out he jumped, and then
discovered the booby. We took the regiment to Barbadoes.

At Barbadoes, some of us were asked to dine with the governor,
Lord Combermere, where was the admiral, to our dismay. The
dinner was half over,—I cannot tell how it was we were so late ; the
admiral was black in the face—tremendously angry. We none of
us had half a dinner. I thought to help myself to some delicious-
looking jelly—it was *marble*. The plate was gold or silver gilt, and
everything in very grand style. We were all very glad to walk off
again, and to have a good supper at Betsey Austin's.

We went to Satcha, St Kitts, Nevis, and Montserrat, and then
again to St Kitts. When at Brimstone Hill, a garrison at the west
side of the land, we dined with the 63rd regiment. Brimstone Hill
is called and considered a second Gibraltar ; seated on a high hill,
and approached by a zig-zag road. Horses were sent down to bring
us all up ; mine was the adjutant's,—and be hanged to him ! He
had the trick of throwing his head up ; and just as I mounted, with

[1] In the Navy List in 1817 the *Antelope* is shown as a troopship.

my head forward, he threw up his own, and hit me under the chin.
I thought all my teeth were out. I was scarcely able to touch a
thing at dinner. We slept at the Hill; the admiral, I remember,
in the officer of engineers' house, as being the best in the garrison.
We were again at Barbadoes; then to Dominique and Montserrat;
and had a prime day up the Soufrière, a burning mountain; here
we tied eggs in our handkerchiefs, and boiled them in the hot water
cracks. The ground seemed very treacherous; very thin-skinned,
with a quantity of small cracks, which were very hot; they were
lined with very bright-looking sulphur. My epaulette and things
in my pocket were all ruined by being clouded dark with sulphur.
We dined at a Mr Dobridge's, some distance in the country, and
had a great scampering, by moonlight, over the sands coming home.
The crab holes in the sand made the ride very dangerous. I had
a wretched beast of a horse, that would not pass as bad a one
ahead. At last I unbuckled my sword and put it under the tail
of the brute ahead of me; he started, jammed to his tail, as horses
will, and on my attempting to recover my sword, it drew, and left
the scabbard behind, to the intense delight of all hands. Away
went the horse with my scabbard tucked under his tail, when he
stepped into a crab hole which threw him forward, and released
the scabbard. The beast kept out of my way after this.

We went again to St Kitts. Here John Harvey and I dined
with the president, meeting the admiral, Captain Sayer, and many
others. Several parts of the road were paved to keep them from
being washed away, it was so steep. On our way homewards we
overtook and passed Captain Sayer, in his kittereen; he called out
to us, 'For God's sake, be careful!' However, away we went, and
passing by a planter's, and wishing to know the time, I absolutely
rode up some steps leading from the road to the verandah round the
house. The planter rushed out, hearing the noise, told us the time,
and insisted on leading my horse down the steps,—and perhaps
well for me that he did,—I don't know. However, it was very
polite of him. On the sandy shore by the town was a long wharf
on piles, and a small house at the end. Of course, in a man-of-war's
boat, we landed on it, and encountered a dapper little lawyer,
seated and writing; he started up, with—'Really, gentlemen, this
is an intrusion; I sit here writing my work; the whole is private
property.' And on our apologising, he said: 'Well, I'll excuse it
this time; but I must not let you pass quite free—do me the favour
of tasting this,' and he pulled down a case of brandy and noyeau,
had some deliciously cool water, and he begged us to make use of

his wharf whenever we chose to land.   He was a clever character,
and at hot water with Governor Probyn ; and one day in court,
seeing the governor in the gallery, he said : ' A poet has said, an
honest man is the noblest work of God ; now who is there here that
will not say, Governor Probyn is an honest man ? but who again
will say that Governor Probyn is the noblest work of God ? '

We went to a sandy island not far off, and landed to take
possession, or rather to establish our right.   It was a desolate place,
overgrown with impenetrable forests.   There was a massive banyan
tree whose lateral branches throw out a small *thread*-like string
that takes root and eventually thickens to the size of the parent
tree, and here was one covering a large space of ground.   In one of
the main forks was a mighty ants' nest, about the size of a round
drawing-room table ; the ants had a covered way running up one
of the stems.   I cut off a part with my sword and, on returning in
half an hour, saw myriads at work repairing the breach.   They
seemed to be divided into large flying ants, soldiers who did nothing,
working ants and very large ones that crawled about at their leisure.

We were at one time at Nevis, where at some distance off we
were invited to dinner to meet the admiral and others ; horses were
sent for us, and the captain's being rather frisky, I exchanged with
him ; we had a gay party and a merry ride home in the evening, a
black boy running by the side of each horse.   John Harvey did not
like this and persuaded the boy to mount behind him, the boy
saying ' The horse no carry two, Massa ' ; and sure enough the horse
became restive, lashed out and threw both John and the boy over
his head.   My horse went well, but in following Mr Carter, the
secretary's, horse, I was induced to put my foot under his tail, and
the horse kicked out and hit me on the knee, luckily without injury,
but the beast threw Carter, whose game arm hung on the horse's
neck and so saved him from a fall : and here I became aware for the
first time that Mr Carter had no joint at the elbow.   I noticed of
course that he bent forward to shake hands ; he was a clever painter
in water colours.   It seemed he met with an accident as a boy, and
had his arm strapped across his chest ; the consequence was the
inflammation fixed the joint and the arm became stiff.   I also came
to grief, my saddle got loose and slipped round, and I was off but
never let go the bridle, and so brought up the horse all standing ;
I adjusted the saddle again and we had a very merry ride home.

In June we were at St John's, Antigua ; here we detained an
American brig for a breach of the navigation laws ; the admiral had
compassion on the poor fellow and desired me to give him a passage

to St John's, three or four miles off. After a little while Jonathan
observed, ' I think, Mr Lieutenant, one of our boats could give yours
a licking.' I said, ' Very probably : a boat built for rowing might not
sail so well, and one built for sailing might fail in rowing, but we
think we have got the right sort '—she was a double banked boat
rowing ten oars, and we had our sails set at the time. ' I don't
mean that, I mean that one of our crews could thrash yours.' The
coxswain jumped up with ' Shall I pitch him overboard, sir ? ' and
the two stroke oars at the same time made a move, when I said,
' Shut up, you fool, if you dare to say one word more I'll have you
overboard, and tow you on shore by the main sheet ' ; the fellow
turned green, but held his tongue. I dare say in their navy the
men are stout able seamen, and he could but notice that our boat's
crew were mere boys. The thing came to the admiral's ears, and
he attacked me for not having him overboard, but in two or three
days after said, ' I believe you acted right, John, but at your age I
think I should have had him overboard.'

I may as well here repeat an amusing story told to us by a
Colonel Walker, who as lieutenant and aide-de-camp of Sir Thomas
Hislop was taken in the ——— frigate during the American war. He
became a colonel, and in the Quarter-Master-General's Department
at Demerara. An American brig arrived with coals, the whole
cargo was purchased for the use of the troops. The captain was a
most quaint object, a blue tailed coat, the buttons of the waist
almost between the shoulders, his gills covering the side of his face,
and in no way would one ever have taken him for a sailor. The
three colonels, Walker, Berkley, of the Adjutant-General's Department, and Popham, agreed to ask him to dinner ; Jonathan accepted, dressed in all his glory, and there were three or four others
at table. The first toast at a military mess was generally ' The
King ' : the Yankee spluttered and spit but drank the toast. Colonel
Walker then drank to the health of the President of the United
States, which greatly pleased the American, who said ' Thank you,
Mr Colonel, this is an honour I did not expect ; I will report it to my
countrymen ; thanks again, Mr Colonel.' A few minutes later, when
up got the Yankee : ' I beg to give a toast, Mr Colonel, a bumper if
you please, here is to the health of the King of Great Britain.' ' Why
we have already done this.' ' No, no, *spit him out,*' and this was his
sputtering with ' the,' spit, ' King,' spit, and so he conceived he
had saved his conscience as a thorough republican in not drinking a
Royal toast. The company was of course excessively entertained,
and thought it best to pass all off as a good joke.

At St John's, Antigua, we were all seated comfortably after
dinner, when there was a noise as if an empty cask was rolled on
deck, and soon after another shake as if a romping of mids. on the
quarter-deck. Out ran my brother to look after them, and by this
time there was a regular trembling of the ship, and everyone knew
then that it was an earthquake. The carpenters were called to
sound the well, it seemed almost as if the ship had taken the ground :
all was safe and the thing passed off ; but on shore there was a
great destruction of crockery in many houses, but no other damage.

We became acquainted with Parson Havercomb, and I went
there to luncheon and had land crabs stewed and porter, only Miss
Havercomb at table. The crabs were most excellent and I asked
who got them. ' Oh, William Charles.' ' Is he not the sexton ? '
' Oh, yes ; but why do you ask ? ' She turned pale and ran out of
the room with the idea she had eaten crabs caught in the church-
yard, where, indeed, there were abundance. But it was not so ;
these crabs are kept in brick caves about three feet deep and regularly fed on guinea corn, and become quite fat. Parson Havercomb
was a schoolfellow of my uncle Harvey, at Canterbury, hence our
acquaintance.

Walking on shore, visiting some negro huts and sugar works,
we were entertained with sugared drinks by an odd-looking manager
of a mill turned by oxen, a very quaint-looking individual indeed.
The drainage of the works was an abomination ; molasses running
into treacle, with all descriptions of noxious insects, cockroaches
innumerable, centipedes, beetles, moths, &c. Coming off I took a
humming-bird's nest, cut from the fork of a manganeel bush. Knowing how acrid the sap of this shrub was, I took the precaution of
wearing gloves. The nest, the size of a section of a hen's egg, had
a young unfledged bird in it and the tips of the little thing's wings
glued to the sides of the nest. The parent bird, one of the tiniest
of its sort, followed me a long way ; I quite felt for the little creature.
After I got to my ship, knowing the virulence of the poison, I
washed my hands, notwithstanding which, when I got up in the
morning my skin was red and inflamed wherever the hands had
touched it, and the little bird was gone—eaten by ants ! The nest
is still in existence in the drawing-room of my old friend John
Griffiths, to whom I gave it in 1819.

How events crop up in one's memory. As I write I remember
John Harvey getting the barge for a trial sail ; she had no ballast,
capsized, fortunately not very distant from the ship ; two boats
were instantly sent off and picked them all up. A day or two after,

Harvey, Mildmay, and myself were asked to Dr Osborn, of Orange Valley, and we went in the barge with two seamen only, Butler and another. It was a most glorious trip; the barge, with proper ballast, behaved well. We took four or five hours' sail to get into a snug bay where we anchored the boat, and we had an hour's ride to Orange Valley, a pretty place surrounded with orchards of oranges and limes, most fragrant. The admiral, Captain Sayer, and Carter the secretary, were staying in the house. I don't know that anything in particular occurred except that I sat next to a Miss Daniels, a niece of Dr Osborn, and was desperately smitten; I had no eyes or ears for anything but her. We stayed the next day and were off to our ship on the third.

We had many friends at Antigua, several to whom we owed a return, and so gave a second breakfast on board, a long table laid out on the poop-deck, shaded by the awnings and a number of flags, and afterwards got up a very respectable dance which we kept up till late in the day.

We had a midshipman, John Cochrane, a very admirable chess player. The admiral, who was fond of the game and not by any means a bad hand at it, used to send for Cochrane, who would generally beat him two out of three. We always knew how the game went by the temper of the admiral, and once or twice we asked Cochrane to give him a game to put him in a good humour; this was no go. Cochrane would be outside the mids.' mess-place and play two games with anyone without seeing the board, and it was marvellous how rapidly his skill got wind among the islands. Directly we anchored some challenge would come off for a trial of strength.

We went to St Vincent and some of the officers, a large party, went up the Soufrière, now only a deep crater, for it had blown itself out some years before. There was a mighty lake nearly filling up the crater. From this we went to Gros Islet Bay, St Lucie, a very snug anchorage, shut in on one side by Pigeon Island, connected with the main land by a bridge of rocks. On Pigeon Island is a fort called Rodney Fort—a barrack, mess-house and a hospital. In September we were at anchor with two schooners. The admiral did not like the look of the weather, had the studding-sail, booms off the yards, all top hamper moved, and the ship made snug in every way aloft, and then up anchor and away to sea; the wind at the same time chopped round to the westward, a most unusual thing, and we started directly to the eastward, the wind continuing light, and by the time we were about thirty miles off and towards

evening it came on to blow with great fury. The wind being always
from the westward, we had to run directly against the easterly
swell. Towards night we could only shew a reefed foresail, with the
clew garnets led into the waist. I had the first watch, six hands
at the wheel; at last the plunging and trembling of the ship was
such that both compass cards in the binnacle were jumped off their
needles, and in a short time the ship suddenly broached to. We up
with the foresail, but to no use, it blew clean out of the bolt ropes;
but the ship lay to quite snug, and I went to my cabin and found
water coming through the ship's side, covering the floor. I turned
in, and notwithstanding a wet pillow, had a good night, finding in
the morning more favourable weather, in fact, by noon it was quite
fine. We kept knocking about for a fortnight and then went to
Barbadoes; found sixteen or seventeen merchant ships on shore.
But the hurricane did not equal that at St Lucie. I was employed
with stream anchors and cables assisting ships in getting off.

At Barbadoes we heard of the sufferings of the inhabitants of St
Lucie. To such an extent, that the ladies of Barbadoes made a
subscription of clothes for their benefit; and by the 9th of November
we embarked Lord and Lady Combermere and staff, and took them
down to Gros Islet Bay. On first making the land, we were struck
with astonishment at the total change in the whole face of the
country. We left it the day before the hurricane a beautiful rich
green, and everything in a most flourishing state. It had now the
dreary appearance of a severe European winter. We were not
aware till now that the mountains and high hills were covered with
large timber trees; hitherto, from the closeness and thickness of
the foliage they appeared to be underwood only. An officer came off
to us in a canoe, half-dressed; we laughed, saying he had been in
the wars evidently; little thinking how true it was, he literally had
lost everything. We went on shore on the 7th, and I was asked by
the admiral to keep my eyes open, and report to him my observa-
tions. The amount of destruction which there presented itself is
beyond my powers of description. The barracks, officers' quarters,
mess-house, and hospital were level with the ground; one large
timber beam I noticed sticking in the ground, and a single iron
bedstead so jammed between two rocks that I could not move it.
On rowing over to the village, in the bight of the bay, three houses
out of about three hundred were standing; the rest with the church
(the great bell in one of the pews) were almost quite destroyed; one
of the three houses was shifted fifteen feet from its foundation
without going to pieces. The two large tamarind trees, under

74

which the negroes always met to dance on Saturday and Sunday evenings, were torn up by the roots, which by their spread in the sandy soil nearly equalled the branches in circumference. The woods, with which the island particularly abounds, were more or less destroyed, according to their exposure to the force of the gale ; many, in truth, which were left standing had only a few of the ragged stout branches remaining. In the deep ravines, the wind appeared to have acted in a whirl, for immense trees were completely thrown down, and twisted up in heaps in the most astonishing manner. The barracks, hospital and all the works on Morne Fortuné, except the magazine, were well nigh demolished. Castres, the chief town, suffered but little ; but all the vessels in the harbour, which is considered as snug as any in the West Indies, were driven on shore,—all the smaller ones high and dry. The inhabitants say that the great hurricane in 1780 was nothing equal to this. The Government House was unroofed ; the shingles (a species of wooden slate) driven miles into the country. One of the governor's children was killed in escaping from the house.

While at St Lucie, we got leave for the barge to take a party of us some distance to leeward of the island to look after a tree we had cut down. We found the tree ; but the rainy season had commenced and the wood was surrounded with water ; by cutting the tree in halves, we contrived to get both parts to the boat, and by hanging it on each side brought it safely to the ship. I also caught a large scorpion, which I shut up in a piece of bamboo wood and secured. The tree had remained on the ground but three months, and when sawed into planks, it proved drilled with the tree maggot, a thing as thick and as long as one's finger.

At Barbadoes I was officer of the guard. A very suspicious-looking craft was in the offing: she looked a corvette and had English colours flying. I boarded her, saw no guns, but a number of young men on deck in all sorts of military costumes, some with swords and braided frock coats ; I went between decks, fitted with cabins on either side for the accommodation of the young fellows, and I found from inquiries that she was destined for the Spanish Main, and that all these young men were to join Bolivar in his endeavours to upset the government of the country. Among the lot was that genius young Searle ; she merely called in for a few supplies and then started off again, and I may as well end the story of Master Searle. In four or five months from this he appeared to have seen and had enough of the hand-to-mouth service in South America. Finding there was no pay and only to trust to what they might get in the way of plunder for their support, he did one of the few wisest things, *i.e.*, cut away, returning to Barbadoes on his way home. He dined on board, and my brother honoured a bill for £10 on his father. The fellow with great solemnity exclaimed at table, ' Although I have torn down the cockade, I still drink success to the cause ' ; and he chose afterwards to say that he left our service through *my* tyranny —I could not avoid pitching into him. He afterwards was midshipman with his father who commanded the *Hyperion* frigate on the coast of South America, where he picked up an enormous freight. For some offence young Searle got into a scrape and drew his dirk on his father. Eventually his end was a sad one : he was killed in a duel at Portsmouth.

At Barbadoes we became acquainted with a Mr Griffiths, the father of one of our mids. He lived at Castle Grant, known all over the country, and at sea, by a gigantic pair of cabbage trees in front of the house. He had a remarkable horse, Peacock, that would not allow anyone to remain in his seat who had mounted him on the off side, and it was our object to trick him by getting him against a gate, but it would not answer, he bucked and kicked till his rider was unseated. A lot of us were spending the day with Mr Griffiths, and late in the evening set off for Bridgetown, first a kittereen with three and after a time three more mounted, I on Peacock. It was very dark ; we saw something, it proved to be three horsemen coming towards us, and we dashed through them ; then something else before us, which we thought to be the kittereen : in an instant, when too late to swerve, it was another kittereen coming towards us with the wife of the attorney-general and another lady in it. Too close to avoid the collision, the shaft glanced from Peacock's shoulder, took me in the thigh and fairly lifted me to the crupper. In two days the admiral, who always contrived to know everything, took us to task for not stopping to inquire after the ladies to apologise, for they were greatly alarmed. But the worst was poor Peacock : a swelling formed on the shoulder which caused his death. Mr Griffiths never knew of the accident, nor did we of Peacock's death till many weeks after. Mr Griffiths was a highminded gentleman and a man of great literary attainments, a classical scholar, quoting Juvenal, Horace, &c.

One day after dinner, we heard great cries of distress as from a man under punishment, which much disturbed our quiet ; at length Mr G——, seeing it, sent out to inquire and in a short time was answered—' It is William Charles, sar, him pretend to be sick, stay at home and when the hands in de field at work, him tief all and eat

all the suppers and him get toko for yam, cowkin, sar,' and so this
well satisfied us all.

As usual we moved about the islands Antigua, Trinidad and St
Vincent, and here we paid a visit to the Botanic Gardens, well
worth seeing, though they were not kept in very good order for
want of funds. We were much struck with the variety of strange
shrubs, nutmeg, spices, cinnamon. I cut two cinnamon stalks and
carried them to Canterbury ; they did not last long, someone found
the *taste* agreeable, and in a short time they were gnawed and
skinned ! I also picked a quantity of leaves of the nutmeg, two of
which are still in my writing book, as strong and as pungent as
when first picked. There was a running stream and a small waterfall
of about three feet only ; but it afforded us vast amusement. 'Long
Jones,' our marine officer, was six feet six inches in height, and he
was the first to go in for a bathe, the water being about five feet
deep, and we got him to put his head under the fall, and the consequence was, the sudden weight of water so unexpected jammed his
head against the rock with great force ; all to our delight.

From this we went to Barbadoes and down to Tortola and St
Thomas. At Tortola there is a remarkable range of rocks of great
size, forming a barrier, enclosing a gigantic sort of harbour. I got
leave for the barge, and with two or three others beat up to the
ridge ; it was difficult to find our way in, clear of the coral bottom,
we were obliged to thread our way. There was merely a village of
huts for fishermen only ; the ridge appeared to be the effect of an
earthquake ; the rocks, of the size of a large house, were thrown one
upon the other, forming numberless caverns and baths of clear
shallow water and a fine sandy bottom. Some of the caverns are as
light as day, others quite dark and with large fish, which we were
too prudent to disturb, fearing there might be sharks among them.
We had, however, our bath, so deliciously cool. To this day I am
fully impressed with my feelings of admiration and wonder at the
stupendous upheaving of the earth and convulsion of nature in this
movement of such tremendous rocks. It certainly could alone be
the work of an earthquake ; well, we turned back and after a
pleasant run of a few miles rejoined the ship at St Thomas, greatly
gratified with our day's outing.

At Barbadoes we gave a boat-race ; all boats of the squadron
joined, and we built a huge kitchen and roasted an ox whole, stuffing
him with a whole pig, a quantity of yams, potatoes, &c. It turned
out first rate.

October 25 we heard of the death of my father at Canterbury at the age of seventy-four.   He was a strict but a very kind father, and we all loved him dearly.

At this time I got two cases of noyeau from Martinique for Doctor Griffiths.   One day we dined with the 25th mess, and in the evening sent down our claret, &c., to the beach, where we sat under some overhanging rocks, called the Regent's Feathers.   We were suddenly out of water ; there was a well near composed of empty flour casks, and the business was to get water.   At last I volunteered, and with a jug in my teeth went down.   The well was not over six casks deep, but after I was down the getting up again was the thing.   I remember the number of heads looking down and saying, ' Well, Boteler, how goes it ? ' and with quite a job with elbows, knees, and back, I managed it.   But I would not try it again, my knees and elbows came to grief.

While at Barbadoes a transport arrived with stores and provisions, and I, with a party of seamen, was employed a week or ten days clearing her, and to my surprise had five shillings a day for the work.

We had an occasional encounter with the sharks, and it was often in this way.   Mr Cavan was the meat contractor for the navy, and when his schooner arrived crammed with oxen, there would be one or two deaths, and the beasts were thrown overboard.   The sharks were soon attracted to the spot, and you saw them agitating the water, tugging at a bullock's head or leg.   We manned a boat, and with a slip-knot soon managed to secure one and tow him on shore, amidst the yells and noise of the negroes, who were delighted at the chance of making short work of the creature.

A sloop of war, Captain Willes, arrived from the Island of Ascension, and gave the admiral and ourselves each a turtle, a magnificent pair of over two hundredweight.   We took our one to the dockyard and turned it into the mast pond till we wanted it, and then sent the jolly boat with the butcher for the creature, and it was a rare puzzle.   It upset everyone who attempted to seize it, biting the butcher very badly.   At last we sent off to the ship for a stout net, and so secured the brute, and we had many meals off it, besides giving a quantity to the warrant officers and the midshipmen.

And now, before I close my *Antelope* adventures, I must bring forward a most remarkable man, James Butler.   He first turned up in the *Agamemnon*, and attached himself to my cousin, John Harvey, whom he never after left.   In the *Agamemnon* he shewed great powers of mental arithmetic.   A question arose in the forecastle as to the division of a leg of mutton, costing so much, and what each man's share was.   Butler, who was near, answered it

78

off-hand. He was confined in irons for some offence, and got the
sentry to read questions from Benythorn's Arithmetic, and so went
into fractions. He then studied reading and writing, teaching
himself. The first time I knew him was in the *Sceptre*, in 1812,
when five of us came down to Plymouth in a six inside coach from
London. I was surprised at seeing the care taken of my chest,
which I found placed in a snug berth in the cockpit. For three or
four mornings my shoes were cleaned, my clothes brushed and put
into the head clew of my hammock. When one morning, waking
up, I called out, ' What are you doing there ? ' ' Beg your pardon,
sir, it's me, Butler, sir ; I am taking care of your things, if you will
allow me.' I was too well satisfied, and Butler, all the time I was
in that ship, attended to all my wants. He remained with Harvey
and I joined another ship and lost sight of him for a time. The
next time I met him was on the *Antelope*, when, although looking
after John Harvey, he never left my side. In fact, for the three
and a-quarter years I never once went to bed without his kissing
my hand. A more faithful and attached fellow I never met with.
He was an able seaman, refused a petty officer's rating, that his
services might not be interfered with. He was also a good astro-
nomer and mathematician. We had an order from the Admiralty
to take sights of the stars during our watches for the latitude of the
ship, and a list of the principal planets and stars supplied us with
their declinations. Butler would take the look out on the weather
gangway, and as I walked forward would remind me that Arcturus,
or Sirius, or Andromeda, as it might be, would be shortly on the
meridian. He was ever ready to help in this way. An officer of
engineers one day came on board saying that a question was puzzling
them as to finding the distance of a balloon from certain angles or
something beyond this ; and that they had not a man that could
solve it. Butler was sent for, and after scratching his head, said
he must ask for a slate, and in a few minutes gave the answer.
Butler was exceedingly near-sighted ; very ingenious ; with a
diamond drill he mended china in a most masterly way ; and he
built a large windmill, about four feet high, that would hoist up its
own bags of wheat, and perform all the functions of a real mill.
When the ship was paid off he went on shore and lived with Henry
Harvey as his groom ; and it was a sight to see him manage a
restive horse, and his contrivances with a pulley to haul his head
to the rack, and so groom him. But one day the horse got loose
and pinned Butler for a time up in a corner, whence it was difficult
to escape. I should have said that Butler's last service was the

care of me for a fortnight at Mr Griffiths', where I was ill, at the paying off of the *Antelope*. After two or three years with Henry Harvey, Butler lived with John Harvey, in a cottage at Woodlands, near Canterbury, where he had his hammock slung in a loft with a step-ladder to it. I lived at that time at Wickham, three or four miles from Woodlands, and Butler used now and then to bring me a hare. When Harvey left Woodlands, he established Butler and his housekeeper 'Annie' in a cottage, and there I paid him a visit. He came out to see me, went into his cottage, would not take leave, but sent Annie out to shew me a penknife I had given him twenty years back. Poor old fellow! his heart was in his mouth, and he felt it was our last interview. He died shortly after, aged eighty-two.

My *Antelope* history draws to a close. While at Barbadoes, waiting for our relief, Admiral Reynolds,[1] in January, 1819, and having nothing to do in my watch, I stretched myself on deck for a sleep, when I was roused up by the mid. of the watch saying, 'Eight bells, sir' (*i.e.*, Four o'clock). I found myself in a pool of water, wet through. I went below; and on waking up, had great difficulty in breathing, an oppression on my chest, and otherwise very ill. Dr Neill came to me, and instantly applied a large blister; and I was very ill for a week, when I was roused up at hearing a salute: our relief had arrived. It took but a few days to settle all arrangements between the two admirals; when we up anchor for England. I was totally unfit for duty, and was put on the sick list, the admiral sending for me, telling me to make use of his cabin whenever I found the noise in the wardroom too great for me; and he otherwise was very kind. I was told to keep quiet, and not attempt any duty. As we got on our voyage, I felt better; gave an 'At home' in my cabin—noyeau and other drinks, salt junk, and American crackers. Speaking of what we three brothers could do on half-pay as to a horse, that it would be as well to have a long backed one, that we might ride double, laughing; when Dr Neill startled me by saying, 'Don't be too sanguine, John.' I wondered for the moment, but gave no further heed.

We had three passengers in the wardroom: an officer of the 63rd, a merchant, and Alfred Lomago, whom we suspected to be a Jew, and Aaron (not Alfred). One day we had a leg of pork for dinner. I asked Limago [2] if he would have some. 'Oh, yes; very fond of

---

[1] Rear Admiral John Harvey's successor as Commander-in-Chief, Leeward Islands station, was Rear Admiral Donald Campbell, whose flag was flying in H.M.S. *Salisbury*.

[2] The spelling Lomago followed two lines later by Limago is a typical Botelerism.

pork.' But I noticed his gorge turned on it ; he played with it for a time, but sent it away.

Strange that all this time I have forgotten our cow, our greatest friend, supplying the admiral and ourselves, morning and evening, with milk, and occasionally even the midshipmen. She embarked at Portsmouth, a very pretty little Alderney ; she never had a calf ; and considering the variety of food she had in harbour, clover, banana stems (very succulent), and other rich green substances,— then at sea, as this supply failed, hay, bread dust, pea-soup ! and, above all, her *pint of grog !* a pint of water, added to the grog tub, that she might have her allowance. She was often landed (would not look at the bull !), but would jump every fence and run down to the boat. In the morning she was let out of her pen, and had a cumbrous game with the butcher ; gambolling and racing about the decks, till her house was made tidy, and then retreating to it as steady as an old pump bolt. On the way home we were caught in a gale, and she had to be slung to the beams ; the consequence was almost entire loss of milk, and the bulletin of the cow's health was anxiously looked for ; but her milk came round again, so that in fact, except during this interruption, she supplied us all with milk for three years and a-half. She was landed in the Downs, like a mad thing ; three men with her to prevent her horning every dog or horse she came near. She was taken to the admiral's residence at Upper Deal, there to live in clover the rest of her days. When Admiral Griffith Colpoys in the *Newcastle* came in—an old friend of our admiral's—he asked about a cow, and what description of one to get ; the admiral proposed his taking his cow, and so she then and there embarked. How she behaved, and what became of her, I never more heard.

While at Barbadoes, I omitted to mention a tall, uncouth Scotch assistant-surgeon joining. As soon as he had announced himself with long strides on the deck, he commenced with, ' I was at the Battle of Algiers, sir—at the Battle of Algiers, in the *Granicus*, sir ' ; and the admiral could not help saying : ' Well done, little *Granicus*.'

When we made the land the admiral sent down a handsome present of a case of champagne (three dozen), which we much en-joyed. Well, on the 17th March, we ran up to the Motherbank, the quarantine establishment, and were visited by the quarantine officer. In such cases the admiral appears at the gangway to answer all questions on oath. ' Where are you from ? any fever there when you left ? have you had fever on board ; and when last ? ' and many other queries of the same sort. At last, ' Have you any sickness ? '

' Only one officer, and he is in consumption.' I was close to the
admiral, and you might have knocked me down at the moment
with a feather. I quite understood then Dr Neill saying, ' Don't
be too sanguine, John.' Other officers present felt for me, and were
as much surprised as I was ; however, we anchored at Spithead.
No Mr Martin appeared, so he was in jail. On the 20th we were
in the Downs, landed all the admiral's baggage as well as our own
for Canterbury, and on the 28th were at Sheerness.

It was thought best that I should be away from the ship while
paying off, and so I went to Mr Griffiths with old Butler to wait on
me. The day before paying off, I went up to London to consult
Dr Maton, an eminent physician and a personal friend of my brother
William ; he examined me with great care, and then said '' he did
not see any immediate danger,' prescribed, and desired me to pay
him another visit at the end of a week. I did not know what to do
with myself, so mounted a coach for Rochester to put up again with
Mr Griffiths. At Gravesend, I met the Rochester coaches coming
up full of our paid-off men, some on the roofs with a fiddler dancing,
one hung in his hammock underneath, a black fellow inside—the
men would not allow him to be on the quarter-deck. I was much
cheered, had to get down and take a sip of grog with many. I was
a sort of medium in the ship between my brother and the men,
getting off several from punishment, and so was rather a favourite
among them. I got off the grog drinking pretty well, reached
Rochester, and at the end of the week paid another visit to Dr
Maton, who said the same thing as before, that ' he did not see any
immediate danger, but that I was to go down to Canterbury, mount
my horse, and take gentle exercise,' gave me medicine for a week,
and so my consultation with him ended. I ought to have said that
on my way to Canterbury I directed my baggage to be left at the
Bull Inn, Shooter's Hill, and walked myself to the Royal Military
Academy and inquired after my brother Robert, a cadet. ' Oh,
he is just coming down stairs,' and in a minute I espied a long-
legged fellow as he seemed, skipping along.

We were mutually delighted ; the meeting so unexpected. I
asked him to come up the hill with me, and if he could eat a second
dinner. ' Oh, yes, of course I can ' ; and so we had as good a dinner
as they could give us, and when we parted, quite under the rose, for
I half feared he might be offended, I put a sovereign into his hands.
' Oh, thank you, John '—to my relief ; and he never forgot this *sov.*
Well, I reached home at last, found the old lady looking very well,
and my sisters the same, but for a time I missed my father very sadly.

CHAPTER V

THE *Seagull*, TENDER TO THE GUARDSHIP AT SHEERNESS

WE were living in a large house belonging to Sir John Fagg, and we shortly after moved into a smaller one, bought by my father and left as a residence for his widow. My brother Richard came down to superintend some requisite repairs. It was a nice snug residence and had been occupied by a Miss Kenrick. My brother Henry, whom the Admiralty promoted when the ship was paid off, did not stay long with us, but went into lodgings at Deal, and my brother Thomas, after six months, went on a pedestrian tour through France, Italy and Austria. We became intimately acquainted with a Mr Salisbury; I went with him across the Channel to Calais for a day by a sailing hoy, the only sort of passage boat, and from which we had the nuisance of landing in a small boat. About this time my brother William paid me the contents of my money-box, £9. 19s. 6d. As boys, we had each a money-box; every 2s. 6d. or other tip coming to us was put into it with a paper of the amount and interest added at the end of each year. My brother Thomas, who was his mother's favourite, had near £20 in his box. I went down to Lydd with Mr Burton to look over his house, he having the living, an unexpected gift of the Archbishop, and soon after this he was married to my sister Eliza.

In August I have a pleasant remembrance of an agreeable visit from John Griffiths, and we went to the Canterbury races twice on horseback. In November I went to Sheerness to pay a visit to my uncle, Captain Thomas Harvey, commanding the *Northumberland* guardship there. In December, at a ball, I was taken by surprise at finding the dance was a quadrille; in the West Indies and elsewhere, nothing was known beyond the simple country dance. So my sister Julia, another lady, Henry Hodges and I, put ourselves into the hands of Philpot, the dancing master, and took regular lessons in the zephir step, balancez, riggidoun, passez, &c., and I

soon mastered all the ins and outs of the quadrille. In December
I went to Rochester to stay a few days with Mr Griffiths ; in
February, 1820, dined with a large party at the Fountain to cele-
brate the accession to the throne of George the Fourth.

On the 1st of February, I received my appointment to the
Northumberland at Sheerness. During my eight months on half-
pay my state of health did not trouble me much ; in fact, I don't
think I ever thought about it, but on going on full pay I could but
notice what a pale-faced fellow I was, so much so that I thought
people turned to look at me, and I was doubtful if I could do my
duty, but this feeling went off and I enjoyed myself. I could see
the captain [1] go on shore for a walk, got leave and followed him.
He was quite a companion, and was most delightful company, full
of anecdotes.

We had a tender, the *Seagull*, a cutter of about fifty tons. I took
my turn in her three months at a time, together with Lieutenants
Cole and Bowker. One of our mids., who had served six years after
passing, wrote to the Admiralty enquiring if it were requisite to pass
a second time. Whether from the quaintness of the letter or their
own sense of justness I do not know, but by return of post they sent
his commission. This caused Daniel Griffiths, son of our friend at
Barbadoes, to try the same, the answer being that ' their lordships
saw nothing in his services or the style of his letter to entitle him to
their consideration.' From this time poor Griffiths seemed to go
astern, and in a quarrel with his father; then in London, both father
and son were found dead. At the inquest both appeared to have
pistols, but it was a question which shot the other first and then
himself. Mr Griffiths had a pair of clean white kid gloves on, and
as they did not seem to be soiled, the verdict was against the son for
shooting the father.

The first lieutenant was a cricketer, and we had two or three
pleasant matches some distance from Sheerness, and a picnic dinner
after.

We had a new gun, General Millar's, and the Admiralty came
down to inspect its prowess. It was a sixty-eight pounder,
chambered, a short gun, weighing about forty hundredweight, a
lump, with timbers, part of the keels of ships lately dug out of
Sheerness dockyard, bolted on the sides, forming a large bull's-eye,
which was chalked on it. The gun had a sight fixed, and in six
shots the mark was a perfect wreck. The gunner asked to fire a
shot from the old thirty-two pounder, and with merely a chance

---

[1] His uncle, Captain Thomas Harvey.

84

sight put the ball right into the bull's-eye. 'There,' said Sir Joseph Yorke, 'that's something like a shot.' He was all along throwing ridicule on the sighted gun. Pity the gunner did not try a second shot ! The mark was moored about 1,200 yards from the ship, and at low water there were several persons hunting for and picking up the large shot.

Towards the close of the year there was a great fire at Sheerness. We landed a party of seamen, who did excellent work in pulling down some old houses to check the fire, for the hoses were cut, supposed by the Jews ; and about the same time one also at Chatham, far more destructive. It raged two whole days. Our surgeon was asleep at the Chest Arms, and when called merely grunted, and turned to sleep again. The chambermaid, exasperated, came a second time, calling out, ' You hardened villain, will you lie and be burnt ? ' and the doctor then saw the flames rushing past the window, jumped up, but lost his watch. He related the story with great gusto.

A never-failing attraction to me was the extensive works going on at the dockyard, taking in very many acres of ground ; and a vast number of old men-of-war, that had been partially buried for many years, the *Sussex*, *Lennox*, &c., were removed, and among them was the *Vindictive* frigate, one of the latest buried, and forming for many years the port-admiral's residence and office. These ships, worn-out men-of-war, were originally sunk and filled to make the ground for the dockyard, in which there were only two or three small docks. They were inhabited by the scum of the town, the refuge of the worst characters of the place. Many deeds of darkness and crime were there committed without a possibility of detection, so that their removal was a grand clearance of rubbish. I have a map shewing the names and positions of the old ships, and it shews an odd record of former times. Some very large granite docks were being formed, and across the centre of two of these was a balk of timber as a way from one side to the other. With cocked hat on and my sword as a walking-stick to steady me, I used to cross them. One day a marine officer attempted to follow, got half-way, when he suddenly called out he had lost his head, turned back running. Nothing would tempt him to try another journey.

The *Hyperion*, Captain Searle, arrived and paid off. I received an order from the admiral, Sir John Gore, to take charge of her till the first officer was appointed. She was wretchedly low between decks. In the gunroom the officers could not sit at table without two inches of the legs of the chairs being cut off, and in my cabin I had to go under the hatchway to put on my coat. The *Brazen*, Captain Fisher, came in to refit, and he asked if I was not tired of a ' guardo,' and would not prefer active service, and go with him as his first lieutenant. Not if I know it, not for Joseph. He was a born fidget, never seemed to trust any officer, even to sweeping the deck. I simply declined.

While in the *Seagull* my sister Agnes and Miss R. Curling came to Milton to pay Captain Harvey a visit. I pulled up the Swale to Milton and there waited for them. As soon as they came we set off amidst the cheers of the oyster boats, who fancied it was a small elopement. They were two or three weeks on board of us.

Our purser, Mr Peche, was a character, a stout, very stout man, so much so that we had an idea of cutting the segment of a circle in the table to fit his corporation. Peche was our caterer, and let us know he carried his money in a pocket constructed in the back of his trowsers. Being married he lived on shore in Mile Town, about a mile out of Sheerness. Three of us agreed to waylay and rob him, and had got crape disguises for that purpose, when by chance, another, not in the secret, said to him, ' That is a disreputable road to Mile Town, I wonder you do not expect to be robbed some night.' Old Peche deliberately pulled out a pocket pistol, saying, ' My dear fellow, I have something here to answer all that.' We never went near him : he would have shot one of us to a certainty. The captain living on board, and keeping a handsome table, had always the first lieutenant, the lieutenant of the forenoon watch, an idler, *i.e.*, purser, master or surgeon, and a mid. or two, making six at his table every day. Consequently, as one was in the *Seagull* and others married, it so happened that Peche and I were alone at table. ' Well, old gentleman, a bottle of port,' and one was had. ' Another bottle, old man.' ' You don't say so,' and without my help, who had the bell rope over my head, he would grasp it, calling to the steward, ' Another bottle of port.' That discussed, I would again propose a pint. ' No, no,' but up would go his hand. ' A pint of port, steward.' By this time the captain's dinner, that was an hour later than ours, was over, and the officers would come down. ' Here you are, you never dine by yourselves that you are not swiping.' Peche was impenetrable and did not seem to hear them, but on my proposal would up with his hand : ' Another pint of port, steward,' and another after this closed the day—two bottles and three pints. The same now would be the death of me.

On the *Northumberland* being paid off we had another purser,

John Archdeacon, who was in the *Antelope* with me, and Peche
had an appointment to the ships in ordinary. On board the *Brune*
frigate, and his wife with him, there was a terrible scene : his wife
was found hanging to a beam, but the old man got over it very well.
The last I heard of him was his going down by coach to Tiverton,
one inside passenger only, and they got on most comfortably
together, when, on stopping at a road-side inn and moving the
luggage, old Peche called out, ' That's my baggage ; what are you
about ? ' The gentleman turned : ' I beg your pardon, sir, is your
name Peche ? I am General Peche ; I seldom meet anyone of my
name. My carriage is here, and I live half-a-dozen miles off the
road. If you are not particularly engaged and will come and stay
a few days with me I shall feel greatly obliged.' Old Peche made
no objection. The result was some months later Peche was the
richer by £1,000 left him by the general.

I used to walk to Sittingbourne and waylay the Canterbury
coaches, pick out a crowded one and roll along the dusty road,
getting down to walk up Barton Hill, as was the custom. Who
should get out from the inside one day but my brother, on his way
to the Sessions, he being Recorder of Canterbury. Well, of course,
we were glad to see each other, and on the top of the hill he went
outside with me for a stage, when he said, ' I think, John, I will
get inside again ; I travel so much that some day I may meet with
an accident, and I think I shall be safer inside.' Some months
after this he said, ' You wondered at my preferring the inside ; do
you know I have been three times upset in a coach, and each time
outside ? ' The first time was going into Cambridge, deep snow ;
they had six horses ; when turning a corner in the street the leaders
pulled the second off their legs, and over the coach went—soft
snow and no one hurt. The second time, he was on the mail, and
going down a long lane, a road waggon was seen before us ; the
coachman called, giving them a tune, and pulling aside for more
room drove against the bank, and over the coach went, falling against
the waggon, my brother scrambling up the tilt, and there, as he said
(stretching his long body over), ' I saw all the commotion below me.'
But the job was, after the coach was righted, to get down again ;
however, by getting at the front of the tilt and with the help of the
waggoner he descended all right. The third time was still more
singular : the coach, while stopping in the streets of Canterbury,
drove against the pavement, which was a foot or more above the
street, and over the coach went, hurting no one but one of the
ostlers.

My brother was senior wrangler of his day at Cambridge, a great
mathematician and most agreeable companion. I used to enjoy
our long walks together, though I often felt myself in the witness-
box, he was so particular in all he said. He was Recorder of Canterbury and Fordwich, Sandwich, Deal, and Hythe, and latterly, Commissioner of Bankruptcy at Leeds. Poor man, he held it but a
brief time ; he was killed on the railway on his return to Leeds from
Kent. It was a most shameful display of carelessness. His train,
the mail, broke down passing a goods train ; they sent back word
for another engine but went on quietly at four or five miles the
hour ; passing a station it was suggested they should wait. ' Oh,
no ; tell them to be careful.' They had barely passed when up
came the pilot engine. ' Where is the mail train ? ' ' Just passed
—the lights are hardly out of sight ; mind what you are about.'
Instead of which they dashed into the mail train, upsetting a second
class carriage off the line and ramming the buffers of the engine into
the first class carriage, breaking my brother's legs all to pieces.
When the door was opened he called their attention to a gentleman
on the opposite side, saying, ' I think he must be very much hurt,
he groans so,' and then added, ' I fear both my legs are broken.'
With saws and chisels it took them over half an hour to clear him.
He was very quiet, only complained of feeling very cold ; fortunately
they were within two or three miles of the house he had taken. The
clergyman of the place hearing a noise in the street looked out, and
seeing a person being carried past and knowing my brother was
expected, followed him to his house. Two surgeons from the Leeds
Hospital were soon in attendance, his house was only two miles from
Leeds. The surgeons' report was that one leg must be amputated
at once, it only hung by a mass of torn flesh. My brother merely
asked for five minutes to add a codicil to his will, which Sir Nicholas
Tyndal said ' was as clear an instrument as could possibly be
written.' The operation was then proceeded with, my brother
sighing and saying, ' I did not think it would have been so painful.'
A messenger was sent down to Eastry to acquaint the family. His
son William was on Betteshanger Downs when the messenger passed,
and he was speculating on his object. The Misses Boteler could
not wait for him but set off at once ; the brother lost that train
but reached the house in time to be just recognised by his father,
and so it ended. The railway sent the body to Eastry for burial,
paying all expenses, and at a public dinner, ' King Hudson ' said
compensation, to the amount of £10,000, would be made to the
family. This was not done, and Sir Nicholas Tyndal advised my

nephew to see Mr Hudson, who was then living in one of the large houses at Albert Gate. He could not get hold of him for a long time, and then he offered Mr Boteler £1,000, which he refused, reminding him of the £10,000. ' Oh,' said Mr Hudson, ' the thing has gone by, the interest has ceased, but here is £3,000,' which my nephew accepted.

We had a mid. named Coode ; his father brought him to us and gave me a £10 note to take care of for him. While at the Fountain Inn the waiter asked if any gentleman had dropped a £10 note. It was an Essex note, and by its peculiarity I recognised it. He soon after came in again to say the chambermaid begged to remind me that she had found it ; my answer was ' Honesty is the best policy,' and I sent out 12s. to her. Some days after a mid. came down, telling me that a woman was alongside wishing to see me. Looking through the port I saw it was the chambermaid ; she came down and I asked her what she expected. ' Why, sir, as you said " Honesty was the best policy," why, sir, I leave it to your generosity, but I am told I am entitled to one-half, but I will put up with less.' I said, ' I shall give you nothing more ; as a servant of the hotel anything you find belongs to the landlord, and you might be prosecuted for theft for retaining it.' She was in a taking when I said this, and declared she would not touch the next note she came across, and remarked that she once picked up a watch and that the gentleman gave it to her for her pains.

Captain Harvey became an admiral and the first lieutenant a commander, and in July we were paid off and re-commissioned the same day, our new captain, Thomas J. Maling. He took up his quarters with Mrs Maling, at Upnor Castle, and we were moved up to Salt-pan Reach, half-way between Sheerness and Chatham ; here we had literally nothing to do. I liked to take long walks on the marshes and with a ship's pistol, almost like a young musket, shoot water rats. I got so expert that I could kill four rats out of six shots. I, one day with our first lieutenant, Meredith, walked over to Cooling and dined with my old school-fellow James Boys, curate there. At a rubber of whist the cards were going against Meredith : he began dealing them into three packs, Mr Boys remarking, ' Were I playing for great stakes, I should object to that, for I can do so and give myself all the trumps,' and he did it to show us. I name this, for many years after, when residing near Barnstaple, at our whist club one of the members, Ignatius Davis, did this, and I objected, he saying, ' Shew me a rule against it,' which I could not, but another member wrote to *Bell's Life*, whose answer was : ' The gentleman is right, there is no rule against it, but the sooner you leave off playing with him the better.'   We did not do this, nor did we tell him of our letter to London.   It is a known trick of cards ; no doubt our friend was not aware of this, but since then the new rules of whist expressly forbid such a shuffle.

At Gillingham I was very intimate with Colonel Boys and his family; he was the grandson of Commodore Boys, Lieutenant-Governor of Greenwich Hospital, whose history is a remarkable one. He was in the merchant service and mate of the *Luxembourg* galley, and when at Jamaica, was nearly wrecked in a hurricane,[1] and one of the ship's boats was so injured that the captain desired she might be destroyed, but being a Deal boat, Mr Boys had an affection for her, and he had her repaired, and this boat, as it turned out, was the means of his safety.   The ship was loaded with sugar and rum, and when some days at sea, two black boys went below to draw off some rum, and spilling some, thoughtlessly put a light to it, and instantly the flame was beyond their control and the ship was hopelessly on fire.   They got the little boat out—she was but twelve feet long ; in endeavouring to launch the long boat, the tackling caught fire, and those who could got into the small boat, twenty-three in all, shoved off, leaving the remainder to their fate, and all shortly after were burnt in the ship.   The boat had neither masts nor sails and only three oars ; there were no other provisions but a little biscuit that one of the men had in his pocket.   It was soon seen that the boat could not possibly swim with such a crowd of men who were obliged to sit close to each other on the boat's gunwale, to keep out the sea.   They were consulting by lot who should be thrown overboard, when the two black boys, thinking they were to be sacrificed, jumped into the sea and perished.   In a day or two, three more men went mad and jumped overboard ; during this time a sail was made from the men's shirts, an oar turned into a mast, the boathook a yard, and they contrived to steer for the north ; they sucked each other's clothes, but the crew rapidly died, the survivors reduced to the dreadful necessity of cutting the throats of the dying and drinking their blood.   It was strange, Mr Boys remarked, that they at night passed or fancied they passed ships ; they could even hear sheep bleating, and thought how hard-hearted the crews were not to notice their shouts.   They had frequently seen the land (or thought they had), which always turned out ' Cape Fly Away,' and they all had stretched themselves out to die, when

[1] In 1727 ; see the notice of William Boys in Charnock's *Biographia Navalis* (1797), Vol. V, pp. 233–9.

Mr Boys turning in the boat thought he really saw the land ; he shut his eyes for a time fearing he might be deceived, and that it was a cloud ; on looking again he felt sure and roused the others, who directly looked up and began to row with the single oar—there were then only five alive, the captain, surgeon, carpenter, another, and Mr Boys. They soon came upon some fishing boats, who, seeing such spectres, at first turned away ; but on the poor fellows holding up their hands in prayer, they gained more courage and took them in, and they were taken on shore ; one of these men died from joy, another, the captain, from over eating, Mr Boys begging them to restrain. Mr Boys entered the navy, became a commodore, and died Lieutenant-Governor of Greenwich Hospital. It was singular, on Deal beach no twenty-five men could ever get into the boat. I well remember at Gillingham, four pictures of the scene hung in the dining-room, and Mr Boys religiously observed a yearly fast at that time.

While in Salt-pan Reach, Mr Griffiths brought all his school down the river in the *Blue-eyed Maid*, one of the very clever Sheerness passage boats. I was on the look out for them, went on board with half a bread bag of biscuits. I took the helm and made one of the boys, Lewis Jones, very happy, in imagining he steered, by having his hand on the tiller with mine ; we had a very jolly day going to Sheerness and out to the Nore.

During my command of the *Seagull*, I would get Meredith and C. Andrews of the Artillery to join me. I used to take them to Faversham, put up at the Ship, and be the guests of Mr Hilton and his family, with whom we went to the Faversham balls ; jolly fun ! The next morning in a post-chaise we would go to Maidstone, put up at the Bull, dine with the cavalry mess and go to the ball in the evening. Great fun again, and the following day in a chaise to the Rochester ball ; these balls always followed each other in this rotation. At Rochester my head-quarters was the Bull.

I must not forget a visit I paid to my brother, a lieutenant of the *Barracouta* brig, fitting at Woolwich with the *Leven*, Captain William Owen, for an extensive survey of the East Coast of Africa, and Mozambique Channel and seas adjacent. I dined with Captain Owen, quite a scientific party ; among others was Captain Edwards the pump maker, and Dr Carpue the nose maker, and with the party was one of the doctor's patients ; till you looked close you would never suspect that his nose was formed from the skin of his forehead : a piece of a triangular form was cut away, turned and formed over an artificial bridge, the edges brought into contact with the cheek, which was prepared to meet it and so grew; the only thing was, that the circulation was so imperfect, that when the cheeks were red the nose might be white or *vice versa*.

Just before my appointment to the *Royal Sovereign* yacht, I paid another visit to Woolwich to see my younger brother Robert, who with fourteen other cadets was waiting his commission in the Arsenal, where I found them in handsome rooms. I was there on the sly, and brought with me two or three bottles of rum; the officer, Captain Durnford, came round to see all snug, desiring the lights to be put out, &c.: at this time I was standing up in one of the cadets' beds, and as soon as his back was turned, blankets were pinned at the windows, lights in, fire lighted, a whole posse of eggs boiled and a hare cut up and stewed, and we passed a very respectable and agreeable evening. The next day, there were races on the common, and I was in an artillery waggon, very sweet with a Miss S——, a niece of the General, Sir Alexander C. Dickson (I think). The winner of the race was a Mr Williams, a cadet, afterwards Sir W. Williams of Kars. He was not supposed to race and was in a blue funk for fear of being detected.

In the evening there was a ball, at which I and my brother were, and I had the supreme felicity of dancing with Miss S——.

I also paid a visit to Eton to see a brother Edward, living at a dame's in charge of Twisden Hodges, a boy at the school.

At another time I went near Maidstone, to see my sister Julia and her husband Mr Hodges, a clergyman, who was doing duty at Loose. The hops, I recollect, were protected by high quick hedges, so high that a waggon was drawn by the side, and a man on a ladder placed in it with shears to clip them.

CHAPTER VI

LENT TO THE ROYAL YACHT—VISIT TO THE BATTLEFIELD OF
WATERLOO

AT this time a succession of most gratifying and pleasing appointments fell to my lot, and a happy, active, and exciting career was before me. Early in June I received an unexpected order to join H.M. Yacht *Royal Sovereign*, fitting for sea at Deptford Dockyard, taking with me three midshipmen Wilmot, Smith, and Evans. A King's lugger was put at our service to take us up the Thames. We were glad to escape this and got leave to go by land ; so off we started by coach from Rochester, got down at the Broadway, Deptford and walked to the dockyard ; being asked our business at the gate, no small stir was made when we announced ourselves officers of the yacht, the warden himself, an ancient lieutenant, offering to shew us the way. We found the yacht in the basin, being regilded and painted, the hull purple, the royal colour. She was a beautiful ship, richly gilt, with a family head, as it is termed, the King, Queen and two or three children in a group. Her ports were all circular, with carved figures round them, of the size of a two-year-old child ; her stern was covered with figures.

I stepped on board, asking of a quartermaster who was the commanding officer. ' The master, Mr Franklyn, sir.' On his coming on deck, I announced myself and introduced my young companions. The officers had just sat down to dinner, and I found the surgeon, purser and clerk at table in the lords' room, where the captain and officers all mess, together with any attendants on royalty that may be on board. I directly inquired as to mess affairs, and was told the expenses, beyond the usual allowance of ships' provisions in yachts, had hitherto been paid, but he was not sure how it might be while fitting out. ' And as to wine ? ' ' Oh, I have charge of the wine stores and it now depends on your orders.' So I had no great hesitation in ordering a bottle of port and sherry. I do not

remember the number of our crew, but they consisted of dockyard
riggers, all old men-of-war's men, thorough seamen, of good
character, and mostly married men. Our proper captain was
Charles Adam, commonly called Charlie Adam, more like a midshipman than a staid post captain. He entertained and amused us
greatly with the story of his being turned back from post captain to
a midshipman, not *his* fault he said, but his uncle, Lord Keith's, who
made him a lieutenant under age, then commander and post captain,
following rapidly according to the usage of the service, and as captain
he brought home a frigate and went to the Admiralty in uniform.
He laughed in telling us that Lord Spencer, or Sandwich,[1] addressed
him as Mr Adam, and he directly knew it was all up with him.
But the strange thing afterwards was, that he became midshipman
of the watch with the man who was his first lieutenant in this
frigate. He was four or five months a mid., and then quickly
advanced, and after all was a young man of his rank. Captain
Adam was in Scotland to be married, so his place was supplied by
Captain Sir Jahleel Brenton, but who did not join us till we were in
the ' fair way,' moored with a ' lump ' on each bow and quarter, to
prevent any clumsy collier running foul of us and spoiling our
gingerbread.

In two or three days I was sent for to the Admiralty and saw
Sir George Cockburn, the senior naval lord, about our mess arrangements. He said that ' hitherto the yachts had been under the
Board of Greencloth, that all was wrong—would you believe it, sir ?
the mess expenses were nearly a £1,000 in six weeks ; I shall give you
a £100 ; you will keep the main bills only as vouchers, the smaller
may go as extras. You will keep a gentlemanly table, your fish,
soup, joint and occasional game, and for wine, port and sherry ;
and if you have a friend at table, a little champagne and claret will
do no harm.' I told him I perfectly understood him and would
allow no extravagance. But I did think his bill of fare most liberal,
it quite staggered me. When the table decker, a sort of butler,
having charge of the plate, and the cook came down from Carlton
House, our living became sumptuous. The first cook left us the
next day with an attack of gout. Another young man came, and
on being asked his business, for I took him for a gentleman, said he
was a cook, so I sent him down to his own dominions. He soon
came back saying, ' He was told he must ask my leave ; that he
wished to return to the palace for two or three more jackets and

<hr>

[1] The First Lord was Lord Spencer. The details are given in O'Byrne's *Naval
Biographical Dictionary.*

94

other trifles.' He was a first-rate artiste and it was a sight (with his white dress, cap also, and a belt with knives in it) to see him handle pastry, &c. But we were all a little tickled, not having seen much of high life, at a *menu* sent in French, even English was not allowed for plain roast beef. He had lately returned from Paris where he had received instruction under a celebrated *chef*. At the Admiralty, Sir George also told me we were going to Antwerp with the Duke and Duchess of Clarence and the two Ladies Fitz-Clarence,[1] that I was to engage a respectable woman, sufficiently used to the sea to attend the ladies, and that she was to be entered on the ship's books as able seaman; consequently, I went to Greenwich and secured the wife of one of the pensioners.

And this reminds me, one Sunday, Wilmot and I went for a stroll in Greenwich Park, and on the ' hill,' as usual, found some old pensioners calling the attention of the London holiday folk to the wonders of their telescopes mounted on triangles, and so to us as we came forward, ' Don't be surprised, young gentlemen, if you see those ships close to you, &c.,' and we led them on to tell most marvellous stories of a sea life, and to our question as to how they managed to find their way across the ocean, ' Why, gentlemen, you see, at noon we shoots the sun,' and this of course excited our unbounded astonishment. By degrees we led them to the West Indies, and asked what ships they were in. As this chaff was going on many got round, including other pensioners. Some, I suspected, began to smell a rat, notwithstanding our apparent innocence. One told us he was in the *Orontes*, Captain Cochrane, and then I suddenly recognised him as our seedy, dissipated, drunken schoolmaster. ' Was Mr Cross your first lieutenant, Cross by name and cross by nature ? ' At this he started, pulled off his cocked hat, made his bow, making sure we were naval officers. I asked if he remembered any of the midshipmen. At first the surprise, then the mirth of the other pensioners ! ' Well, two or three; one John Harvey, a mischievous young gentleman.' ' John Harvey Boteler, you mean ; why, don't you recollect me ? you used to get drunk in our berth, and got your head greased and floured.' At this there was a roar of laughter among all those about us. Then after a little we left, asking him to dine on board the yacht the next day ; and we had just sat down to dinner when a warder called on board ' that there was a pensioner at the gate saying he was to dine on board, and we don't believe him.' We said ' All right ! ' and on board he came in his Sunday's best and a large bouquet at his breast. He was most

---

1 For the Ladies Fitz-Clarence, see Burke's *Peerage*, *sub* Earl of Munster.

95

amusing, but his old habit floored him, and he was wheeled in a
barrow to the dock gates, put into a one-horse two-wheeled 'bus, the
things plying between Deptford and Greenwich, and sent home.
Two days after I received a flaming copy of verses expatiating on
my kindness and hospitality, and the glory of his visit.

When moored in the river we had several visitors, and one day
a large wherry with silk awnings and cushions, and with six men in
nautical dresses, and a party of ladies, rowed slowly round us.   I
invited them to see the yacht, and offered my arm to the best-
looking lady and took her round the ship.   All at once there was a
shout of ‘ A man overboard ! ’   The cries ran like wildfire ; the
ladies began to scream.   I ran on deck, found the master, a fiery-
eyed, red-faced little Welshman, in a great state of excitement.
‘ What’s all this, Franklyn ? ’   ‘ I couldn’t help it, sir ; he began to
abuse the King, and I hustled him to the gangway meaning to kick
him into his boat, but she had dropped astern and overboard he
went ’ ; and there he was, his bald head above water, paddling and
splashing like a dog.   A wherry took him up, and he *would* be landed.
By this time some of the other men began to shew their teeth.   I
told them to be silent, that any person who presumed to abuse His
Majesty on board his own yacht would inevitably be kicked overboard by the officers, and so they all with great haste hustled into
their boat.   As it turned out they were not gentry.   This never got
into the papers ; it would have gone well with Franklyn had it
reached the King’s ears.   Franklyn told me that on showing the
man the companion, a richly decorated staircase, as the entrance to
the royal apartment, ‘ Ah,’ said the fellow, ‘ just the thing for fat
George, when beastly drunk, to roll down.’   ‘ What, sir ! how dare
you, sir, to abuse His Majesty on his own quarter-deck, and before
one of his officers ?   Go along, sir, out of the ship, sir ! ’ and so it
ended.   It was a lesson to us ; we always afterwards required cards
to be sent up before we admitted visitors, at least, questionable
ones.

The captain at last came on board.   The articles of war were
read, to shew the crew they were under martial law and naval
discipline ; and next day we started for and in due time anchored
in the Downs.   There we passed a few jolly days.   My mother and
sisters were in lodgings on Walmer Beach, and I had many relations
in the neighbourhood ; we had two or three parties on board, and I
was in a nice position for entertaining them.

A few days after, the Duke and party came off.   It was blowing
fresh, and there was some difficulty in keeping the barge clear of the

accommodation ladder, the yacht was rolling so. Sir Jahleel was
crippled and lame from wounds, and I had to step down the ladder.
'Take care of the Duchess, sir.' Then: 'Now, girls.' They
required no help, but skipped past me quick enough. We soon after
weighed. It turned out an ugly night, blowing hard, with many
squalls of rain ; and there was much sea on. We had two first-rate
North-Sea pilots ; as also Sir Edward Owen, himself a noted pilot,
having been commodore of an in-shore squadron of frigates off the
Dutch coast, winter and summer for many months. Captain Rich,
his relative, was likewise with us. The Duke, Sir Edward, and our
captain were on deck all night, and, of course, I could never go
below. The yacht had the character of being, and was, a most
excellent sea-boat, but she did kick and roll about famously.

In the middle of the night I heard a *squeal*, divined the cause, and
sent for Mrs Davis to the royal apartments. I watched her coming
out. And, ' Well, what's the matter ? ' ' Oh, nothing, sir.' ' Nonsense—out with it.' ' Well, sir, the young ladies were pitched out
of bed, and I found them in the lee scuppers, rolling over each
other.' They were in George the Third's bed—a standing four-
poster. So, little chance of lying quiet or safe in blowing weather.

As we neared the low sandy coast, the wind moderated, but it
continued thick, and we had some difficulty in striking the proper
entrance to the Skeld, when it (the weather) cleared, and we worked
up the river, which winds immensely and, in parts, quite turns
back. We had much work ; bracing-up on one tack, then perhaps
on another, then before the wind, and up or down studding-sails. I
never before or since had so to knock a ship about,—but I was
backed up by most able and willing hands.

While this was going on, the two young ladies came on deck.
One, Lady Augusta, was very beautiful,—at least I thought so ;
such eyes and expression ; I could not keep mine off her. I was
indeed desperately smitten—mind ! this was just sixty years back !
I fancied she did not quite object to my admiration, so, at a lull in
working the ship, I took courage, and walked up to her, and was
soon in full swing. I began by being sorry that they had such a
disturbed night ; that I heard the half-scream and, divining the
cause, sent Mrs Davis to them. They looked at each other, laughed,
but affected to repudiate anything in particular. I said that ' All
used to the noises on board ship, knew what was happening ' ; and
so we laughed and talked, when up came the Duke—' Well, girls,
what is Mr Boteler talking about ? ' ' Oh, papa, he is admiring
the Dutch scenery ; the mud walls, &c.' ' Oh ! you wear glasses,

sir ; how do you manage with the telescope ? ' ' I merely alter the focus, your Royal Highness, and keep them on.' ' True—true ; pray are they gold ? ' ' Yes, sir ; I had a little extra cash, by chance, and I invested it in gold spectacles ; I should be glad to get rid of them at the same price.' ' Oh ! ' again ; then ' I think you want a pull at the main-top-gallant-brace,' and off he went. ' Oh, how could you answer papa so ? ' or something like it. I said, ' What an odd question to ask, if they were gold ! ' I mention this to show, as it turned out, the noted retentive memory of the royal family.

He had seen me in 1828, when he inspected the *Albion* after the battle of Navarino, and by the same token walked off with one of two of my pen-and-ink sketches of that action, hung up in the captain's cabin for him to look at. On my promotion to commander I went to the first levee at St James's Palace ; on kissing hands the King said, ' I promoted you, I believe, Captain Boteler.' I only bowed, I did not like to say ' No.' Then ' I know all about you, sir, but there is something I do not quite make out,' holding his finger up near my face and moving it up and down. ' I wore glasses, your Majesty.' ' True, true ; *gold* spectacles ! ' and down went his finger, and I backed astern scarcely knowing where I went. There were the Duke of Wellington, Sir Robert Peel and others about the throne. But no doubt it was nothing to them, he was always full of questions, and when old admirals came before him, at his early levees, it was ' Have you read *Peter Simple* ? ' shaking hands with them and laughing— he being noticed in that novel as ' Massa King George's Pickaninny, Prince William Henry,' &c.

In the evening we anchored off the city of Antwerp, and our company all left us. The next day some of us went on shore to visit the picture galleries, churches, &c. Wilmot and I went to the cathedral, up the high tower and even clambered up outside the main spire for some distance, higher probably than any other persons. We endeavoured to make a party the following day, and in a *char à banc* to start for Brussels and Waterloo. But it fell through, so Wilmot and I hired a *voiture* and pair of horses and started by our- selves ; great fun on the road, both in high spirits, greatly entertained at the frequent baiting of the horses on dark brown bread and beer ; we reached Brussels about six, and put up at the Hôtel de Flandre, where we came across our captain, Sir Jahleel. I sent up my card, not quite certain how he might take my having left the yacht under charge of the master. But he came down himself, was glad to see us and welcomed us, asking us to join him and Captain Rich at

98

dinner and all go together to Waterloo. This was most kind and glorious, nothing could be better. Next morning we had a *very* early breakfast and the four rode to the village of Waterloo, had a second breakfast there, after which our captain, being lame, mounted a broad-backed Flanders horse, and we others, accompanied by La Coste (Napoleon's guide), set off walking for the field of battle, and although seven years had gone by since the fight, the effects and remains of the battle were everywhere plainly visible, branches torn off the trees, walls broken down, and at the two farms ' La Belle Alliance ' and ' La Haye Sainte,' the barn doors were riddled with bullets ; monuments, &c., all are too well described in various books of that memorable day for me now to repeat. The fields were well covered with luxuriant crops of young corn, and on my noticing several patches of wheat of darker colour and a foot higher than the rest, La Coste said, ' Vary reech, vary reech, sir,' and he made us understand that bodies of dead men and horses were there buried. In Waterloo Church we were shown a small slab over the grave of the Marquis of Anglesea's leg !

Well, we returned to Brussels and Wilmot and I to Antwerp ; while waiting at Mecklin or Malines, Wilmot purchased a lace veil. ' Do you not sometimes sell us English lace for Brussels ? ' ' Oh, no, sir, it would cost more than our own.' When in the Thames and the Custom House officers came on board, Wilmot at once declared the lace, it was for his mother, Lady Wilmot. The following day it was returned from London, being English lace after all, to poor Wilmot's great disgust.

When I got on board I found the yacht's crew stupid as owls, from the lot of Hollands drunk ; very cheap here. So I at once took strong measures against any further tippling, by having the master-at-arms at the gangway knocking holes in stone jars and slitting bladders of spirit. I was informed that this was only meant for their wives at home. After a little, I thought it a pity to waste so much good stuff, so had all future seizures put into ' breakers,' and when any extra work or bad weather happened, the ' *main brace was spliced* '—in plain English, a tot was served all round ; this quite won the hearts of our fine crew and won me high praise.

When our captain returned, we up anchor, worked down the river, and in quick time were up the Thames again, expecting to be laid up, instead of which to our great delight, for yacht service was very fascinating, our own captain, Charlie Adam, joined, and we next day were off for Dover Roads, and in a day or so embarked

the Crown Prince of Denmark and suite for Calais. On their
leaving the yacht a diamond ring was presented to the captain and
one hundred sovereigns to me for the ship's crew, and which I gave
to the purser to be distributed among them as prize money. I got
into conversation with one of the party, a Danish nobleman, Count
Altenbourg, I think, and speaking of my three years' service in the
Great Belt, and of the Island Romsoe, uninhabited, ' Oh,' he exclaimed, ' that is my property. I had a cottage there, but there
were so many English men-of-war about, and such frequent landing
of seamen, that I was obliged to abandon it.'

In Calais Harbour we lashed alongside the pier. A French
officer, without a word to us, planted a sentry at the landing brow
to prevent anyone coming on board unless passed by an officer. A
gentleman, a Lieutenant Foley, whom I knew, wanted to come on
board, and began to argue the point with the soldier, who, with scant
ceremony, progged him in the stomach with the butt of his musket,
doubling up poor Foley for the rest of the afternoon. Among our
visitors were Beau Brummell and Tylney Long Wellesley Pole,[1] or
however those names may properly stand. We invited both to
dine. Mr Pole declined, saying he was going home to an early
dinner, seven o'clock. This to our unsophisticated minds seemed
utter nonsense, and he also informed us that his creditors had
allowed him sufficient to pay his shoe-black ; £2,000 a-year ! Mr
Brummell accepted and was most entertaining. He told us of
his meeting George the Fourth on the pier, when he landed with the
Duke of Wellington, on his road to Waterloo, and picking up the
King's cap, blown off, and returning it and of his receiving a gracious
bow ; as also of his managing to have a bottle of fine cognac and a
papier mâché box of snuff that he knew was the King's favourite
mixture, put by his side at dinner, and it was said His Majesty at
the first pinch recognised it, and was sure that Mr Brummell alone
could have sent it. Just after writing this and reading it to my
wife, she startled me by saying she had lately seen the same, almost
verbatim, in some periodical, only that it was maraschino and not
cognac. Sixty years have gone by since then, and from that
time to this I have never heard it spoken of or was I aware it was
known.

We returned to England and were ordered to Sheerness to be in
readiness to join the *Royal George*, yacht, about taking the King to
Scotland. It was blowing very strong and we had to beat from the
Nore into Sheerness Harbour ; the yacht worked like a top, tack and

---

[1] Succeeded in 1845 as Earl of Mornington.

tack without a fault. The day after, Lieutenant Hope superseded me; he was for promotion, I was only lent. On this day some officers of the 71st Regiment dined with me. Just before we sat down a quarter-master spoke to me, wanted to measure my finger for a ring which the yacht's crew wished to give me; he said, ' You have been more strict than any officer yet, but you were always just, the men feel very grateful,' and other compliments. I declined receiving any token of their satisfaction, holding that it was not an officer's place to receive either approbation or the contrary from those under his orders. Notwithstanding, I am open to confess that I should have taken it with unfeigned satisfaction had it been given to me. However, so it was. All did not end so quietly: although the dinner was late in breaking up, yet, just as I was leaving to rejoin the *Northumberland*, those of the crew that could, rushed on deck and gave me three very hearty cheers.

It being my turn with the other two lieutenants, I took command of our tender, the *Seagull*, a cutter of fifty tons only, a good sea boat, but very wet in the winter months. She was a sort of half-tide rock, as much under as above water. I wore fisherman's boots above the knees, as the only way of keeping tolerably dry.

We were mainly employed for the suppression of smuggling within the limits of the admiral's command. With our six and four-oared galleys hung up in the rigging she looked before the wind like a donkey with a pair of panniers.

My first movement was to the Nore, and there, with the *Royal Sovereign* and two or three men-of-war, to wait for the *Royal George* yacht, with the King on board, coming down the Thames in tow of a steamer. It was a dark and very still night, and the measured strokes of the paddle wheels was a new and most peculiar sound to us. Steam then was in its very infancy. His Majesty was received with cheers from the men-of-war, all showing brilliant lights as the yacht anchored for the night. My crew of twenty, with some friends, sang ' God save the King ' as the yacht passed. I was told it was very effective and striking in the still evening. I went on board *my* yacht for a chat with my late messmates, and returned with a large basket stuffed with good things by the table decker and young cook.

After the King's Scotch visit was over, and the yachts laid up, I was ordered to Woolwich, to inspect another and a larger cutter, to replace the *Seagull*; I saw several of my late yacht's crew, they seemed, I thought, to avoid me, slipping into different storehouses as I came near. At last I came full butt on the quarter-master who

had spoken to me about the ring ; with his hat off, he said, ' Oh,
sir, we are ashamed to meet you, but we did, sir, subscribe a day's
pay for a ring, and gave the money to Bowley, the joiner, for his
brother, a working jeweller, and he, like a scoundrel, ran away with
it all.'   He again said I was the strictest officer they ever had, but
they ' all so liked my kind ways,' &c.   And thus really ended the
ring affair.   I felt much gratified, though I must own I was sorry
to lose the ring.

CHAPTER VII

THE *Ringdove*—JAMAICA—SUPPRESSION OF PIRACY

ABOUT September [1] it was rumoured that a squadron on the war establishment was hastily fitting out for the Jamaica station, with the *Gloucester*, Sir Edward Owen, for the suppression of piracy, which had reached strong and atrocious lengths. I was ordered up the Thames, and was quickly back with about thirty seamen for the *Gloucester* picked up at our rendezvous on Tower Hill, where, from a public-house window, a large Union Jack floated, with a notice under, that men were wanted, &c. I well remember our difficulty in working through the narrow and crowded Pool, and the jeers and chaff of the collier men, when a square-bowed barge shoved the iron corner into the cutter's side close to my bedstead, calling out ' Never mind ; uncle pays for all.' At the rendezvous, the news was confirmed that Sir Edward was to relieve the admiral and hoist a broad pennant as commodore of the first class.

I had another trip to the Tower, bringing back a second batch of men. I found the *Gloucester* already at the Nore, and I entered by telegraph into negotiations for an exchange with one of her lieutenants, but could not bring him to book, though he had no desire for the West Indies, and in fact did not go after all. Sir Edward had not joined the ship and did not, till she was at Portsmouth, from whence about October he ultimately sailed. I had in the meanwhile got my uncle, Admiral Harvey, to name my wish to Sir Edward, but it seems the complement of lieutenants was full. However, two or three weeks later, I imagined, through the influence of Sir Edward, I received a letter from Captain Rich, that he was to commission an eighteen-gun brig for the West Indies, and would feel pleased to have me as his first lieutenant ; I was overjoyed ; the very thing I most coveted. Soon after I got my appointment [2] and was

---

[1] 1822.
[2] Appointed *Ringdove* (Commander George F. Rich), December 3rd, 1822.

allowed to leave the *Northumberland* without waiting to be superseded. Captain Rich told me that Sir Edward had nothing to do
with my appointment, but that he himself took a fancy to me from
what he saw of my management of the yacht, &c., and our long
talk during the visit to Waterloo. I wish I could be more fluent
with my pen, better describe the scenes about me, and be less
egotistical, but really I only write on what I saw myself, acted and
heard.

The brig was new, without her masts, and in the basin of the
dockyard; we rapidly entered men, and were hulked in the old
Pearl frigate. It turned out a bitter cold winter; at one time we
were obliged to hoist the boats out of the water to clear blocks of
ice floating down the harbour, and the cold was such that several
birds fell on our decks with icicles on their wings and tails. The
daily work at the dockyard was wretched enough, snow, sleet or
freezing; we could not get the eyes of the lower rigging over the
mast-heads, without taking it to the pitch house to be thawed, and
this pitch house many a time had I to chase the men out of, only to
go through and in again at the other end; poor fellows, I could
but feel for them. A black fellow, John Crow! was particularly
cunning in dodging me, and I heard him boasting how he ' done
the first lieutenant.' One morning I recollect my mackintosh
cloak froze stiff enough almost to stand alone. I was anxious to
be well manned, and became particular in entering none but good
hands; and walking outside the yard one day I came across a man
who was a petty officer with me for three years in the *Antelope*.
We were mutually pleased at meeting, and when I said I was first
lieutenant of the *Ringdove*, fitting for the West Indies, he said,
' Do you want hands, sir ? I shall be glad to sail with you, sir; you
may put my name on the brig's books, and if you let me remain on
shore for two or three days I will pick up some good hands for you;
there are several about that want ships, but are looking round for
comfortable ones '; and by his crying me up, we soon got many
prime seamen.

Beyond the yard gates, the long gunwharf wall, besides our
printed placards for men, was chalked with ' Happy, flying, saucy
Ringdove, she's your chance, good officers.' I was thought well
of by the *Antelope's* crew; not difficult to account for this. My
brother Henry, a most active, smart officer, was first lieutenant,
and on him wholly rested the punishments, discipline and management of the ship. By the way, also, he was somewhat of a Tartar,
and made me, the second lieutenant, run about almost as if a mid-

shipman. Men occasionally begged me to intercede for, and get
them off from threatened punishment : ' Indeed, sir, I was not to
blame, but your brother wouldn't listen to me ' ; and on enquiry,
and finding the case close upon what they stated, I used to speak to
my brother, and generally got them clear, though with an impatient
' Well, well, that will do, don't plague me more, tell the fellow to
be more careful for the future.'

In due time the fitting was complete, the hulk left and the crew
on board. Within three days nearly all officers and men had severe
colds, sore throats, &c., and no wonder—every portion, between
decks, joiner's work, all description of stores began to thaw—and
there was great dampness throughout. The captain came down
before leaving the harbour, shewed me his orders for the West
Indies to join the pennant of Sir Edward Owen, calling at Plymouth
for final letters, and also at Barbadoes.

During all our fitting out he was on leave, and only once with
us, so I had full swing, and my own way. The ship's corporal was
not worth his salt, not half strict enough, never sufficiently on the
look out ; let one man run (*that* not perhaps to be well prevented),
but he let him carry off his hammock, bed and bedding, and his
bag of clothes, not yet paid for. He was stupidly inefficient. I was
excessively angry, had his buttons cut off on the quarter deck, and
on my complaint he was discharged by Admiralty order. There
were two scamps on board. I told them they might do in harbour,
and *significantly* added they would find it very different when we
got to sea. They took the hint and ran. But—and it set my back
up—like the other man they carried off bed and bedding. After
being inspected by the Admiral we went out to Spithead : this is
always a good step—we are more by ourselves, things shake into
their places and all soon get to rights.

The *Seringapatam* came in, her Captain Samuel (black) Warren,
a Sandwich man I knew a little, so went on board and had a pleasant
chat. While on the quarter deck an officer said, ' Are you first
lieutenant of that brig ? the old story, when the cat is away the
mice will play,' and then with a glass I saw them parbuckling a
cask through the bow port, Lieutenant Madden and other officers
walking the deck. I could make out two of the men and a knot of
others were on the gangways screening from the officers what was
going on. Though vexed, I could not help laughing to myself at
being so hoodwinked. It never would have happened had I been on
board. On returning to the brig, ' Why, Madden, where are your
eyes ? how could you let the men get a cask of porter in, and you

all parading the deck almost looking on ? ' He was greatly taken aback, in fact could scarcely believe it. I let a little time go by and then went to look to the men's berths, &c. ' Hallo, what's all this? (*sniffing*). You have been upsetting porter, where is it stowed?' (*sniffing again*). An awful smell of porter there was. ' No porter, *shir* ; no blessed porter at all, shir,' speaking very thick. Not a vestige of a cask could I come across, it was ' shaken ' (as the term is at sea), staves and hoops all thrown overboard ; more than half the crew were screwed, it must have been drunk marvellously quickly. I noticed the men watching me from the corners of their eyes. I do not believe they even knew how I found it out. They only fancied I suspected it. But a few days later, I got under weigh to shift our berth nearer the Motherbank to be more in a fair way for a start down channel. All evolutions in a man-of-war are methodical and on system. Smart and sharp as possible of course. To furl sails, ' Man the rigging,' the men clustering on the lower part of the shrouds, then ' Way aloft,' and up they all scramble, and wait on the inner part of the yards till ' Trice up (the studding sail boom), lay out,' and out they run, furl away, and down as smartly as they can. One of the men, the second captain, began to crawl or steal out (as it is termed) before my order. I called out, ' Lay in, you, sir, directly.' The man smiled. I had him down saying, ' What do you mean by grinning when I hailed you ? ' He said he laughed because the captain of the top said, ' I told you he would catch you.' It was usual for some officers in those days to strike the men. I seldom or ever did, but in this case I was irritated and hit the man with my glass : I often thought afterwards it served me right, for I split the glass. But the man, who was a fine active fellow, dashed his hand across his face, and with something like a tear in his eye, said, ' It's all along that d——d porter.' I never struck but one man from that time till I retired from the service. The man after that became the first lieutenant's fancy man—so the others called him. He lost his jacket overboard. I gave him a new one ; for we became great friends, and the man quite loved me. But to the porter ; he was one of those whose face I made out with my glass.

By the end of the month we were off for and anchored in Plymouth Sound, where we were stuck till the 14th March, to our great disgust, for we were all most impatient to start for the West Indies. Our captain had a friend on board, a Mr Paget. He was my *bête noir*. He gave his opinion oftener than I liked, twice interfered and stopped our weighing. We set him down as a sort of

106

Jonah, the wind so often baffled us. At last we began to think we should never get away till he was gone, and true enough, the day after he took leave, we were able to sail and anchored in Carlisle Bay, Barbadoes, on the 7th April. Our purser was a bit of a chemist, and by sponging joints of mutton with diluted pyroligneous acid, contrived to keep the meat good all the passage ; the last leg was cooked the day before we anchored, a trifle gone, but this was from carelessness of the signal men, in not hanging a flag over the meat and screening it from the fierce sun. Our captain in attempting to make a short cut by passing near the Azores, instead of following the common route of running well to the southward, and so fall in with the trade winds, fell himself into the 'Doldrums,' getting becalmed, the ship rolling about, flapping the sails and of herself going round and round the compass, exposing her stern and consequently our poor mutton to the blazing sun. We crossed the Line at night, but we were hailed from under the bows by Neptune saying that he would pay us a visit next day and welcome his sons to his dominions, and then went astern in a tar barrel, the light shewing a very long while. I was, of course, up to *answer* his hail ! The next day he came on board, appearing on the quarter deck in a gun carriage, a dolphin on his trident, and his wife, such a wife and such a dress, and his son by his side, and his barber, physician, constables and a retinue of monsters of the deep, porpoises, &c., wolloping and rolling about his car. As a matter of course the captain received him, and from a tray brought up by his steward, a small glass of rum was given to his godship and attendants. I put on an old jacket and presided at the fun and soon got wet through and through. My ' fancy man,' Jackson, was the barber ; I let him understand when I held up my finger he was to give whoever was in his hands a close shave. There were two razors, both made of iron hoops, one smooth, the other notched, but this last was only used on those who resisted and roughly fought. The captain's clerk was a stupid, idle and lazy fellow (a pudding and spotted faced young fellow). I was obliged to rout him out of his cabin, by having his bed and bedding taken to air. My finger was up for him and for him only. I had a notion he suspected me, for soon after he dashed a bucket of water in my face. Our captain was a sporting man in Berkshire, fond of hunting ; which indeed kept him so much from us while fitting out ; he had two young grooms on the ship's books, and as the second was floundering out of the water after being shaved, more water was thrown over him by his fellow-servant ; I shall never forget his look, and ' *Oh, Henry !* '

We anchored in Carlisle Bay, Barbadoes, on the 7th April, remaining but two days, and then off for Jamaica. I had a run on shore to visit my old haunts, for I was at the station when mid. and mate of the *Orontes*, in 1814, and lieutenant of the *Antelope* in 16, 17 and 18, and with another had supper at Betsy Austen's tavern. I was originally attracted to the house by seeing in the principal room two engravings by Pocock, of the *Brunswick*, my grandfather's ship at the battle of the 1st of June, 1794, as also his portrait. Excepting some great disturbance in the atmosphere, turning at times to a hurricane, the wind is invariably from the east, and consequently fair all the way to Jamaica, and this gives any new ship a great opportunity to get thoroughly to rights, and even to paint outside as we in fact did.

As a passing remark I find in my diary, that I by chance preserved for this year, that I had no fear of the climate as to fever, but that I did not like an occasional pain in the chest and left side ; of a necessity, I was most actively employed I may say day and night, subject to all calls, disturbed at any hour ; and these pains annoyed me. I feared I might break down under them. But enough of this.

A rather strange thing happened ; the officer of the middle watch had a glass of grog—the tumbler slipped off the capstan head, and the bottom, with the ship's roll, went under a carronade slide. In the morning watch, at washing decks when all officers and men are barefooted, the broken glass came out, and the mate, Mr Westbrook, trod on it and cut his foot deeply, just under the ankle. A vessel must have been divided ; the surgeon was a very long while in stanching the blood. A species of fever set in, as also a sympathetic swelling of the groin and on the thigh. He was moved to the Naval Hospital. The swelling of the groin disappeared, but another shewed on the thigh, there was a large malformation of the bone above the knee, and the fear of the surgeon at the hospital was, that the main artery might be turned from its natural course, and that at the necessary operation the poor fellow might be dead before a tourniquet could be applied. The tumours were connected with each other as was ascertained by the feel, and a knife was obliged to be passed from one to the other ; it succeeded, there was an enormous discharge for days, and poor Westbrook was reduced to the verge of death. But he got over it. I may as well tell the ending. Prior to the operation I was at sea, and one day said to my surgeon, ' I dreamt of Westbrook last night, that he was about ; I wonder how he really is.' ' Gone, sir, depend on it.' The operation was a dan-

108

gerous one, but when, some weeks later on, I was myself brought to the hospital, I found him on crutches, getting well fast and stout, and with such a wonderful appetite that a patient on low diet was put on full, that Westbrook might have the benefit of the difference.

The floor of the ward was waxed and kept well polished by Sarah our black nurse, and woe betide anyone who ventured in without using the small square of drugget for the feet, and so slide about without disturbing the polish. Though very ill, I could not help laughing to see Westbrook's crutches slip from under him as he was trying to help another patient on the floor, both enjoying the fun, and unable to get up without assistance.

We anchored in Port Royal on the 16th April [1823], the harbour full of men-of-war. *Sybille*, with the flag of Sir C. Rowley still up, the *Gloucester*, Sir Edward Owen, *Thracian, Phæton, Eden, Tyne, Grecian* cutter and the old *Shark*, a sort of receiving ship always at Port Royal, and then also a wicked, long, low, snake-looking pirate schooner, captured only a week back. I name all these ships, for really, though sixty years ago, they are now vividly before me. But the pirates : after all our exertions, *mine not the least*, we were too late, the work was done, an end was put to piracy, as I shall soon relate.

I first went on board the *Gloucester* and was most kindly received by Sir Edward Owen. I saw my two young cousins and late ship-mates Thomas and Henry Harvey [1]—both became admirals ; the latter still in being ; the former, Tom, dying some years back, after commanding on the Pacific station. Two old messmates in the *Antelope*, Oliver, Master Attendant of Port Royal Dockyard, and Lieutenant James, first of the *Eden*, and a whole host of young mids. from the *Gloucester* came on board to see me.

I was here in 1814, when midshipman of the *Orontes*, two or three days after Captain Stackpoole of the *Statira* was shot in a duel. The circumstance was most remarkable. A ship came into the port in a very smart style, the sails furled, yards squared, ropes taut and all snug. Captain Stackpoole enquired, and finding Mr Cecil was the first lieutenant, ' Oh, I have a bone to pick with him.' It seems, and so I heard at the time, that a young mid. speaking to Captain S., not knowing the meaning, said he had just seen Mr Cecil : ' he says you draw a long bow.' ' The deuce he does—I will

<hr>

[1] Sons of Vice Admiral Sir Thomas Harvey, K.C.B. Both entered the service in December 1822 as Volunteers, First Class, on board the *Gloucester*. Rear Admiral Thomas Harvey died at Deal, April 8th, 1868 ; Admiral Henry Harvey died at Walmer, May 27th, 1887.

long bow him.' Cecil on going below received a note, and looking
grave, his brother officers enquired the cause. Cecil said, ' I have a
note from Captain Stackpoole : he requires an apology for something
I have said long back derogatory to his honour. I have not the
slightest recollection of ever speaking of him, and certainly not
against him ; I would readily apologise to anyone else, but he is a
noted duellist and a dead shot, and it might be supposed I was in
fear of him,' and to this effect he answered Stackpoole's note. The
next missive was calling him out, and the meeting took place next
morning under the Twelve Apostles Fort. Stackpoole said, ' At
the eleventh hour, will you apologise ? ' ' You know, Captain S.,
it is impossible.' Now Cecil had never fired at a mark in his life.
The surgeon was his second, and told him to fire immediately he
let go the handkerchief. Cecil's shot hit Captain S.'s right hand
little finger, from that to the upper arm, turning into the chest.
Stackpoole, staggering back, rested his pistol on his left arm and
fired, and in falling exclaimed, ' Good God ! have I missed him ? '
This is an ugly thing to record, but it was so talked of by all. Cecil
took to the mountains, fearing arrest, needlessly. The challenge
was from his superior officer, and he got private notice from the
admiral to return and take his trial by court-martial. He was on
the list as first for promotion, but of course could not take the place
of one he had himself killed. He was engaged to a cousin of mine
in Kent, and was a modest quiet man. The circumstance of the duel
dwelt so on his mind, that within three months he was attacked with
yellow fever and succumbed under it.

Stackpoole was constantly shewing off his dexterity with the
pistol ; he used to have the hencoop put on the frigate's taffrail, and
at twelve paces kill the first bird that put its head through the bars.
Archdeacon, our purser in the *Antelope*, was purser of the *Statira*
at Spithead, about 1813. He told us that Captain Stackpoole had
lodgings at Portsmouth, usual with many captains, and that he was
in the habit of opening the officers' papers and taking a look before
the postman took them off to the ship. Some a little growled at
this liberty, and it came to the captain's ears. In regiments and
ships alike, there is generally some talebearer to make mischief.
One day the captain came off ; all officers, of course, to receive him,
the marine guard presenting arms. As soon as they were dismissed,
he turned round saying, ' I understand, gentlemen, that you find
fault and are annoyed at my looking at your papers,' and bowing
round, ' Mind, I am Mr Stackpoole, at your service at any time.'
Archdeacon replied, ' When it comes to my turn, it shall be across a

handkerchief '—as he told us he was determined that they should both fall together. Nothing further occurred in the matter.

And now to turn again to the pirates. My memory fails me, and not being present, I am unable to repeat the whole of this very stirring story, told me by Chadwick, mid. of the *Gloucester*, and who was present and took part in the whole proceedings. It became known that a pirate schooner was sheltered in a small river or creek in the Isle of Pines, south of Cuba, a great resort of pirates in general. The Admiral's tender, Joe Geary, mate, commanding (The ' Dick Gaskin,' of *Tom Cringle* [1]), was anchored in the mouth of the creek, also one of the *Gloucester's* boats with Lieutenant Layton,[2] Stroud and Chadwick mids., there to wait till more strength joined them. Layton wished to reconnoitre, and against Geary's advice, took the schooner's six-oared gig, and with Stroud set off up the creek. The evening was closing in and in that climate there is little or no twilight, and it soon became very dark and also exceedingly still, not a breath of air. All at once a single shot startled Geary, and another, and directly after a whole volley of musketry. Geary jumped into the cutter fully armed and pulled up the creek. They had not got far, when a hail from the shore ' Is that the cutter ? ' ' Yes, who are you ? ' ' Lewis, sir, for God's sake take us in, we are all murdered.' They pulled in, and through the thick jungle took in Lewis and another, both wounded. From the two men it was learned, that there was a path each side of the creek and perfectly screened from the water by the impenetrable luxuriant foliage, that most likely someone tracked the gig all the way up, and the men said just as they came to a broader part or a sort of opening two single shots were fired, and then a volley, four of the crew of six were killed ; two, both wounded, jumped overboard, and Mr Stroud was about to follow when the lieutenant said, ' You won't leave me.' ' What's the use of staying ? Come yourself, sir—we are sure to be murdered ! ' Whether Layton could not swim or whether he chose not to leave the boat, no one can say. Stroud jumped and was not long in the water before he was shot through the head. All that night a strict watch was kept at the mouth of the creek to prevent the pirate escaping, and next morning early, Chadwick was sent down to leeward in the cutter to meet the *Icarus* brig, Captain Graham, who was beating up to join in the proposed attack. The story caused intense excitement in the brig, some of her men went

---

[1] *Tom Cringle's Log.* By Michael Scott.
[2] Lieutenant Thomas Layton, crossed off the Sea Officers List for 1824 as ' killed 20th February '.

aloft, and there remained looking with all eyes for any movement,
particularly as they neared the creek in the evening. I am not
sure that it was not another day before they got there. Captain
Graham questioned Geary closely as to the possibility of the pirate
slipping out at night. When able, Captain Graham, Geary and
Chadwick with the pinnace, cutter, and two brig's boats pulled up
the creek, a party of marines and seamen in the paths on both sides
keeping pace with the boats ; as they got on the stream narrowed
and the trees were nearly meeting overhead, and it seemed as if no
vessel of any size could get up ; but suddenly there was an opening
widening into an open lake or lagoon and *no* schooner ! Captain
Graham turned fiercely on poor Joe Geary, ' You have let the pirate
go by, sir, after all. She has slipped through your fingers ; I
thought so from the first.' This was not fair, but as the talk was
going on the sergeant of marines called out, ' There is the lieutenant,
sir, don't you see him ? there, sir, tied to a tree,' and indeed a sicken-
ing sight, partially sitting on the rocky ground, his head drooping
over his chest, and his stomach ripped up, and his bowels on the
ground before him. All cried vengeance against the murderers if
caught ; and then what to do ? From exposure to the hot sun and
heavy dews at night, the corpse was so dreadfully decomposed, that
it could not be moved from the spot, and the ground being all rock,
and no tools that could make anything like a grave, a very fierce
fire was made and the body burned.

A little off they came upon a fire, not very long left, for it was still
burning ; but what pirates or how many had been there was not
known. Chadwick was sent to a small fishing village on the side of
the island next to Cuba to make enquiries ; he could get no information ; most probably they were in league with the pirates. I don't
quite know how, but they came across a man who it was thought
had been one of the pirate's crew himself, at any rate he volunteered
to shew their hiding places. He got the name of ' pilot ' and was
the leader of the hunt and when he had the chance never let one
escape his knife. Captain Graham sent a party to the village and
secured all canoes, so as to prevent the escape of any of the mis-
creants, and Chadwick some time after was sent over to Cuba for
two bloodhounds ; they were of a dull leaden colour, had smooth
leather-like skins, no hair, the size of a common spaniel, but with
longer legs, not very ugly, only very fierce eyes. The pursuit soon
commenced and it was over six weeks or more before the last pirate
was killed, for none were taken alive, they were either cut down
resisting or shot running. I mistake ; four got away before the

canoes were secured ; two of these returned at the close of the hunt
fancying the English had left long before, these two were taken and
hanged.   The first adventure with the ' pilot's ' help was thus.   He
said some would be sure to visit one of their resting places, a hut
not far off.   Here the party, rather late, hid themselves in wait ;
soon a fellow ran in, jumping the fence of a pigsty, and fell right
upon *Joe* who was ensconced there ; the man was utterly astonished,
still he made a hard struggle, and before other help came Joe's
cutlass was through his body.   Soon another (a mulatto) came,
went to the hut, looked about, became apparently suspicious, gave
a shout, listened and began to move away ; up jumped Geary and
gave chase, his foot caught in a root and down he went sprawling,
others followed ; the pilot, heading all, overtook and killed him
with a thrust of his long knife over the shoulder.   Many encounters
of this sort, mostly with two or only one pirate.   Their fires were
two or three times come upon, still alight, and from articles left, it
was evident the place had been but just quitted ; blood was twice
found, they probably had quarrelled.   Several very stirring encounters took place, I have no clear recollection of them as told me
by Chadwick, they were every one most thrilling.   It was not till
after the death of ten or more that the bloodhounds were sent for,
and a few more *scented* out.   The last found was the captain.   One
evening a marine had taken his kettle to a stream among rocks
some distance off, and there came upon a man washing the wounded
stump of his arm.   He started to run ; the marine fired and missed ;
it was late and getting dark but they were sure of him now, and the
hounds next morning were put on his scent and instantly took it
up and, with one sharp bark or yell, silently set off in pursuit.   In
a short time they were heard baying, and when the party came up
there was the captain lying dead and stiff, most likely worn out
with fatigue and mental agony as well as exhausted from his wound.
What became of the hounds this deponent sayeth not.   But what
of the schooner itself, where could she be ?   The ' pilot ' led the way
to the ' lagoon ' and after picking about with a pike or boat-hook,
struck upon the vessel, for there she was sunk, her masts cut away ;
she was raised and turned out a very beautiful craft.

The capture of the pirate schooner *Zaragozana* we found at
Port Royal may be more shortly told.[1]   She was known to be in
another creek at the Isle of Pines.   The *Thracian* 26, and *Tyne* the
admiral's tender, Joe Geary's schooner, were sent to cut her out.
Prior to their attack the pirate gave up a boat's crew of the *Gloucester*

---

[1] There is an account in *The Annual Register*, 1823, pp. 42-3.

with Tom Smith, mid., who was with me in the *Royal Sovereign*
yacht. How, and it is most strange why I should forget, but how, I
repeat, the boat and crew were originally captured I know not.
But to Tom Smith ; I must digress ; it leaked out in trying to get
from him the strength of the squadron in the vicinity, and his
refusal to tell them, that they hung him by the neck three times till
he was black in the face and well-nigh strangled ; with much
difficulty we used to get the story from him, ' Well, Tom, did you
ask for mercy ? '—' No, no use.' ' Did you cry ? '—' No.' ' Did
you laugh ? '—' *No.*' ' Then what did you do ? '—' Nothing at all,
so at last they let me alone and patted my back.' It was a real
treat to hear him. The pirate schooner was moored, and by springs
held broadside to the sea, our boats dashed alongside and boarded ;
the first men on board fell and were wounded ; they called out, ' Mind
yourselves, the beggar's decks are greased,' and not a bad dodge
either. Had the pirates stood a little better it might have gone
worse with many. But it was soon over ; sixteen or seventeen
were killed, close upon twenty jumped overboard and swam on
shore, and the captain who stood by the long gun to the last, and
twenty-three were made prisoners and taken to Jamaica, where
they were tried before Mr Scarlett, the judge (brother to the late
Lord Abinger), with a post captain on either side on the bench ;
four were admitted King's evidence, the other twenty condemned,
all Spaniards, one only an Englishman, the greatest scoundrel of
the whole. He ought never to have been a King's evidence, but his
account was clearer and more to the understanding than that
obtained through an interpreter. At the end of May they were
hung at Gallows Point on the Palisades, a long neck of sand connecting the town of Port Royal with the main Island of Jamaica,
and forming the snug and roomy harbour. I witnessed the execution ; early in the morning the *Gloucester's* boats, manned and armed
and with a guard of marine drums and fifes, went up to Kingston,
returning in procession towing the launch with the captain
(Aragonez) and nine pirates, the drums and fifes giving out the
' Dead March in Saul,' ' Adeste Fideles,' &c. The following
morning the other ten were also executed—a fearful sight. No
men could go to their death with less apparent concern. Before
the captain first went up the ladder he called upon his men to
remember they were before foreigners and to die like Spaniards.
The gallows was a long piece of timber, with ten hooks, supported
by two uprights. Each of the condemned, with a rope (with an
' eye ' at the end) round his neck, walked up the ladder ; the eye

114

was put on the hook and the culprit pushed off. The negro hangman then seized the rope, riding the pirate's shoulders, and after a jerk sliding down by his feet. Though certainly merciful in hastening death, yet it was very horrid to witness. This was undoubtedly a wholesale execution, but it completely put an end to piracy; there was no more.

I cannot resist turning back to an event, now quite seventy-one years since, leaving a much stronger impression on my young mind and nights of terror, than this great execution, *i.e.*, the hanging a seaman at the yard-arm of the *Venerable*, at Spithead, in 1811. He had cut a boat adrift from his ship and deserted to the enemy, and was sentenced to death by a court-martial. Many men-of-war were at Spithead; a boat from each ship went alongside the *Venerable*, two of the crew went up to man the hanging-rope—two of the worst hands are generally sent for this office. I was mid. of our boat with a lieutenant. The culprit was marched along the gangway (I could see his head as we lay off on our oars) to a stage or grating rigged over the cathead; the rope, leading from the ship's waist, was rove through a block at the yard-arm, with a knot two or three fathoms from the criminal's neck, so that when run away with it brought up at the block with a jerk and so hastened death. Standing but a little while on the grating, the chaplain by his side, a gun was fired under his feet and he then launched into eternity, the body swinging like a pendulum long before it became still. For several nights after, my sleep was disturbed by what I had seen.

The pirate captain had two of his fingers amputated on board my ship: he never winced; but when the surgeon talked to him, that he was more like a gentleman than a pirate, a tear stole down his cheek. He was of noble family in Spain, was aide-de-camp to the governor at the Havannah, got into serious scrapes, mostly at the monté tables, and was dismissed. After a while an English merchant took compassion on him and admitted him to his office; he kept steady for some time, then broke out once more and ran away to the haunts of the pirates in the Isle of Pines. I do not imagine he at that time had any notion of joining, but he took one cruise with them, took interest in their adventures, so much so, it was said of him, that they induced him to remain and he soon became their captain, and was as reckless and cruel as any towards the unfortunate people who fell into their hands.

When Sir C. Rowley was supposed beyond the limits of his command, Sir Edward Owen hoisted a broad pennant as commodore of

the first class, entitling him to a captain. So, as we before understood, our captain, Rich, was posted into the *Gloucester*, his first
lieutenant, MacClean, made commander; another Captain Rich
appointed to the *Ringdove* and I went to the *Gloucester* in the room
of MacClean.[1] We were very busy refitting the brig, so an eighteen-
oared barge was sent for me and my traps. All my brother officers
were on deck to take leave of me, and I observed many men lifting
their hats to me, and I had got but a little way off when I heard the
twitter of the boatswain's pipe, and in an instant the lower rigging
was manned and three hearty cheers given me. At this very
moment while writing, I almost feel as much as I did then. It
was not only a great compliment but *totally* unexpected; I had
been from first joining, as I thought, an unusually strict officer: at
the moment I felt almost overcome. ' You will answer the cheer,
men, for me '—when, with a slap on the thigh, up went the oars,
the boat's crew, with hats off and standing, gave three cheers, and on
the *Ringdove's* ' one cheer more ' down went the oars with a splash,
and we pulled away to my new ship. At that time in the morning,
before the sea breeze (or *Doctor* as it is called) sets in, the sea is like
molten lead, sweltering hot and still to a degree, and any noise is
echoed from the shore, and *this* cheer, of course, was heard by all
the ships. ' What's up ? There is some decent fellow leaving that
craft '; and so under such auspices I joined the commodore's ship,
and I noticed many fellows peering at me through the ports.

Various recollections are crossing my mind, and I note the bad
with the good. Before three days went by I was not made happy
with the change of ships. The *Gloucester's* officers were not well
assorted, the mess was poor. I received from the little brig three
times over my mess entrance in the big ship. Some had their wine,
&c., in their own cabins; one actually messed there by himself.
They smoked in the wardroom, as I thought putting it on a par
with a pot-house; in those days no smoking below was permitted.
Besides all this I had nothing to do, so at variance with my late
active life. One small employment amused me for two days. The
commodore wished me to make a drawing of a new gun and carriage,
and take it to him at the ' Pen,' the name of the colonial residence
of the naval commander-in-chief. How he came to know I could do
anything of the kind I never made out. The commodore was
without any doubt a first-rate officer and commander in all essential
points, but I never considered he had his ships in happy and comfortable order. As long back as 1812, I went on board his frigate

----

[1] The Navy List shows Boteler as appointed to the *Gloucester* May 1st, 1823.

116

at anchor out of sight of land, keeping watch off the Texel, and even
then as a young mid. I was quite struck with the apparent disorder
and untidiness of the ship. In the *Gloucester* to prevent drunkenness he ordered *wine* for breakfast, which agreed neither with the
taste or stomach of the men, and there were three tumbles from
aloft, the men getting stupid with too much. It was common to
arrange with a messmate to have two or three days' grog and go
without one or two, and this many continued with wine. The crew
were also harassed with over-much exercising ; at daylight, ship at
anchor, it was ' All hands loose sails,' then make and shorten sail,
then beat to quarters, exercise one side, and then both sides, boarders
and firemen, buckets and arms all mustered ; then the retreat, furl
sails, call the watch and wash decks. The men had no night watch,
but the officer of the middle watch, going to his cot at 4.20 A.M., had
to be at his quarters and station by about 5.30. Many times when
going below I have fallen asleep, my head on the wardroom table.

When the *Gloucester's* crew were turned up, hats off, to hear
Captain Rich's commission read, he addressed a few words to them,
saying that he was aware there was a great amount of drunkenness
among them, that it was the root of almost every offence on a man-
of-war, and the chief cause of all punishment ; that he never looked
over drunkenness, and he desired them to mark his words, if any
man got drunk he would give him two dozen, if he repeated it then
three dozen, and if a third time, he would try him by a court-martial.
' Pipe down.' Five men were drunk that very afternoon—they each
received two dozen with the cat the next morning, and the same
night two of these were again very drunk, and four fresh ones.
The captain kept his word ; the two had each three dozen, the
other four two dozen. This at once sobered them ; there were
but two that offended while I was in the ship.

To vary our dull life we got up a picnic under Fort Augusta,
two from the *Gloucester*, Jackson and Bell of the *Serapis*, which had
lately taken the place of the old *Shark* harbour depot ship ; Shaplin,
acting lieutenant of the *Thracian*, Berkeley, of the 33rd, and St
John, of the artillery, commonly called ' Jack Shark.' I mention
all these as some will appear again in my yarns. We were joined by
some quadroon and mulatto ladies. How they came, where from,
or who invited them I have no remembrance. Though in a questionable grade of *society* yet they are scrupulously well behaved, and
never permit any approach to a liberty. We had a band from
Kingston, and in one way or other kept it up, dancing and otherwise, till past midnight. One thing made a strong impression on

my memory—the attack of sand flies. They buried their small
head or nose in the back of our hands. The terrible mosquito was
nothing to be compared to their bite or sting. We had quite a job to
get to the large boats, that could not get near from the belt of coral
rocks. Being night, the little channel of water could not be seen,
so we had canoes, ticklish enough at all times, but on *such* an occasion
—well, mine turned over twice, and Lieutenant Jackson, worse off
than any, he got floundering among the coral reefs. I only know
we were on board about three o'clock.

And so St John, called Jack Shark, he was always successfully
at war with those ugly brutes. He had a small cask anchored
among the men-of-war with a strong line, three or four feet of chain
next the hook, often with a puppy dog on it for bait. He then
would seat himself under a shed on a jetty on open piles, and there,
while watching the cask, amuse himself with a bow and arrow,
shooting fish swimming about the piles—fish of all fantastic shapes
and beautiful colours—prismatic red and silver fish, purple, gold,
and other coloured fins and tails; one with a deep blue streak,
edged with a narrow white one, from the dorsal fin to the tail; and
another odd creature that he never could hit—a triangular-shaped
thing, in a shell as hard as a crab's—a tough leathery stuff for its
tail to move on—and it had teeth like a rat's and as sharp. If
St John did not see it, some would call out, ' A shark, sir ! ' for
there was the cask moving about, and St John would start off in a
canoe with his sergeant and four negroes, and was soon towing the
shark on shore. The parade ground extended to the water : it soon
got wind ; a number of soldiers were ready to take hold of the rope
and race with the creature to the officers' quarters, cheering as they
ran ; St John, himself, mad, striking at the shark as it floundered
about, and once, they told me, a very large one, he actually in his
excitement jumped across the brute's back.

But his crowning adventure was his encounter with a very extraordinary creature, there called a conch-eater, or devil fish. I never
saw the fish, but it was described to me as a species of ray or skate
of immense size. I can scarcely imagine this to be a flat fish, both
from the very peculiar structure of its mouth, and from its appearance
on the surface of the water, all the tribe of flat fish generally keeping
at the bottom. Whether St John had intimation of the fish being
seen in the harbour I do not remember ; at any rate, in his canoe,
sergeant and negroes, when he came upon and harpooned it, it
dashed off at speed, tearing a length of rope through their hands
before they could attempt to check it. The creature made directly

118

out to sea, carrying off the canoe with great swiftness. After a time they gradually shortened in the rope, and when near enough, gave the fish a thrust with a bayonet at the end of a boat-hook. Away went the fish again, taking a length of rope with it. One or two more attacks of the same sort ; at last, when very close, the sergeant dug the bayonet deep into him. The monster made a violent struggle, jumping, as St John told me, nearly out of the water, breaking from the harpoon, and away it went, leaving the canoe and its exhausted crew beyond the (Morant ?) Keys, several miles from the harbour's mouth, and it was late at night before they got back—St John's hands burnt and blistered with the friction, and they were very sore for many days. And now for the marvellous construction of the tongue ; it was absolutely stone !—about the breadth and length of our three forefingers, and bent downwards. The grain or strata was peculiar, the upper half running with the tongue, the lower diagonal, as if for support in crushing shellfish, and this feeding plainly shewn by the wear and scratches on the top of the tongue, so that Quace was not far out in calling it conch-eater. The roof of the mouth was *paved* with closely packed *pebbles* of the size between a shilling and sixpence. I saw the tongue, and made a drawing of one caught or procured by St John. To finish with this fish : early in the following year I was in England, and, full of this story, went to London and called on Mr Wood, a naturalist. He was a very talented man, published several works—one in particular : Wood's *Zoography*, illustrated by Daniel—and father of the present Rev. J. George Wood, whose entertaining and instructive books on ' Natural History ' are well known and most popular. Mr Wood brought down several large folio books, two and three feet square, on fishes, chiefly French. Rays were found, and though no *stone* tongue, yet one was described as having the roof of the mouth encrusted with stony knots, or knots as hard as stone. In the end I felt rather small ; he evidently thought I was somehow greatly mistaken, or had got an idea of the thing without foundation. Soon after this visit, Sir Edward Owen returned to England in the *Gloucester*, Berkeley and St John passengers ; so I set off to Sheerness, found St John's address, wrote and had all my story confirmed, and this I sent to Mr Wood. I quite forget the result of this. I was only too glad to shew the truth of my story.

CHAPTER VIII

And now to continue my personal yarns. After the execution of
the twenty pirates, the lieutenants of my ship were all and always
admiring the pirate schooner, now called the *Renegade*, an appropriate change, though not equal to her own : *Zaragozana*. It was
known she was to be taken into the service, and the talk was as to
who the lucky one would be to command her. There she lay astern
of us, her raking lower masts only in—a long, black, wicked and
snake-looking craft. In two or three days only from the hanging,
a midshipman came, with ' The captain wishes to see you in the
cabin, sir.' ' What's the matter now, I wonder ? ' One is startled
being sent for in this way, thinking generally something wrong.
' Oh, Boteler, have you heard anything of going in the *Renegade* ? '
' *I*, sir ? No, sir.' ' Just like the commodore, with his tin pot and
spoon, fancies everyone can be off at a moment's notice. Well,
you are to have her, and your first trip will be to pick up freight.'
' Oh,' said I in my rapture, ' never mind the freight, sir, give me the
schooner.' ' No, no,' said he ; ' but about the freightage : I am told
by Sir C. Ross [1] and Captain Newcombe that as you will be manned
from this ship, I am entitled to the freightage.' I again said, ' Hang
the freight, give me the schooner.' On his remarking he had no
wish to take me by surprise, I had time to get cool, and, begging
his pardon, told him it was clear he could not share, and when
before in the West Indies, our tender commanded by a midshipman and manned by the ship, and so actually belonging to her, yet
the midshipman had the freight money ; and, I added, ' Though
manned from the *Gloucester*, she will be a separate command.' He
laughed, and said he thought it would be so, but he considered it
but right to have it all clear. So I made my bow as happy as a

---

[1] Captain Charles B. H. Ross, Resident Commissioner at Jamaica—not then
' Sir Charles '.

king. When I appeared in the wardroom it was: 'What's up, Boteler ? ' 'Oh, capital news for me, I am to have the *Renegade*.' 'Nonsense, man.' 'Indeed it's all true.' 'You be d——d.' They were like a swarm of angry bees. 'You, why you have only been in the ship a week, and we all old hands.' 'Well, all I can say is that I am as much surprised as you; it is the last thing I could possibly have expected or thought of.' They all soon cooled down and congratulated me on my good fortune. The next morning, by telegraph, I was sent for to the ' Pen.' The commodore received me most kindly, as indeed he always did, said that my order to command the schooner, and various instructions, would be sent to me before night ; that I had fourteen days only to get ready for sea, for by nearly that time an officer might arrive from England and take my place. I said I had heard I was to pick up freight. 'Ah ! by the way, Rich fancies he is entitled to the freightage ; don't you give in to this.' I said I had already settled that with Captain Rich, and on thanking Sir Edward for sending me for treasure, he replied that he always liked to give an officer a lift on his first command to help him towards his outfit, &c.

In the course of the day my order to command the *Renegade* came. A crew was selected from the *Gloucester*, and my whole establishment consisted of two mids., assistant surgeon, two quartermasters, boatswain, gunner and carpenter's mates, twenty-nine seamen and nine marine artillerymen ; to my fancy a very respectable and sufficient turn out. It was a most eligible command for my rank, the best on the station. The following morning early I took my crew to the dockyard and on board the schooner, hoisted the pennant and read my commission, and then directly to work. I found her in an awful mess ; plundered of rigging and furniture by ships fitting out. There was a tremendous amount of work before us and we had to set to with a will. We took out the bowsprit and foremast to examine the heels, both decayed. I was glad to shorten the latter three feet. I was fairly frightened at the length of the spars, and I should like to have served the mainmast in the same way, but time was too precious. I should here say for two days we returned to the *Gloucester*. I then quartered the men over the capstan house or rigging loft, a long shed open at the sides, like those for carts and waggons in a farmyard ; at one end two rooms for the surgeon and mids., at the other, two for myself. I very seldom dined there ; often on board the *Gloucester*, many times with the captains of different ships and the Commissioner of the Dockyard, Sir Charles Ross. My two mids. Tony Robinson and

Mitchell, the first an old passed midshipman and my shipmate in the *Antelope*. Of course I knew him well, and doubted if I ever should get work out of him : he was full of fun, always laughing, and openly ignored work, had been too long a mid. for that ; and so it proved. I at once lectured him on starting : ' Now, Master Tony, I know you well, you really must turn over a new leaf and do your best ; we have no more cats than can catch mice ' ; and ' Oh, sir, you may depend on me ' ; but deuce a bit. I sent him with a party on some duty, and in less than an hour he was off somewhere else. I was then sharp with him, he only was merry, promising to mend his ways ; but it was no go, and I returned him to his ship, and got Evans (with me in the ' Yacht ') in his room, and we went on swimmingly.

Tom [1] Oliver, my three years' messmate in the *Antelope*, was here, Master Attendant of the Dockyard. He lived three or four hundred yards from the dock gate, and insisted I should always have ' second breakfast ' with him. His establishment was an old negress and her daughter, a fair mulatto. Just at one o'clock a little black boy would come with ' Miss Laurette send him compliment, and glad ob your company to second breakfast, sir.' Jack never waited for a word, but darted on board the schooner, looking about him, handling the ropes, whistling in imitation of the boatswain, till I began to move, when off he started at a run to Johnny Forang's store for a bottle of porter and, with this under his arm, was alongside of, and keeping step for step with me till we reached Oliver's door. We always had a nice luncheon, and the porter between us, then a siesta. The old negress would, seated by my sofa, fan me with a large bunch of feathers to keep off the mosquitoes. I disliked it for a time, but in the end got used to it. It did not appear long when it was ' Come, John, rouse and bit, there's the dockyard bell.' One day a tall slip of a negress came instead of Jack, and next day, asking him who she was, ' Him Sarah, sar, um call him sugar tong, him hab such long legs.' I see the girl before me now, with her woolly head and scant chemise, her only garment.

We all worked hard, shipwrights busy laying down a lower deck ; two two-ton iron water tanks appearing two feet above the deck, they acting as a sort of table. Bins constructed against the vessel's sides for provisions and stores, part tinned for biscuit in bulk ; a cabin for mids.' mess, and one for the doctor to be made ; and also much work on deck, constructing circular sweeps for two thirty-two pounders. We hove the schooner down both sides, keel out, her

<hr>

[1] Actually William.

122

bottom seemingly sound in every way. Then it was no small job
mounting the heavy guns and slides, as well as fitting two twelve
pounder carronades as broadside guns, and to arrange the fashion
of all this, I had to go to the gun wharf at Kingston, and confer
with the ordnance officials. The rigging, not pilfered, was very
perfect. The shrouds, stays, all wormed, and the strops of blocks .
covered with red leather.

When the schooner was captured she had little ballast, but was
loaded deep with plunder : silks, satins, brocades, silver and gold,
wines, brandy, liqueurs, noyeau, calico, cambric, &c., and I was at
a loss as to how much ballast she would require. I drew ten tons
first, it made no impression, and I drew two tons more. This
evidently was not sufficient. I was ashamed to shew my ignorance
in demanding more. So I *stole* over two tons just before dark, the
men still at work. Near us was a stack of iron ballast ; hooks were
put into the holes of the pig iron, and ropes led from them to the
schooner. When quite dark and all quiet, we began to haul away.
As the first pig fell from the stack, the negro sentry, not far off,
jumped from his box ; then, as another fell and clattered over the
stones, he called out, ' What um dat ? whom dere ? de Debil sure,
him dancing wid um iron.' He shouted again, and in his terror fired
off his musket, and bolted for the guard house. Our men, highly
amused, ran to the ballast stack, and brought off what we wanted,
and all was quiet on board before the officer of the guard and
sergeant came down with the sentry as prisoner, who was not out
of his terror, but with great volubility declared the Debil himself
was dancing with the ballast, that he saw his long tail moving on
the ground. I let the officer into the secret, that the poor fellow
might not be punished for leaving his post.

I had to make a daily report of our progress to the commodore,
who had me up on a Sunday, extending my time of sailing till the
14th June. I was still pressed for time, and he allowed me to
telegraph for the crew to work and hoist a convoy signal for Carthagena. The commodore, I repeat, so kind in all he said—I don't
know how I ever got so much in his good graces—never lost sight
of me, and when at the Admiralty stood my friend in several ways,
and without one single application on my part.

As events, trifles certainly, come now across my memory, I must
indulge in recording them. I one day dined with Captain Newcombe, of the *Phæton*. He had a most strange head of hair, so
exactly resembling a coarse scratch wig that many bets were lost
and won on it, and knowing this, whenever he saw anyone looking

at it, he would pull at one side lock, then another, and also at the
back, as if adjusting a wig—he took many in.   At this dinner, with
others, I met the commissioner, Sir C. Ross, and I took him to the
yard in my boat.   At the challenge of the first sentry, he quite
forgot the patrol,[1] though given by himself.   'Hang it,' said he, 'I
must bolt ; they will be sure to take me to the guard house,' and
off he went, knowing how to double round the different blocks of
timber, &c., leaving me in the lurch and to be taken to the guard
house.   Of course, the officers saw me to the schooner, but not
before we had a parting glass.   The commissioner enjoyed the joke
afterwards.

We completed provisions and water to four months, hauled off
from the dockyard jetty, anchored in the fair way, and the next
morning at daylight, up anchor and ran out with the land wind
under our square foresail, having under convoy, seven schooners,
and one Columbian brig ; saluted the commodore with thirteen
guns, he returning eleven—our salute rather an odd sounding one—
a big gun, then the twelve pounder, a thirty-two pounder, and twelve
pounder.   I ought not to leave out the bumboat woman, and who
washed for me, Dolly Johnson, a jet-black negress, a splendid
figure, supple, and most graceful in all her movements.   I had won
her gratitude by getting her the washing of three of the *Gloucester's*
officers, and the 'bumboating' of another ship.   We had just
cleared the harbour's mouth when Dolly paddled alongside, saying,
'I not let you sail, Massa Boteler, without wishing you health and
happiness,' and standing up, swaying and bending over the vessel's
side, 'May Goramighty bless you and de kooner, and send you
good luck and plenty ob dollar, and I bring you yam, plantain and
banana for de cruise,' and away she went, scouting any payment.

When outside of the Keys the pilot left us, just as the 'sea
breeze' came down on us, strong as usual ; so down square-foresail,
and make sail on a wind, the schooner kicking and plunging about
at a great rate.   From myself downwards, not one had ever been in
a schooner, and it requires some considerable experience to sail them
properly ; the foremast is kept stiff enough with a stout stay and
four shrouds, the mainmast must be allowed full play, swinging
backwards and forwards to the pitch of the vessel.   I wished I had
examined its heel with the chance of taking two feet off its length.
I kept for a time in dread fancy that, like the other mast, it might
be decayed, give way, and the mast tear up the deck.   We were
soon obliged to reduce sail, for she was, every now and then, gun-

<hr>

[1] Doubtless a misprint for parole.

wale under. In resetting the fore-and-aft foresail, after reefing, the gaff broke in half, it was quite rotten ; it took us some time to fish it, &c., and so retarded us that our convoy were all ahead, and I was obliged, with a gun, to signal them to shorten sail. When all was right with us, we walked on, and soon took the lead, steering away for Carthagena. Long before noon I was dreadfully sea-sick, as were also more than half the crew ; I got over it soon, but four or five fellows were almost helpless for days. For two days the wind continued strong, the schooner burying the bowsprit frequently. I found she leaked very much, and the water was nearly up to the cabin decks, wetting some muskets, a cask of flour, and two bags of letters, my mail—such a job in drying these, the address of many barely legible. In squalls the schooner did not lay over more than with the general strong wind, but *that* was mostly gunwale under !

Daylight made the land, and inside of the convoy, running along shore, there was a puff of smoke, a report, and at the same instant, ' whiz,' and a shot right across our bows. ' Up with the colours and pennant.' I suppose they either did not make out our colours, or would not believe them, for another puff, report, and a shot across us from the low fort. We went to quarters, cleared away the two thirty-two pounders ; I was determined to give them a couple of our heavy pills, but the marine artillery uniform settled the question, the fort dipped their colours twice, and sent off an officer to apologise, that they took us for a noted pirate, &c.—in fact, we had not yet painted her out of her former likeness. One of our convoy, the *General Conran*, ran within hail, and pointed out to us the Popa, a convent on a high hill directly over Carthagena. I ran into five fathoms, and anchored for the night, making signals to part company. Daylight next morning we ran in and anchored off the Gate St Domingo. I sent Evans on shore, who soon returned with my passport, to wait on the Governor, to whom I delivered the commodore's letter—secret to me, but of considerable importance—as also a verbal message. Nothing else passed, so made my bow, and accompanied some merchants to their different houses, all being anxious for news. They told me the Governor wished much to get English men-of-war again into the harbour, and threw every obstacle in the way to prevent us anchoring off the city. An insult had been offered to the *Carnation* by the commander of Boca Chica Fort, and I was not to go into harbour, or put myself under their control, till ample apologies had been made.

In the afternoon we were off for Chagres, two schooners only under my charge, *Judith Farmer*, and *Columbine*. Fresh breezes

and squally weather, storms of rain, thunder and lightning, early
in the morning a sudden shift of wind, in a squall taking us on the
larboard quarter, jibing the mainsail, and the lazy guy being fast
to the stern boat's davit, carried that, with a part of the hammock
irons, bulwark and sweeps, over to the starboard side, besides
making a complete wreck of the starboard quarter. I had warned
the mid. against this change, and he ought to have been more prepared, but he was not up to schooner sailing, indeed, we all had
much to learn. Looking over the bows, found the knee of the stem
was badly sprung, in fact, nearly in half. The carpenter had
pointed it out to the shipwrights at the dockyard, but it was not
thought so bad, nor had they time to make the defect good. However, there was a spare shackle bolted through the stem, and to
this we gammoned the bowsprit, making it more secure than ever.
Nothing further took place on our way to Chagres, except in the
fish way. We observed the *Columbine* haul in a lot of fine fish, and
she hailed us for a boat, which returned with two splendid dolphin !
We had neither a hook or line of any sort ; but we were lucky in
our fishing also. Looking over the stern, which overhung very much,
I saw a number of fish, sixteen to eighteen inches long, poking their
noses almost against the rudder. The wind was very light, and we
moved but slowly through the water. With a boarding pike,
leaning over the taffrail, I managed to spear several, but only
landed two, the pikes having no barb. The next catch was a small
shark, about six feet in length, just after the men's dinner, and no
doubt he was attracted by or had picked up something thrown overboard ; and also no doubt he was ravenous,—indeed, for the matter
of that, I never knew them otherwise,—at all events, he kept close
alongside by the gangway. I again hung over the side, with a
slip noose just before him, one of the men tempting him on with a
piece of pork at the end of a string ; it answered admirably, and as
he got sufficiently through, I caught the brute behind the pectoral
fins, and we hauled him on board. I gave him, of course, to the
crew. A famous dinner to them—a shark of that size eats well.
The last catch was a shoal of flying-fish, suddenly spattering about
the deck—it was getting dark, and a lantern going aft to light the
binnacle took their attention ; they always fly at a light. Ships
often take them by shewing a light ; as we more than once did after
this.

I must indulge in relating one trifling circumstance. I was on
the best terms with all ; but I messed by myself : in so small a craft,
we might perhaps have comfortably lived at one table ; it did not

agree with my notions of preserving discipline. It was my idea when I had the *Seagull*, and when my captain (Maling) suggested it to me, I objected, and he allowed that perhaps I was right. Still no one day passed that one or other was not at my table, for a few minutes, and in a very small way. Part of my sea stock was two or three cheeses, and a few dozens of porter. After my dinner, when cheese was on the table, I used to ask through the skylight, ' Who's on deck ? ' A most *ready* answer, ' I am, sir.' ' Will you come down and have a glass of porter ? ' Well, some cheese, and a glass each. Then—and it was always the same—helping myself to a little, then a little to him. Then, so again to be quite equal, I always saying, ' First to himself he did serve out, for fear it would not go about.' This quotation was never stale—the porter was too much appreciated ; there was invariably a pleasant smile. In all my life I never did more fully enjoy a glass and a half of porter. I could willingly then have daily finished the bottle myself, but I found the enjoyment so great on both sides that it became a standing affair. We once joined our dinners. I had bought a very large turtle for four dollars, and it gave two days' dinners to the whole crew—a large portion for me and the mids. Their servant was a marine, and having been at Ascension, where turtles abound and were supplied as rations to the garrison, he was supposed to be *au fait* at making turtle soup, and he had from me nearly a whole bottle of Madeira, and we all dined together. The soup, though excellent, was not quite so strong of the wine as I expected. There was a small smash of crockery in the galley ; in reality the ' Jolly ' had helped himself to a very undue portion of the wine. Still we had a merry evening. We always had our coffee together on deck, in basins, lounging against the big guns. I have a pleasant recollection of this also, all as plainly before my mind's eye as if only yesterday.

One fine day we had general exercise—great guns and small arms, with shot. We found the foremost thirty-two pounder answered better on its sweep than the after one, it having a different sort of slide ; and lucky it was we tried the twelve pounders with shot. They performed well, considering the small space they had for recoil. Only two of the side ringbolts drew, not having been clinched by the shipwrights—a serious thing, had we come to any fight. On the same day we cleared all the side bins, and found one hundred and fifty pounds of bread wet and totally spoiled, and we were obliged to throw it overboard.

In due time we made the land. High and mountainous. At

daylight next morning we stood in ; of course, could make nothing
as to where Chagres was, till the Spaniard hailed us, and we desired
him to lead ; and as we closed in made signal for a pilot with a gun ;
none came off.   More light winds ; and an hour after anchored in
five fathom soft mud under the so-called *Castle*, a bare ruin at the
mouth of the river.   This castle, more indebted to Nature than art
for its strength, has a few honeycombed guns mounted on rotten
carriages, and garrisoned by about one hundred half-bred mulatto
militia men.   As my friend Lord Dunboyne used to say in his
strong brogue, ' What's the use of having eyes in the back of your
head ? ' but it seems strange to me now, why, while fitting out at
Port Royal, I never asked a question about Chagres ; but this is
sixty years back, and I had not an old head on young shoulders !

After setting the crew to work, refitting the rigging and repairing
the sails, Mitchell and I went into the harbour with the letters, and
seeing only a few wretched straw huts, could not suppose it to be
the town of Chagres, particularly as one of our men, Jones, whom
I took as a guide, said the town was six miles up the river, ' a well
built regular Spanish town.' On the strength of this away we
pulled ; at six miles, no town ; still he persisted in his story. ' When
were you here, and for what purpose ? ' ' Two years back, sir, and
for cattle ; don't you hear them, sir ? ' and as it happened, there
was the lowing of some in the woods.   The stream was running
down pretty strong, and we kept close to the shore for the chance
of eddies and more still water ; an impenetrable mass of luxuriant
vegetation growing into the river.   The mangrove, the most remarkable, its roots beginning three or four feet above the water and
striking downwards, too close to admit the boat's stem in, but in
places sufficiently apart to see four or five yards in and quite alive
with reptiles, lizards, guanas, gigantic toads, snakes, &c.   They, as
we approached, kept most perfectly still.   I said ' Oars, men,' and
the boat quietly drifted for a time.   The lizards and guanas very
beautiful, the colours of the latter most gorgeous, and as it puffed
out a large swelling under its throat, with all the prismatic colours
of the rainbow, I never saw or thought anything could equal it.
The creature was about four feet long, all still and quiet ; my admiration was great, when the charm was suddenly dispelled by the man
Jones, giving a strong pull with his oar.   ' It's a dragon, sir.'   The
fellow was a cur as it soon proved ; however, we pulled away again
and about ten miles up came to a large Indian village on each side
of the river.   I put the boat on shore for a minute and tried by
signs to find where Chagres was.   A well-dressed man who gave me
128

a light for my cigar said : ' Chagres, Chagres,' stretching both arms
up and down the river ; no doubt he meant all the river was Chagres,
but it was enough to persevere a little longer. At a bend of the
river, a low point, there was the most beautiful clump of very tall
bamboos, their tops hanging and waving over the water like ostrich
feathers ; after passing this point, the dense foliage still extending
into the water ; but the background began to rise and soon became
quite mountainous. We were by this time, I should think, twelve
miles up, and I told the boat's crew that I doubted Jones' story,
and I left to them to pull or not, that there was a dollar each if we
succeeded in finding a town. So they cheerfully stretched out
again, the river began to narrow, the foliage all evergreen, more
rich and enchanting than ever ; the evening was closing in, the trees
larger and nearer added to the increasing darkness. There was a
large white stork standing on one leg in the water, it allowed us to
be very near before it stretched and flapped its long wings and
noiselessly sailed a distance, and then again stood in the water till
we were close as before, and away it went and continued to do the
same several times. Our men called it their ' pilot.' It now really
became gloomy, almost dark ; birds took to roosting ; parrots innumerable, clawing about the branches with bills and feet, and
such screaming and chattering ; brilliant lantern and fire flies flitting
all round us—the whole scene wonderfully enchanting ; but there
must be an end to it all ; the situation became serious.

I again said, ' Oars, men,' and turned the boat down stream and
let her drift. I had put a bottle of rum in the boat and served some
to the crew, who were greatly pleased, it was so unexpected. But
Jones exclaimed, ' Oh, sir, you won't go through that Indian village ?
we shall all be murdered.' ' Silence, you fool, and keep your tongue
to yourself.' We had gone up quite sixteen or seventeen miles ; I
let the boat drift for a time to relieve the men, then paddled on
gently, and when in sight of the lights of and near the village, being
a wee startled at what the man Jones said, we dashed on with a
strong pull to run the gauntlet, when all at once crash, we ran into
a long canoe, and bearing in mind what the man Jones had said,
both Mitchell and I out with our swords, and the men with the
stretchers ready for a scrimmage. Jones, we thought, would have
jumped overboard ; he never heard the end of it. The Indians
were far more startled than we were, and only seemed anxious to
get clear. The canoe was a toldo, the greater part covered with a
round roof thatched with dried leaves, carrying merchandise to
Cruzes, a small town at the end of the river, the nearest place to

Panama, fifteen miles further on. Well, our (in some respects) most agreeable excursion ended by our getting on board the *Renegade* at 9.30 P.M., after a continued pull of seven and a-half hours.

Very early next morning, I landed and delivered the Panama letters to the commandant, and let the merchants know that I should be in again about the 6th or 7th July. This was the most wretched hovel of a town I have ever seen or heard of, nothing whatever to be procured but bread. I sent Evans up the river to cut some bamboo for yards and also to get a turn of water ; tremendous heavy rain before he was two miles off ; at ten he returned. I engaged a French pilot to take us alongshore to Portobello and further among the San Blas Keys, where it was supposed a Spanish pirate was harbouring ; this according to the commodore's orders. In a couple of days I ran in and anchored at Portobello—an intelligent black fellow, captain of the port, came off—and on landing I was received by the governor and a Spanish gentleman (Elhana) ; could get no news of any suspicious vessel being in the neighbourhood ; so after lounging about for a time returned to the schooner. The forts that formerly were of such magnitude and strength were then mere ruins with but four or five effective guns in them. I could not help admiring the remains of Spanish grandeur in the Custom House, a massive stone structure built on arches ; and they shewed me one of Benbow's round shot sticking in the walls of a church. From alternate squalls and calms I could not get clear of the harbour till the evening, and then helped her out with our sweeps ; the current was running strong along shore to the eastward, and we kept well out to sea to pass Green Island. The pilot wanted us to keep away, and well it was I did not trust him ; for about nine, Mitchell called out the Cadagas Keys were right ahead, and not far off. We hauled up north and N.N.W. as high as she could lay ; not much wind and we were dropping rapidly on the rocks. Out boat to tow and also the sweeps ; we just cleared the tremendous breakers and thanked God for our fortunate escape. We all could plainly hear the lizards, grasshoppers, &c., and the cry of birds. I pitched into the pilot, threatening to pay him nothing ; this did not appear to trouble him, he felt amply repaid by our and his escape. For nearly a whole week I had a very anxious and trying time ; our Admiralty charts were by no means perfect. My instructions were to examine the San Blas Keys, a nest of low sandy islands in the very bight of the Isthmus of Panama. I did not venture nearer than four miles of the coast for two days after leaving Portobello, for the chart gave that extent from the

130

land for a long reef.   I had seen the breakers, and the pilot had said
we might throw a biscuit on shore—plenty of water ; but I stood out
to sea.   By chance, looking on deck from my dinner, I asked him
how much water : before he could answer, the quartermaster said,
' I can see the bottom, sir ' ; directly sounded four, five, then three !
five, six, seven ; this gave me breathing time, and the pilot quite
caught at my threat to send him off, and wished to go, but I stopped
him, for the man aloft called out that there were breakers a mile
out to sea ; but soundings kept regular from seven to six and four,
and on going aloft myself I made out, what appeared to be a shoal,
was a mass of trees, wood, and pieces of wreck.   I could do no
better than stand directly out to sea ; we had our boat out and the
anchor ready, continued to sound, and when quite six miles off, the
water again shoaled seven, seven, six, six, half-six, and then mark five.
I really feared we were in a serious scrape, but this did not last
long ; it was from five to seven, thirteen, and no bottom.   I then
started the pilot off in his tiny canoe, a doré, giving him a little rum,
water, and some biscuit, thinking myself well clear of him and the
rocks.   I have been minute in all this ; the whole danger and
responsibility strongly impressed on my memory, with a succession
of squalls, calms, thunder, lightning, and torrents of rain.   We
cruised about for a week, looked into the entrance of Mandigno
Bay and close to San Blas Keys ; being low we could see over them,
breakers between them, so went no further ; one morning we were
not far from five schooners—they scuttled off right and left.   I gave
chase to two of the most likely ones, from their roguish appearance,
to be up to mischief, gave them two shots from the thirty-two
pounder, and as we overhauled them too rapidly for escape, they
both hove to. They were dreadfully alarmed, taking us for a pirate,
notwithstanding my colours and pennant ; they were traders, and
so were the other three.   One of the captains, in his delight, I suppose, gave me a fine turtle of about fifty pounds weight.   They
used to say I had the bump of locality, for I never forgot any land
I had once seen, and at the end of my week I was well pleased to
make out a remarkable sugar-loaf hill, ' El Migel de la Bora.'
Though intent, when last at Chagres, on following the *Columbine*,
who led us in, yet I had noticed the configuration of the land, and
did not forget it.   When close, I sent Evans in for news : he reported
that the Spanish pirate schooner had run into Chagres the day after
we left and landed a prisoner, and, strangely enough, had again
been off the river's mouth just before we shewed ourselves ; he had
some intimation of our vicinity, or suspected it, unfortunately for

us ; I should much like to have come across him. My orders were clear ; I could not go to the westward.

Anchored near the castle ; sent the boat up the river for water, and noticed she was followed from the town, as I afterwards learnt, by a guard-boat, the commandant suspecting she was after money. I afterwards saw and talked to the commandant, and I told him I would not smuggle. I found a letter from a Panama merchant, a Mr Ferrand, that there were 50,000 dollars ready for me, hoping I would delay my sailing till they could be sent to Chagres. This put me in high spirits ; the letter dated two or three days back. I made acquaintance with a creole Spanish gentleman, Monsanta, and slept one night in his wretched hut ; I in a net hammock hung right across the hut, he on a stretcher like a long camp stool. When about dark in came a lot of copper-coloured Indians, and with scant ceremony lay down for the night, and such a chorus of snorts and grunting. I could not help laughing *at first*, for soon my nose was awfully offended. I breakfasted with Monsanta ; he took a great fancy to my mackintosh cloak, offering two doubloons for it, saying, ' No money will buy that cloak on the Panama road,' and this he kept repeating. After going by water over forty miles, the rest of the way to Panama leads across very high ground, noted for torrents of rain. He absolutely stowed the cloak away, and it was two or three days before I got it again, and that was managed by our surgeon, who called and hunted it out for me. Monsanta only laughed. In conversation he warned me to be careful when going to my boat in the evening ; a knife might be thrown at me for the sake of plunder. All there were most dexterous at this. One person shewed me how it was done. He held the knife by the point, handle downwards, swung it once or twice backwards and forwards, then let it go, and it quivered in a mark on the door ten or twelve paces off. These assassins have a great horror of a pistol. I wished to let them know I carried one, a rather large five to six-inch barrel, but hardly knew how to go about it. One day at the Custom House door, talking to the commandant, some huts were on the opposite side of the street. On every hut is always a long pole from end to end for two or three John Crows or turkey-buzzards, or whatever the proper name may be—long, lanky, ill-favoured creatures, the only scavengers of the place ; a dollar fine for injuring them. They stand quite still, only occasionally putting out one leg, then a wing, these wings generally drooping as if the bird was oppressed with extreme heat. Now I was a tolerable shot with a pistol, and when in the *Northumberland*, anchored half-way up the

Medway, I used to take a stroll in the marshes and shoot water rats.
I have often killed four out of six shots. So I said to the commandant, taking out my pistol, ' If it were not against your law I
should like to pick off one of those birds.' ' Oh, captain, I will
give you leave,' and I was fortunate to bring one nasty creature
down. On first shewing my pistol most drew back ; after the shot
all crowded round me to look at and handle the pistol. Such a
wonderful pistol ; it was the pistol, not my skill. No one after this
ever came near me at night : on the contrary, all got out of my way.

My two mids., the doctor and I dined with the commandant,
Sr Simon Ospino ; also Monsanta and two or three others. He
could only afford straps on his shoulders for epaulettes, but no
epaulette. The floor was dried mud, and I had some difficulty in
steadying my chair. But what a dinner ! In all my life I never
before or since sat down to its like. Of course in Spanish style ;
the manner of bringing it on, one dish after another, and from fifteen
to seventeen of them, all highly seasoned. As a sort of confession,
never did I eat such a dinner. My wish to taste of each may be
partly the reason. We kept it up till past eight. It was a wild
stormy evening, and that was the time I slept at Monsanta's.
During dinner the commandant said, ' Tell me, captain, tell in
confidence, tell me in honour how much money you have on board.'
I replied, ' $6,000 or $8,000.' He pulled his eyes wide open with a
finger at each. ' Oh, mine God, it is impossible to stop you.' I
then added, ' But, mind, I have smuggled nothing ; your own people
bring them off at night.' And it was in this wise. Our look-out
men would hail a boat—no answer ; then a canoe with one Indian
would drop alongside, and a hide bag of $2,000 would be handed
up and the canoe off without a word or any acknowledgment from
me. On another night a hide bag with more doubloons and two
packages of plate, and so on nearly every night. The Custom House
people did, however, seize $900 and some plate about to be put into
our boat. After some unusual heavy showers the stream increased
to great strength, and several canoes broke adrift, I imagine from
the Indian village twelve miles up. They would all have drifted out
to sea had we not secured most, and we had five astern when their
owners came down next morning to look after them, and greatly
delighted the poor fellows were to find them safe with us. In one
was a small turtle ; our men had it on deck covered with a swab.
The owner peered about and discovered it, in doubt what to do, but
I settled it by offering a dollar, and he was overjoyed to so easily
part with it. I once witnessed a curious scene, the cutting up a

very large turtle. First were the butchers and a small lot of copper-coloured fellows round the creature ; then a circle of many women, some of them with a piece of flesh in the palms of their hands, held upwards as high as the shoulder, keeping up a wonderful gabbling ; behind them many children as naked as when born, and behind all a few dogs and several of the nasty John Crows, two of them at the end of a long piece of intestine, tugging with all their might, jumping off the ground, their wings partly spread. They would run in between the legs of all, and neither were or expected to be repulsed. It was a strange sight. There was another remarkable bird, the size of our rooks, a water bird by its webbed feet, but it took to trees like other birds. It was either exceedingly stupid or it was not acquainted with a gun. Three would be close together on a branch ; our doctor from our boat would pick off the middle one, the other two remaining quiet, and waited till both were shot ; and here, again, returning to the town from the river, the gun was examined with much admiration. ' A gun to shoot so well,' &c. ! At last my time was up, and Mr Ferrand, who took a passage with me to Carthagena, told me that the merchants at Panama had met, and agreed not to send their treasure in a *one* gun schooner ; that, notwithstanding their faith in me and my crew, the pirates were so daring and numerous they declined risking their money. The fact was, as I afterwards learned, the money was not all ready to meet their en-gagements at Jamaica. And now comes my closing adventure at Chagres. The evening before sailing, on stepping into my boat there was a cask in the stern sheets, from which arose an unpleasant odour. ' What's all this ? ' ' Some beef and pork, sir, of one of the passengers ' ; and I had it bundled to the bows of the boat. The doctor said he thought there was money in the cask, but I remarked it was not likely to be there without my knowledge. On reaching the schooner I jumped on board and dived to my cabin. Dr Wilson remained in the boat, still thinking of the money. There was much quiet ground swell, and the vessel was lifting and rolling much, and as the cask was placed on the gunwale of the schooner she suddenly raised up from the boat and overboard went the cask, sinking immediately. Up jumped the doctor, calling to me, ' It's all gone, sir ; money must be there, it sank so fast.' I directly desired them to buoy the cask with some heavy iron, that it might be found the next morning. I landed and at Monsanta's met some merchants, and to my question I was told they believed money was in my boat—$1,500 belonging to Jose, a Portuguese. ' Well,' I said, ' it's all overboard.' But to make sure, he was sent for, and

134

came in a great state of agitation and excited anger; water stood
in large drops on his forehead and trickled down his cheeks.
Through Monsanta, ‘Did you send money off in my boat?’ ‘Si,
si, $1,500.’ ‘Well, it’s all gone.’ ‘Ugh, ugh!’ ‘Why did you
not let me know?’ A great angry grunt, ‘I did tell you.’ ‘Nonsense; how could I know when I can’t speak a word of your
language?’ And the brute in his rage at my saying it was all overboard put his hand to his knife. I started back and drew my sword,
saying if he dared to shew his knife I would run him through instantly; at the same time several threw themselves on him. As
he became quiet I told him I had buoyed the cask, and as there was
but five fathoms water, it might be dived for. I took leave of
all and went off; soon after Jose followed with two Indians seated
on the gunwale; and after bargaining for $50, one oiled and crossed
himself and dived, said all was right, talked with his companion,
when both said they must have $100; both went over and both up
marvellously soon, said they felt the cask but would not try again
without $150. At this, Jose was in a towering passion, downright
refusing, and for that time all ended. I could not wait for the
result, but up anchor and started for Carthagena. My belief was
that the Indians got frightened at the thought of sharks, which were
numerous, and never meant to try again. I must not leave out
that, the evening before, I was at a ‘Dignity’ in a larger hut than
many, and was greatly amused with the waltzing and *minuets*. All
with unbounded ceremony and propriety.

The passage to Carthagena was by no means agreeable, such a
continued succession of storms, squalls of wind, with heavy thunder
and lightning and torrents of rain, as also calms. We pumped dry
every four hours. She made eighteen inches in the twenty-four
hours. Lifting the cabin hatch to examine the money—and we had
over $8,000 and 1,000 ounces of silver plate—found two of the raw
hide bags rotten and stinking. We made canvas bags instead, and,
strange to say, we three times failed to count the money so as to
agree with the sum named in the bill of lading. The dollars turned
black with the bilge water. I had only one black sheep in all the
crew, and was never under any difficulty; but this one had made
much disturbance below about the provisions, instead of complaining
on the quarter-deck. He was almost mutinous and I put him in
irons for four or five days. And here I may add as a trifle, I had a
squabble with my poultry. They had been confined in rather a
small coop and I let a few out to stretch themselves: three directly
flew overboard; it was nearly calm, a chicken takes some time to

drown and we out boat and picked them up; I then had all the others taken out and threw them overboard, with a rope yarn tied to a leg: none ever flew over after that.

It seems to me just now I have time to recollect other things that I omitted to log before. First, the schooner was infested with all the noxious insects of the climate, centipedes, cockroaches, red ants, &c., in myriads ; with every lump of sugar in my tea, up would float four or five at least, and when a cold chicken was put on the table, on my lifting the dish an inch and letting it fall out they came in swarms, by degrees, as I repeated this, absolutely covering the table ; but I got used to them and never troubled myself to pick them off every mouthful. In another point I was far more pleased. In most vessels there is a band of timber round the inside, called a shelf piece, on which all the beams rest. In the *Renegade* this was unusually deep, and as the schooner heeled over and jumped, the very morning we met the sea breeze on leaving Port Royal, out came three or four cigars ; then more and more, and many more still when we put her on the other tack. As I before observed, when captured she was full of rich plunder, and no doubt was afterwards well searched, but the shelf pieces were not examined to their depths. I did not get less than from 300 to 400 ; they were first-rate cigars, the finest cigars, the finest Havannahs. I gave 100 to the mids.

Towards the afternoon we made the land, and could plainly distinguish the Popa. Soon after we carried away the log line, fortunately not before, for we had none other in the schooner. We ran in and anchored close off the St Domingo Gate. I sent Evans to the governor, who limited our stay off the town to twenty-four hours. So I went myself, and after some talk and a laugh, he allowed us to remain three or four days. Mitchell and Evans beat up the quarters of different merchants to give them notice of when I should sail, and that money must come off early. With Mr Robinson I drove into the country on a *volante* and was detained by a bull-fight, the rope being right across the road ; two of us dined with Mr Robinson and each brought off $2,000 in doubloons (about 140) ; in another room for secrecy a cambric handkerchief was on the table, and rows of gold rolled up, and then tied round the waist ; I did not half like it, fancying the sentry at St Domingo might stop me, and what could I do ! The next day Evans took our boat past Bocachica Castle, on to the harbour, a pull of twenty-two miles. I could see the boat over the low neck of land, and wishing to lighten the labour made signal for a pilot to take me off the harbour mouth, and he

startled me by saying it was the governor's order to take us into
the harbour. I directly wrote to the governor desiring his explicit
intention. He answered very civilly that it was wholly a mistake
of the pilot's, &c. So I up anchor and picked up Evans with
$60,000. I slept at Mr Nicholson's and before breakfast took off
$3,000, but I declined doing this again. I returned on shore to
breakfast, we dined again on shore ; I did not feel over well ; Mitchell
and Evans brought on board between them $6,000. In the after-
noon an English schooner, the *Anne*, one of my late convoy, came in
in distress, having sprung a leak. I sent our carpenter, who soon
put all to rights. The next day Evans, the sharper of the two mids.,
again went his twenty-two miles and brought on board $60,000,
and the following day, his last trip, $12,000 more. This time the
boat was very strictly searched, I did some extensive shopping, and
being so rich gave a demijohn of claret to the mids. ; the governor's
aide-de-camp had been twice on board, and each time impressed
on me the sin of smuggling, and he told me Captain Rowley [1] was a
very bad man—' he was rob a woman,' and which I found meant he
had run away with a nun from a convent.

Four passengers, merchants' clerks, came on board with their
traps as also the governor's woolly-headed aide-de-camp, who when
in my cabin very deliberately pulled several packages of fine gold
dust from his pockets! By eight the breeze commenced and we
up anchor. The schooner was quietly rolling with the ground swell,
and I noticed one of my passengers getting very uneasy, changing
colour from white to livid and green ! then ' Oh Madre ! oh Padre !
oh Dios ! ' repeating this and ' Oh Senora de la Popa ! ' and at last
with a shout ' Oh la Plata, la Plata, la Plata ! ' and off went his
linen jacket, and then his waistcoat with a bang. It was literally
quilted with doubloons. It was, he thought, the weight of so much
smuggled gold that disturbed his conscience and caused his sickness !

But we were off. I had engaged a pilot to take us to Savanilla
and Santa Martha. I was feeling ill and the passage was most unpleasant, for one day we got on well, the second day the fever was
on me. I have a troubled remembrance of falling and being caught
by the quarter-master and put to bed ; in two or three hours I rallied
sufficiently to know what was going on—we were making no way.
The schooner behaved badly, missed stays constantly, she was too
light ; we filled empty tanks and casks with salt water, and got the
twelve pounder guns below : all would not do, we often lost ground ;

---

[1] Presumably Captain Joshua Ricketts Rowley, till recently Flag Captain to
Sir Charles Rowley, Commander-in-Chief.

at last I gave up Savanilla and pushed for Santa Martha, where I
had notice that $100,000 were in waiting for us. My fever inter-
mitted, but I suffered great pain all over, particularly in the eyes
and back, and I had fits of delirium : we were on short allowance
six upon four, we had a young leopard and monkey on board, and
my fancy was I had to eat them ! As we were always prepared for
meeting a pirate, our boarding pikes were secured round the main
boom, a stand of arms was placed against the foremost bulkhead of
my cabin, so that they could be reached from deck through my
skylight, and I had a pair of ship's pistols at the head of my cot.
In my different attacks of delirium in many serious illnesses, the
wanderings of my fancies have always been fixed on my memory
for years after. And these pistols, I see them now as I did then, as
they turned their gaping muzzles towards me with a fiery ball
staring me in the face ; a species of terror was over me, and I was
not satisfied till they were removed. I had a raging thirst, nothing
seemed to allay it ; the mids. gave up a portion of their small allowance of water for my barley and rice mixtures. When first floored
by the fever, forgetting that the man M'Kenzie was already freed
from his irons, I desired he might be released ; I feared he might be
forgotten and so remain in irons till we reached Port Royal. He
felt this act of mine and let me know he meant to be a better man.
    At last we got on so badly, provisions and water running so
short, that I felt obliged to give up St Martha and stretch across to
Jamaica. There is a nest of dangerous shoals called the Morant
Keys, on one of which are two cocoanut trees, they are directly in
the passage to Port Royal. A few miles off running for the land, I
was in doubt whether I should be to windward or to leeward of
them. At last at midnight we were in smooth water, shewing us
to be to leeward, at daylight pretty close in. Got a pilot and
anchored in the harbour all snug. The opening to the harbour is
very narrow and all ships large or small have to run very close to
the shore. My young friend Oliver's boy Jack, always on the look
out, espied the schooner, and not seeing me on deck ran off at once
to Dr Lang of the Naval Hospital. ' Oh, Missa Dr Lang, him
Renegade come, sir ; I no see Missa Boteler, him sick, him dead,
him sick, him dead ! ' and within an hour of anchoring Dr Lang
came off and I was in bed. He put his hands under my arms,
lifted my eyelids, felt my pulse, and then—' It's better than I expected : you have had a narrow escape. Come to the hospital : I
will soon set you up. Don't wait for the commodore's order—I will
arrange all that.' Before the evening Oliver and little James, both
138

with me in the *Antelope*, two or three of the *Gloucester's* officers, and
others came on board to see me, and before dark, a barge from the
Gloucester took me to the hospital, with a white cap and a high
broad brimmed Panama hat. I was supported along the deck into
the boat. I noticed the men eyeing me very gravely; it is always
considered a bad case when sent to the hospital. Dr Lang was
there to receive me: I was put into a warm bath, had a cup of tea
with milk, a luxury, and then to bed with mosquito curtains, and
its legs in saucers of oil to keep ants and other abominations from
crawling up. The black nurse, Sarah, flourished a towel to drive
the mosquitoes out, tucked me up and I was soon asleep: such a
blessed change from the sweltering heat of my cabin with continued
stamping and other noises overhead, to a delicious cool room and
all so still and quiet. My rank entitled me to a separate room; but
that wing of the hospital was not yet finished, so we were five in
one large room; two lieutenants of the squadron were there and also
the captain's clerk of the *Ringdove*, my *bête noir*; poor fellow, he
was almost on the point of death, his body swelled, nothing would
move his interior; at last Dr Lang administered, at that time, a
perfectly new medicine, croton oil, a single drop in some water,
desiring Jeffries, if he felt at all qualmish, to call the nurse and send
for him. The effect was wonderful, we all thought he would have
died from exhaustion.

I felt so happy and comfortable, Dr Lang was most kind and
attentive. I feared there would be difficulty with the treasure, I
alone knowing the marks, but on the third day the merchants let
me know all was right, only that some of the shippers had sent
Columbian milled doubloons instead of Spanish, and as I had signed
for all as Spanish, I was at a loss of half a dollar on each, and there
were twenty. The wording of my receipt for bags so-and-so,
should have been *said* to contain so much. However, the same
evening gold was sent to me to the value of over £200 all in gold; I
felt so amazingly wealthy. The next day, Wednesday, the fever
left me and I began to be dosed with calomel for a nasty pain in
my left side, and I thought more of this than the fever, but I was
on the mend, and next day walked across the room—no small feat,
I was so dreadfully weak; I gradually mended and began to look
for my dinner; as I got on, I had a daily visit from my little friend
'Jack' sent by Oliver, but it was invariably 'Miss Laurette send
him compliment and glad to know how you am, sir,' often bringing
some delicacy—split chicken, pigeon, custard pudding, or what-
not; when well, I insisted on paying for all; it mainly helped to

bring me round. Jack never waited for an answer, but seized my little telescope and to the door that looked out on the harbour, soon again to my bedside with news, ' Him commodore got him long mast up ; the *Thracian* go to sea this morning.' ' Did she, Jack ? ' ' Yes, massa, why you no hear him salute ? ' and so it was ; he generally found something to tell me.

Our hospital establishment was Dr Lang, two assistant-surgeons and a tall black man, William Charles, the most delicate fingered fellow, such a gentle touch, he was most expert in dressing a blister. Then there was a little negro, Tom Hercules, the barber, and last, Sarah, nurse, a dark mulatto, an attentive and most excellent help ; she slept on a mattress in a corner of the ward—slept I suppose she did ; but we had only to whisper her name and she was instantly by our bedside. She never touched anything till after our dinners, and then seated at the top of the stairs, a pail by her side, containing a wonderful mixture, soup and broth, a salt herring or two, the remains of our dinner, chops, chickens, and what-not. The two negroes at the bottom of the stairs, always so, and it would be, ' Missa Wiyam, you take something, sar,' and down would go a chop, and then, ' Missa Hercules, you this,' and again went some delicacy which they caught with dexterity, and so it went on full one and a-half hours till the pail was empty, and not another thing did Sarah touch till next day. I used to plague her in accusing her of cannibalism ; she would get angry : ' I no eat man, but um like um dog good.' We made her own, I think in desperation, that she once tasted a man's hand. She had many dresses, given by different patients, chiefly of highly-coloured *glazed* calicoes ; but on Sundays she appeared entirely in white : shoes, stockings, gloves, bonnet, veil and parasol.

As I got better and talking of the *Renegade's* cruise, I mentioned my passenger with his waistcoat quilted with gold. ' Why, Boteler, did you not search their trunks ? depend on it all had false bottoms : what a Johnny Raw you were.' It never for a moment struck me at the time, but I did think they were very heavy ; one thing, illness was on me. I heard that passengers' trunks were examined in one of our men-of-war ; they had false bottoms, and very many thousand dollars turned up ; there was great inducement to smuggle, for the export duty was three per cent., and our freightage two per cent., and even should the fraud be discovered by us, they would save three out of the five per cent. No wonder the Carthagena people sent me presents of brandy, liqueurs, and claret. By very moderate suspicion that 5,000 doubloons (*i.e.*,

140

$80,000) might easily have taken little room in trunks, a loss to me of £160 at one per cent.—the full man-of-war's freight is two per cent., but the commodore has half, and Greenwich the other half per cent. I explain this now, but it never troubled me at the time ; I considered myself a lucky fellow, and well off. As I got rapidly better, my diet became more generous, porter, &c. ; and Dr Lang advised me to get some good old madeira from Johnny Ferron, a Frenchman, whose store contained every conceivable or inconceivable thing imaginable.

One day my two young midshipmen cousins, Tom and Henry Harvey, paid me a visit. I was walking in the broad verandah, and to prove how strong I was, I said : ' See me run.' But the running step was totally beyond my power. I seemed nailed to the floor. It amused them, and they each got a doubloon from my golden store. Their father, Admiral Tom, never forgot this ; nor has his son Henry, now an admiral, for he named it to me two years back at Walmer. St John and Captain Rich called to see me and us. The latter rather coarse ; he meant well, but it jarred on our weakened nerves. ' You all want stirring up ; a good rope's ending all round would do you good.'

In a few days I was able to walk out and call on Oliver, and at the end of three weeks was discharged. When going off to the *Gloucester*, less than half-way, one of the rattling West India storms came on ; tremendous thunder, rolling with wonderful echoes over the Blue Mountains, and a perfect continued blaze of lightning all over the harbour, and of course torrents of rain ; all over in a few minutes, and then such perfect stillness, the noises of various insects could be distinctly heard. I wet to the skin, from head to feet. I went up the ship's side ; most of the officers were there to receive me ; all congratulating me. ' Well, Boteler, glad to see you again ; you have weathered the crabs this time ; a rich fellow, too.' Then the surgeon shook hands, started, and said : ' My dear fellow, what is the matter with you ? you must go on shore again.' And so it was ; I was in a high fever : from being shut up so long, and enfeebled with illness, the sudden check to the perspiration, through such a drenching, was too much for me. The surgeon himself went with me to the hospital, taking great care, covering me up with cloaks ; and there I was for six long weeks more, at first very ill. I scarcely knew at times what passed around me. I lay ten days on my back, touching nothing but a little soup ; but my hearing was unusually acute. I heard someone coming up the broad stairs say he came to see Boteler ; the reply being : ' Poor fellow ! don't

disturb him ; he is going as fast as he can.' This naturally much
startled me ; and as soon as I could go to my desk I wrote to Joe
O'Brien about disposing of parts of my little property. I did not
send the letter ; it was a queer production, and I kept it some years
as a curiosity.

My illness had taken the form of fever and ague. First, a
hideous fit of shivering, followed by a burning heat, all closing with
profuse perspiration. During the hot stage my legs (and such legs
as they were !) were sponged with concentrated vinegar and water.
While so ill the commodore sent Dr Wilson to sound me as to my
going to England, which I directly decided on, feeling quite certain
I could never do a day's duty in the climate ; and it was fixed that
I should start by the first packet. Shortly after, the commodore
himself visited the hospital, and with the negroes it was ' See um
big commodore, wid um white foot.' He was dressed entirely in
white. How things turn up in my memory ! Scarcely a morning
passed that someone did not call for a chat with us, and to tell the
news. One morning a lieutenant told us Mr St Clair [1] was promoted.
' St Clair, whose vacancy has he ? ' ' *Boteler's.*' There was an
instant pause, a whispering, and pointing to me on my bed. The
officer was dreadfully shocked ; came to my bed ; so very sorry ;
said it was known I was very ill, and that morning my death reported. I must not forget Dolly Johnson. Day by day she would
sit by my bedside, holding her hand to my forehead, and changing
it,—so deliciously cool. A black woman's skin is velvety and cool,
and the hand often as cool as a dog's nose. I cannot express the
comfort the cool hand was to my burning forehead. In due time
three captains with their surgeons came and invalided me, and
two or three others ; and Dr Lang gave me a certificate, which
insured me the Government £40 towards expenses of my passage
home ; and Hooper and I secured two adjoining cabins in the
Sandwich packet, Captain Adoniah Schuyler.

There was a death in the next ward, Tom Marriott, commanding the *Union* schooner. I knew him at Sheerness, when in the
Northumberland. There he had a cutter ; we dined with each
other often. He made a dreadful noise. We all were wide awake,
listening with awe to his strange soliloquy, going over some events
of his life. ' Tom, you have not been quite a bad fellow, have
you ? ' and so on. I could repeat much that he said, it was all so
impressed on my memory.

I left the hospital, having been there nine weeks to a day, landed

<hr>

[1] Presumably the Hon. E. G. Sinclair (Lieutenant, October 22nd, 1823).

142

at Greenwich, where a kittereen was in waiting to take me to the commodore : a large party at dinner. The change was too great for me, and I *did* think I had been so abstemious ; I breakfasted with the party next morning and was very ill after. Sally Adams, the commodore's mulatto housekeeper, took me in hand ; they are all good nurses. She gave me a great dose of castor oil, just pressed from the green nut, very different from the filthy, rancid, abominable stuff in England. The *Gloucester's* surgeon was telegraphed for, but he found me already better. I stayed four days at the ' Pen,' a large party each day, and in the evening of one dancing till late. I felt so ashamed of my *white* face. One of the young ladies, very pretty, quite won my heart, she would neither dance herself or let me, I was not strong enough ; she kept by me half the evening. Very early next morning the kittereen took me to the foot of Stony Hill, on which was quartered the 33rd Regiment ; it was 1,500 feet above the level of the sea. From the kittereen I went the rest of the way on a mule, the guest of the colonel, Fogarty ; I never was quite aware why he noticed me, but in 1776 and 1777 he, an infantry officer, did marine's duty on board the *Prince of Wales*, the flagship of my great-uncle, Sir Henry Harvey ; or the commodore might have named me for two or three days' change of climate. It was a change : that night I had a blanket and counterpane over me, and wore cloth trousers at the mess dinner. I never shall forget being waked up from a sound sleep by the band of the regiment under my window playing ' Sul marginè dun Rio.' All my children, from babyhood and upwards, when restless or ill, in turn, with their heads on my shoulders, were *buzzed* to sleep with this tune. Four days only on Stony Hill, and in that short time a wonderful change came over me for the better ; I absolutely felt quite strong. I went first to the Pen, found the commodore very ill ; in the afternoon took leave of Sir Edward and all the others. To Greenwich in the kittereen and on board the *Gloucester* to dinner. What a change again ! sweltering heat. Slept at Laurette's.

The next day took my baggage on board the packet, dined again on board the *Gloucester* and took my leave of all ; four or five had tea with me at Laurette's. The next morning, my last in Jamaica, called on St John and Berkeley and on Dr Lang at the hospital. In the evening I gave a grand dinner to some of my messmates and others—I could if I chose name nearly all ; champagne, muscat, old madeira, noyeau, and choice fruits. The packet boat was at the end of a rocky point to take me off, and I got on board the *Sandwich* at 10 P.M.

This rocky point all at once brings to my memory a curious mischievous adventure that might have turned to a serious affair. At low water it was the resort of pigs to pick up any offal; a midshipman of a small ship anchored pretty close in, with more deviltry than reflection, floated a line with corks, and a baited hook, soon got hold of a pig, who, unable to fight against the pain, walked into the water, squealing all the way. The astonishment of the negroes was great; 'See um d—n fool; what him go dere for? Him surely mad, or the debbil in him; him surely be killed; nebber see such a ting before, golly,' &c. I am not sure if it ever came to the knowledge of the authorities. As soon as the sea breeze set in we up anchor for Old England.

I had over-taxed my strength yesterday in my various calls, that for two or three days my leg was on a camp stool, with a swelled ankle. Our passengers were a Mrs Courtney, Lieutenant Hooper, a naval surgeon, master and purser, Mair (a young merchant), and a brown *gentleman* (an opulent saddler) with his jet-black, woolly-headed little girl of twelve. He would seize the child by the head, swear at her, 'You debil, I give you a lunger in the eye, make um fire-fly; or I lace your jacket well, make um wale rise'; the little creature never moving, only looking at him apparently with wonder. He made himself exceedingly disagreeable, throwing himself back in his chair, rattling his keys in his trousers' pocket. 'I am a man of substance, my house hab seven doors. A magistrate say to me, "You hab trouble with your slaves, send them to me and I will give them cow kin,"' and much in this way. At last one day he burst out, 'What are you all? vagabonds on the face of the earth;' this was too much, Hooper started up and brought a pistol from his cabin, with 'Now, sir, if you dare to say another word I'll shoot you like a dog.' Down went the big brute on his knees with a flop: 'I beg your pardon, sir, and, gentlemen, I humbly beg your pardon; I neber do so again,' and so it ended; he was well behaved the remainder of our passage. Mrs. Courtney was present, got frightened, fell on the deck, struggling and hysterical. We did not know till afterwards how near the chance was of a birth taking place. In our innocence we thought that, like poor Mair, she was suffering from dropsy! The two surgeons took her to her cabin and soon quieted her.

Nothing very unusual occurred in our way, only one night, the wind round the compass, thunder and lightning in squalls, then calm; we were invited on deck to see *two fly-by-nights*. There they were, a faint blue light at each mast head, and if the packet rolled

144

over much they would dance to a yard-arm and back, to the great discomfiture of the men reefing topsails. They all lost no time in getting on deck again. To many it was no joke, others laughed over it, and to the caring man, ' How did you like that fellow shewing you a light ? ' &c. I had heard of these small meteors, had never before seen any and, in fact, did not credit them. About this time, in this region of baffling winds, we saw many waterspouts, and once a splendid lunar rainbow. I cannot say much for the navigation. Adoniah Schuyler was drunk for four days together, and at another time he never left his cabin for a whole week, and during those days no sights were ever once taken for the chronometers, and often not even for the latitude. The packet, or rather the gear, was the captain's property, and he kept a dilapidated suit of canvas on her till it was blown away, when new sails were bent, and when running in a strong wind across the Atlantic we altered four points on either side of the proper course to find which would be easiest or least trying to the masts, yards and rigging, quite ignoring the importance of his mail. During the voyage our table was well kept. I contributed much towards this, and no great credit to me either. I had a demijohn of brandy, two dozen of claret, and two or three dozen of other good wines. I could not well take it into port, so it was always produced, but Hooper, twice my fellow-patient at the hospital, had the run of my store at any time he chose. One thing reduces my liberality. I saved my friend's and my own pockets from the charge of using the packet's wine. One of the crew died of fever on the way.

Made St Agnes light, got a pilot and some nice fish with him, tacked about Mount's Bay, Penzance, and next day ran into Falmouth Harbour, and to our great dismay were ordered into quarantine till released from London ; six weeks this day from Port Royal. Poor young Mr Mair warded off death, and we thought he would have lived to see his family at Liverpool. But the quarantine upset him ; he turned his head to the wall and died the next evening. He was buried the following day, a guard of militiamen to keep all away. The fourth day we were released. In these days of quarantine we had to pay our own mess, and we installed the purser, Willie, as caterer. I found ' Adoniah ' not far from a Jew. He got as much for the passage from each as he could. The brown fellow paid for self and child £120 ! and he took his passage back to Jamaica by the next packet. I paid £70, Hooper £45, and the others between £30 and £50. I never thought in a government vessel there could be two prices.

To follow out the oft-repeated story, on landing in Old England
I absolutely kissed the stones, most grateful to the Almighty for my
safe return after all the illness I had gone through. The whole of
us put up at the Royal Hotel; I walked out for a little shopping,
and went to bed with fever and ague, but it went off by the morning.
This day nearly the whole party set off for their homes. By noon,
in a fly, I drove to Captain William King, a post captain in charge
of the government packet service here. He and Mrs King and two
girls, Laura and Julia, I had intimately known at Sheerness and
elsewhere. Their jump up and start of astonishment as I went in,
the very last person they could possibly expect to see. They so
commiserated my breakdown: Mrs King took me in hand, was so
kind, it quite touched me, for I was as weak as a rat. I dined there,
and the following day as well. He was a noted smart and strict
officer, known in the service as ' Billy King.' He astonished the
captains of the packets in stirring them up, and he had a great row,
I being present, with Bull, of the *Marlborough*, the chief man in
the packet service. He did not like going to sea with a foul wind,
Captain King saying, ' It is your business, sir, with a mail to go out
and look for a fair wind, not wait for one.' ' My topmast is sprung,
sir.' ' You should have looked to that days back, sir,' and he rang
the bell. Answered by his coxswain : ' How long will it take to
shift the *Marlborough's* topmast ? ' Said the coxswain, ' Well, sir,
'tis but a *stick* ! ' He was a frigate's man, but the answer disgusted
Bull ; and he burst out with, ' Wouldn't send a dog to sea in such
weather.' ' Dog or weather, sir, out you go as soon as your topmast
is ready,' and out he was next morning, weather somewhat finer.
Captain King soon quite changed the whole conduct of their slow
ways.

On the third day after sending off my baggage to Canterbury by
water, and passing my fruit through the Custom House—a lot of
shaddock, forbidden fruit, and a few pines—I set off very early for
Exeter ; breakfasted, I remember, at Truro. I thought it was
wearisome up and down hill through Cornwall, and we were at
Exeter by eight. Next day for Bath, which we reached by seven or
eight. I put up at the White Hart, which I note for two reasons,
because I was often there in aftertime, and because, although my
dinner was by no means extensive, yet it was brought in by the
landlord and five waiters, each with something, if only a sauce-boat.
Of course I made sure I should have to pay in accordance, whereas
the charge was most moderate in every respect. The following day
being Sunday, I remained at Bath, and was at my old quarters,

Spring Garden Coffee House, by the evening of Monday. Stayed a few days in London. We all had to pass a medical board at the Admiralty, and each pronounced proper cases for invaliding.

One day I met, full butt, Lieutenant Chaplin. He started back with 'Good God! I took you for your ghost. When I called at the hospital they told me you were going as fast as you could, and Dr Lang's opinion was you would sink under your frequent attacks.' I found he had sailed for England in a merchant ship, and from incompetence of the drunken captain had got on shore in Crooked Island Passage. As a naval officer he took command and got the ship off; then, the captain still incapable from drinking, and the mate being no navigator, he agreed with the passengers to put the ship wholly under his charge. He lost three or four men from fever on the passage, but brought the ship safely home. He entered four men off Plymouth, and on reaching London was found fault with for so doing by the owners, who rewarded him with £100, considering he had also his passage free. He took this, but when it came to the ears of his navy agents they made a great outcry that such a mean act of an English merchant was never before known, and the end was, that Chaplin was paid several hundred pounds, even then less than would have been awarded had he sued for salvage. Well, I got home to Canterbury, staying two days with Dr Griffiths at Rochester, and then meeting my young brother Edward, just in orders, and curate of Cliff, next Rochester. At last at home, but with a heavy heart, thinking to be a burden to my mother, and lost to the service.

CHAPTER IX

INVITED to both my uncles Admirals John and Thomas Harvey, the latter anxious to see me and hear of his two boys, and to him I first went, he living in his father's (Sir Henry Harvey's) house at Walmer; still shaky in health, for in a walk to Deal and hurrying back in rain, fever and ague set in, pulse 154; in two days I was well, and with the exception of two or three very slight touches, those attacks ceased, and I heard no more of them. I distributed my shaddock and forbidden fruit to friends; they were greatly prized, and with the peel of the shaddock I made a lot of first-rate rum-shrub. Events of my half-pay life on shore are not fixed on my memory as those afloat. I followed my family in the summer to Herne Bay, had long walks with grammar and dictionary and made very fair progress in French. Once or twice found my way along shore to Whitstable, the scene of my cruising ground when I had the *Seagull* cutter; and this cutter *will* conjure up many recollections. I had been as far as Harwich, and on shore had a present of a fine hare, which I hung over the stern with other meat, and on running into Whitstable Bay, where one or two other cutters lay at anchor, proud of and to exhibit my game I turned among them before picking up my berth. That night I lost the *hare*, it was 'cut out'; two days after I dined with Lieutenant Woollnough of the *Swan*, and we had a fine *hare* for dinner. I had little doubt the hare was mine. Woollnough sat very low in his chair, but he had the longest legs I ever saw, he seemed split up to the breast bone. Another of my cruising companions the *Asp*, Lieutenant Jones, tender to the flagship at Chatham, dining with him and talking of names, I said: 'What a common name yours is: there are more Joneses hung than others.' 'To be sure, Boteler, the Joneses are well known, and many rogues take that name and get off, but who would ever take the name of Boteler? it is never heard

148

of, and he would be suspected at once.' He turned the tables on
me nicely, and we had a good laugh over it. One day Lord Darnley
in his cutter yacht *Elizabeth* came in and Jones went on board to
pay his respects ; I did not, and it chanced they both sailed together.
The *Asp* beat the *Elizabeth*, and as Jones perceived this, to please
his lordship, he quietly dropped a spar astern and towed it, soon
causing the *Asp* to slacken her rate of sailing. Jones little thought
of the consequences. Lord Darnley was so gratified at beating a
King's cutter of such known good sailing qualities, Jones calling
on him perhaps contributing a little towards it, but he invited
Jones to dine, and hearing of his length of serving and his having
no interest, he said it ought to be looked to, not fair that an active
officer should be put aside without hope ; within two months Jones
was a commander, got a ship, and in less than three years was a
captain. So much for being shrewd and a little polite.[1]

I thought my half-pay time would supply nothing for my
memory—quite the contrary, a crowd of recollections now rise up.
My brother Richard who had for nine years been Commanding
Royal Engineer at Spike Island, Cove of Cork, was just appointed
to superintend the powder manufactory at Waltham Abbey, and
small arms works at Enfield. I stayed three or four weeks with
him, lodging at Waltham Cross ; we passed an agreeable time together. He had seen much service, was in Spain in 1808, and at the
retreat of Corunna in the scramble in getting off he was the only
person to reach a transport, which absolutely cut and sailed for
England with him alone ! Captain Thomas Boys, with whom I
afterwards sailed, then commanded the *Zealous*, and was on shore
at Corunna in his barge anxiously looking out for my brother. He
was the next year, 1809, with the expedition to Walcheren, and like
a vast number of the army caught the fever that destroyed so many
thousands of our troops. He was one of the few that got over it,
and was again in Spain and through the whole campaign. At the
siege of Badajos he was desperately wounded : four captains of
engineers had been picked off before him, and he had scarcely taken
charge of the breaching battery and shewed his head over the
rampart, when a musket ball, first going through two parts of his
cocked hat, entered his forehead, twisted and lodged behind the ear.

---

[1] The Navy List would fix this story on Captain William Jones (Lieutenant of
1811 ; Commander May 1st, 1826 ; Captain August 18th, 1828). He was one of
five William Joneses, all Lieutenants in 1826, who were distinguished by letters
after their names ; his letter was C. From the Navy List and O'Byrne's *Naval
Biographical Dictionary*, he would not appear to have commanded the *Asp* during
the period of Boteler's half-pay, but this is hardly the point in Boteler's story.

His servant was close and caught him as he fell; all thought he was
killed.   The ball was extracted as also afterwards two pieces of the
hat.   After some time at sick quarters in Lisbon he got round,
resumed his duties to the close of the war.   At the siege of St
Sebastian he was again wounded, but laid up only for a few days.
I must here name one day's little occurrence :   I was walking by his
side, and in crossing a road in a sloppy muddy place and in picking
my way was about to step on a stone.   He rather rudely pulled me
back, saying sharply, ' Don't do *that*, John.'   I looked surprised.
' No, I can't bear to see you ; I never do ! ' and then he told me
that a few days after the siege he went into the citadel, and in
crossing a street in a wet slushy state he made a long step for what
he took to be a white stone—it was a man's stomach! and it squashed
under his foot, covering him with no pleasant odour.   From that
time he had a horror of picking his way !

About this time we heard of my sister Julia's death in child-
birth ; she had married my schoolfellow T. Hodges, a clergyman,
from our school direct to Oxford ; he took first-class honours, which
Dr Griffiths thought did himself and the school great credit.   We
went to London and my tailor, Solomon, made me a suit of mourning
in six hours ; we went down to Hastings by the night coach and
attended the funeral next day.   Poor Julia, she was a favourite
sister with all of us ; her youngest daughter (Sharland) died only a
few months back.   I remained at Hastings with my mother and
sister all the winter and spring of 1825.   Mr Hodges had four
private pupils, each paying him £300 a year.   His mother at Canterbury became dangerously ill, and he asked me to take charge of his
house and look after his young men while away—something on my
shoulders—and I thought the best plan to keep them in order was
to amuse them.   We had two or three walking excursions.   I took
them to Lord Ashburnham's, a show place, and we were particularly pleased with the dairy I remember ; and one day was a grand
one for them : a man-of-war anchored off the town ; I knew her
captain, Willes, and in their own boat I took them off to the ship ;
several of the officers knew something of me, of course my young
friends were shown over the ship and they were delighted with their
trip.   My sea yarns also greatly entertained them, never tired of
hearing my different stories ; and of course my adventures with the
pirates so lately gone through stood as first in their estimation ;
for ten, twenty and thirty years after, I have met these (then lads)
and they invariably referred to that time and the delight I gave
them.

Having quite got rid of all attacks of fever and ague, and perfectly recovered in strength, I went for a most interesting walking tour through the South of England and Wales ; and on my arrival in London at my old quarters, Spring Garden Coffee House, I found several letters and my appointment to the *Albion* two or three days old.[1] My agent not knowing where to send it, there was a to-do, and real bustle. I wrote to our servant at Canterbury to start my chest off to Portsmouth, and I went myself next day to Rochester to take leave of Dr Griffiths and my brother Edward, and Robert with his commission, and at the Engineer Barracks where I dined with him, and late at night called at the halting place of the road waggon and saw my chest all right on its way to Portsmouth. The following morning from the top of the London coach crossing Rochester Bridge I hailed my brother on a pontoon with a big gun and a party of sappers at exercise,—they looked like marines adrift on a grating. He gave me an answering cheer, and I saw no more of him for years. My brothers, William, Henry, and Richard, met me in the course of the day, the latter making me a present of a handsome naval sword, knot and belt, and in the evening I went by the night coach and joined my ship at Portsmouth.

The *Albion* was completely fitted and on the point of leaving the harbour for Spithead. Some changes had taken place among the officers. My old messmate Dr Neill had left, as also the first lieutenant, a first-rate officer, and who had fitted out the ship—his place taken by a most inefficient man, who had been fifteen years unemployed,[2] totally unfit for his duty ; he went by the name of ' Molly S.' He had the habit of shrugging his shoulders and giving a cough before speaking. He was perfectly incompetent. I could but pity him, and having been myself a first lieutenant, as also in command, and always actively employed, I had a certain *esprit de corps* that prompted me to help him, and I did so in stationing and quartering the men, often ; and on my naming any one he would give his usual shrug and cough and bolt away, leaving me to do as I chose. Lord Yarborough was on board with Captain Ommanney for a passage to Lisbon, our destination. But while unmooring at Spithead we found our orders were for the Cove of Cork to embark the 42nd Highlanders for Gibraltar, Lord Yarborough saying, ' Don't send me on shore. I shall like of all things to go to Gibraltar and see my old friend, the governor, Sir

---

[1] Boteler was appointed to the *Albion* August 30th, 1825.
[2] The Navy List shows John H. Servante as the *Albion's* First Lieutenant. ' Fifteen years unemployed ' is inaccurate ; but perhaps he is not the officer intended.

George Don'; and so off we were—such confusion, first beating to quarters, the same man called for different guns, and it was a long while before the lieutenants could report the state of their different commands. I was third lieutenant. On our way to Cork there was a great breakdown. Molly S. could not even work the ship; he would get her in irons, unable to get her out again. My station was on a gangway, and I used to prompt him, till one day the captain, who had a forbidding and stern manner, called out, ' Don't prompt him, sir, leave him to himself and attend to your own duty.' Of course this silenced me, but it ended in his relieving me from watch duty, appointing me a day officer, with orders to the first lieutenant to follow my suggestions ; in fact I had the full internal management of the ship—an unpleasant office, putting me in an invidious and anomalous position. However, I made the best of it, and made all as little irksome to the first lieutenant's feelings as possible. Before this, during my watch, I made the men up and down courses till they did it more smartly, and this brought up Lord Yarborough, who complimented me on the occasion. I did not half like this, and I said, ' From a thorough seaman as he was known to be, and in command of the finest and largest yacht afloat, I accepted the praise, but I did not think I could take praise as a naval officer from any other civilian.' He took it well, shook hands, saying, ' Gad, sir ! you are right, I honour your reply ' ; and he was ever after a great friend, years after noticing me and inviting me to his Christmas parties at his mansion in the Isle of Wight, and to many dinners on board his yacht, the *Falcon* ; and he made me two or three handsome presents before leaving the *Albion*.

Our captain was at the general's, in Cork, to hear all about the regiment. He did not admire being used as a troop ship, and was not over gracious ; and when a young *aide de camp* asked with rather an air, ' What are you going to do with the colonel's carriages ?' he burst out with, ' D—— his carriages, sir ; I have no coach-house for his carriages.' So there was a split at starting, and the colonel, imagining he had a sea-bear to deal with, determined to go in a transport with the head-quarters, and send the strength of the regiment with us.

I had been before in a ship with a regiment on board, and knew all arrangements requisite, and soon after, when a young officer came on board, I at once talked to him, and said ' we should prepare cots for them, that all would sleep in the cockpit, where flag screens would be, and that each of us would take two or three in our cabins

for dressing, &c., that the regiment need prepare nothing, that the
whole would mess with us as best we could make of it.' The young
fellow was shy, and, suspecting what was in the background, I said,
'You are probably thinking of what payment is required?' He
was so pleased to come to the point, and produced a bag of sovereigns.
I told him we had laid out all our spare money in completing, &c., a
stock for our station, in every respect ; that of course we must have
extra live stock, and must charge them £4 a head, and that that
would cover every expense ; and so all went smooth enough. My
brother officers were pleased that I had taken all trouble off their
hands. In a day or two a large steamer came alongside full of
soldiers, and a staff officer with embarkation papers came on deck,
and here was our incompetent first lieutenant shrugging his shoulders,
coughing, and standing like a born ass, without an attempt at coming
forward. Of course I could do nothing less than take the officer to
him, and tell Molly to introduce him to the captain, who was on the
poop swelling with anger at seeing such imbecility. I should be
sorry if any one reading this would think I had made myself
officious, and meddled too much. Our second lieutenant, Paddy
Norcott, never cared to interfere or put himself forward in any way,
and for the credit of the ship, for the honour of the service, I felt I
could do no less. I was officer of the watch on that morning ; as
batches of ten or twelve soldiers came up the side, I had sergeants
and corporals of marines, and leading seamen ready to shew them to
their mess places between guns on the main deck, as also to take
their muskets, knapsacks, and handsome plumed bonnets to the
gunner's store rooms, a great relief to the poor fellows, who would
encounter discomfort enough without being hampered with accoutre-
ments ; and so all went smoothly enough. There were about fourteen
officers in all, headed by brevet Lieutenant-Colonel Campbell, a fine
soldier-looking fellow, and we contrived that all in some way should
be at our dinner, in these days, three o'clock. Some at the rudder
head, some seated on fire buckets, all making the best of it. On the
following day, the wind getting up, and the weather threatening, it
was up anchor ; we had little room to drift, and it was requisite sail
should be on her as soon as the anchor was out of the ground. So
the capstan was manned entirely by the Highlanders, stout, brawny
fellows, and they put their chests to the bars with a will, calling for
the pipers, and then such a screaming and skirling set up as was
seldom heard on board a man-of-war ; in the meanwhile, the seamen
were aloft, and on the yards, and all ropes in hand ready to make
sail when required without a minute's loss of time. Then, heave

and away, and as the ship canted, " Let fall, sheet home, hoist away '
—the capstan going steadily round, the din of the pipes increasing in
noise !   The anchor was speedily catted, and we went rapidly out of
the harbour, holding seaward, at from ten to twelve knots.   As the
ship felt the full sea of the Atlantic, she began to pitch and surge
about at a great rate, the wind increasing to a gale, and we were
soon reduced to a close reefed main topsail, reefed foresail, and
storm staysails ; two seas tumbled over our sides, finding their way
into the cockpit, where we had just put the women and children
for safety.   The cross sea was very trying, the ship tore about
wonderfully, and the anchor, not being sufficiently secured, broke
partially adrift, and we had to cut the cable below, then the
lashings at the bow, and let the anchor overboard, or it would
have pecked a hole in the ship's side.   Of course the troops were
in a pitiable condition, sick to a man—indeed, for that matter,
so were very many of the ship's crew ; and a lot of them, not
sick, were more than half drunk with the grog the soldiers and sick
seamen could not themselves drink.   Some of us did not fare better.
Lieutenant Read went to his cot, Lieutenant Ramsay to his cabin,
and here, as a confession—though I don't mind owning it a bit, for I
was like Blackwood's ' Joe Pippins, the lad of wax who couldn't
help himself '—but there was I carrying on duty on the quarter-deck,
holding on by a copper belaying pin as sick as a dog ! And the
provoking thing was, to see Colonel Campbell under the poop
awning, his arm round a stanchion, looking on quite comfortable and
at home.   I never fairly got over sea sickness, *i.e.*, if I chanced at
once to get into bad weather after being at anchor or in smooth
water a few days ; but if I sailed in fine weather it might blow hard
enough the next day, and I never cared at all.   I remember in particular, once starting with despatches for Lisbon, going into bad
weather and being very sick for three whole days, and on the second
day, our boatswain, a smart little fellow, a thorough seaman, lifting
his hat with—" I beg your pardon, sir, anything wrong ? ' very
insinuatingly.   ' Wrong, no ! '   ' Nothing wrong, sir ? say the word
and I'll put it to rights in no time, sir ! '   ' What makes you think
anything wrong ? '   ' Why, sir, you look so pale, I thought you were
angry about something ! '   No sickness, however bad, ever kept me
from duty.   I had only to dive occasionally to my cabin.

But to the *Albion* : the gale increased ; we had got well out to
sea, and were obliged to heave to ; ship, rigging and gear all new, it
was a busy time with everyone in making all snug, looking to the
guns, ports, and all fittings.   I had the first watch, and when about
154

to be relieved, reported to the captain that there appeared a trifling
lull and that we might bear away on our course. ' Do so, sir, with
both watches ' ; and at eight bells, before the next officer took charge,
I up with the helm, the ship made two or three heavy laboured
plunges and there was a crash and outcry below : the massive iron
tiller had gone right in halves ; the ship flew to again and remained
quiet ; we could not get the stump of the tiller out, and so were
obliged to knock away the covering of the rudder head in the wardroom (our mess place) and then ship a spare tiller, and of course,
also down went our mess table, as well as the two after cabins on
each side, that the tiller might have proper play. If we were put
to straits before in arranging for so large a party, what was the case
now—the tiller working from side to side and taking up fully one
half of the wardroom, leaving us the fore part only to do the best we
could ! Our captain kept at all times a handsome table and had not
only his own officers there, but also constantly officers of the squadron
wherever we chanced to be ; he was always most hospitable, and
here in our difficulty he shewed out well, inviting the colonel always
and five or six of the regiment to dine every day. I never knew a
captain more, or as liberal, at his table. My three uncles (as
captains), Sir John, Sir Thomas and Sir Edward Harvey, kept the
same table, always having there the first lieutenant, the officer and
mid. of the forenoon watch, and an idler, as the master, surgeon,
purser, and marine officer were designated, the chaplain generally,
so that there were invariably six at table. We had a very tolerable
band almost exclusively maintained by the captain, and his purse
was open on many occasions.

But again to the ship : the tiller was soon in proper management,
we took to our right course, the wind continued strong, and we made
a rapid passage, and were at Gibraltar on the fourth day. The past
two days the sea had gone down, the sun was out, the weather
warmer, and the troops began to crawl on deck, cluster on the booms
and air themselves. I could not avoid noticing the general intelli-
gence of the men ; I often talked with them, some bringing a well-
thumbed map, questioning me as to where the ship was. Our friends
were so little or rather so short a time with us, that we considered
£4 too great for their passage, and we pressed them to take back
£2 each ; they would not hear of this, but as a sort of compromise
would be greatly pleased if we let them take two of our English
sheep on shore with them. It comes across my recollection, though I
scarcely feel it worth mentioning, on the way we most unwittingly
caused great offence, and it was not easy for a time to clear ourselves.

At someone's suggestion we had a haggis on table. Some took it as a joke, they being a Scotch regiment, whereas we really, in our innocence, meant it as a compliment, and when looking for approbation became aware of their annoyance ; none touched the haggis, and we ordered it off. I was, indeed we all were, very energetic, endeavouring to soften matters, that they ought not to suppose for an instant it a joke at their expense ; in the course of time they came round, and all was as before. The principal opposer to good fellowship was a young sandy-whiskered subaltern, who was inclined to be *cantankerous* on the slightest chance.

We were well received by every regiment of the garrison, particularly by the 23rd Royal Welsh Fusiliers, and by the 42nd of course. At the 23rd mess, our mad Irish lieutenant, excited by Jack Tupper, a noted fast fellow of the regiment, mounted the long table, and amidst handsome cut glass shades, engraved with the Prince of Wales feathers and R.W.F., danced the whole length to the band's tune of ' Rule, Britannia,' without breaking a single thing. I mention this as a contrast to what took place at Lisbon a few months after.

The *Constitution* was in the bay, with the American commodore Rodgers' pennant flying.[1] There was a terrible feud between the officers of the garrison and the Americans. How it originated I did not know ; duels were frequent ; one officer, a Captain Johnson, was out three times. At last a stringent order was given for the arrest of any two or three seen together, till a satisfactory explanation was given. The last duel was fought in a boat, the principals at the bow and stern ; the seconds were on each side, making themselves, I imagine, as small as possible. There was a rather ridiculous story told us, of the reply of an American officer acknowledging the health of his commodore : ' Though I say it that should not, Commodore Rodgers is as brave a man as Julius Cæsar, and as pretty a fighter, by God ! '

We left Gibraltar for Lisbon, our future station, and where we found the *Ocean*, with the flag of Lord Amelius Beauclerk, the *Windsor Castle*, Sir Charles Dashwood, and *Genoa*, Captain Bathurst. The Portuguese Government were in some alarm of an attack on the throne, and a strong battalion of marines was sent out and distributed among the different ships. A considerable time prior to this,[2] and before an admiral took the command, there was an

---

[1] Commodore Rodgers's broad pendant was flying in the *North Carolina* ; the *Constitution* was one of his squadron (see *Commodore John Rodgers : A Biography*. By Charles Oscar Paullin. 1910).

[2] For these events of May 1824 see *The Annual Register*, 1824, pp. 181 *et seq.*

émeute, stirred up by Don Miguel, the king's second son. The king himself, Don John VI., was frightened; and without notice, for secrecy, had his barge manned for a row on the Tagus. He desired to keep out to look at the English; when discovered, the yards were manned, and a salute fired; then he suddenly pulled alongside the *Windsor Castle*, went on board and claimed the protection of Sir Charles Dashwood. In the evening his two daughters joined him. There was a great commotion on shore. Ministers and dignitaries backwards and forwards. The next day, a royal barge was coming off and in it Don Miguel making for the ship: the king kept close. Presently the prince dashed alongside; and as he was striding across the deck for the cabin, was stopped by the officer of the watch, saying that: 'No one is permitted to cross the quarter deck of a man-of-war without permission.' 'I wish to see my father, the king.' 'Very well, sir, I must report it.' The king, in a fright, refused to see him, and requested he might be made a prisoner. So Miguel was taken below, and put into the first lieutenant's cabin, with his four attendants and two bulldogs! It was said that two of these attendants were convicted felons. At stated times a lieutenant had to see that he was safe. On the first visit one of the dogs was ready to fly at him. The next officer had a pistol, ready cocked, and declared he would shoot the brute if he only shewed his teeth, and not wait for his attack. He was shut up two or three days, and then transferred to a frigate for conveyance to Trieste. She was to sail in the morning; and that night, at the king's request, our boats rowed round the ship, and such was the king's fear of his escape, that he was not satisfied till Sir Charles Dashwood himself, in his barge, also rowed guard.

It appeared a relief to all when the prince was off, and ministers begged the king to hold a grand levee at the palace. He said No, he owed his throne, and perhaps his life, to the protection of the English, and on board an English man-of-war he would hold his court. And a very grand affair it was: a throne was sent for, the quarter deck decorated, a larger accommodation ladder fitted. The whole city in a stir; splendid barges, public and private; ministers, and the whole nobility came, and such a scene was never before witnessed. Handsome presents were made to Sir Charles and Lady Dashwood. It was ill-naturedly reported that Lady Dashwood was a wee over-grasping; had expressed a wish for the king's likeness, and which, of course, could only be set with brilliants; it was said, this came to the ambassador's ears, and the upshot was, an Admiralty order came out forbidding captains having their wives and families on board their ships. Captain Ommanney had been refused, when appointed to the Lisbon station ; and it was this that interrupted the good feeling between him and Colonel Dick, of the 42nd, who wished to take his wife in the *Albion.* Captain O. did not feel inclined to have the colonel's wife when he was not permitted to have his own. When Lord Amelius hoisted his flag his first act was to bundle Lady Dashwood and Mrs Sykes on shore. I dined two or three times with Captain Sykes at his lodgings ; I do not know what made him notice me, but I think he knew Admiral Harvey. The *Windsor Castle* left in the spring of 1826.[1] We were all amused at hearing of an officer going on board the *Windsor Castle* a very foggy day, and saying, ' I thought I had lost myself, but it's all right, I see the old Head of Kinsale.' Lady Dashwood was leaning out of a front cabin window—she was a daughter of Lord Kingsale.

As I said before, a battalion of marines was sent out, and on Sundays the admiral closely inspected them on board each ship, they drawn up from the poop round the gangways, forecastle and back. I must say something of the admiral ; I had very much to do with him and, as it turned out in the end, was very much noticed by him : I greatly liked him. He was a character in many ways, in speech, dress, and bearing ; rough, abrupt, but in no way ill-natured ; very stiff in carrying out his orders, which did not always please his captains, our captain for one, for he made him kill his pigs of which we, as well as the captain, were very proud. He was a good officer, a thorough seaman, and a *close*, first-rate diplomatist, and the ambassador's right-hand man, and his advice or opinion on the disturbed state of the country carried great weight. He was short, rather stout, and his bow, with one foot forward, was *rich* ; he went to sea almost a child, just eight, which at once may account for his failing in orthography. I had three or four notes from him, no two consecutive words spelt right. For a time he lived in Lord Beresford's quinta, and one of our officers, who had never seen him, took him for the gardener, his trousers too short, one stocking down, with a whip chasing a dog off the premises. The officer burst out laughing. ' What,' said the admiral, ' did you ever see a Beauclerk that couldn't run ? ' All the Beauclerks were cricketers, his brother, Lord Frederick, in particular. Well, one Sunday, as the admiral came on deck with his queer bow, he began with, ' The

---

[1] The evidence of the Navy List is that the *Windsor Castle* left the Lisbon station in 1824 (before Boteler's arrival on the station). Captain Dashwood was relieved by Captain Downman on November 25th, 1824. Captain Dashwood was knighted at home on April 20th, 1825, having been created G.C.T.S. on March 28th, 1825.

packet is in : any letters, Captain Ommanney ? ' ' No, my lord.'
' I hear there's a new mine just discovered in South Ameriky. There
is a river called Coquimbo, and on the river is a town also called
Coquimbo, and near it a mine likewise called Coquimbo, and very
productive it is, I understand,' the last word rather raised with a
sort of grunt. Soon after this three ten-gun brigs came out from
Plymouth ; the officer, who brought out the brig I afterwards
commanded, had heard this story ; went on board the flagship
and asked, ' How is Coquimbo ? ' ' Who, sir ? '—and out it came,
and ever after that the admiral always went by the name of
Coquimbo. And when a frigate arrived from the Brazils the admiral
invited one of her lieutenants to dinner, Tom Best, son of Judge
Best (I do not know whether *then* Lord Wynford). After taking
wine he said, ' What news, Mr Best ? We look for news from ships
coming from abroad, eh ! ' ' No particular news, my lord.' ' Oh,
yes, there was some talk of a new mine lately discovered ; I forget
the exact name, Co—Co—Co—— what, *Coquimbo*, eh ? ' Those
at table had a difficulty in restraining a laugh, Tom's face perfectly
innocent. From the admiral's look and manner there was no doubt
he knew his cognomen. Tom Best and I were thought very much
alike and at our wardroom table we were pitted against each other,
the difference being only that his hair was cut short. Four years
after this, in the Gulf of Paria, Trinidad, and early in the morning,
working up to the anchorage off Porto Spain, and going alongside
the *Mersey* to pay my respects to Captain Courtney, the officers
called from her gangway, ' Hallo, Tom, have they sent you back
again ? ' Tom Best had a short time before invalided from her,
so the likeness was still carried out.

For some considerable time I had been doing the duty, in a great
measure, of first lieutenant. In a flagship, any officer, however his
standing, can be appointed first lieutenant ; not so in a private
ship, and it was very unpleasant to me. Things got so bad that the
captain threatened Molly S—— with a court-martial for incompetence unless he invalided, which he did, and the same day Johnny
Waugh, the second lieutenant, let me understand, with a laugh, my
services as a prompter were no longer required. Waugh was not
long the senior, for on Lieutenant Read invaliding, another, John
Drake, was appointed from England. Read was the one in such
bad health at Portsmouth, and supposed unable ever to go to sea
in the ship.

CHAPTER X

IN April three brigs came out, *Falcon*, *Reynard*, and *Lyra* as tenders
to the *Ocean*, *Genoa*, and *Albion*, whose captains were desired to
name the officers they considered best calculated to bring forward
and instruct the young seamen in seamanship, &c. So I was
named ; the same day I took command of the *Lyra*, with a crew of
seventy-five in all ; warrant officers, boatswain, gunner, and carpenter, came out with them ; I had a mate, three mids., assistant
surgeon, about thirty petty officers and good seamen ; the rest,
forty, the younger part of the *Albion's* crew, and there I was as a
sort of drill-sergeant. I was already pretty well up to my work,
but it is marvellous in a variety of ways how one's eyes are opened
by this sort of command, and how young mids. are brought forward
as well by the responsible duty, charge of a watch, &c., in those brigs,
knowing in a month far more than could be learned in a whole year
in a big ship. It was only three months back that I had a letter
from an admiral, then a mid. of the *Albion*, lamenting that the captain
had not sent him with me. We were anchored close in shore, and
with several merchant vessels near ; I could not sleep, but kept
awake, puzzling myself as to how I should clear them next morning.
A brig is a deep-waisted craft, and it seemed I was shut up and could
not see my way ; the change too from a big ship to so small a one
half bewildered me ; I never closed my eyes, and just at daylight I
heard a commotion, and down came a mid. : ' The ship's on fire, sir ! '
' Where ? ' ' Forward, sir, by the galley.' I jumped out ; here was
a to-do ! the men had not yet been stationed for quarters or for fire.
The fire, however, was soon put out ; it seemed that some wet clothes
had been hung by the galley fire, were drawn to the bars, caught
and set fire to some hammocks hung close by. The powder magazine
was not far off, and this at first caused a panic ; I did not so wonder
at the younger part of the crew being alarmed, but was surprised

to see, with many over the bows to escape a blow up, one of the finest of the *Albion's* seamen; he also was perfectly ashamed when I took him to task for shewing such a very bad example to the others. We had a variety of orders from the admiral for the management of the brigs, and the bringing forward of the young seamen, that we were at all times to be ready to receive him, as he should visit us on any day. He very soon sent us out for a fortnight's cruise, to run in and out of the two channels, the north and south, at least once in the twenty-four hours, shewing our number to him, to make ourselves acquainted with the entrance of the Tagus, and for our help we were to have a pilot; that he expected at the end of the fortnight we should be competent to pilot ourselves; still at any time if we felt from bad weather, or otherwise, any fear, we were at liberty at once to engage a pilot; under no circumstances did I ever take a pilot after this: I took my own soundings, made my own marks, and constructed two or three charts, and felt perfectly at home.

My first independent trip was in May to Madeira with despatches for the governor and our consul, and I never forgot the admiral's caution to put to sea if a swell set in, as I might expect bad weather to follow; for the remembrance of this caution stood my stead in after years. I did not make a good landfall, in fact, I missed the island, and was two or three days knocking about till I found it. The consul asked me to give a Mr Jenkinson a passage to Lisbon; I was quite ready, but when I began to arrange things I found it was his sister, Miss Jenkinson. This was a very different affair: it was beyond my notion altogether; a young lady, what in the world could I do with her! I had no accommodation for a lady, and I got out of it by quoting the Admiralty order I so lately mentioned; I believe after all it was only my shyness that was in the way. She was a relation of Lord Liverpool; and she told me the misery of a passage to England by a small vessel was unbearable, that she could not put her hand out of bed without touching someone, the space was so confined; and the worst was that 'Coquimbo' pitched into me. I had a pipe of madeira for the ambassador lashed on deck, and hung between the boats' davits four splendid bunches of bananas, intended for the ambassador, admiral, Captain Ommanney, and one for myself. I rather doubted one of the young mids. I had known him at Jamaica, so I said, as we started, 'Now, Master Boys, if you can't keep your hands from picking and stealing—mind! you peck at *that* bunch (mine), and don't touch the others.' He screwed up his face; a day or two after I heard the click of a carronade overhead, and knew it must be from someone stepping on it, and on looking up my skylight

I saw Boys retreating with a banana in his hand, so I sent my steward
up with my compliments, that when Mr Boys could not help taking a
banana, I hoped he would have the decency to do it when I was
not looking on. On the steward's return, ' Well ? ' ' Yes, sir, I
gave your message.' ' Well ? ' ' He turned very red in the face,
and the other young gentlemen all laughed.' Twenty or thirty
years after I had often a pull at him on this. We made a better
run back to the Tagus.

In June I had another very pleasant trip to Oporto ; from bad
weather and contrary winds it took us twelve days ; at the mouth of
the river Douro is a nasty bar, a ship may get in at once, or she
may be delayed a week, month, or even longer. The river Douro
rushes down very strong at most times, but madly after much rain.
It so happened I got in the first day. The consul was on board,
bringing two pilots and a large boat on each side with anchors and
hawsers to let go and check us clear of danger. Such a clatter the
fellows kept up all the while, and seeing me wonder the consul said
all was right when they were noisy, that they were silent enough if
in any danger. My business at Oporto was, in conjunction with the
consul, to settle some disturbance among the English merchant
seamen. From the lateness of the vintage, the ships were kept
unusually long waiting for cargoes, and having nothing to do, their
crews got into all sorts of mischief. Two that could not be brought
to reason I pressed ; three or four were imprisoned for a short time,
some admonished, but all in the end quieted. I remained five days
at Oporto, met with much attention, the Portuguese Admiral and
some notables coming to see me. Some of my men, finding they
refused to take or change their English money, went in rather a
riotous body to the palace. Despite the sentries and guard, they
would see the governor and have it out. To their utter astonishment, down came the governor, the Marquess Saldanha, one of
Wellington's colonels. ' Well, my fine fellows, what's the row ? '
The men off hats. ' Lord bless your Honour, we did not know
you'd talk to us this way ; it's these Portuguese fellows won't take
our money.' ' Oh,' said Saldanha, ' I'll manage all that,' and he
desired someone to give change for all they had, and he gave them
a glass of grog each ; all this to their intense delight, and when I
was sent for and came I found the fellows lustily cheering the
governor, who was laughing and highly amused. One day at the
Cathedral I saw a lot of hands, feet, toes and fingers in wax, hung
up as offerings or rather mementoes of cures, and among them a
little framed engraving representing a stag hunt, and at a precipice

was represented a man, the hind heels of his horse at the very edge, the body hanging beyond as if at full gallop, and overhead a full-dressed little guardian saint waving her wand, some dogs dead underneath and a *stag* at a distance, and this all arising from a man escaping a tumble over a small bank at a *hare* hunt ; but it was from the miraculous appearance of his patron saint that he was saved from destruction.

I remained in the Douro five days. The bar was up and I could not get out. I passed the time agreeably enough. Dined one day with the French consul, large party and a dance in the evening, another day with Mr Noble the English consul, meeting the governor Saldanha, admiral, chancellor and other swells. I became acquainted with a Mr Gould, who asked for a passage to Lisbon. The afternoon before sailing a boat came alongside with two large cases which I made out were Mr Gould's. I thought it all very well to give him a passage, but a little growled at carrying a lot of large baggage. When on shore, the consul said, ' So Mr Gould has sent off some wine for you.' I expressed my ignorance. ' Well,' he said, ' if it is so, you are in great luck, for to my certain knowledge he has not laid any wine in for the past ten years ' ; and it was so, two three-dozen cases of the finest old port. He breakfasted with me next day, and soon after breakfast on the day following we were in the Tagus. Such a windfall of first-rate wine was a wonderful chance. While pretty well in shore, almost every evening there was a hail, ' Boat ahoy,' and the answer, ' Aye, aye,' meaning commissioned officer. ' No, no,' is for a mid. or petty officer. The name of a ship, as *Albion*, is for a captain, and ' Flag ' for an admiral. A boat would come alongside and a lieutenant or two. ' Well, Boteler, are you for the opera to-night ? ' ' Yes, I think so.' ' Then give us a lift in your gig, will you ? ' ' Certainly ; in the meanwhile, step down till I go.' Well, great praise was generally given at the neatness of fittings, &c., and handsome turnout, and one would say, kicking the side lockers used for seats instead of chairs, ' What do you stow here, potatoes ? ' ' You know pretty well what is there. Steward,' and out would come a bottle of my prime port ; and that was one way to lessen the stock. With these officers I often dined on board their different ships, and it was an agreeable return for their hospitality.

The admiral never let the grass grow under my feet, as with the other brigs we had little rest. Always in and out and cruising outside. One day he sent the masters of the squadron to sound the entrances of the Tagus ; at another time off in a hurry to find and

recall the *Ocean*, cruising with her tender out of sight of land, and
this was in bad weather as to wind; but I came across the ship and
made signal to speak : she hove to, and as I passed near, the contrast
between an eighty-gun ship and a brig ! She seemed a castle
towering above us, and I did not know where to throw my voice,
not catching sight of her captain, who *coolly* desired me to come on
board. There was no help for it, but it was no joke, we kicking
about, our little boat risking a smash under our channels, but when
we got under her lee it was perfectly smooth water, like landing
under a rock. A whole week Captain Ommanney. took a cruise
with me, and although he was on board, ' Coquimbo ' obliged me
to run every day within the Cachops and shew my number to him,
and this, I remember : Captain Ommanney left the remainder of
his wine with me, as well as all other good things he had for our
mess. Another time I was sent to survey the Burlings, four or five
islands of rock, three or four miles off Cape Peniche. There was a
remarkable cave that I entered with my gig, disturbing myriads of
sea pigeons, puffin and bats, and I found to my surprise the cavern
went right through that point of the island. I took a succession of
accurate soundings and made a neat chart of the whole for the
admiral, and it pleased him much. Anything of this sort always
gratified him ; for this and other things I imagine was the cause
of his frequent invitations to dine. He seldom called me by my
right name when asking me to take wine. One day he pulled slowly ·
past the brig, jerking his thumb across his chest, this two or three
times. I could scarcely know what he wanted, and to my young
officers, ' What in the world does he mean ? ' All were at a loss to
conjecture. At last I said, ' Upon my word I shouldn't wonder if
he does not want me to up anchor and follow him. Well, if wrong
it is only excess of zeal. Hands up anchor,' and in a few minutes
I was after him, he quietly paddling on. As I came near a man
was under the waist netting with a coil of rope ready for his boat,
when the admiral called out, ' You'll give us a rope, won't ye ? '
and in an instant the coil was thrown, almost knocking down the
bowman of his gig. Up the side he came with, ' I said you'd understand me ; I knew you'd understand me. Hand those things up '
—one or two small hampers. ' Make sail down the Tagus, will ye ? '
—and so I had him on board till the evening, his hampers opened and
a fair dinner made up. He had some colares and lavradio, sorts of
bastard port, poor stuff for the interior, and when he got a taste of
my fine port did he not fully enjoy it and stick to it, and with no
objection to the second bottle ! He became quite cosy, and he was

most excellent company, very *queer* though. At last, full of satisfaction, he threw his heels on the locker seat. 'This is what I call
sticking the spoon in the wall.' An odd idea; I never heard it
before. He made me shave a merchant vessel too close, so much
so that my topmast studding sail boom hooked one of her braces.
One of our active topmen soon cleared it. I saw the admiral slyly
put his coat aside to exhibit his *star*, at which the merchant captain
lifted his hat, although just before I expected he was on the point
of exclaiming at our running foul of him. I felt quite at home with
the admiral; he was absolutely complimentary; still I was not
sorry when we parted. I might at any time get a bear's hug.

I frequently, as time went on, dined with the admiral, as also
with Captains Ommanney, Sykes and Bathurst. In those days a
captain's dinner hour was three o'clock. On one of these occasions
Captain Ommanney said, 'Come, Boteler, we will have a run down
the Tagus with you,' and it was up anchor in no time, and I had
them on board till our return at ten. It gave me an opportunity
to produce two bottles of my prime port, which they much appreciated, but what pleased me most was the handsome compliments
paid me by Captain Ommanney on my management of the brig.
For some reason that no one could make out the admiral was in a
horrid bad temper, quarrelling with everyone and finding fault at all
things. He called alongside with many questions as to our readiness for sea, and leaving two cases of liqueurs with me, but with no
address, I fancy for Cadiz or England. The next day the secretary,
Harry Munro, my messmate some years back, hinted England
to me.

To show how *close* the admiral was, I dined with Captain
Ommanney, who felt annoyed at the admiral's sending me off
without telling him, and he said there was no fear of my moving,
as the ambassador intended waiting for another packet from England
before taking action. While at tea *Lyra's* signal made ' Prepare
to weigh,' and mine to ' go on board the flagship.' There I received
orders for Falmouth or Plymouth, whichever I could easiest make,
to take despatches from the ambassador, to tell no one and to take
no letters. I was off in no time, and had not gone far when a signal
from the *Albion* to pick up a boat which I saw pulling after me;
I answered the signal of course, but continued on; the signal was
then repeated with a gun—my reply being, ' Am charged with
despatches,' and out I went to sea under all sail. The Falmouth
packet *Marlborough*, Captain Bull, started at the same time; we
were in company two days and I dined with him; he was the same

who got such a setting down from Captain King when I was present two years back ; as the wind headed us I beat her much, crawling dead to windward of her ; we made a tolerable passage though rather a lengthy one. Our navigation was made easy, Captain Ommanney having lent me the ship's chronometer, a first-rate watch ; years back they were not supplied by Government, and but very few captains owned one. The best London makers sent yearly a certain number to the Observatory, Greenwich, to be tested and rated ; the best performers would get the Government reward of £300 and the chronometer taken for the navy. So ours were all prize watches, our reckoning was perfect to a mile. I ran with a strong breeze past the Eddystone light, and right into Plymouth Sound, landed with my despatches to the admiral's office. And here I was greatly surprised at the flag lieutenant, from Lady Saumarez, asking me in to luncheon and at her apologising, not asking me to dine as they were engaged elsewhere ; but that the admiral would be glad of my company next day, and that there would be a dance in the evening. Well, I thought, it must be something to come with an ambassador's despatches, for in no other way could I account for such marked attention, I only a lieutenant. The next day at dinner, on Sir James's right, he asked me if I was at all related to Captain Philip Boteler, &c.[1] However, three years after this, the cat was out of the bag ! When at Portsmouth in the *Royal George* yacht and commanding the *Onyx*, I was honorary member of the *Victory's* mess, her chaplain asked if I dined with them that day. ' No, I dine with Dr Thomson (the yacht's surgeon) at Southsea.' ' When were you asked ? ' ' Yesterday ! ' ' Ah ! ' said he, ' you take my place ; well, I owe you a dinner. You remember coming to Plymouth with despatches from Lisbon. I was with Commissioner Shield at the dockyard. " There's young *Beauclerk* [2] in the Sound, I have just sent my barge off to ask him to dine." " Beauclerk ! Commissioner, his name is Boteler." " What, what ! " said Billy Shield, " here, messenger, run down to the King's stairs and stop my boat." ' So there it was, Sir James and Lady Saumarez evidently took my name to be Beauclerk, coming too as I did from Lord A. Beauclerk. What's in a name ! Had Billy Shield been aware I was a Harvey Boteler, he would have

<hr>

[1] Captain Philip Boteler (Captain March 26th, 1762), of whom there is a notice in Charnock's *Biographia Navalis*, Vol. VI. In extenuation of Saumarez's interest, it should be noted that having recorded Boteler's dismissal from the service, Charnock concludes : ' we consequently have no farther information concerning him, nor do we even know whether he be now [1798] living or not '.

[2] ' Young Beauclerk ' was Lord Frederick, then only a midshipman. He became a Lieutenant in 1828.

known he owed me a dozen dinners to one as a Beauclerk, for like
Captain Ommanney he was made both commander and post captain
by Sir Henry Harvey,[1] and was most intimate with my uncle Sir
John Harvey, calling each other by their Christian names, and very
often staying at each other's houses. At Lisbon I had scraped the
brig's copper with two anchors coming up with our own and was
put into a dock for twenty-four hours, a little copper only torn off.
While waiting for orders from the Admiralty, I was receiving a
variety of boatswain's stores for the Lisbon squadron, all very
weighty, coils of rope, several hawsers from five to ten inch, bolts
of canvas, and for the stowage of these I had to strike four guns
into the hold, and then the commissioner came down and proposed
I should take the *Ocean's* bower cable as well, a twenty-five inch
fellow. I said, ' Impossible, sir.' ' Impossible ! there is no such
word in the service.'[2] ' Very well, sir, all I can say then, is, that
200 men cannot put it on board, unless you allow me to go alongside
the sheer hulk and have the brig's masts taken out, and after all
the brig would never swim with it.' He did not like it as I spoke
out, but it was not attempted.

The Admiralty orders arrived and I started ; I never before
knew the feeling of an overloaded vessel, as she lifted *heavily* to the
least sea, one's feet seemed glued to the deck. It was sensibly
felt by all on board ; I was never quite satisfied with myself for not
reporting it. Still, with important despatches I feared to make a
difficulty, and so I went on, and when clear of the Land's End,
meeting some swell, the brig seemed to feel the overweight so much
that I up helm and ran back for Falmouth, intending to get rid of
some of the dead weight and start afresh ; but in an hour's time
the wind suddenly chopped round fair ; so I took the hint and again
turned round. The weather kept fine, and on the seventh day ran
into the Tagus ; the admiral laughed with a growl at the authorities
of Plymouth Dockyard expecting I could take the *Ocean's* cable.
At Plymouth six of my men deserted ; the admiral did not blame
me ; Captain Ommanney was out of countenance, though he
said but little. At Plymouth I was greatly gratified at hearing
of my brother Thomas's promotion to commander: he richly
deserved it.[3]

[1] For the services of Commissioner Shield, see Marshall's *Royal Naval Biography*,
II, 89–91. Boteler seems to be mistaken in attributing Shield's advancement to
Sir Henry Harvey.

[2] Cf. *The Sailor's Word-Book*, by Admiral W. H. Smyth (1867) : ' IMPOSSIBLE :
A hateful word, generally supplanted among good seamen by ' we'll try'.

[3] Dated September 30th, 1826.

But to the Tagus: there was another scare with the royal family,[1] and 600 or 800 marines were landed in the boats of the squadron and took up their quarters near the Adjeuda Palace, and at first the *Falcon* and then the *Lyra* was anchored near them as the medium of messages to the flagship; a table was kept for the officers, about fourteen, by the palace. I being in attendance was one of the party, and a famous set out it was, both in dinners and liberal supply of wine. The head servant was very clever with the table napkins: for many days he contrived to fold every one different, cocked hats, boats, swans, fans, stars, crescents, moons, sun-flowers and other strange shapes. To be ready in case of emergencies, the big ships were spread, *Albion* at anchor below Belem Castle; one day the admiral sent for me merely to say he should not want me, and soon after made my signal to weigh, to carry a letter to Captain Ommanney. I was engaged to dine with Captain Bathurst, and in returning, to save time made too short a cut and all at once found myself fast in the *mud*! The tide running down like a sluice, there was no help for it; I made signal for assistance, down top-gallant masts, topmasts and lower yards, cleared the booms and got all spare masts, yards, &c., over the sides lashed all round her, as shores, and she fortunately stood perfectly upright; boats from the squadron were speedily alongside, guns and shot were taken away by the *Albion's* boats, and we started our water to lighten the brig. Admiral came alongside only to ask if we wanted anything, and made no row; also Admiral May, the Portuguese admiral, with two launches to assist if required, and the *Genoa's* boats laid out our anchor in eight fathoms, and the *Falcon* anchored near us for the night. Captain Ommanney was on board two hours, so we were neither in want of assistance or attention. Paddy Norcott, our master, White, and Douney dined with me, and before midnight we floated and hauled into deep water, and as a wind-up spliced the mainbrace.

I got into the admiral's especial good graces by merely a chance trick. He always had something to keep the brigs moving, more for the sake of exercising the young hands than anything else, and he had a signal of four flags 'Brigs to weigh, run down the Tagus, exercise and return at sunset.' I was always up early, and one morning I noticed the admiral in his dressing gown in the stern gallery. I jumped off the poop and watched him with my glass through the chink of a port, and I saw him eyeing the brigs, and

<hr>

[1] King John VI of Portugal died March 10th, 1826. For the consequent unrest, see *The Annual Register*, 1826, chapter xii.

then pull at a bell rope ; I suspected mischief, and 'Swabs aft, dry
the deck quick, men ; carpenters ship the capstan bars, pass the
messenger, unbit the cable and bring to '—all smartly done, and, as I
conjectured, an officer appeared, took some order from the admiral,
and directly four flags were on their way to the mast-head, and
though rolled up as flags always are, I had been long enough as
signal mid. and lieutenant to make out their colours, so up went my
answering pennant also in a ball, and when their stops were broken,
my pennant also showed out, and 'Hands up anchor,' and round
went the capstan merrily to our song—

> 'Green grow the Rushes O, Green grow the Rushes O,
> The parson kissed the tinker's wife all among the Rushes O ! '

—the men breaking out with the words, they were so pleased at my
method of getting such a start over their rivals the other brigs ; and
it was a start, we were under all sail long before their anchors were
out of the ground. It soon fell calm and the three were together,
but the wind got up again and became fresh up the river, and here
we had our second victory. We first beat the *Falcon*, and then the
Reynard, and we had barely managed this when my recall was
made and a signal to dine with the admiral ; they told me he said
nothing till after breakfast, and then while watching us he broke
out : ' I'll teach those young fellows what they are about ; if one
brig can answer my signal as smartly as the *Lyra*, I'll let the others
know they shall do the same or I'll have the reason why.' And at
dinner, after as usual asking me to take wine as Mr Boutly, or perhaps
Boughly ! ' I don't know what those two young fellows were about
this morning : I'll teach them to be more on the look out.' I never
told any one of my spying the admiral and seeing his preparation
for our signal. Lapidge [1] of the *Falcon* never alluded to it. But
little Worth [2] of the *Reynard* was at me more than once ; he was a
smart officer in many ways and was always jealous of me and my
brig. ' How do you manage, Boteler, to get your anchor up and off
so soon ? I consider I can work the *Reynard* as well and as smartly
as anyone, and I don't understand it.' Precisely the same thing
happened in every way two or three months later, and the admiral
had both the other officers on board, not at all sparing in language.
Captain Ommanney also talked to me about it, commenting freely
on my smartness, when, not liking so much blame bestowed on the
other brigs, I let it all out, to his great amusement, more particularly

[1] Lapidge belonged to the *Ocean*, from which the *Falcon* was manned.
[2] Worth belonged to the *Genoa*, from which the *Reynard* was manned.

as he thought the admiral was hoodwinked by it and annoyed at his own lieutenant being so much beaten.

Captain Ommanney was never on very good terms with the admiral, and he more than once had me in his cabin to talk over some order that displeased him. I tried to get him to put a better face on it, and though he would not see the order other than with repugnance, I had reason to know he was pleased with my softening the matter. I merely mention this as shewing the confidence he had in me, and I think I have reason to be proud of all this. He was stern and forbidding in his manner, but for two and a-half years that I sailed with him I never but once had an angry word from him, and that was undeserved, as he found out. We were in company with the *Asia*, Sir Edward Codrington, and the *Genoa*, working between the Island of Chios and the main. I had the middle watch, with orders to let the captain know whenever we went about. He had before desired me to tell him when I relieved the deck, as he could then sleep. He was very tired as I was aware. I had twice acquainted him that we had tacked. It fell calm, and the ship of herself went round and round, which I thought not necessary to disturb him about, and then as the breeze came on I called to tell him the pilot wished to go round. ' What tack is she on ? ' ' Starboard, sir.' ' What is the reason you have not told me of her going round ? ' ' She did so of herself, sir, during a calm, two or three times, and I did not like to disturb you as the ship in no way had neared the shore.' He was very angry, followed me on deck, and severely reprimanded me before all the watch. He asked me to breakfast next morning out of my turn : I had a headache. I was invited to dine the same day and again made an excuse. The following day he once more asked me to dine. He evidently was making the ' amende,' and I could no longer decline ; particularly in the service it is an act of duty to dine when asked, and he received me so kindly and made himself so agreeable that I quite forgave him, but I had felt very much hurt indeed.

About the end of October, the *Lyra* was sent out for fourteen days' cruise under the orders of the *Falcon*. Great surf on the bar, by no means a pleasant sight, and though we once pitched the bowsprit in the crest of the sea the tide carried us out. The *Falcon* missed stays twice ; we never did. Lapidge one day made signal to try rate of sailing : to my surprise she beat us. I suspected we were out of trim, and by moving several fathoms of chain cable forward we at once came up with him, and then could spare him top-gallant sails, and, under all circumstances after, retained a de-

170

cided advantage. After a week the *Falcon* was recalled, and we too, soon.

November 25th,[1] while dining with the admiral, and after his usual odd way of taking wine with me, ' Are you ready for sea, sir ? ' —'All ready, my lord.' ' Provisions and water complete ? '—' Yes, sir.' ' Young gentlemen all on board ? '—' Yes, my lord ; it would not do to let them on shore in sight of your flag.' *A grunt!* ' I want you to go to England after dinner.'—'May I make her signal to prepare for sea ? ' ' No, you told me you were all ready.'—' So I am, my lord.' Another grunt. ' The ambassador's despatches will be here soon, when you will be off ; no word to anyone '; and when the bag did come he sent me to the brig in his own gig. When alongside, ' Up boats ' : all started and turned to look at me. ' Hands up anchor ' : then another inquisitive look, and while heaving round, ' What's in the wind, sir ; not for England ? '—' Yes.' ' All my linen at the wash.'—' More goose you ; I always told you never to do this.' But off we were, and reached Plymouth in half a gale of wind, after a rather quick passage, ran at once into Hamoaze, and gave the bags up at the admiral's office, a little surprised at my getting in in such weather. The despatches were of great import-ance ; in twenty-four hours of their receipt in London the Guards were on their march to embark in one of the guard ships for the Tagus, as well as some other regiments, and I received Admiralty orders to hold myself in momentary readiness to take back despatches, and I was sent into the Sound for that purpose.

The guard ships at the different ports were in a great state of commotion, the *Windsor Castle* in particular ; most of her officers married men, little expecting to be disturbed. She was ordered to take the 60th Rifles, and well knowing the help I could be to them, I went on board and explained all that was necessary in carrying troops. They were most thankful, but only two officers could well attend ; the others seemed beside themselves at the sudden move, worried with the visits of tradesmen and others, creating greater confusion. I dined with a regiment of the garrison, and then met Jack Tupper, of the 23rd, who were ordered to Lisbon from Gibraltar. I was quite glad to give him a passage to the Tagus, and had all his baggage sent me next morning. The *Windsor Castle* was sent into the Sound, and the 60th Regiment was em-barked. The ship's lower deck guns were sent to the gun wharf, and the powder hoys alongside at the same time the regiment was embarking, and as a matter of course all fires were put out, and no

---

[1] 1826.

breakfast could be prepared. I went on board, and seeing the confusion she was in, sent back for forty-five of my crew to assist,—a
ten-gun brig helping a 74 ! I found the 6oth's officers huddled
together in the wardroom ; nothing to eat or likely to get till the
evening. With the hands from my brig I hoisted in Colonel Bun-
bury's horses—beautiful animals. He a heavy stout fellow. It
seems strange that another ship's officer should be doing this—but
it was well I did ! The men were catching the horses by their tails,
to ' *steer* ' them into the ship, they lashing out, and serious mischief
might have occurred had I not been there. The *Windsor Castle's*
officers never interposed, they were too much occupied with their
own private affairs. I never could imagine such confusion and
consequent inattention to duty. Seeing no chance of dinner in her
till late, I invited Tupper and a friend to have dinner with me.
Tupper could not go with me, having received orders from the
Horse Guards to embark in the *Windsor Castle* ; and so they both
dined with me, and at seven, when I took them back, the wardroom
was then only just sitting down to the first meal of that day. The
Windsor Castle sailed. There was little chance of much comfort for
the soldiers. I can in no way understand the repugnance of the
ship's officers to the military ones messing with them. At such a
time it seems to me a bounden duty, to use no other word, to make
soldier passengers comfortable at any inconvenience it may be to
ourselves. How different we acted in the *Antelope* and *Albion*, and
how ample was the repayment. We gained the good opinion of
the two regiments, 25th and 42nd, and of the whole garrison at
Gibraltar.

In two or three days despatches from the Secretary of State
came down and we sailed for Lisbon. We had a quick passage of
six days, and running down the coast of Portugal with a fair wind,
I steered so as to pass fully fifteen miles clear of the Birlings. The
Apollo frigate, Captain Dixon, with forty-four sail of her convoy,
was wrecked in that neighbourhood during a gale, right on shore, it
was said in consequence of an indraft ; I do not credit this, still such
was the received opinion.[1] An uncle (afterwards Admiral Sir
Edward Harvey) was one of her lieutenants and escaped on a raft
to the shore and then, by manning some merchant ships' boats,
helped to save several of the crew, though over 120 were drowned.
Bearing all this in mind I kept well out, and twice during the night
had the log board brought down to work up the brig's place, and I

---

[1] For the wreck of the *Apollo* (Captain J. W. T. Dixon) on April 2nd, 1804, see
James's *Naval History of Great Britain* (1886 edition), III, 261–4.

repeated a caution to the officer of the watch to keep a good look
out and call me if required ; that the rocks would appear as four
or five ships under all sail. I kept awake and heard the officer call
'Keep a good look out there forward.' 'Aye, aye, sir.' Then,
'Keep your eyes open there.' 'Eye, eye, sir ' ; and directly after
'Three ships right ahead, sir.' I jumped on deck, and we absolutely ran inside of them ! It was of no consequence, I had recently
surveyed them and knew every inch of ground.

We soon rounded Cape Roca and in smooth water, at daylight
began to thoroughly holystone the decks ; there was an outcry from
young Faber's cabin. I had not seen his face since we started. A
quartermaster went to enquire the matter and came to me laughing :
'The young gentleman fancied the ship was on shore on the rocks,
sir.' The fact was he had just got asleep as we were in smooth
water, and having heard my direction about the Birlings, and
probably dreaming of the rocks, was suddenly woke up by the
grinding noise of the big holystones over his head, and so fancied
we were grinding on those rocks.

I ran up the Tagus, and just as my boat returned with pratique
from the quarantine office at Belem Castle, a gun was fired from the
flagship. 'Hallo, what's that ? ' Our signal to assist ship in distress
with compass pendant N.W., and looking round, to my great
surprise, there was a line-of-battle ship on shore at the mouth of
the river. I made all sail and was soon alongside, and stepped over
her launch about to lay out an anchor. I asked the name of the
ship—'The *Spartiate*, sir '—and ran up the side ; said to the first
lieutenant I was sent down by the signal to assist, and was ready
to offer any advice the captain would be pleased to accept. 'Captain
Warren is on the poop, sir.' I then said the same to him, also that
I considered myself a perfect pilot for the Tagus, and was ready to
offer any advice he was pleased to take. 'Repeat that, sir,' which I
did ; and 'Then I put the ship into your hands, sir.' I was a little
taken aback at the moment, still felt confidence in myself. I first
noticed her position ; she was on shore on the middle ground
between the two Cachops, striking heavily at times, her deck waving
from cabin to forecastle like a maggot's back ; topgallant masts
struck, topsails sheeted home but down, all perfectly quiet and not
the slightest confusion. Her master was sounding some distance
to the south, the anchor was dropped in the direction I wished, and
I asked that the capstan should be manned and a good strain put
on it. The master by this time had returned and reported more
water on the port bow, and that the anchor was in the wrong place.

I said, ' Yes, sir, but there is less water beyond his sounding.'
Captain Warren merely said, ' Do as this officer desires,' and I asked
if the ship could be made a little lively by sending the crew with a
rush from one side to the other by the boatswain's pipe. I was
surprised myself at the effect it had. As she rolled over she gave a
jump, and with my own distant marks I saw she made a slight
move. I desired the spanker and after sails to be set, and a continued strain kept at the capstan ; over an hour at this work when,
after a jump or two, the ship moved and reached her anchor. I
called out, ' Cut, sir, if you please.' Both first lieutenant and
master exclaimed, ' We can save the anchor, sir.' Captain Warren
again quietly said, ' Do as this officer desires.' The cable was cut
and, with the after sail to help, she turned up the river, and I remarked to the captain it was too nice a time to hesitate, that had
she checked the wrong way nothing could have saved the ship.
Indeed, as it was, the *Spartiate* was one of the few ships that ever
got off that dangerous shoal. Two pilots were on board, and it
appeared in attempting the northern passage, close under Fort St
Julian, their courage failed and they ran the ship on shore in trying
to cross over to the south channel ; keeping well to windward, I
steered by my own marks, much inside the usual ones. One of the
pilots seized me by the arm saying something I did not understand,
but a passenger, Colonel Ward, assistant quarter-master-general,
and who knew the language : ' He says, sir, you are running the
ship on shore again.' ' What is that ? ' said Captain Warren ; ' tell
him if he again speaks I will hang him at the yard-arm—I have a
mind to do so now.' They both retreated and never came near me
afterwards. By this time we were in the usual track and in the
fair way, and I asked to go on board my brig. ' No, sir ; you must
keep charge till you anchor the ship ! ' Here, to me, was a dilemma :
I had been so long in the little brig that I felt at some loss how to
take an eighty-gun ship to her berth, and I had actually taken her
too much in shore, and only just contrived to start her into deeper
water and let go the anchor, run out two whole cables and let go
the other, and then to the first lieutenant, ' You may now moor
her,' and my charge was over. Captain Warren sent for me to his
cabin, shook hands, thanking me for my services with handsome
compliments on my skill as an officer, seaman, and pilot. It was
a memorable event in my sea life. No captain ever likes to refer
to getting his ship ashore ; but had Captain Warren stated the
circumstance to the Admiralty and the part I played in getting her
off, there is no doubt but I should have gained my promotion. He
174

was on board the flagship before I reported myself, and I was startled at the admiral with other commendation saying 'I had anchored in the exact place he had desired by his flag lieutenant ! ' This was only a lucky chance ; no flag lieutenant had been near me, he had been waiting at the south side of the Tagus in the usual track of large ships.

The *Windsor Castle* had already arrived, had disembarked the Rifles and had left for Gibraltar to bring the 23rd Fusiliers ; the next day the men-of-war boats took the Guards to the block-house square led by the flag lieutenant [1] in the *Ocean's* gig. It was an attractive and imposing sight their forming up in the square, the regiment's splendid drum and fife band playing the while. I had never seen these bands, and was much charmed with the stirring and agreeable music ; drums of different sizes, as also fifes, flutes and piccolos. The King's mind seemed much relieved by the arrival of the troops ; he was always pleased to see the captains of the squadron, as also the lieutenants ; three or four of us would occasionally call at the palace, and he made a point of seeing and making us welcome. One day, Captain Ommanney invited me to a walk on the south side of the Tagus. I had that morning a letter from Dr Griffiths, and among other news said it was reported I was to be first lieutenant with Captain Kearney White, and on my mentioning this to the captain—' Yes, hang him, he wrote to me to let you go.' It was strange that I never heard anything of the matter till then.

I scarcely know how to enter on the subject of the abominable filthy state of the streets of Lisbon ; the rise and fall is such, so hilly, as to admit of the most complete sewerage, which, excepting in a few streets, was only on the surface—every description of filth thrown or rather emptied into the streets, and no other scavengers than dogs ; and these dogs, the ugliest of all brutes, are numerous, have their own districts, and take care that no strange dogs intrude ; during the day they are stretched lazily at full length and seldom move aside for any person, at night they are lively enough, rushing about. Returning late from the opera, in a hurry to reach our boat, it would be dangerous to move beyond a walk ; an attempt at a run, a whole pack would be at your heels ; I have stopped short and with a back stroke of my sword endeavoured to hit them —they generally eluded me ; I once only succeeded, and then such a yell. I have known a dead horse to remain in a street two whole days before being removed ; in the main streets it was requisite

[1] Lord Amelius Beauclerk's Flag Lieutenant was Lieutenant M. M. Wroot.

to walk in the middle at night. I do not say in the streets, that inattention to common decency went so far; but in the outskirts barely 200 yards off, three or four of us were walking to attend an afternoon party at the postmaster's, Sir Edward S., when from a hole in a blind wall six or eight feet overhead out burst a cascade of sewage: all escaped but our unlucky first lieutenant, who was obliged to turn back; we were cruel enough to wonder if the scavenger dogs would be after him. We were told that the city was in a far worse state before the French had possession in 1808, when Marshal Junot set them at work in cleansing the streets. In the centre of a small square was a beautiful column about twenty to twenty-five feet high (a figure at the top); the shaft was spiral, the pedestal on a flight of four steps, and till the French occupation, two of these steps only were apparently above ground, the whole of the square being covered with hardened refuse, the accumulation of years.

I was sent up the Tagus to Santarem, there to wait for the admiral. Having a day to spare, in company with one of my mids., Graham Gore (who, when a captain, perished with Franklin in the Polar Seas), rode across the isthmus to St Ubes or Setuval, famous for its extensive production of salt. I well remember the delicious fragrance while riding through a large fir plantation, and the crackling of the cones by the heat of the sun. Returning from St Ubes, and not far out, we met a string of mules, loaded, and on the two last a woman and children; the muleteers by their side. They said something that we could not understand; but hearing an out-cry, on looking back, we saw two fellows with poles beating them. As we supposed, they had imagined they had warned us of them. For they followed us, evidently with no good intent; and I am half ashamed to say that two of His Majesty's officers felt ' retreat was the better part of valour.' We had no weapon, nothing beyond a switch, and could stand no chance against their poles, that they are noted to use with great dexterity, and with which they could easily knock us off our horses. So we put them to a canter; they were but sorry nags, and in the deep sandy road soon began to flag; we therefore pulled up to a walk. Our pursuers came up gradually, and when very near, we made another spurt forward, and the same thing two or three times, when they suddenly changed their course, as I fancied, to cut us off. We therefore changed ours, and in time, for we saw them at a point where we should have been, had we continued on as we had intended. The fellows gave a shout as we passed, and gave up the chase.

At this time St Julian's was garrisoned by marines with Captain
Ommanney as governor. One day I was sent down to bring back
the admiral, Captain Warren, Harry Munro (the secretary), and
flag lieutenant, who were dining with the 'governor.' I also was
at the dinner. In due time, the admiral was for moving; but the
governor said another bottle of claret would do no harm, and
Captain Warren remarked that I was passing the bottle rightly, to
keep my head clear as their pilot. The admiral's and my gig were
at the landing place, and as his gig was outside, the admiral desired
two of my young crew to carry him to his boat, and as they began
to stagger under his weight, he called out, ' Come, come, none of
that ! ' he thinking they were about to succumb under him, and they
said afterwards they nearly did so. The brig was under weigh ; I
reached her first, jumped on board, and veered the gig astern ; the
admiral soon followed, and as he stepped on deck desired me to
make sail, and we had only to fill the main topsail when the brig
gathered ahead, not taking half the time a large ship does. I
heard a scuffle on the poop and there was the admiral and quarter-
master endeavouring to free his gig which had got across mine and
run over, two of the admiral's men in her drifting astern; we instantly
hove to and sent the gig off to tow the swamped one back, but we
drifted faster than she could tow. I told the admiral I could pick
them up. ' Well, have your own way then ! '—so I filled, made a
tack, and again round and got hold of both and prepared, by his
desire, to hoist his gig in. All this time we were drawing towards
the other side. I said, ' Go about, my lord, if you please.' ' Don't
you be in a hurry, sir ' : we were then trying to hook her on by the
stern ring, but could not get hold of it, and no wonder—the gig was
cut in halves and the other half gone. I again called out, ' Go
about ' ; ' Not yet, sir.' ' By George, she'll be on shore ! ' and sure
enough, up she went on the beach and no mistake ; and now was
more bustle. We had to hoist our own large boat out to carry our
anchor and hawser astern to help her off, for there was just a quarter-
of-an-hour more flood, and in that time we floated her off and let go
our anchor in deeper water ; on going aft and talking to the quarter-
master, he told me the admiral wanted him to cut my boat's painter
when it was too late, and had he done so he would have cut the
admiral's knuckles ! When I said something to the admiral he
replied, ' Had you an axe, sir, I could have saved all the mischief.'
' Here's one,' I said, ' close to,' holding it up to him. ' Who is to
know your stow holes ? '—who indeed ! But whenever I have had
the ordering I always had an axe hung up for emergencies. Well,

we remained snug for the night. I offered the admiral supper. 'No, thank ye ; but if you have a glass of claret I shall be obliged, to wash the cobwebs out of my throat.' The admiral turned into my bed, and thinking he might wake up at daylight I drew a tarpaulin over the skylight, put a swab on the bull's-eyes over the bed-place and also stuffed oakum in the keyhole. At the first of the flood it was up anchor with as little noise as possible, and I then thought to give the admiral some light and desired the tarpaulin to be partially moved off ; not fancying it enough, desired the quartermaster to pull off more, but the admiral, expecting another covering up, called out : ' No more of that, I've had enough of that,' no doubt fully alive to all our schemes ! I heard Captain Warren say, ' It was no fault of young Boteler.' I breakfasted with the admiral, who was very gracious.

About the last week in April I was once more sent off with despatches from the ambassador, and desired by the admiral in a private note to give Dr Ward, surgeon of the Grenadier Guards, and his servant a passage to England. On nearing the Cachops the tide turned, and as the wind was against us we could not beat out, and were obliged to anchor in Passo d'Arcos Bay, and as the tide again turned we attempted to weigh, but the chain cable had got foul of a rock and we could not get the anchor ; we unshackled, buoyed the end of the chain and sent a report to the admiral with cross bearings of the anchor and made sail. The wind had freshened, and meeting a strong ebb, a considerable broken swell was raised on the bar, the brig several times pitching the bees of the bowsprit into the curl of the surf, and making the top-gallant mast fairly tremble : I could not help an exclamation of ' Hang it,' ' Hold on,' or something like it, when the doctor caught hold of my arm by way of remonstrance or reproof. This to the commander of a man-of-war, though small, and in face of all hands was a trifle over the mark, and I directly desired him to go below ; and when clear outside, went to the cabin to look at the chart. The doctor began to apologise, 'At such a time, sir——' I said, ' The fact was you were frightened '—which he *clinched* by allowing he did offer up a prayer for his wife and children. ' And for yourself too, I suppose '—I had no patience with him. This did not interrupt companionship and good understanding between us, but I never could imagine a gentle-man in his position, a surgeon of such a regiment, to shew so much ignorance on various subjects of everyday occurrence ; in history, geography or science, it was all the same. One evening in the cabin, two or three of the young mids. with us, we were talking of
178

the compass and the wonder how the Romans found their way over
to Carthage, if at sea two or three days through an adverse wind.
'Yes,' said the doctor, 'how puzzled Julius Cæsar must have been
finding himself out of sight of land when he invaded Great Britain !'
A laugh from one of the young mids., echoed by the other, made the
doctor fancy he had made some mistake, and that was all. We had
an exceedingly pleasant passage as far as smooth water and moderate
winds went, though, just after striking soundings seventy-six fathoms
near the Scilly Islands, we ran into a thick fog, but the soundings
continued so regular and the arming of the lead showed so clearly
our position that I went on, till I made sure we were close to the
Lizard. I went over the side, hanging on by a man rope, looked
under the fog, and saw the surf breaking on the Lizard Point.
'A gun ready forward.' 'All ready, sir.' 'Fire !' and thud, the
deadened sound of a gun in a fog. Directly after, ' Ship ahoy, you
wants we ? ' and alongside came a Scilly pilot, glad to exchange
his potatoes and fish for our rum, biscuit and money. He could not
tell us more of the Lizard than I knew myself. We went on till
we turned for Falmouth, cautiously feeling our way with the lead, a
hand in both chains calling the soundings. ' By the deep nine.'
' And a half eight.' ' By the mark eight,' and so on, for the fog
was more dense than ever. The pilot said, ' No occasion for the lead,
sir: I know where we are, sir.' I replied, ' I never fully trust anyone,
and good-bye to my commission if anything goes wrong and no lead
going.' And so we went on, under topsails only, gradually shoaling
the water to six and five fathoms, when a man forward, ' Right
overhead, sir, a castle, sir.' Let go the anchor, for the pilot could
not say on which side of the entrance it was, and he wanted to take
his boat to find out ; but I ignored this, and sent him in my boat,
thinking he might be off and leave us in the lurch. In the meanwhile, I went below to look at the chart, and there I found the
doctor pulling on his boots, ready, as he said, to go on shore. He
imagined, by hearing all going on on deck, that we were in the
harbour ! I don't recollect the name of the castle, but it was the
one on the right hand side, and we up anchor, and were stretching
to the other side, and I said, ' Well, pilot ? ' ' Not yet, sir,' when
a man again hailed, ' There is another, sir, right overhead.' ' What
are you about, pilot ? ' ' Oh, sir, you overruns *we*.' The fact was
he had been more used to merchant vessels, and we had slipped
through the water faster than he thought, and we anchored. The
doctor asked to be landed, and seemed most happy to get out of
the brig and clear of all the *risks* he had encountered ; but he was

cunning enough to ask me to take his servant and baggage to
Plymouth. I then went to Captain King, still in charge of the
packet service. Surprised at again seeing me so unexpectedly,
' Why, where are you from ? ' ' Lisbon, sir.' ' But I mean, how
did you find your way in such a fog ? It is more than some of our
packets will do.' ' We must not hang back with despatches.'
' What ! despatches, sir ; you should have said so at first,' this in
a sharp voice, and a quick ring, answered by his coxswain. ' Here,
take this bag at once to the " Royal," and see it sent off without
delay by special messenger ' ; and there ended the officer, and I had
a long talk with him, Mrs King and daughters. I could not wait
to dine. The fog a little cleared, and I was away again for Plymouth,
reaching next afternoon, and remaining eight or ten days till more
despatches came down from the Foreign Office.

Once more off for the Tagus. During a calm, rainy day off Cape
Finisterre we came upon several turtles, and caught many asleep on
the surface. With the log of my proceedings I had to furnish the
admiral with a track chart of our passage ; and to note the place
where the turtles were taken, I sketched one ; and a lieutenant of
the *Albion*, who was on board before we anchored, very cleverly
turned it into a caricature of the admiral, with his broad gold laced
coat, helped by the divisions of the turtle's shell, with his short arms
and legs and small head, and in that state I took it to the admiral.
But Harry Munro, the secretary, caught sight of it in time. I have
this chart by me now, with the turtle sketch on it.

Long before this time the 23rd Fusiliers were brought from
Gibraltar in the *Windsor Castle,* and a most uncomfortable passage
they had in consequence of the ship's officers declining to have
them in the wardroom mess. It seems to me inconceivable that
any naval officer could make any objection to a joint mess. The
excuse of being put to inconvenience, even if great, would be paltry
indeed. What a contrast to our arrangement with a regiment in
the *Antelope* and *Albion*. But so it was. The 23rd were put to
the expense of purchasing all mess requisites, and to mess by themselves in the gunroom, a deck under the wardroom, and when at
sea often with the lower deck ports barred in. There consequently
was little cordiality between the ship and regiment, whose officers
declined the dinner invitation of the captain. The Admiralty
certainly leave it to the option of the ship's officers as to taking the
military to their mess. When the army left Lisbon and marched
into the country the regiments broke up their general mess to mess
by companies, and the day before, the 23rd had a large party at
180

dinner. It was rather a wild and noisy to-do, and Paddy Norcott was *persuaded* (?) to mount and march down the table to the tune of 'Rule, Britannia' as before at Gibraltar ; but the tables of a Portuguese barrack were not as substantial as ours, in fact were made up by four or five Pembroke tables, one of which gave way, and down came Paddy on me, reducing my chair to splinters, all ending in a general smash of bottles and glasses. One wineglass alone escaped, and this I secured, and in a day or two after engraved on it the whole scene : table giving way, Norcott falling on me, and a dragoon officer with his lace-barred shell jacket at the head of the table. Three or four of us slept on mattresses on the floor of an adjoining room, tormented by myriads of *fleas*. The engraved wineglass I was keeping as a memento of that parting dinner. The 23rd begged hard for it, and alas ! when exhibiting it, one of the younger officers let it slip out of his hand, and it was smashed.

I have little else of any consequence to note ; a rather eccentric lady, a Mrs Ward, whom I had met once or twice at dinner at the chaplain's to the English resident at Lisbon, paid me a visit on board my brig, coming off in such weather she ought never to have faced ; she was in a riding habit and with high gentlemen's boots, wet through and through. I begged her to make use of my cabin and bed place, and my steward would carefully dry at the galley fire any clothes she liked to put aside for that purpose. About an hour after she came on deck laughing, said that she had been made quite comfortable, and the upshot or end was a present of a Westphalia ham, a cheddar loaf cheese and a dozen of porter ! The other small affair was the falling in love of one of our lieutenants, Johnny W.,[1] with a Miss Hornby, a great beauty, going by the name of 'La blonde Anglaise,' he also being a remarkably fine-looking young fellow. At her leaving for England he *mooned* so and became so unhappy that he applied to be superseded, and soon after left the ship. I mention all this as the end was strange, as I shall hereafter relate ; in one way, poor fellow, he regretted this, as he shewed with tears in his eyes when he came on board at Portsmouth, from having thrown himself out of being with us at the battle of Navarino.

[1] Waugh.

CHAPTER XI

Return to the Albion—Battle of Navarino

About the end of June [1] the *Albion* and *Genoa* were ordered to the Mediterranean. I felt very loth to give up the brig, and was offered by the admiral to remain if I chose. 'You know the brig and the brig knows you, I believe.' On consideration, I thought it best to follow the fortunes of my own ship, and so returned to the *Albion*, and well I did, for I should have lost Navarino and the stepping stone it gave me to my promotion. Captain Ommanney would not have a pilot, but trusted the ship to me ; we were at Gibraltar two days and made welcome by our friends the 42nd, and on to Malta, and there we remained several days. The *Isis*, Sir Thomas Staines, arrived. Sir Thomas, who had lost his left arm in action, was hit in the other when fighting a duel, causing a stiff elbow, so that he never after could bring his hand within a foot of his mouth. I met him and Lady S. at dinner at the commissioner's, Sir Charles Ross, the same I knew so well at Port Royal. Sir Thomas had his glass and tumbler with a long stem, and a long-handled knife and fork in one, and with these he managed very well ; at a signal, his wife came round, took his handkerchief to blow his nose, he laughing—'that it was not every husband who would allow their wives to pull their noses.' He was often irritable, particularly when his face was itching, and he used to hurry to the cabin, throw himself into any easy chair, and with a carved ivory hand at the end of a porcupine quill play with his face, and this soon soothed him into a smile ; anyone can fancy the torment of an itching face and no means of touching it. It was Sir Thomas, when commanding the *Briton* frigate, who first discovered Adams, Christian, and others [2] of the *Bounty*, at Pitcairn's Island.

---

[1] 1827.

[2] Staines's statement in 1814 was that there were then on Pitcairn Island ' only one man (John Adams) and seven women of the original settlers '. The Thursday October Christian whom Staines ' discovered ' was the son of Fletcher Christian of the *Bounty*.

At Malta in August it was intensely hot; it was the first time of my acquaintance with the sirocco wind: the leaves of a book I was reading curled up, an ivory flute cracked with a report, as well as one or two glasses in the buffet. We, the *Genoa* and ourselves, soon after joined the *Asia* with the flag of Sir Edward Codrington,[1] and worked through the Archipelago to Smyrna, passing between Chios and the Main, and here was a most melancholy sight. The town of Chios, but a few months back, was the scene of a horrible massacre of old and young; the women alone spared, and that for the harem of the Turkish butchers; the town had all the beauty of an eastern city, large buildings, flat roofs, dazzling white, relieved by cypress and other evergreen trees, but scarcely a living person to be seen; we anchored in Vourla Bay, four or five miles from Smyrna.

I went on shore with a watering party; a single fountain to supply our wants, and there were the boats of an American and Austrian frigate for the same purpose. The American lieutenant said, 'Well, sir, what's to be done? you are the big ship, and I suppose will help yourself.' I answered, 'The water runs freely, and we may as well dip our buckets in turns.' This greatly pleased the Yankee, and we got on amicably together. Very soon I noticed our men's eyes shining: they evidently had found something stronger than water, and on a rising ground I came upon a ring of Turks, seated cross-legged, with grapes, figs, &c., and jars of milk (?), one of which I kicked over and there was no mistake of its *mixed* contents. The Turks were at first angry, wagged their beards and rolled their eyes, but afterwards smiled; no doubt they had sold the milk at a good profit. When on shore, after the men's dinner, I brought a pound of our priming powder, to their unbounded delight. I gave it in acknowledgment of their so good-humouredly taking my kicking over the jar. Before going off they gave me three brace of red-legged partridges, and the next day sent on board more game.

While in the bay we invited the American officers to dinner. We agreed to *taboo* certain touchy subjects. There was still a certain restraint till one of the Americans proposed a toast, 'Here's to John Bull and Brother Jonathan,' and it seemed at once to break the ice, we were more sociable. I noticed they hung much on being of old families, one saying, 'We are of the *Jenkinsons* (I am not sure of the name) of Hampshire. We figure *in your Hume*.' They affected

---

[1] For much detail explanatory of Boteler's succeeding narrative see *Memoir of the Life of Admiral Sir Edward Codrington*, edited by his daughter, Lady Bouchier (1873).

some nicety in chewing, introducing a small piece of negrohead tobacco, more like Spanish liquorice, under the lip. They looked down on our very white deck, seemingly loth to soil it ; divining their thoughts or wishes we sent for spittoons from the lower deck, and they were made happy. On board their frigate we were rather surprised at the quantity of polishing belaying pins, copper railing of the companion hatch, monkey tails, and even the breech of the quarter-deck carronade, and we heard that their crew complained bitterly of this incessant work.

One morning, with Captain Stevens of the marines, I went up to Smyrna in the *Asia's* tender, the *Hind* cutter. We called on the British consul, and were taken by him to some Turkish dignitary and there had coffee brought in by two female black slaves, shapely and graceful in their walk—one with a silver tray with small china cups of exquisite coffee, in other cups of filigree silver ; the other slave with a gilt fringed towel over each shoulder, and holding a large china basin of rosewater. With the coffee was a saucer of sweets and flat shovel teaspoon ; I took some of the sweets, and was told that I should have kept it in my mouth and drank the coffee over it. On our way to the boat we met the pasha governor, with an armed Turk before and two others behind, all swaggering along taking the street to themselves ; most of the population on their knees and all prostrating ; one poor fellow of necessity crawling on his hands and knees, his feet swollen and tied up in flannel—he had been bastinadoed.

The three ships soon after left Vourla, and in my middle watch, in a strong wind, I heard something give way aloft, and on sending the carpenter up found the foreyard badly sprung in the slings, and in the morning, by signal, we parted company and ran for Volo, a horseshoe shaped island (Archipelago) forming one extensive harbour. A French line-of-battle ship was at anchor, and the only vessel there, fitting a jury mainmast, and, to the disgust and the annoyance of every officer, by clumsy mismanagement, bad seamanship, or otherwise, we all but ran foul of her. We were not long in fishing the yard and then joined the admiral off Cape Colonna, ' A range of columns long by time defaced.' From this the squadron returned to Malta and put into quarantine ; having come from the East, the difficulty next was to get our linen washed, but as there was such a quantity among the three ships, some women readily took the work, going to the lazaretto and putting themselves a whole month in quarantine. In three days, when about to leave Malta, the linen came off, with small attention as to the right owners ; I had some of
184

the *Asia's* and *Genoa's* ; but when outside changes were made, I, at least, came well off, losing nothing. Before sailing I should say a ship came in that had communicated with the Russian squadron, and asking the men what sort of ships they were, the only reply was, '*Lumps* of ships, sir.' With our own squadron, while cruising some distance from Navarino, in the middle of the night we suddenly came upon and passed right through the Turkish and Egyptian fleets ; all were at quarters, a light shewing at each port—it was a very fine sight ; we glided silently past, all perfectly still, no sound beyond their boatswains' pipes, and they were rather loud. I suppose this was the concerted rendezvous, for shortly after we were joined by the French and Russian squadrons. I do not well remember that we were many days in company, but I do recollect that one day, whether to try the rate of sailing, the power of our allies, or what not, in following the admiral's motion we commenced beating to windward, a rather fresh wind, so as only occasionally to bear top-gallant sails over double reefed topsails. The English clawed to windward very soon. Both French and Russians carried full topsails, and that was too much : a Russian lost a topmast, and they all fell to leeward of the French, who kept better up with us.

18th October, 1827, we were close off Navarino and the *Dartmouth*, Sir Thomas Fellowes, was sent in with a message to Ibrahim Pasha, the Commander-in-Chief of the Egyptians. On his return the next day the French and Russian admirals and the captains went on board the *Asia*, and late in the evening a general telegraph, 'Prepare to enter.' Too dark to make out more, but even with this it was not thought there would be a fight—at least, the *Genoa* made no preparation ; for the following day when, after the men's dinner and our substantial luncheon, we bore up for the harbour, passing through a continual wreck of men's mess tables, cabin bulkheads, partitions, and what not thrown overboard from the *Genoa*, she not having cleared for action. However, we went in single line, the French following also in single line, the Russian in the same way ; and we, the third ship, had just let go our anchor, when the battle began. The battle began about half-past two, and ended near five. The destruction of the Turks was complete ; many set fire to themselves, and blew up during the action ; scarcely any hauled down their colours ; and some fanatics would fire a shot when their ship was almost knocked to pieces, and this caused our firing to continue longer than necessary. In fact, when orders were given to cease firing, there was difficulty in restraining them. The captain of the gun would say—' Not yet, sir ; please let us have another shot ;

see, sir, she has just fired ' ; squaring his elbows, as a man might
do in his eagerness to continue a boxing match, while someone is
trying to pull him away.   One ship of the line was burned during
the action, while drifting away ; and three others, that went ashore
under the rocky cliffs of Old Navarino, set fire to themselves, and
blew up with tremendous explosions.   We saw many of their crews,
poor fellows ! crawling in a zig-zag line up the face of the cliff.

The evening of the next day, several bodies began to float,—the
usual time is the third day, but it is sooner with bodies that have
been burned.   On the 4th day we left the harbour ; I had a division of
boats to tow out the *Asia* and *Sirène*, the French admiral's ship ; the
whole harbour was then strewed with floating corpses ;—so much so
that frequently we had to toss the oars to clear them.   While towing
the French ship, an officer on her cathead kept calling out, ' Pull,
John, pull, John—well done !   Pull ! '

I here introduce, as an account of the battle, a letter I wrote to
Admiral Sir Erasmus Ommanney [1] at his request :—

PENZANCE,
Feby., 1882.

MY DEAR OMMANNEY,
Thank you very much for your nice letter, I was greatly pleased to
hear from you, and you conjured up a host of recollections of Navarin ;
my memory is exceedingly accurate and vivid, and respecting that affair,
I made notes of many interesting occurrences happening during the action,
as also those of a day or two after, as well as making (not bad ! !) pen-and-
ink sketches.   First I must bring you in.   Soon after the blowing up
of the frigate we had boarded and cut adrift, I ran on deck for a minute
to try and get a general view of the state of the action.   I shook hands
with the captain, who was frowning, shaking his head, touching his nose,
where one or two drops of blood were falling.   There was Commr. Campbell,[2] his head bound round with a blood-stained handkerchief, no great
harm ; then Johnny Drake, and last, as also least, your own small self,
your hands on your knees, looking with strained eyes through the spare
quarter deck port ; and I don't know why it should be so on my memory,
but I never think of that hasty visit that I do not see you.   Capt. Stevens
came from the poop to shake hands ; he had always an idea of being killed,
and had asked me to see that his little property should be sent to his
family at Canterbury, where we both then lived.   I said, ' The work is
getting warm, I will ask you to do the same for me,' and turned to go

---

[1] Admiral Sir Erasmus Ommanney, K.C.B., F.R.S., died December 21st, 1904,
aged 89.   He entered the service in 1826 and was nephew of Captain J. A. Ommanney
of the *Albion*, in which ship he was present at Navarino.

[2] The employment of Commanders as First Lieutenants of line-of-battle ships
was introduced in May 1827 (on which subject see *Naval Administrations, 1827 to
1892*, by Sir John Henry Briggs, 1897, pp. 2-3).   Commander John Norman
Campbell was the officer appointed to the *Albion*.

186

below, when I heard a shout, and looking round saw poor Stevens across the front rail, shot through the body; when the action was over, one of the young marines came to Lieut. Anderson, asking, 'What shall I do with this, sir?' holding up a hand by a finger; 'please, sir, it was Capt. Stevens''; he had picked it up and put it in his cap, and worn it the rest of the action—was not this a genuine piece of most kind feeling? I fear I shall be very egotistical, though, as naturally all my recollections are from my own acting and feeling. Our two quarter boats were both swamped astern; fortunately a pinnace of the *Genoa* floated alongside, and after dark I went in her to the flagship to report our state, and with a hurried account of our killed and wounded, and to ask for any orders, and a perfect job I had to find my way; alongside the *Asia* I found Sir Edward Codrington in the act of getting into a two-oared boat belonging to the *Hind* cutter, to go to the *Genoa* to see his old friend Capt. Bathurst, who was mortally wounded and dying. I of course offered my boat, and took him. I had an interesting talk with him respecting the battle and cause of commencement. Early next morning I again was sent to the admiral with other reports, and I told him I had observed some officers, apparently of rank from their fur-trimmed cloaks, on board the Turkish admiral's ship. 'Thanks, sir, tell Captain Ommanney to send for, and bring them to his ship.' Here I must add that I had asked the captain, in memory of old times, he having been made a commander and captain by my great-uncle, Sir Henry Harvey, if he would put me forward if there was any boarding, hence it was my being so much employed. And so I was sent in the barge with Lieut. Anderson and a party of marines, and the Greek pilot to interpret, and boarded the Turkish admiral, foul of another 80 gun ship, each with one mast only, and such a wreck, 1,040 killed and wounded between the two. Your recollection of the corvette you boarded with me was nothing to be compared to the perfect shambles of this ship between decks. They held red ropes as we mounted the sides by an accommodation ladder almost cut to pieces. The marines . were drawn up on the quarter deck with Anderson, and a part of the boat's crew with Langtry; the Turkish officers seated in a ring cross-legged, none moving, only rolling their eyes at us. I was ushered into the cabin, walking through the bulkheads, half standing, was put on a sofa, two Turks with cushions to put under me as I turned from side to side. The Turkish admiral and first captain had got away, but I brought on board the second captain, the secretary, and his three assistants, brothers. I also brought away a large ensign, two or three smaller ones, and several flags; with four pair of large silver mounted pistols, which Langtry slung across his shoulders for me, and last, a hanging compass from the admiral's cabin, a gorgeous thing, crimson and gold, prismatic colors. By the way, as this compass was taken across the deck by Anderson, most of the Turks bowed and salaamed it. This large ensign, which I gave to the captain, I imagine to be the one you named. The flag of the frigate we boarded was not brought away, for by the time our men got aft as far as the companion, flames sprung up from the cabin, where preparations were made beforehand for firing the ship to escape capture. One of the Turks told me this was arranged in most of the ships.

Our purpose, the next day, for boarding the corvette on shore, was to

bring away canvas and spars for cots for our wounded ; you remember,
I dare say, what a pull we had in a fresh wind, to get back to our ship.

I have two of my best sketches by me now, done 51 years back ; they
came to me in an unexpected way. While staying with the Ommanneys
at Northbrook, soon after my promotion in 1830, I drew them for Emma,
and till last May had forgotten all about them. Admiral Borlase, my
neighbour, called saying he had a letter from Admiral Lowe asking him
to find out if I was the Boteler, a lieut. of the *Albion*, that he saw by
O'Byrne's *Naval Biography* that I must be 85. If I was that person,
Mrs Chambers (Emma Ommanney that was) had desired by her will that
they should be returned to me.

One strange circumstance I often relate of the recklessness of men-of-
war's men. At my quarters there was a squabble among the powder
boys waiting at the fearnought screen for their powder. ' What's all
this row about ? ' ' Please, sir, it's big Knight getting all the powder '—
he had already three cartridges in his box. I gave his ear a pull and told
him to be off. Two minutes after, coming back, there was Knight and
another boy fighting, and the best part of the crew of two guns standing
round and encouraging them ! Would anyone dream of such a freak ?
To the captain of the gun : ' What can you be about, sir ? ' ' Beg your
pardon, sir, we could not help it, sir,' and away they went to their guns.
Captain Edward Pelham Brenton, without asking my leave, introduced
my plan of the battle into his *Naval History*.[1] I a little took him up, he
should have paid me the compliment of asking my permission. It was
very different with Admiral Sir Charles Ekins, who wrote to me, hearing
I had made notes of the battle, asking for any information I could give.
I sent him my plan, as also a letter explaining. He introduced the plan
in his book, with some extracts of my letter complimentary of the justice
of my remarks. He also wrote me a handsome letter of thanks and a
copy of his work, a *History of Naval Battles*.[2] Young Gray at my quarters,
I was close to him, he was in the act of giving the captain of the gun some
grape shot, when he suddenly turned round, laughing to see the grape
scattered on the deck. I saw what it was, and he too directly also. He
turned pale, and said : ' Oh, sir, it's my right arm.' He was taken below
and the arm amputated, but the next day Dr Hillyar found the bone
splintered higher up ; I gave up my cabin to him, and it was taken out
of the socket. Poor little man ! he said as an apology for groaning :
' This is a great deal for a little fellow like me to stand.' At the Naval
Hospital, Malta, he had lockjaw and got over it. When the Duke of
Clarence, as Lord High Admiral, came on board at Spithead and inspected
us at quarters, he noticed Gray, saying : ' Why, little man, you don't say
a shot found you out, such a small lad should have been spared ; what's
your name ? Well mind, the Duke of Clarence cannot always find
Mr Gray, but Mr Gray can always find the Duke of Clarence ; when you
pass, let me know and I will promote you the next day.' But alas,
both he and his brother, both wounded, were so noticed and made much

---

[1] It faces p. 626 in Vol. II of the 1837 edition of Brenton's *Naval History of Great
Britain*.

[2] Boteler's plan faces p. 348 of the 1828 edition of Ekins's *Naval Battles of Great
Britain*.

of that they lost their heads, each took to drinking, became irreclaimable
drunkards and were turned out of the service. When the ship was paid
off, he went to London and stayed some days with Drake's brother, in
the Temple. He told us that one day his boy, a regular little flibberty-
gibbet, ran in saying : ' Haven't you a brother in the *Albion*, sir ? He
has been in a great battle.' ' Well, Jack, run out and get more news.'
Shortly after, he came back : ' Yes, sir, a great battle with the Turks,
that the *Albion* boarded and took one, notwithstanding their three-edged
skimmiters.' And while dining there he told us that one morning young
Gray asked Jack to wash his neck, and when he let fall his shirt over his
shoulders the boy started back with horror, and " Lor, sir, was that cut
off with one of them three-edged skimmiters ? '

I mentioned before that I brought from the Turkish admiral's ship
three brothers, one with the loss of his arm, died at Malta. His brothers
were anxious that he should not be buried on shore, I imagine not liking
the contact with Christians, so we took the body out and buried him at
sea. Before this, they found the corpse, as is the custom, sewn up in a
hammock covered with the Union Jack, they pulled off the flag and cut
several of the stitches to give his spirit an opening for flight. Another
case of the reckless mischief of one of the men. The six after guns,
24 pdrs., are inclosed in officers' cabins : their partitions or bulkheads,
composed of light frames with canvas panels, hung on hinges and bolted
to cants and screwed on the deck. So that when orders are given to
clear for action, carpenters unbolted them, removed the cants and hooked
the partition overhead. I had a gun in my cabin, and on a brass hook
over it, on a beam, I had hanging a valuable fowling piece. I had been
moving about at my quarters, desiring the captains of guns to fire at
particular ships, when coming near my cabin I found a stupid fellow
squatted on his hams and snapping my gun (a flint lock) over some loose
powder scattered on the deck, running a great chance of an explosion,
the smoke between decks was so densely yellow and inflammable, as also
spoiling my gun ; an involuntary kick *en derrière* sent him sprawling, and
the captain of the gun looking round gave him a staggering box on the
ear as he was getting up on his legs, and the second captain bestowed
another that almost floored him again. It seemed most strange, considering we had sixty or seventy killed and wounded, that anyone could
think of any but his own duty ; but stranger still, this recklessness was
not confined to the men. The captain's clerk, Mr Stewart, was stationed
on the poop with slate and pencil to take notes, not a desirable office in
this place at close quarters, and with wild bad directed firing, the most
exposed part of the ship. Being so near the enemy, the marines, instead
of being divided among the guns, were all on the poop. Lieut. Anderson,
who three or four years back died a general officer and K.C.B., picked up
a stray bullet and threw it at Stewart, hitting him on the shoulder ; he
started and once or twice shrugged his shoulders, apparently to ascertain
how far he was hurt : he had been twice wounded and knew from experience
how little one knew how much he was injured unless the wound was
severe ; he then looked to see if it was a spent ball after killing a marine
close to him, or if the ball had glanced from the mizenmast. He then
again *felt* himself, and turning round saw Anderson laughing. He shook

his head, saying, ' Oh, sir ; that's too bad.' And it was too bad, and
a most foolish joke. Some on being hit and fancying themselves wounded
might have shewn fear, and had this been so, the joke would have been
greatly regretted. The next morning our first lieutenant, Johnny Drake,
gave Anderson a severe lecture on the folly and cruelty of the act, relating
at the same time the case of a fine old officer of the King's German
Legion, a cavalry regiment, for some years part of our military force.
This officer was never known to be taken by surprise, but one of the
young officers thought to disturb his nerves, ran to him in the middle of
the night reporting something dreadful demanding his immediate attention. The old fellow deliberately dressed, buckled on his sword, went
down and finding it a hoax, turned in again, taking no notice or saying
a word till next day at mess, when, turning to the young officer, he said,
' It is well for you, sir, that you are at this table now, for had I shewn
the slightest tribulation when you called me up last night, you would
have been a dead man long before this ; never you attempt to play off
such a joke again.' We all applauded Drake.

I have before said that on anchoring we had just manned the rigging
to furl sails, when the action unexpectedly began, and it was ' Down, men,
to your guns.' Our anchor did not immediately hold and we drifted on to
a double-banked Turkish frigate, her spritsail yard crossing our poop
hammock nettings before the mizenmast ; over this the first division of
boarders scrambled, led by the first lieutenant ; she was soon mastered,
and directly after was found on fire, and our boarders forced to a hasty
retreat. The boatswain, a fine fellow, lost his arm while on the bowsprit
by a shot from the Turk's foretop ; then, notwithstanding the hurry to
get back to our ship, three of our men ran up her fore-rigging, stormed
the top and threw two Turks headlong over the top-rail. Several acts of
pluck were shewn by our men ; one in particular by a man, a simple
good-natured fellow—the butt of all the mischievous boys, who used to
take him by the forelock leading him about the decks, he only laughing,
and ' Don't 'e, don't 'e ; now please don't I '—well, this man to the surprise
of all was among the leading boarders, using his cutlass most effectually
with great pluck and daring. The other remarkable case was that of the
second captain of the foretop, a stout Irishman. The marines are never
told off as boarders ; their only arm, the musket, is not only cumbrous,
but an ineffective weapon on such occasions ; still three or four could not
resist the exciting temptation, and followed the seamen boarding. From
one of these the topman seized a musket, and taking it by the muzzle,
swinging it from side to side with ' Make a lane there I ' he fairly scattered
a group of Turks right and left, literally making a lane. Many of the
boarders omitted to bring their pistols, and as we overlooked the main
deck from the gangway, the Turks fired from below, when one of the mids.,
young Hinds, with a happy thought, said to the first lieutenant, ' Give
them cold shot, sir ' ; and this was acted on with marvellous effect. Their
shot, as in our ships, are in semi-circular holes round the combings of the
hatchways, so just at hand to throw down on the Turks. The first
lieutenant spoke of this afterwards in great praise of the little fellow.
The great difficulty was in clearing the frigate from us—she was moored ;
one cable was easily cut at her own hawse-hole, the other hanging slack

190

could not so easily be divided, and the only person at this was a passed
mid., Mr Langtry ; and he had but little footing, standing in one of our
cutters swamped and flush with the water. I had myself lowered an
axe to him from the wardroom windows and encouraged him to persevere ;
he was nearly exhausted when the cable parted, and the frigate was but
little over her own length from us when she blew up with a thundering
explosion. Those at the guns felt no effect of this ; certainly I in no
way did, but below, the concussion was so great, that the gunner in the
magazine thought the explosion was in the ship and that she might be
on fire, and he with his men rushed out, locking the door. Before the
magazine is a light-room and three lamps in a glass case give light to
the men filling powder, &c. The shock was so great that two panes of
glass were shaken from the sash ; most providentially, those panes were
not those on the magazine side, or the powder dust would have ignited
and the ship would have inevitably blown up.

Our men were greatly fatigued, particularly as we twice lifted our
anchor and warped farther off to clear burning ships ; we had difficulty in
rousing them up asleep at their guns ; and this reminds me of the custom
in the Russian service. By the blazing light of a burning ship close to
the Russian Admiral I saw the men on the poop in ranks as soldiers (this
late in the night). Next day one of her officers came on board bringing
a wounded man whom they took from the burning ship they had towed
clear, finding he was English. I noticed to this officer his men on the poop,
and asked if they were kept so. ' Oh, yes, sir.' ' What, all night ? '
' Certainly, they sometimes drop, but get up again.' Off and on I remained on deck nearly the whole night ; I never felt the least fatigue, or
any way drowsy. I suppose excitement kept me up. As I have just
said, I was on deck nearly the whole night, I don't know that this was
from entire choice, but the Captain, who was very tired, had asked me to
be on the look out, and to report anything worth his attention. I slipped
down about nine and found my messmates at work on what they could
by chance get for supper ; they had come upon a small keg of American
crackers and a reindeer tongue in my cabin and finished them, having
the grace to reserve some for me, their owner. We had sat down to a
good luncheon at one, nothing after, no dinner. Returning on deck the
whole scene, if I may so term it, so striking, such a contrast, the apparent
perfect stillness, to the two or three hours' din of battle ; the deafness of
those between decks, the difficulty of hearing a word or making an order
understood ; some of us did not recover our hearing for two days. Then
again, the blaze of light from burning ships shewing a clear view all round,
followed perhaps by an explosion, a blinding flash, then dark as pitch.
It was on my mind that fire rafts might be drifted down on us, as several
piles of burning wreck floated past ; a large one, not on fire, came near :
I jumped into a boat to tow it clear ; it was merely a mass of mast, yard,
and rigging, and a poor fellow entangled in it ; we got him into our boat ;
his right arm was off at the shoulder, only some small strips of flesh
hanging down ; he was so grateful, lifting my hand to his forehead
and lips ; we assisted him up the side, and he walked down to the
cockpit where the surgeon attended him, and two days after we landed
him.

It was quite late, I think about ten, I went on the poop and, seeing
some flags on the deck, told the signal man to roll them up and return
them to the proper locker. Under an ensign we found an unfortunate
Turk (moaning) ; how he possibly could have got there was a marvel ;
he must have returned with our retreating boarders unnoticed. He was
awfully wounded, and with such injury he yet could not possibly have
followed the boarders. He must have been cut down on our deck, yet
no one seemed to know it. It seems incredible, but I can vouch for the
fact, and the surgeon named it to me the next morning with ' How could
you send that man to me ? the skull at the back of the head was absolutely
cut through, hanging down the neck shewing the brain.' Still, supported
by the quarter-master, he walked down the ladders and lived, to the
surgeon's astonishment, till next morning. We all could talk of different
incidents, but none agreed as to the order in which they occurred. The
one who seemed to set us right was the chaplain in the cockpit to assist
with the wounded—and, by the way, he was himself there wounded : he
knew when the boarders were called, also twice the firemen. I should
have related that when the frigate, we had sent clear by hauling astern by
her jib guys, blew up, she was so near that two or three pieces of her
falling timber passed completely over us, and as our sails were loose we
had a most narrow escape. Had a sail caught fire nothing could have
saved the ship—no surer method of burning a ship, than to loose a sail
and set fire to it—I saw at the close of the action two of the Turks set fire
to their ships in this way. Still we were twice on fire, once in the lanyards
of the lower rigging, probably fired by our own carronades, which are too
short to clear the rigging.

We were mostly engaged with our larboard guns, but at one time a
few of the other side were directed at a frigate broad on the starboard
bow, and which was sunk outright by a single broadside of the *Breslau*, 74,
a French ship passing near as she came into action ; this ship our men
called their ' chum '—her shot might seem to be fired at us. However,
when Lieut. Ramsay, who had the foremost guns on the main deck, came
aft, he found the mate of his quarters firing *into* the Frenchman ; he
reprimanded him of course, but almost directly after he caught him again
firing into the French ship ; then Ramsay blazed out, and calling him
a ' dolt, fool and ass ! ' ' Why she is firing into us,' was the young man's
angry reply. There was no mistake in the matter. A *Breslau* officer
named it to me : he thought the shot came from us, and it proved so, for
there was our mark on the shot sticking in his foremast. Our captain
never knew of this, or it would have been a decisive reason for passing
him over among those recommended for promotion. Two were made
Lieuts., one of them Langtry, his junior. He had not conducted himself
over well prior to the action. He became ill on arriving at Spithead, and
was sent to Haslar Hospital, and there died, poor fellow, I have little
doubt from a broken heart.

Another circumstance connected with a midshipman, Mr Boys, I
must relate : heavy in mind and body, by no means brilliant, he was
quartered at the foremost guns on the lower deck—our men were not over
well instructed in gunnery, knew how to load and fire, and nothing more
of the management and property of the guns. They invariably over-

loaded, nearly always with two shot, sometimes with three, and when the gunner on the following day examined the guns and drew the charges, in one was found *four* round shot. The guns, consequently, were very lively, springing back upon their breechings, jumping off the deck. I had a trifling knowledge of gunnery, and on my own responsibility sent a message to the gunner in the magazine to reduce the charges, as we were at close quarters. In those days we had flint locks, fired by a hide lanyard; one of these broke and the gun twice missed fire, when Mr Boys jumped to the breech and pulled the trigger: the gun went off, and with its rapid recoil violently struck him in the stomach, leaving him like a dead man by the combing of the hatchway. As his arm hung over the back of the man carrying him to the cockpit, one of his messmates shook it, saying ' Good-bye, old fellow,' making sure he was killed, as indeed all thought. He was long unconscious, but on stripping him, the surgeon could find no wound—it was supposed the wind of a shot : I don't believe in any such thing, though many do—well, he was put on a mattress by the purser's cabin. Soon other wounded came down, and the assistant-surgeon told Boys to make room for them, that nothing was the matter with him, and to return to his quarters. He staggered up and went to the after guns on the lower deck, as much exposed as any part of the ship : in fact close to him a mid., Mr Forster, was killed, his head shot clean off. The same evening his name was among the wounded sent to the Admiral. The next morning when an amended list was made out, the surgeon said to me, ' By the way, here's young Boys, his name must be withdrawn.' I objected, as it would seem so strange ; that in fact he was sufficiently hurt to be carried below perfectly insensible. In a day or two it became whispered he had shewn the white feather, and I found it originated through the assistant-surgeon. I called upon the lieutenant of his quarters to take the case to the captain : enquiries were made, the surgeon and assistant-surgeon called into the cabin, and the captain severely reprimanded the assistant for his attempt to take away the character of the young fellow. This did not satisfy me—I called young Boys, told him a stain of cowardice was on him, and unless some strong measure was taken, it would stick to him and ruin him in the service, and though a peacemaker, in this case I was not ; that he must ' go below and insult the assistant-surgeon before everyone, whatever the consequence might be, and do not come near, shew yourself or speak to me till you have so done.' For two days I kept patient, but could stand it no longer. I said, ' Well, sir, did you do as I desired ? ' He pursed his mouth up : ' Yes, sir.' ' Well ? ' ' I went down and told Mr * * * he was a great blackguard.' ' Well ? ' ' He turned very red in the face.' ' Well ? ' ' I said he was himself a paltry coward to attempt to take away the character of a young fellow.' ' Well, what else ? ' ' All the midshipmen laughed, and I told him if I were big enough I would give him a good thrashing.' So I took him by the hand well satisfied. He was growing fast into a big stout young fellow, and when four months after, at the Blue Posts, Portsmouth, the mids.' house (humorously noticed by Marryat), and where the coffee-room is upstairs and Mr Boys and others were there, when up came the assistant-surgeon. Boys jumped up and attacked him furiously—two waiters attempted to interfere, but the mids. prevented them, and it ended by Boys getting the doctor to the head of the stairs and pitching him down headlong.

While with me at Jamaica, in 1823, he lost two front teeth from a fall. I never shall forget his enormously swelled face; his two teeth were lost when the gun gave him such a fling and they afterwards went as part of his wound. Then, again, when agent of transports carrying troops to the Mauritius, the ship was caught in a typhoon. Poor Boys had his leg broken, and as the report said, lost two of his teeth! The ship was nearly lost, and only saved by battening down the hatches. Though the ship was saved, five of the soldiers were suffocated below. To stay some reports unfavourable to Mr Boys, the general, on the ship's arrival, in general orders greatly complimented Mr Boys for his conduct and ability in bringing the ship safely in. The Turkish brothers afforded us some amusement; for a time they declined wine, but soon returned the compliment of drinking their health by the like way, and afterwards asking each other '*Omar vino*,' but persisted in calling it sherbet. A Turk is never happy without his pipe. In those days smoking was never permitted in the wardroom, but under the circumstances I asked for an exception to the rule. Anderson produced his long cherry-stick, amber mouth piece and red clay bowl pipe. Both looked at it with longing eyes, and when presented to them, one drew a very lengthy pull, handed it to his brother, threw himself back in his chair, pouring out a perfect volume of smoke, and so they passed it from one to the other, shewing most perfect delight in their countenances. A Turk considers it beneath the dignity of man to shew any feeling, such as crying, laughing, &c. But one day after dinner I was exhibiting a feat, holding up my right foot behind me by the left hand, as also my right ear by the other, stooping down and picking up my hat from the deck by my teeth. I often did this, but once by the vibration of the ship, before I could unhook, I pitched my head into my hat ready to break my neck. This was too much for Omar's sense of dignity, and he burst out with a wild laugh; his brother shaking him by the shoulder with 'Omar, Omar!' It was no go, he continued his laugh, and was ready at all times to do the same. Another change came over their habits: at Malta we were sent into quarantine, though only for four days; several boats pulled round the ships with ladies. The young Turks affected shyness—wrong to look at unveiled ladies; they began to look through their spread fingers, then more openly, till at last they called each other whenever ladies rowed past. They were very grateful for all kindness shewn them, and when they left, Omar tore up a valuable sealskin cloak and put a square under my pillow.

Yours faithfully,

J. H. B.

The English and Russians went to Malta, as also the *Breslau*, which our men called their ' chum.' The rest of the French squadron went to Toulon.

We became very friendly with the Russians. *I*, in particular, was intimate with several; and whenever a Russian came alongside, it was—' Where's Boteler? Here, Boteler; here are some of your

Arctic seals, or Polar bears.' We dined with each other. They beat us at this; their pastry was equal to any confectioner's. They began with gin and cheese; the first in tiny glasses, the latter of the size only of dice. Sitting by Utomeski, a Tartar prince, and asking him for the salt, he called his servant to give it. I said: ' You don't mean to say, in these enlightened times, you have in Russia such superstitious notions about salt.' ' Well, Sir Boteler, what do you do in England ? if you spill salt on the table, do you not take a pinch, and throw it over your shoulder ? ' I laughed, for he fairly had me there. The Russians are great copyists. Soon after we anchored, an officer from their flagship, the *Gangout*, came with the carpenter to ask leave to measure our bulwarks. Theirs were so high that, standing on the quarter deck carronades, one could not look over the hammock nettings. Then, with 150 Maltese shipwrights, all their bulwarks were cut down, like ours. With their lofty top sides, no wonder they lagged to leeward, it was like a back sail to them. At another time the request was to copy the sails and rig of our boats, and they were turned over to me who had them under my care, and being next to a Deal man, I had our boats with fore and mizen lugs only. Again, when about to sail for England, I was asked to send out some hanging lamps, as over the table in our ward-room ; and a number of books and some other trifles ; they giving me a bag of forty gold ducats in payment. At Spithead, we found the *Vengeur* on the point of sailing for Malta, and I had just time to get everything and send them out in her.

A 74, the *Alexander Newski*, was close to us,—the very ditto of Sir Robert Sepping's last launched a few months back, with the round stern, diagonal build, diagonal decks, plank for plank and almost nail for nail ; and even the stern railing, cast as if in the same mould as that ship. In our dockyard, they generally had a clever artist to note our latest and best inventions.

The strictest discipline was observed in the Russian navy ; no such thing known as an ' unlawful ' order, all must be implicitly obeyed. Punishments, I was told, were very severe : and though within hail of two ships, I never heard the sound of the lash or the cry of anyone under it. The men did not seem active aloft, and I did not see how they well could, as all had heavy boots. I asked an officer, Lieutenant Demetrieff, what he thought of his own men. ' Why, Sir Boteler,'—for in this way was I addressed,—' they are but machines ; they do what we tell them ; they are not like yours ; if our officers fall, none could manage the ship, as your men would.' Their navy is composed of so many regiments, who, when

unemployed, are in barracks.   When afloat, a regiment mans a line
of battle ship and a frigate, the colonel commanding the big ship, the
major a frigate.   When in barracks at home the pay is much reduced,
but when at sea they beat us out and out,—shewing almost gold to
our silver.

Well, again to our ships ; we were made much of, received with
great enthusiasm by the garrison, the troops lining the ramparts, a
royal salute, cheering and bands playing ; a grand ball given, a large
transparency of the battle across the end of the room by a young
artist, George Reinagle, who chanced to be on board the *Philomel*, a
guest of her captain Lord Ingestre.   He made many very faithful
and clever sketches of the battle and published a series.   I called on
him in London, a pair of silver mounted pistols were on the table,
and which Miss Reinagle proudly pointed as George's trophy of the
battle ; they were one of the four pair I brought from the Turkish
admiral's ship and gave him at Malta.

We were three months at Malta, *i.e.*, *Asia* and ourselves ; the
Genoa had sailed early with the body of her captain, Commodore
Bathurst, on board.   We were, between us, most of the time in the
hands of the dockyard, our foremast was so injured, that besides
fishing, it had to be shortened six feet ; both ships had also to be
docked.   A large promotion took place, all commanders posted, and
all first lieutenants made commanders, besides several mids. to
lieutenants ; the admiral also having the privilege of filling the
vacancies consequent upon the death of Captain Bathurst : a post
captain, commander and lieutenant.   The *Asia* and ourselves
sailed for England, and arrived at Spithead about the middle of
March, were then inspected by the Duke of Clarence, then Lord
High Admiral, and ordered into the harbour to be paid off ; we were
lashed alongside of, and hulked on board the *Blake*, while the
guns were got out, the ship unrigged to the lower masts, anchors,
chain cables and all stores returned to the dockyard, in short, the
Albion reduced to a clean swept hold.

Then comes the paying off, an exciting and curious scene.   I
scarcely have the power of describing it with full justice ; the ship
is made scrupulously clean, decks white and spotless, the officers with
cocked hats and side-arms, the men in their ' Sunday best.'   The
Commissioner comes on board, is received by all the officers, the
marine guard presenting arms ; he takes his seat in the fore cabin,
together with the clerk of the cheque, cashier, and four or five clerks,
with the necessary iron-bound cash boxes.   In those days, when
seamen's wages accumulated from the time of entry till paid off, the

amount required became very large, and in the case of a large ship over two and a-half years in commission, reached several thousand pounds. In paying off, the men are mustered aft by open list, *i.e.*, as they stand on the ship's books, a copy of which is always at the navy office in London, and one sent to the pay office at Portsmouth. Then from a string of men on one side of the quarter-deck, three at a time are called into the cabin, and—'William Smith, £34. 6s. 8d.,' repeated by the clerks from different books, to verify the correctness, followed always by the same question, of—'William Smith, how will you have it, the whole now or part ? or you can remit the whole or part to any place in the kingdom, and you will find it there ready for you or anyone you name, for you.' To another, ' £57. 5s. 6d.' ; ' £57. 5s. 6d.' repeated, and the question again : 'How will you have it ? ' &c. 'The whole lot, sir, if you please ! ' Hats are always put on the deck, and into it the money placed, and which the man always stuffs, as it is, into his pocket. Some would say ' Remit every farthing, sir,' and swagger out of the cabin with a defiant air, probably with his pockets turned inside out, knowing whom he was about to face, for there on the gangway the bumboat women who had attended the ship with their account books, eagerly watching the men as they emerged from the cabin ; it was no time to squabble, the man would often open—' You cheated me last paying off, I am even with you this time, my lady ' ; a number of boats were in waiting, many with persons ready to pounce on the defaulter as he left the ship. Some men would be met with—' Take so-and-so, £3. 10s.' ' Eh, what ? ' ' Mutton so much, soft bread and butter, money lent ! ' ' Well, all right ! ' and payment made ; at other times a dispute, which we never allowed to go on, but settled else-where. On the whole, I imagine bumboat people were amply repaid ; all charges high and often false, trusting to the forgetfulness and recklessness of Jack.

While at Malta most of the officers lent money to the men, I among them ; a sort of carnival in the town, and a little money lent was highly prized. I had run rather short when a black fellow, Hercules Taylor, asked for some. I said : ' I was sorry that I had lent already all I could spare ' ; the man put on a comical face with ' I tink, sir, you find im dollar in the heel of the old *tockin* ! ' I went aft, and on turning again forward, he was still on the gangway with such an entreating look, that the dollar was found. ' Ah, Massa Boteler, youm very good ; I gib you double at Portsmouth ! ' He nearly lost his dollar by the threatened bribe ; in but one single instance was the loan forgotten, and all wished to return double and treble what was lent. In my case I was on the hulk's quarter deck, when Taylor rushed past, flourishing a copper belaying pin on his way over the side—' I mash the head of anyone dare touch me ! ' I called out, ' Put that pin down, sir, directly.' ' Ah, Massa Boteler, um forgot you most,' and into my hand was pushed a £5 note, he down the side like a shot, and off in a four-oared wherry, I calling out, ' Stop that fellow, stop him at once ! ' Of no use, he shouting to the men to pull like devils, gesticulating and swaying to the motion of the boat, and why ? Round the bow of the hulk appeared another four-oared boat with a tipstaff to cut him off and to give chase. Taylor got the better of it, probably through his crew being the most willing of the two. There were two fellows alongside dressed as stage coachmen, in box coats of many capes, voluminous belcher handkerchiefs round their necks, *whips*, and a parchment-covered book in their hands to book men for London by the ' Rocket,' ' Nelson,' ' Trafalgar,' &c. I need scarcely add the whole was a fraud.

In the evening at the George hotel we had a parting dinner, Captain Ommanney our guest, all ending in best wishes for a happy and prosperous future. Four of us the next day went to London, Ramsay, Norcott, D'Urban and myself. We put up at the Old Slaughter Coffee House in St Martin's Lane, and passed a very merry fortnight in town. In a room on the opposite side of the street we saw a man striding about and putting himself in all manner of attitudes before the glass. ' Look at that precious fool,' said Norcott ; ' what can he be about ? He must be cracked.' ' Oh no, most likely he is a posture master, teacher of ladies to walk and properly carry themselves.' In a day or two Norcott received a note as from this man to the effect that he had noticed by his manner he was a stranger to London, and by his gait more used to pacing a ship's deck than the fashionable lounge of Bond Street, and offering to give lessons in walking, and on very reasonable terms. Paddy's lower lip began to quiver, the prelude to a storm which burst out ; he calling, ' Waiter, waiter, bring me a broomstick, or chambermaid, a mop handle ; I will break the fellow's head.' He was furious and wished to run across the street and at once attack the man. To pacify him seemed hopeless ; he turned upon us with increased anger, and we had the greatest difficulty in allaying the tempest we had raised. We found he was too dangerous a subject to play with.

At another time, walking in the Strand with a friend, a barrister, the latter said he suspected that man a pickpocket ' by the way he is watching and following us.' ' Oh,' said Norcott, ' let me be at him.'
198

'No, no, you can't do that ; you must keep quiet. I believe I am right though, after all. Keep still, take no notice ; I will let you know.' True enough the fellow was at Norcott's pocket, and at a nudge from his friend Norcott turned sharp round, took him by the shoulders, and bore him backwards into the gutter. Norcott telling the story to us said his friend left him, but a gentleman helped, and an Irishman he was, but the barrister only left to bring back a constable, and the culprit led off to Bow Street, locked up for the night, and Norcott desired to attend next day, when two of our party went with him. He was very desirous it should not be known as to his *calling*, but through a trifling hint it leaked out. Before the magistrate spoke the fellow exclaimed, ' I am innocent, your worship ; I did but touch him and he seized me like a wild beast by both shoulders and threw me down.' ' Oh,' said the magistrate, ' as to your innocence, I have had you here before.' Norcott was asked to prosecute, but pleaded family affairs requiring his presence at home. ' Well, I will take care he picks no more pockets for the next two months. I wish others would act with your courage, it would soon put an end to such pilfering, but it is no more than would be expected from a British naval officer.' A half-crown was given the reporter to omit this, but two half-crowns turned the scale, and a flaming account of the officer's gallantry was in the paper the following morning. And here again Norcott's back was fairly up, and had he known how to come across the reporter he no doubt would have assaulted him.

One day all four of us, returning from an exhibition of waxwork in the Strand, met several of our wounded men. They off hats as we stopped to say a few words. They had been to Somerset House respecting their pensions for wounds ; in less than half-a-minute a crowd collected, people running. We were soon hemmed in by a mob staring at us and making odd remarks. ' These are officers, they have been in battle ; see now the wounded, with their hats all off.' We were obliged to take refuge in Starkie's chemist shop, and it was long before the crowd dispersed, and then only as it seemed to follow our wounded shipmates.

But the crowning morning's amusement was in our visit to the panorama of the Battle of Navarino, sketched and painted by Reinagle and exhibited by Burford at his large room in the Strand. It was a faithful though somewhat exaggerated representation of the battle ; plenty of fire and smoke, as also ships on fire and blowing up, masts and yards falling and all sorts of wreckage and confusion ; Turks lowering themselves from stern windows to escape in boats. After

looking round for a time Ramsay took the showman's long wand and
began with a grave countenance to explain the battle : ' Here, ladies
and gentlemen, is the famous battle of Navarino, and the destruction
of the Turkish and Egyptian fleets by the British and their allies, the
French and Russian squadrons. There you see the *Albion's* men
boarding an enemy's ship, the brave Captain Ommanney, with his
cocked hat on, holding up his sword encouraging the boarders. Here
is a Turkish frigate in the act of blowing up ; her captain sets fire to
her himself sooner than strike his colours. And there, gentlemen,
you observe the Egyptian admiral's ship crippled, her masts falling
over the side and her crew crowding into boats to escape ; many you
see in the water, some entangled in the wreck. One poor fellow ties
himself to a spar and to keep well out of the water, is over-balanced,
and there he is, his legs only appearing ; such is an instance of the
horrors of war. And there again you see the Turkish fireships
all in a blaze, drifting towards the fight, but providentially getting
foul of and burning their own ships only.' And in this way for a
time Ramsay kept stalking round the room, pointing out the wonders
of a sea fight, not in the way I have written it, but more adapted to
the open mouths of many of the lookers-on. At last he gave up the
long wand to the showman, who thanked him, wishing he could
engage his services, as it would increase the number of visitors. I
fancy, though, at one time there was a knot of the company which
suspected we were officers by their whispering and smiling, particularly as now and then we could not help laughing at the absurd
way Ramsay was, with great gravity, explaining the battle.

After attending the Duke of Clarence's levee at the Admiralty
we separated. Ramsay and Norcott I have since often come across,
but D'Urban I never again met.

CHAPTER XII

Royal Yacht—In command of the *Onyx*—The Navarino Court-Martial—Promoted Commander—Marriage and close of service

My half-pay time seemed to pass rapidly away. I paid my brother Richard another visit at Waltham Cross, and at the small arm manufactory at Enfield, a sword was made for me. I saw it forged and tempered ; it was then hung up for the night, having a little oil poured on the blade, and so left till examined in the morning, then ground to its required thickness on large stones appearing above the floor whirling rapidly round, the grinders on iron saddles secured to the flooring by strong chains, for a stone once split with its velocity and passed through two stories and the roof of the building. The sword was then brought down on a log of lignum vitæ wood with a violent stroke on its back, followed by another on its edge, then again, on a broader slab of the same wood, on both sides ; this is a great trial, for the blade sometimes splits with the force of the blow. The last method of proof is by placing the point on the foot of an upright bar, one side of which is a strip of brass, graduated in divisions, and the hilt brought down to a certain mark, bowing the blade nearly to a circle and then very gently easing it back, looking carefully to see if it is at all bent and, after serving the other side in the same way, it was handed to me with, ' There, sir, is a blade that will never fail you.' I took it to a sword cutler in the Strand to be mounted as a naval captain's, and needlessly added, ' You never change a blade.' As might be expected he was not over pleased, turned the blade over and over, saying he saw nothing so particular in it to induce him to change it. I said I had seen it forged, ground, and put to a proof I thought no sword could possibly stand. In due time I called, and, to my annoyance, found half the blade *blued* and etched with the royal arms, naval trophies, and also his name as cutler to H.R.H. the Duke of Clarence, &c. I told him he had no directions for this, that we all knew the process of blueing in a small

way interfered with the temper, and as to his name he had no right
to add that ; in fact, it did not enhance the value of the sword ; that
two of mine came from his shop, the last of which had bent nearly
double killing a dog at Lisbon, and so we parted, neither the best of
friends.

At this time Sir Edward Owen was one of the Duke of Clarence's
council at the Admiralty, and as an instance of my former remark,
of his never losing sight of a follower or any officer who had once
sailed with him, early in April [1] he wrote to me to the effect that his
brother's first lieutenant (Vidal) was returning to England invalided,
and offering me the appointment if I had no dislike to the climate or
service ; that I need be in no hurry to decide, and to say nothing.
My answer was that I had been too long in the service to object to
climate or station, and was ready to accept that or any other appointment at his hands. His brother, William Owen, was Governor of
Fernando Po, having also his frigate on the station cruising about
under the command of the first lieutenant, so that the appointment
was of great responsibility. I made every preparation for a start,
completing a stock of linen and all description of fit out, and was kept
a long time in suspense, not *very* anxious for the appointment ; for,
to confess the truth, I had some apprehension of the coast of Africa's
climate. However, in June, another letter from Sir Edward telling
me that Vidal, after a medical survey, had been ordered to rejoin
his ship, and that if I would name a wish for any other appointment
he would endeavour to effect it.

I left all to him, and nothing turned up till August.   When staying at Sandgate, and while sauntering on the beach, a coastguardsman asked if I was Lieutenant Boteler, giving me a letter from
Admiral Harvey, inclosing an Admiralty appointment to the *William
and Mary* royal yacht.   I was taken utterly by surprise—the very
best thing going. In those days an appointment was followed by
promotion at the end of six weeks only—one of the few prizes of
the service.

Next morning off for London, but too late for the Admiralty ;
and, lounging in the Strand, I came across Johnny Waugh, who congratulated me on my appointment, adding, ' But take care he does
not make you jump over-board before three months.'   ' What do
you mean ? '   Why, being Sir Graham Hamond's first lieutenant.'
' No such thing ; much better than that, my appointment is to the
William and Mary yacht.'   ' Well, that is good ; I do indeed wish
you joy ; the talk in the clubs is that you go with Sir Graham.'

[1] 1828.

The following morning to the Admiralty, and at the proper office, said, ' I come to take up my commission for the *William and Mary.*' ' What name, sir ? ' ' Boteler.' ' It is cancelled, sir ' ; and on my exclamation of surprise, ' Of course, sir, we know nothing.' I begged pardon, and sent my card up to Sir Edward Owen, who said he was sorry I came up, that he was in hopes to have prevented it ; and then he explained that the duke had asked the day before, ' Who have you appointed to the yacht ? ' ' Lieutenant Boteler.' ' Oh, you must cancel it, I promised it to another officer last week ' ; and thus ended a brief dream of happiness.[1] I then mentioned my being congratulated the previous evening on an appointment as first lieutenant to Sir G. Hamond. ' Oh,' said Sir Edward, ' that hangs over your head yet ; we gave him the nomination of his captain, commander, and flag lieutenant ; but we named you and another for his first lieutenant, giving him the choice, and we consider it will be you ' ; and so I made my bow.[2] The same afternoon, at the corner of Dover Street, I was accosted by an Admiralty porter. ' Are you not Lieutenant Boteler ? ' He had seen me at the Admiralty, fortunately remembered my face ; he had a note from Sir Edward desiring to see me. The porter had been to my agent, Sir F. Ommanney, my brother at Lincoln's Inn, and to his house in Gower Street, and was just turning into Dover Street, where Lady Harvey was thought to be staying, when he luckily met me ; he had a fair tip, and I made all haste to the Admiralty. Sir Edward told me he was glad his messenger had found me in time to stop my leaving town ; that the officer Lieutenant Forster, appointed to the *Royal George* yacht, at Portsmouth, was in India, and not likely to be home for three or four months, and that at his suggestion the duke had readily appointed me acting lieutenant in his absence, particularly as it would be some compensation for that morning's disappointment, and he added it seemed the best he could do for me, and though nothing was certain, yet it was fairly a step on the ladder to promotion ; that I would have the command of her tender the *Onyx*, a ten-gun brig, and at any rate be in the way of anything turning up. The *Onyx* was particularly agreeable to me ; I should feel quite at home in her, having so lately commanded the *Lyra*, her sister brig.

[1] The officer appointed to the *William and Mary* was Lieutenant (afterwards Captain) Edward John Johnson. He was a surveying officer of high scientific attainments and became first Superintendent of Compasses and a Fellow of the Royal Society.

[2] Rear Admiral Sir Graham Hamond was nominated Commander-in-Chief, East Indies.

I lost no time, first going to Hastings, where my mother and sisters were for the winter, to pick up my baggage, and on to Portsmouth by the same coast route I travelled three years back. While at dinner at the George, seated at another table were two young fellows whom I took to be mids., and I pricked up my ears at hearing them speak of the yacht, one saying : ' I wonder what officer will be sent down to the yacht.' ' Oh, some nob, I suppose.' That was all, I heard no more. Before leaving the coffee-room I asked the waiter if he knew where the *Royal George* was. ' Well up the harbour, sir, abreast of the dockyard.' It was their turn to cock their ears, and to eye me, rightly divining, I suppose, who I was.

The next morning I went off to the *Onyx*, asked for the commanding officer. The gunner came up and I announced myself, and after several inquiries as to her officers and crew, and general state of the brig, said I should come on board to-morrow after the men's dinner and read my commission ; and when about to leave and call the wherry alongside : ' Won't you have your gig, sir ? ' By this time many eyes were on me, for it speedily got wind who I was ; the gigs were called away, the boatswain at the gangway, the side boys ready, and I was duly piped over the side ; and as we shoved off, the oars dropped and the crew gave way with a full swing. I could not for the life of me restrain a smile, all was so much to my satisfaction ; the first position in the whole service for one of my rank ; none but the admiral likely to interfere with me in any way ; my own captain, Sir Michael Seymour, always on Admiralty leave, so that both yacht and *Onyx* were under my charge.

By noon I reported myself at the Admiralty, and took up my commission, and by the day's post received from Sir Michael Seymour my order to command the *Onyx*, as well as some particular instructions for my guidance in that command : the entry of men, none under twenty-three or over thirty-two in age, and none but of known good character, punishments at my discretion, but advising moderation and leniency, to report to him sailings from and returns to port, caution as to expenditure of stores, &c.

The next day my commission was read, two mids. (not those at the hotel), assistant-surgeon, gunner, boatswain and carpenter, a purser's steward and the crew, ten only short of the full complement of seventy-five. The gunner, Mullins, I already felt an interest in. He was with my brother Thomas during the five years' survey on the East Coast of Africa, as also with him up a river during an encounter with a very large hippopotamus, the skull of which is now in the museum at Canterbury. In a few days I had the brig ready for sea, complete in provisions and stores, and the crew also.

The first night I was scarcely half-an-hour in bed when I was attacked by a legion of bugs; my bed-place swarmed with them. The brig had just returned from the Coast of Africa; the climate there helps marvellously the increase of this noxious insect. Her late commander W. J. Cole was my messmate in the *Northumberland*; he must have been either case-hardened, not caring for them, or they not caring for him. After sleeping on the cabin deck all night, and early in the morning sending for the carpenter to dismantle the standing bed-place entirely, he expressed surprise, for he had never heard the commander complain, nor had he any suspicion of such a colony. All the wood framing was removed, and sacking used instead, laced to small screw eye bolts, and such other measures, that I ever after slept in peace—though what escaped migrated forward and invaded the midshipmen's cabins, greatly to their disturbance.

I seldom dined on board, having been made honorary member of the *Victory's* mess, as also of the *Spartiate's*, Marine Artillery, and 52nd. In the *Spartiate* was Lieutenant Lapidge, who had the *Falcon* at Lisbon, and to whom I gave my hanging compass, when I gave up the *Lyra*, and which he now returned to me for the *Onyx*. ' Ah,' said he, ' when you gave it to me I thought myself sure of promotion, but the admiral greatly disappointed me; the tables are turned, you will get the step first now '—this with almost tears in his eyes. We also *all* thought he would have had Coquimbo's hauling down vacancy.

For over the first week in the *Onyx* the talk here was that I was to be Sir G. Hamond's first lieutenant, and it was known he had written to Captain Ommanney about me, and so much was my position coveted that three officers asked me to give them early notice of my leaving, that they might apply for the yacht.

At the end of three weeks, a letter from Sir Edward Owen, that if the Duke of Clarence continued Lord High Admiral he should retain his seat at the board; but if not, he was a candidate for the command in India and would be glad to have me as his first lieutenant; that he did not quite know how his list stood for promotion, but there were two before me; it was something to say and be proud of, to be nominated first lieutenant to two admirals in succession, both going to India. For several days I was in doubt whether it would not be better to accept this offer at once instead of waiting in anxious suspense, as to the chance of remaining in the yacht. Another letter from Sir Edward put all doubts aside. He had been to the Admiralty and was glad to hear my appointment was likely to be confirmed, that he thought this was too interesting to be kept from me a day.[1]

The same day, 2nd October, I received my first sailing orders to pick up 190 coastguardsmen from New Haven, Shoreham, Worthing, Arundel and Littlehampton, to complete the crew of the *Melville* and *Spartiate*, then waiting at Spithead; and to point out the different stations along shore, I had a chief officer on board in addition to a first-rate branch pilot (Mr Spraggs), on the permanent establishment of the yacht's crew, so I felt quite free from any anxiety as to pilotage; embarked about 130, and when off Littlehampton at some considerable distance from the station, to save time, particularly as it was getting late, I ran in to meet the boats coming off, soundings very regular, chiefly four and five fathoms. The weather seemed uncertain and lowering to windward, and I thought it as well to reef, and in rounding to for that purpose to my surprise we took the ground and the next send she was fast enough, and it was within twenty minutes of high water; we let go an anchor, let her take three or four fathom chain, furled sails, out boat and sent a kedge well out to seaward. The brig lifted and struck rather hard several times, as the tide continued to rise a little. By this time fifty more men came alongside; their chief officer said they had made signal we were running into danger, that the chief officer on board ought to have known better. When fairly afloat we up anchor; our decks were crowded with coastguardsmen, whom in this instance we were glad to make use of in manning the hawser and hauling us off to the kedge, while our crew were on the yards ready to let fall and make sail as the brig canted, and it was altogether a close shave; we instantly gathered way, held our own, and, with one tack only, cleared all danger, and in good time too, for the weather, already threatening, became rough in heavy squalls; by carrying on we reached a snug little anchorage under Selsea Bill,—a ridge of rocks, where we let go two anchors, and so rode out a boisterous night very comfortably, and to ease the brig from unnecessary back sail, I furled the courses, calling for volunteers among the coastguardsmen to assist, answered by two or three *Irishmen* with—' Our nailed boots won't agree with your rigging, sir.' But the main reason was, that the greater part of our passengers were terribly sea sick.

[1] Rear Admiral Sir Edward Owen did in fact get the East Indies command in place of Sir Graham Hamond.

The following morning we up anchors, and ran into Spithead. The captain of the *Melville* rather offended my dignity, in expecting me to take the *Onyx* alongside, and so deliver my cargo. Why, the chance was her topmasts would have been knocked away, and other damage as well. I was sorry the *Spartiate* was off in this way. · I lost my messmates and the pleasant dinner to sit down to after the day's work was over. While off Brighton two guns fired (to hurry off the beachmen) brought two boats full of visitors, but I was forced to be uncivil and refuse admittance. On reporting myself to the admiral, he was well satisfied with my dispatch, and added he felt much for me in last night's gale.

About this time I received an invitation from Captain Ommanney for the anniversary of Navarino. Being under momentary expectation of sailing orders, I was truly sorry to decline. I should have met my old friends, Captains Campbell, Drake, Lieutenants Norcott, Ramsay, Waugh and Langtry, Doctor Hillyar and three or four others. I was to have taken with me a union-jack, as Captain O. did not wish to hoist his Turkish ensign without the union-jack over it. This was the large ensign I brought from the Turkish admiral's ship the morning after the battle, and gave to Captain Ommanney. My next order was to cruise off the Isle of Wight in the fair way to look out for a Russian squadron, expected to pass down Channel ; and I was three weeks on this look out, occasionally running back to shew my number, in case of being wanted for other duty.

I had to apply to the Navy Office for a dinghy. The board consisted of three commissioners, post captains, and they sign all letters, ' We are your affectionate friends ' ; and this official style reminded me of a humorous story, related of Captain John Tower, who, when in command of a frigate, made some alteration which the navy board considered a dilapidation, and consequently put an impress against his pay to some considerable amount, signing the letter as usual ' your affectionate friends,' &c. In his remonstrance to this charge he signed, ' I am your affectionate friend, Jno. Tower.' For this he received a reprimand from the board. But John Tower was not to let them off without a parting shot, and in acknowledging the receipt of their reprimand he begged to say, ' I am no longer your affectionate friend, Jno. Tower.' [1]

The *Melville*, at Spithead, was again suddenly ordered to sea, and being short of men, I was once more sent off with despatches for

---

[1] This story is told of Captain Sir John Phillimore, in the *Dictionary of National Biography*.

Captain Mingaye, of the *Hyperion*, at Newhaven. She was an old
French frigate, and when cleared out and sufficiently lightened, was
floated into the river, and there fixed in the mud as headquarters of
the coastguard. We were soon off Newhaven, and shewed our
number, but there was no chance of further communication, and
we ran back to St Helen's for the night, and back again next day,
and off Newhaven towards evening. The landing was by no means
tempting ; but fearing to be thought wanting in zeal, I set off,
taking with me a blue light, lantern, and a musket, the wind still
fresh and right on shore. By the time we were two-thirds of the
way the sea broke into surf outside of us, and it was then impossible
to turn back, for the chance would be an upset. As we neared, the
pilots on the pier waved their hats to warn us off, but as I supposed
to direct us more on one side. I stood up for an instant, pointing
with my arm, as if to ask if I was steering right. As none stirred, I
kept on, and just as I said to my coxswain, ' It's not so bad, after
all,' a heavy sea broke in surf under our stern, and shot us over
the bar with astonishing velocity, and the boat was so canted up
that I slipped off my seat to the grating, and the coxswain on his
back, heels up. Had the boat's gripe touched, nothing could have
saved us ;—the tide running out so strong. On going on board the
Hyperion, I found a signal had been made to prevent me leaving
the brig. When I landed to report myself to Captain Mingaye,
he began to find fault at my disregarding the signal, &c. However,
I was desired to return to the *Onyx* ; not to attempt it by my boat,
but by the *Hyperion's* life-boat, her officer being Lieutenant Finch.
When near the bar, where the surf looked ugly enough, I chanced
to look back, and there was my gig close astern. I called out,
' What are you about ? Go back to the ship.' ' Ready to pick you
up, sir.' By this time, as we neared the bar, the pilots on the jetty
head exclaimed, ' For God's sake, gentlemen, don't try it ; it's
more than your lives are worth.' Finch turned to me, saying,
' What do you think of it, sir ? ' ' Oh,' I replied, ' you are the
officer of the boat—I am only a passenger.' ' That is it, is it ? then,
here goes ! ' (So like him, as I afterwards found out.) But at the
first attempt the boat was sent back half full of water, and luckily
not keel up, and we returned to the ship. I had no doubt of the
result, but it was not my *place* to say so. I wrote to the admiral
the same evening, as also did Captain Mingaye, of my safety, and
requesting the *Onyx* might be sent back for the men, he supposing
she had gone to Portsmouth. I differed in this ; as it blew so very
hard I thought she would run for the Downs, and I was not far out ;
208

she made for and anchored under Dungeness. The next morning I was sent by coach to Hastings to the quarters of the divisional, Lieutenant Green.

Fancying I should have a wetting over the bar I had left my watch and purse, and was by no means in my Sunday's best (the first lieutenant of the frigate most kindly setting me up in funds), and as soon as the coach was ready I bundled in, it being Sunday, too glad to hide my diminished head, travelling in shabby uniform, cocked hat and sword, and for the same reasons I was loth to shew myself in Hastings, where I had spent two gay seasons with my family, and so left the coach at Bexhill, and walked down to the beach to look for Paddy Norcott, who was in a tower not far off. I soon came across a coastguardsman on duty, who, seeing an officer, brought his cutlass to the salute, and on my asking in which tower was Lieutenant Norcott, ' Indeed, sur, I don't exactly know, the next sentry perhaps may,' and on I went, and the next sentry said, ' Sure, sur, he is in *that* tower,' and there I was received by Norcott most heartily, as also by his wife, who at once exclaimed, ' Oh, Mr Boteler, ar'n't you surprised to see me here ? I have only two antipathies in the world, rats and a step ladder, and when I got out of the carriage there was one right before me. I thought I should have fainted.' But Paddy was greatly excited when he heard I was in a measure cast ashore half wrecked, offered to set me up with every possible thing I might want, &c. I spent an agreeable hour in the tower. He was much disgusted with his quarters and the service, and more so with Captain Mingaye, who in no way would let him leave.

I must here relate Paddy's humorous scheme for getting clear. Two or three months later, when in Portsmouth Harbour, I saw the *Hyperion's* tender, the *Wolf* cutter, coming in, and with the aid of my glass made out Norcott on deck. I was soon alongside. I could not help laughing ; he had on a white cap and an old glazed cocked hat over it. ' Why, what's the matter, Norcott ? ' ' Oh, I am not at all well ; I am going to the hospital to be invalided.' He said this with a grave face, but with a twinkle in his eye. I con- tinued to stare at his very white face. At last he laughed out, ' I don't know how it will end, I hope Dr Mortimer won't see it. I have chalked my face, and I mean to chalk my tongue a little before I shew it.' Some days after I called on him at Haslar ; he told me Dr Mortimer, after feeling his pulse and looking at his tongue, asked what ailed him, and on his reply that the tower was damp and gave him colds and rheumatic pains, and that the coastguard service

disagreed with him, ' Ah,' said the doctor, once more peering into
his face, ' I see, I see,' smiling, ' but we must try to set you up.'
All medicine went out of the window, and he shewed me where it
trickled down a lean-to roof. He was very comfortably lodged,
though only for a time, for all ended in his being invalided.

After a short stay at the tower I walked into Hastings and
reported myself at the coastguard watch-house as ordered. Lieutenant Green was with his wife in handsome lodgings. He received
me with hospitality, and wished me to accompany them to an
evening party. I remained the night and after breakfast went off
to the *Wolf*, which had just arrived from Newhaven with my gig
and crew. What a contrast between the cutter and *Onyx* for a
lieutenant's command ! forgetting how proud I was when my turn
came for three months in the *Seagull* tender to the *Northumberland*.
We made sail for Newhaven, and in the afternoon fell in with the
Onyx. I knew her before in signal distance, and before her topsails
were above the horizon, by a new cloth in her top-gallant sail. I
need not say how pleased I felt at stepping on board, as also with
the hearty congratulations of the young officers. They all expressed
the anxiety they had been in as to my safety, and Maynard, the
senior mate, had hovered about as close in and as long as it was
prudent looking out for me. He saw me leave the *Hyperion* for
the bar, but the jetty was in the way, and it speedily became too
dark to make out any more. The *Onyx* had on board the men I
was sent for, and early next morning we anchored at Spithead,
and discharged them into the *Melville*.

About this time, with one of my mids. in Dudley's shop, a little
man was purchasing a dirk for his son. Smith, the midshipman,
said : ' Do you know who that is, sir ? ' ' No ! ' ' Sir Graham
Hamond.' Directly after, Sir Graham spoke to Mr Smith, asking
what ship he was in. ' The *Royal George*, sir.' ' Pray, who is your
lieutenant ? ' ' Mr Boteler, sir,' pointing me out. Sir Graham
eyed me *all over*, then taking me by the arm and leading me into
the street, said : ' I am sorry you and I have not sailed together ;
if the service knew how I have been treated it would make their
hair stand on end.' He then said something complimentary on
what he had heard of me and that he was glad to make my acquaintance, &c. Whatever he might be *afloat*, on shore I found him
agreeable, friendly, and most hospitable.

While looking out for the Russian squadron, I saw a ship coming
from the west and with signals that I could not make out ; but
on calling the attention of our signal man, I found she was the

Falcon, Lord Yarborough's yacht, who was on board, as her commodore's broad pennant was flying ; I shewed our number and soon after went and paid my respects ; I landed with him and was shewn over one of his estates on the south shore of the Isle of Wight ; I also dined on board his ship, the brig keeping company. The *Falcon* was frigate built, about the size of the *Royal George*, with sixteen brass guns and well and fully manned, and all carried on as like a man-of-war as possible. A few days after I ran over to Cowes and again dined on board his yacht, a large party of twenty, the principal men in the island, to all of whom I was particularly introduced, for the purpose as his lordship told me, after they were gone, of making me acquainted with many I was likely to meet in the yacht season ; and I may here say at his paying off and commissioning dinner parties, I was always included.

Ned Cannon, appointed flag lieutenant, had arrived from the West Indies just in time, and went off to the *Southampton*,[1] at Spithead, and finding Sir Edward was on shore, was about to follow ; but said one of the officers—' Won't you see Lady Owen first ? ' ' Lady Owen, I didn't know he was married ! ' ' Why she is your own sister, man.'[2] Many of her officers I knew, Captain Fisher once proposed my being his first lieutenant ; he was not a pleasant man to sail with, he trusted no one, unnecessarily interfered in most trifling things, had the officer of the watch down continually to his cabin, and was in general a tormenting fidget. Mr Parker, the commander, was a fine fellow, gallant and spirited ; several others I was more or less acquainted with.

I must take this opportunity of relating some anecdotes of Parker ; he was master's mate (in those days so-called) in the first of my seagoing ships, the *Majestic*, and I was put under his care ; on parting he gave me his miniature, in water colours, by the ship's painter, and he had from me a silver pencil-case, these we each kept for over forty years. While a *young* mid., off Brest, his ship captured a French merchant brig, and a prize crew consisting of Parker, a quarter-master and seven or eight men was put in her, to take her to Plymouth. The morning after leaving, a suspicious vessel was seen to windward, and there was no doubt of her character, she was evidently a privateer, for she soon made all sail in chase. Parker

---

[1] The *Southampton* (Captain Peter Fisher), commissioned as flagship of Rear Admiral Sir Edward Owen, Commander-in-Chief, East Indies. One of her lieutenants was Lieutenant Edward Cannon.

[2] The actual facts eliminate ' Ned Cannon.' Sir Edward Owen married in 1829 Selena, daughter of Captain John Baker Hay, R.N. Lady Owen's brother, Lieutenant James Beckford Lewis Hay, became Flag Lieutenant to Sir Edward Owen.

ran as long as he could, and finding that the Frenchman was rapidly overhauling the prize, and that there was no chance of escape, suddenly thought of a ruse. He placed his men, each with two or three ropes to let go, so that a few could do the work of many ; took in all his studding sails together, down with the helm and hauled up directly to face his adversary; having, at the same time, all the stray hats and caps on handspikes, &c. just above the bulwarks, and men crawling about under cover, moving them so as to make it supposed that she was well manned. The privateer for a time continued to near, then hesitated, shortened sail, and then, fortunately for Parker, made off, Parker continuing the *chase* ! and then bore away and took the prize safely into Plymouth.

At another time in the *Majestic* (the year before I joined her) while in the Baltic, the ship took a Danish lugger, with one brass six-pounder and six swivels. Parker and a strong crew were put in charge to take her to Gothenburg, the *Majestic* away through the Belt for Carlscrona ; two or three days after, Sir James Saumarez in the *Victory*, with two other ships, passing through the Belt at daybreak, found themselves not far from three or four Danish luggers and row boats. All scuttled away to escape, the English following in chase, firing their bow guns ; all were getting clear off but one, which, to their surprise, down with the Danish and up with English colours, and commenced firing away at the others. This was Parker, who, on being questioned by Sir James and telling his story, was reprimanded for his temerity, Parker saying—' If you had not come across us, I would have had one of those luggers at night ! '

But Parker's crowning exploit was in the Mediterranean, when a midshipman in the *Standard*, Captain Thomas Harvey. Early one morning a large merchant ship was seen, and it being a fine day and little wind, two boats were sent away in chase ; one with a lieutenant and Parker, the other with a mate ; the crews well armed and eight marines as well. The ship took no notice of the boats, but kept on ; soon all were out of sight of the *Standard*, and I believe the recall was made with one or two guns. A breeze had sprung up and the ship soon sailed away, but the boats followed. Many of the details I never heard—at least, I have no remembrance of them, it was in my midshipman days ; nor is it in my mind where the event happened, excepting that it was on the African Coast by Tripoli or Tunis. However, the main facts were, that at night the boats found the ship fast to a battery, and not a merchant vessel, but a Turkish frigate armed ' *en flute*,' and, notwithstanding, the chase was reck-

lessly unsuspicious, or not dreaming of an attack, the greater part
of her officers and crew had landed ; finding they were not challenged,
in fact, not discovered, both boats boarded over the bows, cheering
and shouting, seemingly to increase their number. The Turks were
paralysed at once and began to jump overboard and swim on shore.
There was of course some resistance. The lieutenant was killed,
some of the men also killed and wounded, and the mate shewed the
white feather ; but Parker encouraged, and gallantly led them on,
cleared the ship of the rest of the Turks, cut the hawsers away from
the fort, loosed a sail or two, and brought the ship off. When much
too late, those on shore and in the fort began to stir themselves ;
they all were completely taken by surprise. Lord Collingwood was
in the offing and, attracted by the firing, had stood on and met the
boats with their prize. Parker wished to screen the mate and let it
be supposed he commanded when the lieutenant fell, but the men
would not allow it. The poor fellow was permitted to leave the
service without further notice of his offence. Lord Collingwood was
immensely pleased with Parker's gallantry, and promised to promote
him directly he served his time. I only remember Parker speaking
of this *but once* and then to say that, being very tired, he had gone
into the cabin and fallen asleep on a sofa or bed, and how *frightened*
he was at being suddenly disturbed by some noise, and putting his
hand on the bald head of a Turk, for he thought all were out of the
ship.

After this long digression I must return to the *Onyx*. The day
following my visit to the *Southampton* I was ordered to the westward, the *Southampton* weighing at the same time, and we both
started together with a foul wind, which towards evening became
fresh, and rather strong before midnight. Our pilot wished to run
back. ' Where is the frigate ? ' ' Holding on, sir.' ' And so will
I.' But when they reported she had given it up I then also up
helm and anchored at St Helen's, rather in shore ; the frigate
further out. I went on board and breakfasted with Sir Edward
and his lady, and what had ' the commodore ' come to !—for many
years he was always ' the commodore ' even long after he was an
admiral—there was a piano in his cabin !

When I left I said I should go through the Needles, and he remarked I should take nothing by it ; we shook hands and off I went.
Before reaching the Needles the wind fell and the tide against us ;
we anchored. Looking at a house I saw numbers in different panes
of a window, three, eight, five, and they told me it was Sir Graham
Hamond's house, and in the signal book I found it was asking me to

dine ; my answer was, of course, in the affirmative. As my boat was
being manned I saw the little man hurrying away for a pony, and then
as I pulled on shore he was coming to the landing-place with one of
his children. He really seemed glad to have me ; he and Lady
Hamond were so pleasantly agreeable and hospitable. They made
me promise never to pass their house if possible, but always to land
and see them. When I named my visit to Sir Edward that morning
Sir Graham became irritated, said he heard Sir Edward had talked
of going through the Needles passage, that he wondered he could
have the face to shew his flag in sight of his house. Sir Graham was,
no doubt, badly treated, he was put to the expense of £1,000 or £2,000
in preparing an outfit, and was then put aside ; of course, he never
received his appointment, as in that case it could not have been
cancelled. I never heard or could make out the real story. It was
something in one's life to say that, as the chosen first lieutenant of
two commanders-in-chief going to India, I had on the same day
breakfasted with one and dined with the other.

On the 2nd January, the 'demand' was at the *Victory's* mast-
head, and on looking out to sea I saw a frigate with her number
and the Union under it, shewing her name to be low in the alpha-
betical list of the navy, the list being divided into three parts,
the Union above for the first part, and in the middle for the second.
Down to the cabin, and by the signals there she was, as I suspected,
the *Undaunted*, from India. It was not long before I was on board
and introduced myself to Mr Forster, telling him I was keeping his
place warm in the yacht, hoping he would not join for three days.
It was news to him ; he was not aware of his appointment.

It was the first day of my dining with the admiral,[1] and his
saying, as I made my bow, ' I am sorry we are to lose you just as
I am beginning to know you,' did not tend to raise my already low
spirits. It was a large party, Sir Augustus Clifford, the captain of
the *Undaunted*—the lion of the day, so much Indian news to tell
and which he told well. By my side was Captain John Absolom
(commonly called ' Absolute ') Griffiths;[2] a very Tartar in the service.
With a squeaky voice he began, ' Pray, are you John Harvey
Boteler ? ' ' Oh, then you are the officer my friend Hamond was
to have as his first lieutenant. He wrote to me to make inquiries,
and, I need not say, all was in your favour.' The next morning
I was at the admiral's office, saw the secretary, Mr Brenton (brother

---

[1] ' The admiral ' was Admiral the Hon. Sir Robert Stopford, K.C.B., Commander-
in-Chief, Portsmouth, with his flag in the *Victory* (Captain the Hon. G. Elliot).
[2] His name actually was Anselm John Griffiths.

214

to Sir Jahleel); the only news was that Forster's appointment to the yacht had come down, and dated in September, therefore telling nothing new. As an excuse for my evident anxiety, I told the secretary I had fair reasons to expect confirmation to the yacht, and so, of course, felt the suspense. That evening my senior mate, a *cantankerous* fellow, ever ready with bad news and never, if possible, giving good, told me he had seen Mr Forster, who had said he should come on board to-morrow. I had packed up all my things and had my chest lashed up ready to send to the dockyard, for conveyance to Deal by a Government lighter. In the morning the postman squinted down my skylight. '*No* letter for you to-day, sir '; and so I had a whip on the yard in readiness for my chest, for I could not bear the idea of seeming to linger. Very soon after I heard the peculiar trickling of a small rope overhead, and knew some flag was being hoisted, and on my calling out, ' What's all that ? ' ' Your signal from the admiral's office, sir.' I jumped up, opened my chest for uniforms, &c., for everything was packed up, was on shore in no time, for I felt sure something important was in the wind, and I caught myself almost on a run, then checking my haste, thinking what a fool I was to so hurry and not take it more easy, but still I had difficulty in restraining my speed. I saw the secretary, who told me I was going off immediately with secret orders, and that the admiral wished to see me (anything for delay and for time to use interest at the Admiralty), and being asked and finding that I was ready for sea (for I had all the crew on board for Forster's inspection), ' Here is Hunt the police officer from Bow Street, you are to take him on board ; Brenton is preparing your orders. In the meanwhile Captain Elliot will be glad of your company at breakfast, and, by the way, I am happy to say your appointment to the yacht is confirmed.'

So at once I was *somebody*, hence Captain Elliot's invitation, for till this he had never noticed or spoken to me. Outside was our pilot, Mr Spraggs. ' Any news, sir ? ' ' Yes, we are off directly ; go on board at once, and desire Mr Smith to have all ready for slipping.' I breakfasted with Captain and Mrs Elliot ; she was a very handsome woman, a Miss Ness, one of three sisters, the eldest very plain, the second untidy and slovenly ; they were termed ' prettiness,' ' ugliness,' and ' nastiness.'

And all this time the happy news. How buoyant I felt, my mind and anxiety fully relieved, promotion secured : already, as they often told me, I ranked as the junior commander. Well, I got my orders and with Hunt by my side went off to the brig. It was

blowing strong, wind right out, and a rapid ebb tide. In the act
of slipping, both chain and rope spring parted, and we shot through
the narrows stern foremost, almost as fast as if head foremost. We
soon got her round, and by the time we reached Spithead were
obliged to treble-reef topsails. We ran through the Needles, and
hove to off the Isle of Wight, in the fair way of ships passing. The
facts were that Roland Stevenson, a great government defaulter,
was escaping, and was supposed to be on board an American ship
that was likely to be going down channel this day or to-morrow.
I was to bring her to, take possession, and examine the passengers,
and in case of resistance I was to threaten to bring the ship into
Portsmouth. Nothing passed that day, but the next morning a
large ship came along, and I tied the ensign into a whiff as a signal
to speak. No notice till we fired a gun ; she then hove to, and I
boarded with Hunt, explained the case, looked over the list of
passengers, and examined them as well. The captain was very civil,
though he did not much like the detention with such a fine fair wind.
The next ship bowling along hoisted American colours to my signal
to speak, but took no other notice ; I fired a gun, still with no effect.
I then gave her a shot close across the bows, and on this she hove to.
The captain began to show his teeth immediately we went on board.
In as few words as possible I let him know I was ordered to search
for a person who was supposed to be escaping in his ship. He at
first protested against any search and at being delayed. I then told
him I should take possession of his ship and carry her to Portsmouth,
and I made him produce the list of passengers and have them all up
for examination. I asked what lady passengers were on board.
' Well, this beats all ; what will you require next ? ' ' It is life or
death, and he may be disguised in petticoats.' Hunt whispered to
me, ' You beat me, sir.' I did this mainly to tease the Yankee.
A gentleman came forward, ' One is my wife, sir ' ; another said his
sister was on board, and I said it was sufficient. I also desired the
hands to be turned up and mustered before the police officer, and the
captain again began to bluster, and I let him understand that his very
conduct made me suspicious, and that if an English merchant vessel
under similar circumstances had thrown as much opposition to the
search of an American officer at the mouth of their port he would
not be let off as easily, and I mustered and examined the whole crew,
and wished the passengers a pleasant passage across the Atlantic.
One of them, laughing, said he was glad I had riled the captain, he
was such an unsociable fellow. As I went over the side the captain
offered his hand, which I declined to take, his whole manner had

been so offensive. Late, indeed when dark, I ran into the harbour and picked up the buoy, under sail, as I almost always did. The wind, though fresh, being off the land, there was no sea to speak of, and the policeman never turned a hair. He was most entertaining and very graphic in relating several events as a Bow Street runner. After dinner (two of my mids. with us), he warmed over his adventures, evidently encouraged by the marked attention we paid to them. One was remarkable, and sufficiently on my memory to give it a place here, though with the loss of his animation and peculiar manner and quaint words (not slang) he used, expressing himself. This story was, that he called on a gentleman at the West End, introducing himself as a police officer, and telling him, from information, it was known that he was the next day going down the road (to Uxbridge, I believe), and would travel post, and that also he was to be waylaid and an attempt made to rob him. The gentleman said it was true as to his going, but he would easily settle the other matter by staying at home. Hunt said he would go in the chaise and would take care no harm should come to him, and assured him of safety, and for the ends of justice he hoped he would not give up the journey. Hunt enlarged on the fight he had to induce the ' gent.' to go, but at last succeeded, and they both set off on the journey. At the very place expected, two fellows, mounted, dashed at them; one dismounted the post boy and the other, when about to open the door, caught sight of Hunt, and with an exclamation turned to bolt. Hunt was too quick for him, fired his pistol, and from the man's shout was satisfied he had hit him hard. He then told the gentleman he would go to the end of the stage with him and return to London, and shortly would have the fellow, who could not now escape him. And Hunt went on to tell of the many visits to surgeons for several days, and the difficulty he met with to get any answers at all from some. In the end, at a small surgery he got every information. A man had been dressed for a gun shot wound in the shoulder ; he recognised the bullet with his mark on it, but did not touch it till another person came in to witness his sealing it up ; after this a watch was set and the man captured. I am quite aware of not doing justice to the story, but such are the facts.

One other of his stories has just crossed my memory. A few years prior to this time, smuggling was carried on to a great extent, and in a most daring manner, on the coast between Deal and Dover, more particularly in the neighbourhood of Kingsdown and St Margaret's Bay ; I had myself, in those days, some knowledge of those affairs. The smugglers gathered in force, forming into three

parties, the centre one to run or work the cargo, the other two, on
each side, to face and keep off the coastguard ; strong and well
armed as the coastguard were, several were killed and wounded in
these desperate encounters ; one a lieutenant, afterwards a commander, was riddled with shot, fourteen in all, large and small, were
taken from him ; he was supposed to be lamed for life and had a
pension equal to that for the loss of a limb. I cannot recall his
name, but I knew him well, and he was staying with us in Canterbury, and at that time was able to get about with the help of a stick ;
one shot was still embedded in the leg and could not be got at.

But to the smuggling : a strong party was also on the cliffs,
ready to carry the tubs into the country. Hunt was sent down, and
at the Walmer Castle Inn in Deal chanced to be in a room with a
mid., Simmonds of the *Ramillies*, in the Downs. I knew him also.
Hunt said they had a long talk over their grog, and Simmonds tried
hard to find out his calling ; but Hunt only said : ' You will see me
again, perhaps to-night, and not know me.' Towards or after
midnight, Simmonds, with two men, was somewhere inland of St
Margaret's, and hearing a scuffling of many feet, started forward
and seized a countryman, and with several questions wanted to
know what he was doing and was inclined to detain him, and here
Hunt, telling the story, said : ' That was *me*,' and he appeared
much amused at the astonishment of the young officer, when he
added—' I told you you would not know me, but you must let me
be off, I expect to capture a leading man,' and this he did. He was
convicted at Canterbury, exchequered and heavily fined.

I think I may relate a *trick*, as my father chose to call it, that
the smugglers played him ; I well remember it when a little boy ;
our footman coming in with a ' tub ' of Hollands that, with another,
was just found in the barn. They were a present to my father for
allowing thirty tubs to be in his barn for two or three days ! My
father professed to be angry, but I well remember his praising the
stuff and enjoying sundry glasses of it.

Both brandy and Hollands were always smuggled in tubs of
between two and four gallons each, and this reminds me also, when
a smaller child still, of being out with two nursemaids and two or
three other brothers and sisters, in a bye lane, and unfrequented road
across country to Canterbury, and being overtaken by five or six
men mounted and with led horses, each with tubs slung across
them. We were alarmed : we thought of them as Ali Baba and the
forty thieves. I should not, perhaps, so well have remembered this
—I don't know that anything led to it—but one of the men jumped

off his horse and soundly kissed both the maids amidst much laughing. We never mentioned this at home, we were cautioned not.

I received an order to take £30,000 in specie, from the *Madagascar* frigate, Captain Frederick Spencer,[1] for Gibraltar. Captain S. not being ready, I had the job. I went to the frigate, and was cautioned by her captain to take particular care as to the taking on board. I don't know if he recognised me, when I was with him in the stage-coach from Triphook.[2] However, I did him, and could not help answering that I had charge of nearly 300,000 dollars in the West Indies, and well understood the responsibility.

In a day or two I started, had a tolerable passage, and ran into Gibraltar with all studding sails, thinking to shew our smartness in shortening sail at one pipe ; when, to my dismay, I first noticed a small craft, leaving the anchorage likewise, with a dead fair wind. I knew it was all up with us, and that I was sure not to carry the wind. I at once shortened sail, hoisted out the boats, and took the brig in tow. A portion of the troops were exercising on Europa Point, laughing at us, for it was a joke with them to see a man-of-war being ' back-strapped,' for in fact that was our case, drifting slowly into the Mediterranean sea. I had just before this been amusing the young officers with the story of being ' back-strapped,' not dreaming that we should shew ourselves in so inglorious a posi-tion. However, we got out of it by the *Pyramus* making a signal for all boats to tow ; and they *did* tow us, at the rate of four knots, into the anchorage.

I most unwittingly got into a scrape. Whenever a junior officer enters a port it is his business directly to wait on the senior officer. I was sufficiently long in doing this to get a gun from the *Pyramus,* Sir Thomas Fellowes, to go on board his ship. I was not long in doing so, making my apology, with the excuse of a party of officers coming off, some of whom were old acquaintances. In fact, the sudden appearance of Robby M'Clure, to announce my boat being manned, with his close cropped hair ; the officers shouting, ' Why, Robby, is that you ? ' He had been at the Military College with them two years back. He only smiled. Coming down to report my boat, shut his mouth.

However, Sir Thomas was easily appeased. He did not know the *Onyx,* and wished for news ; and he took me in his boat to the

<hr>

[1] This is probably a mistake. Captain the Hon. Sir Robert Cavendish Spencer commanded the *Madagascar,* not his brother Frederick (afterwards Earl Spencer).

[2] Presumably Liphook.

governor, Sir George Don, poor man ! I was announced to him, in bed. He began by saying he was much better ; that it was but a bout of sciatica ; thanked me for my kind enquiries, &c., &c. All this time I had said nothing respecting his health, but he took it all as meant ; asked some questions respecting my passage out, and finally asked me to dinner. This affair over, I started for the 7th Fusiliers, and called on my cousin Harvey, a lieutenant of the regiment ; and, after a time, I, not unwilling, took a walk with him, over the principal rampart, the lighthouse, the squares, and everything worth a visit in the town ; and from all this to the galleries, mounted with 32 and 42-pounder carronades, in the covered way, by the side of the mountain, running up quite 200 feet on the side of the rock facing the neutral ground, between the rock and the Spanish main, a distance of two or three miles inland. We then went up to the sentry on the top of the hill, asked him if anything was moving, &c., and if the baboons were visible. He had only seen one, they were keeping snug and warm ; appeared angry. Having to leave the face of the hill which appeared to be descending the precipitous face of the rock and the Mediterranean sea, we clambered along some distance down on our own side, when we were disturbed by a stone whizzing by, thrown by a beast of a monkey, and we suddenly saw a whole troop of them clustered together, and we found it advisable to make off ; they were evidently offended at our intrusion ; and we managed to find our way down the rock. These monkeys, or rather baboons, are sometimes a source of great trouble and annoyance to the inhabitants, robbing their gardens with great dexterity ; they have been known to form a flock of one or two hundred, spread themselves in a line from the garden up to the top of the hill, and so throw the apples, or what not, from one to the other, right away. In this way of a morning, some time back, they almost cleared the governor's garden of the remainder of his fruit. No one is permitted to shoot or molest them, they are held in such estimation. A path leads up the side of the rock, which is nearly perpendicular, from the square patch of ground directly under, where a fishing village is established, and remains unmolested. The Spanish forces once got hold of this, and landed a party of men, who in time managed to get up the path and near the summit, when the dog-faced baboons made such a disturbance that the garrison were alarmed, came up in such strength that the objectionable Spaniards were soon hurled back, and beaten down the cliffs with great slaughter.

My cousin then took me to the St Paul's Cavern ; a most won-

220

drous excavation and gigantic in the extreme. We went down by steps cut in the rock, and then, some distance further, by a rope ladder. The stalactites were enormous, hanging from the roof in wild disorder. Many attempts at exploring these regions have been made, and have utterly failed, from coming suddenly upon water,—always on the move, and falling into space. We seemed to be intruding, and were glad to make our way back again.

We had a capital dinner at the governor's ; one of the dishes, beccaficoes, a small bird, was most delicious. The governor asked me to dine the following day, and on my saying I was engaged to dine with Mr Harvey : ' Oh, tell him he must dine here as well ; young Harvey, he will be breaking his neck some day. Why, sir, he drove a four-in-hand trap over the draw-bridges the other day, notwithstanding the warning of the sentries.'

The next day I called on Jack Tupper of the 23rd Fusiliers, and others of my acquaintance in the garrison, and gave out that I should be most happy to take any three officers to England. I left it to themselves to fix who were to be the party, but I could only take three.

I must relate a curious circumstance : we were within an ace of being overrun with rats. I had anchored with two anchors to the seaward, hauling in the stern towards the rock by a nine inch hawser. I had barely finished this, when I saw two large rats crawling along the hawser towards the ship. I gave a mid. leave to have a crack at them, when I suddenly remembered the chance of a shot injuring the rope just in time. Our armourer made a large tin funnel, which when on the rope effectually baulked the expected intruders.

A day or two after this I started for Portsmouth, having Captain Shaw and the paymaster of the 23rd, and Lieutenant Widrington of the 7th Fusiliers as passengers. We had a beautiful passage of six days across the bay, undisturbed by sea enough to slip a glass off the table even, and we had a quiet rubber every evening. I wished to refund a sovereign to each of my guests, they scouted the notion and were so generous to my steward, giving him their bedding &c., that they upset his usual quiet equanimity, so completely turning his head that shortly after I had to discharge him. I dined with the admiral that day, and some of the knowing ones were surprised at a dish of peas which I had brought from Gibraltar.

In April I was ordered to Sheerness and Chatham. I beat up the Medway to Chatham, received a rap on the knuckles for coming up the river without a pilot or order, but all ended in my being asked to dine with Sir Benjamin Hallowell,[1] who was sorry I did not tell him that young Stopford was on board. How did I know that their fathers were acquainted ?

A very little respite and we were off for Jersey. Young Stopford had let the admiral know that he heard his commander say how much he should like to be sent there, ' Hinc illæ lacrymæ.' Every officer on going to any port ought to read up a little, but being so near and having two pilots on board, an English branch attached to the yacht, and a French one as well, I never dreamed of anything wrong. I had anchored in five fathoms, when at night I suddenly woke up, as every seaman on board will from the absence of motion, not upon taking ground. I naturally felt the ' tell tale ' over my cot and found the brig heel over. I rang the bell, and on the officer shewing himself asked what was the matter. ' The brig's on shore, sir, I believe.' ' Of course she is, turn the hands up,' and then down top-gallant masts, topmast, lower yards, and unlash the booms ; and in a wonderful short space of time got all the spare masts, yards, top-gallant masts &c. over the side, and so lashed to the chain plates, ring bolts, and what not, to shore the brig up; and this we did so effectually that she never swerved a single inch, and I began to breathe freely, for I must confess to having been in a mortal funk, not from fear of life, but had she gone over, good-bye to my commission—such a long-legged craft, she never would have righted. The tide left us with *one foot* of water, so that I was enabled to have a gang over the side, with sand and canvas, and brooms, to thoroughly scrub her bottom. I heard one of the men say, ' I believe the commander has shoved her ashore for this purpose alone.' I consider this lost me two or three years of my life, I was in such a terrible quandary. But *gently* hinting of this two or three days after, one of the young officers remarked that I seemed to take little notice of it. I was well out of it all, completed my stores in the way of wine, brandy, tea, sugar, raisins, a great lift for me. Tea, green, at five shillings ; black at four shillings-and-sixpence, whereas at Portsmouth it was twelve shillings and fourteen shillings for green, and for black nine shillings. A large quantity of tea I brought to Portsmouth for the *Victory's* and *Royal William's* mess, making them clearly understand that they were to do all the smuggling.

While at Jersey I crossed the bay to St Aubyn's, hauled along-side of the pier there and remained two days. I dined with Captain White, and met Lieutenant Barnett of the *Linnet* cutter, who

---

[1] Both here and later Sir Benjamin Hallowell is a mistake for Sir Henry Blackwood, Commander-in-Chief at the Nore.

was conducting a general survey of the port. I agreed to give his
wife and her mother a passage to Portsmouth, and they had just
comfortably settled on board when Captain White sent off a note
warning them of the probable consequences to me, that it might
cost me my commission, &c. He had nothing in the world to do
with me, he was at the head of the surveying department for the
Channel Islands and that was all. However, the ladies would go on
shore again. Mrs Barnett was a Nassau creole. Well, we started
once more for Portsmouth, taking their piano and heavy baggage.
I had almost forgotten to say that the rise and fall of tide at Jersey
is forty-five feet; two other places in the world only exceed this:
Monmouth is sixty feet, and at Halifax, Nova Scotia, it is fifty feet.
Hence the scrape I got into.

Sir Thomas Baker had his flag on board the *Cumberland*; I
dined with him and his Countess, a Swedish lady. I was to have
gone to sea with him, but my uncle, Captain Harvey, having a ship,
I went with him.

While at Plymouth I saw a gentleman on the beach waving his
hat, he seemed so much like my brother, who was inspecting commander of the coastguard at a neighbouring station, that I manned
the gig for him, but he was on his way off, by a cutter's boat. He
sent his card on board before him as Captain Smith, R.N., I suppose
that he might be properly received, &c. I found his object was to
get a passage to Portsmouth: I told him we were bound to Jersey
first. ' Oh, just the thing I should like of all things, to see Jersey
once more ! ' I then said we had but little room and less accommodation. He remarked, ' A flag or two on the deck would suffice ! '
My boat being announced as manned, I desired the jolly boat to land
him and went myself to the admiral's office. Calling there the next
day, I found Captain Smith with the secretary. I began by making
excuses for putting him off, that I had seldom my own cabin to
myself, &c. He answered, that he had noticed my unwillingness,
and did not intend going ; that when he commanded the ship's tender
he had made many sincere friends, by giving them a passage. I said
that I had many more friends than cared for me, or that I cared a
farthing about. He replied, by saying he should have brought his
mutton and hamper with him. This I at once cut short, by saying,
' Hang your mutton and hamper, sir,' and he cut his stick.

Well, the following day, we were off for Jersey, but it came on
most dirty weather : for four days we were in a gale of wind unable
to approach the wild rocky coast at all ; on the fifth or sixth day
it moderated, and I was able to run in and anchor. I spent an

agreeable week here. One day I dined with the governor, Sir Colin and Lady Halkett ; he was a fine, handsome man, but had a dreadful wound from a musket ball in the left cheek, received at Waterloo ; he was carried to Brussels, where he was attended to and nursed by one of the ladies who laid themselves out for that kind office. The ball had lodged in the mouth, and on my asking what had become of it, he turned it off with a laugh of not knowing. ' Oh, you know very well, Sir Colin, I have it safe enough up stairs.' She was the lady who nursed and took care of him.

I was just in the nick of time, there was a ball in the evening, and a mid. and a boat's crew came with the standard of almost every nation, and fitted up a room in splendid style. I danced with a Miss Hornby, sister to Johnny Waugh's inamorata at Lisbon, of whom more anon. I dined with Captain Pipon, who wished me to take a cow to Captain Loring at Portsmouth, but this I got off doing ! I also dined with Mr Godfrey and his wife, meeting Captain and Mrs Monins, formerly ' Eliza Jull,' an old flame of mine in days gone by ; I also dined with Hemery brothers, wine merchants, meeting the Duke of Norfolk ; I merely mention this, for in 1868 (forty years after) when at Barton Fields, Canterbury, living in a house next to one occupied by a gentleman named Hemery, with whose family we became very intimate, I chanced to say—' I never met anyone of your name but once, and that was at Jersey, where I dined and met the Duke of Norfolk ! ' ' Did you dine there that day ? I thought it a great honour to walk with a lantern to show his grace the way to his lodgings, the British Hotel.' He was a son to Mr Hemery.

I also put up at the Royal, and had not the wine been first-rate, I should not have got over the day so easily. While at this hotel Mr Hornby called, and after talking some time, he learnt that I was in the *Albion*. ' Oh, sir, you then knew Mr Waugh ? ' ' Johnny Waugh ! as fine a fellow as ever stepped ; if he would only be commonly prudent, he would not fail to inherit his uncle's fortune.' ' You don't say so, sir, I see *they will come together yet* ! ' and he asked me to breakfast ; I was rather late, in fact, breakfast was over, but things came in, and the Misses Hornby were very chatty. Waugh, of course, was on the tapis, their sister was away, but they spoke of Waugh being there, walking past the house several times, looking up, and that they called him the handsome stranger. To end the story of Waugh : seven or eight years after this, walking in Regent Street with Long Ramsay, we chanced to talk of Waugh. ' He is married, and to whom do you think ? ' ' Why, to the girl

224

he was so fond of at Lisbon ! ' 'Not a bit of it, but to her sister, whom he met in the Mediterranean while commanding the *Megæra* steamer, and to whom he chanced to give a passage to Alexandria.'

I had barely got to Portsmouth when I received orders to take on board nine Spaniards, who had been convicted of piracy and brought from Sierra Leone to be again tried in England ; they were acquitted. The master of the merchantman, who had charge of them, had confined them in irons all the way to this country ; consequently a suit of clothes and a sum of money to each, was awarded, and I received an order to take them and land them at Santander or St Andero. One or two of the party might have been pirates or anything as bad, they were rough-looking fellows as anyone might wish to see ; however, they were to be landed, the worst was, what was I to call them ? They were not all Spaniards, and how was I to designate them ? I called them *foreigners* in my letter to the governor, asking his permission to land them ; he took a long time in answering my letter, at last he gave permission that the *foreigners* should be landed. I found my way into the harbour well enough, but caused no little commotion by firing a royal salute of twenty-one guns, to which *in time* the fort replied, but with uncertain time ; the fact was, there were but three or four guns altogether.

I dined with our consul. Dinner was scarcely over, when a communication was sent up that two of our seamen were obliged to be put in limbo for creating a disturbance ; on sending a mid. from the table to settle matters, he found that our men, through an extra glass of ' vino blanco,' had shuffled and double-shuffled before some Spanish girls who were dancing the fandango at a sort of fair. This at first was resented by their cavalieros, still Jack continued with much laughter, and so the thing went on till the ' vino blanco ' became too powerful, and then Jack was moved off to the prison, where our mid. found him calling for more ' vino blanco,' and the soldiers pouring water into their mouths ; however, the best way was to leave them alone, and get them quietly off in the morning.

The next day I had a little jaunt into the country, and the following day set off for Portsmouth ; I was surprised at finding from forty to fifty fathoms sounding, more than half across the Bay of Biscay ; the weather was fine, and as I drew in with the French coast I was surprised at the beauty of the scenery, particularly in the neighbourhood of Penmark. There is a long, very long, dangerous shoal, the Saints, running right out to sea, which took many hours to beat round ; mastering this, I determined to run through the passage between Ushant and the main ; it was rather risky but

I had a leading wind, and keeping well in the middle, I got through,
saving a weary beat. They were making hay on the slopes, and
we were amused to see the country folks running down to get a look
at us; I imagine the sight of an English man-of-war was a great
object of wonder to them. We ran across the channel and were
at anchor in Portsmouth Harbour the following day.

A week later I was again sent to Plymouth and there received
two madmen from the hospital for Haslar. One was a Lieutenant
Hamling, and the other a carpenter. I was much amused at hearing
the assistant-surgeon and midshipman, who went for them, mis-
taking Franklyn (the fiery-eyed Welshman, who was master in the
Royal Sovereign yacht with me, and master attendant of the
Plymouth Hospital) for the madman, and keeping the real Simon
Pure between the two others in the walk from the hospital. On
going on board I enquired after them and was told the lieutenant
was no more mad than I was, and that he was very sociable with
the mids. It was up anchor, and as the men danced round the
capstan, I soon heard the lieutenant cheering them, clapping his
hands, &c.; he cooled directly he came on deck, but could not help
praising our smart evolutions in weighing and making all sail so
quickly; he was apparently rational enough, though I could not
avoid eyeing him askant when he flourished the carving knife.
He was abstemious and refused even a single glass of wine, saying
the medical man had cautioned him on the point; then he began to
drum with his fingers on the table to the tune of the ' British
Grenadiers,' ' The Army for me, Sir.' He took an opportunity to
caution us against the mad carpenter, saying that he would bite us
if he could or if he had the chance. True enough, we were obliged
to muffle him, and one day he affected to choke, and on being
assisted, did attempt to bite the hand that helped him. My friend,
the lieutenant, quite lost himself, beating through the Needles :
he caught hold of the mainbrace, cheering as he ran ; on calling
him to order, he was instantly quiet, but put his tongue in his cheek,
and I noticed the men smile. At another time he jumped across
the waist netting, spurring with his heels, when I again checked
him ; at last in executing a masterly manœuvre in swinging the
brig round a yacht, he could not longer stand it, gave a cheer and
threw his cap overboard. ' Quartermaster, take that madman
below,' and down he went as meek as a lamb. When in Portsmouth
Harbour I went below to put on my sword, &c., to wait on the
admiral ; the lieutenant was very penitent, begged my pardon, &c.,
' but will you allow me to look at it ? ' taking my sword off the
226

table, and requesting to be one of my boat's crew. I gave directions for sending him with the assistant-surgeon to Haslar Hospital: 'Hullo! what's all this? where are you taking me? too bad of your captain; I see, I suppose he is obeying orders'; and then he was quiet enough. Before the week was out I went to Haslar to ask after him, was told he was well, but not to disturb him; I only left a packet of snuff for him, which I heard gave him great pleasure. In a year or so he was discharged cured, was appointed to the coast-guard in the west of England, but in a short time disappeared, and his body was afterwards discovered under a rocky headland. He may have lost his head and tumbled over, or have jumped over.

I was cautioned against going into one of the wards as there was a carpenter there who laid to my charge his being shut up; he was continually muttering my name, with the wish of coming across me. Poor fellow, he was with me in the *Lyra* at Lisbon. I got him removed from my ship for his eccentricities, with the understanding that no further notice was to be taken of his offences.

The *Nightingale* schooner had run on shore outside the Needles' Rocks and I was sent down to her assistance. She was hard and fast, with a hole in her bottom, there were two or three dockyard lumps by her, and she had all the help that could be given. I took her commander and a young midshipman on board, and carried them into Portsmouth; they were with me two days. Years after, in 1848 (twenty years), when walking about the new docks at Cardiff, I was spoken to by the midshipman, who recognised me as one who was so kind to him in the *Onyx*. He spoke of me as such a smart officer in the management of my brig.

In one of my trips to the westward a curious circumstance took place. We had anchored at Swanage and had noticed a boat start off from a schooner towards a rock in the bay, and always being on the watch for any smuggling we kept an eye on her; to our surprise we saw that she had a tin pot and the men kept beating it to attract a swarm of bees, which they hived and carried to their vessel, which soon after weighed and went to sea.

We landed for a walk and went to Corfe Castle, not far off, admiring the strength of the outworks, one tower of which had been mined and thrown down, and there it remained some hundred years without going to pieces. Well, in putting into Lyme I chanced to call at a timber yard to get a cheque cashed by the proprietor, and on mentioning the bees he said, 'It is very strange, sir, they are safe enough in my yard, the vessel was chartered to me.' It seems the vessel had to beat all the way to Lyme, not going three or four miles, tack and tack along shore, and that the bees regularly worked. This is the most singular record of a bee story I ever came across ; that they should be able to distinguish their ship is most marvellous, but such is the fact.

I was hulked on board the *Prothee*, the same I was in in 1822, when first lieutenant of the *Ringdove*. I do not know that I was ever more comfortable or better off, though thoughts would occur to damp my happiness. I was in a situation envied by all of my rank, and from belonging to the King's personal yacht and at the same time in command of a ten-gun brig, felt myself most fortunate, and consequently was generally included in most invitations which take in the captains of the squadron here ; yet for all this I felt and knew I ought to have been in the same position ten years back. The unlucky termination of my West Indian trip in '16, '17 and '18 always annoyed me ; my third look at that country was again unfortunate, with the loss of health into the bargain ; and even the Navarino affair was but an ' untoward event ' to me ; fortune was against me, so many of my juniors present who got the step from sheer good luck ; lastly, even then, when my foot was in the stirrup fortune might have played me a slippery trick and marred my promotion. How all this should have intruded itself I know not ; I had much to be thankful for when I looked round and saw how many were much worse off. The admiral was very kind to me. Lord Yarborough, too, had not forgotten me ; I dined with him on board the *Falcon* yacht last [1] Monday, his first dinner for the season ; our party was thirty-two at table, Sir Robert Stopford and family, Sir Michael Seymour and family, the captains of the ships here, and myself ; this pleased me to be included. I seldom dined at home, six or seven times in the month only. 8th, the admiral's ; Duc de Chartres and a very large party, myself the only lieutenant ; 9th, the 52nd mess ; 11th, Captain Loring's, to meet Lord Yarborough ; 12th, Mr Gaze ; a dance in the evening ; 13th, the admiral, to meet Lord Yarborough and large party ; 15th, Lord Yarborough, and a large party ; 17th, I gave a dinner ; then on board the *Melville* ; and then with one of the officers of the Royal Naval College.

Somewhere about this time there was a court-martial on Captain Dickinson, of the *Genoa*, arising from the Russian ambassador having sent a decoration to the Admiralty for him, to be at their

[1] ' Last Monday ' indicates that Boteler was writing from a contemporary journal. He has slipped up here in copying it. Loring was Lieutenant-Governor of the Royal Naval College, Portsmouth ; Sir Michael Seymour, Resident Commissioner, Portsmouth Dockyard ; and Mr John Gaze was Second Master Attendant in the dockyard.

228

discretion whether he was entitled to it or not, he having fought the
ship, when Captain Bathurst was mortally wounded. The Admiralty
referred it to Sir Edward Codrington, who replied that he did not
see anything in the conduct of Captain Dickinson to entitle him to
the decoration. I believe this was rather a hasty reply of Sir
Edward's, for the Admiralty took exception to it and ordered the
court. It was what is called a ' Roast Beef Court,' all in full dress :
Sir Robert Stopford (president), Sir Benjamin Hallowell,[1] Sir Robert
Otway, and nine post captains. As Captain Ommanney was supposed to be a principal witness, the court was obliged to be delayed
several days, till his recovery from a broken leg from trying a four-
year-old colt. I had two or three times been at table with the
admiral and had given him many hints as to the action. The
court sat some days. I took my stand by a stanchion the whole
time, and never was so surprised as at a portion of the evidence.[2] I
was not aware till then that an officer had been sent to the *Albion*
by the admiral to divert our course in. Till this day I had imagined
we went under the bows of a Turkish 74, so much so that even now
I seem to remember her rampant red lion head with gilt claws and
teeth, but so it was. My name was twice mentioned in the evidence.
Fortunately I was not called. On the third day Sir Edward sent for
me in the cabin of the *Victory*. ' I am told, Mr Boteler, that you
know something of all this. How did I go on board the *Genoa* ? '
' I took you, Sir Edward.' ' You ! I had an idea I went to her in
a two-oared boat.' ' You were about to do so, but I offered my
boat and so took you, and I well remember in answer to my observa-
tion that the action was brought about by mistake, your saying
" Oh, no, they shot my poor pilot going up the side of the Turkish
admiral." '

There was an amusing incident during the trial. A lieutenant,
Smith, of the *Genoa*, was under examination as to the position of
the ship, whether she was raked by the enemy's shot or not, and the
fact was meant to be illustrated by ascertaining whether the shot
that first struck the after part of the port and then the breech of the
gun was, if the gun was *in* or *out*. Had the gun been out at the
time it would have been nearer a raking shot than otherwise. Smith
did not seem to be aware of the question, but said all he knew was

---

[1] A mistake for Sir Henry Blackwood.

[2] The court-martial met on August 26th, 1829, and its proceedings were public.
No one desirous of defending the good name of Sir Edward Codrington will dis-
approve of the complete omission of any mention of the trial in the biography by
his daughter, and in the memoir in the *Dictionary of National Biography*. The
evidence is summarised in pp. 328–59 of *The Annual Register*, 1829, and commented
upon in pp. 133–6.

that it killed two men and two of the captain's sheep. He was
saluted by ' Ba-a, ba-a, ba-a,' by some of the mids. afterwards. But
the joke was whenever a question was put Smith hung his head for
a considerable time, making one feel anxious for his answer, but
instead of this out would roll a mass of high-flown terms, such as,
' When she diverged from that beautiful position,' &c. So that
Moses Greetham, the judge advocate, who was more used to the
evidence of seamen, was sorely put to it, and when Smith used the
word ' consecutive,' said ' Sir,' and Smith began to spell it for him.
Sir Benjamin Hallowell cocked his eye towards Sir Robert Otway,
when Sir Robert Stopford quietly said, ' A very proper word, from
" con " and " sequar." ' ' *Oh*,' said the two admirals. There were
three Smiths : one who invented a target was called ' Target Smith,'
another Smith, an improved life-buoy, ' Life-buoy Smith,' and our
Smith ' Diverging Smith.' Sir Edward tried hard to induce the
court to call for his instructions, declaring he was the object of the
court-martial. However, it ended in the honourable acquittal of
Captain Dickinson. While not in attendance at the court I waited
on Mrs and the three Misses Ommanney, and generally took Captain
Ommanney on board the *Victory* in my boat.

In September I again was cruising westward and got as far as
Lyme, the day before the king's birthday, and my brother, who was
inspecting commander, had arranged a general meeting of all his
forces on the Pinney cliffs, and had prepared a second breakfast
under tents. I got under weigh and joined him there, firing a royal
salute on the king's birthday. I was close in shore, and the cattle,
unused to such noises, were galloping about like mad. Our presence
added greatly to the scene. Towards the evening I took many of
the ladies back to Lyme, and on the way fired a shotted gun in stays.
It missed fire, and when at the second pull of the lanyard it exploded
the brig had altered her course, and the shot flew away, dropping
not far from Mr Holland's small yacht. At a ball in the evening I
let him know how it occurred and apologised. This did not satisfy
him, but he went on as to my carelessness in firing a shot in mixed
company, &c., till I lost my temper, and said I supposed he was in
a terrible fright, and this shut him up for the evening.

In October I received a note from the secretary desiring me to
appear before the commission sitting at the dockyard for revising
the rigging of the navy. They consisted of Admiral Sir Laurence
Halsted, Sir Thomas Hardy, Sir William Parker, Captain White,
Captain Brace and another. They began to ask me if we were rigged
according to warrant, and on my hesitating, said, ' We are not trying

you by a court-martial, but only wish to get at the truth.' I replied,
' No, nor is there a single ship so in the service,' and I explained a
variety of instances, that rope slings were still supplied for hanging
the lower yards when chains were used ; that they encumbered the
ships, rotting in the holds, &c., &c. I never thought to have gone
through such a passing in rigging, but I felt well up to the thing,
and was in no way puzzled till they asked what length I should propose for a top-gallant brace. I said I would bring my boatswain the
following day. ' A very good idea, sir ; secretary, make a note of
that.' The next day I brought little Cable, one of the right sort, a
thorough seaman, active, and well up to his work. But they could
get little from him. When asked a question it was : ' What do you
say, sir ? ' turning to me, and if pressed, it was, ' Why, gentlemen,
the commander knows better than I,' till they absolutely laughed at
his obstinacy. He could give the length of a brace, &c., and that
was about as much as they could get out of him, till a question arose
out of a new way I had of fishing the anchor with a pendant of so
many fathoms ; I said twelve, which was thought too little. At last,
on being appealed to, Cable said, ' *Stretch* it, gentlemen, give us
fourteen ' ; and I came off with flying colours, complimented by the
committee and a warrant put into my hands to be filled up as I chose
for the rigging of brigs. The *Frolic*, 10, at that time was just
commissioned by Captain Swinburne, who was desired to consult with
me and follow all the suggestions that I might propose.[1] ' Stretch it '
seemed to take the fancy of the committee. Years after when in
Devonport Dockyard I met the admiral, who I thought did not
quite remember me, and on my hinting as much, replied, ' Oh yes,
you and your boatswain " Stretch it " I shall remember as long as
I live.'

One day Cable came to me to ask my advice. ' You see, sir, my
name is not Cable ; that is a purser's name. I ran away from a frigate,
joined the merchant service, which did not agree with me, and I
feared to enter again under my proper name, which is Forbes, and so
took that of Cable.' ' Well,' I said, ' you are married, are you not,
and have two or three little cablets ? Stick to it, as you have gone
so far.' ' Thank you, sir, so I will,' and he did.

A few days after my examination I saw the admiral's barge
coming down the harbour and, fancying mischief, disappeared from
the poop, eyeing them through a port ; they lay on their oars a little
way astern, looking at us, making sundry remarks. The same day

---

[1] According to the Navy List, Commander Swinburne commissioned the ten-
gun sloop *Rapid* at Portsmouth in 1829. The *Frolic* was a six-gun brig.

at dinner, at the admiral's, Sir Thomas Hardy and one or more of the committee present, he, Sir Thomas, said, ' We have been overhauling you to-day ; you seem to be but half rigged. Where is your studding-sail gear, sir ? ' ' The yards, sir, stopped on.' ' Your topsail haulyard block ? ' ' The same, sir ' ; and some other questions of the like nature. At last I said, ' If the admiral makes my signal to start off, and wind is fair, in ten minutes I will have all sail set low and aloft ! ' ' And let me tell you,' added the admiral, ' Mr Boteler is just the man to do it.'

After waiting several days in expectation of sailing orders, they at last came, to take some valuable instruments for the *Chanticleer*, Captain Foster, surveying, who was expected at Maranham, on the coast of Brazil, to remain there thirty days, then on to Para for a week, and finally to call at Trinidad, taking Madeira in our way out, and then home. A long trip for us, just what pleased me most. I lost no time in completing my sea stock, and provisioning the brig for four months in every way. I dined with the admiral, and after ' Success to the *Onyx*,' was off the next day. We had a fair run down channel and to Madeira, getting to that anchorage early in the morning. I went on shore and ordered a large bake, two bullocks, and some wine.

When at Madeira in the *Lyra*, in 1826, I was warned by the admiral not to be caught by bad weather, that if I observed the sea set in, to be off directly. I dined with the consul that day and met Captain Gill of the *Sparrowhawk*, bound for the coast of Africa. I noticed the sea was getting up, and in going off at night was asked by Captain Gill to give him a passage to his ship. Seeing that I disliked being on shore made him suspicious. However, next morning the weather was no worse, but I saw that the fishermen were hauling their boats further up, and towards evening the surf was on the increase. Directly I reached the brig, with the watch I struck top-gallant masts, got the studding-sail booms off the yards, and all top-hamper down. In the morning the wind got up rapidly, in squalls of heavy rain. While the wind was directly on shore, it did not seem to blow home, but when it got more to the S.W. the strain on our cable was great. I determined to hold on as long as the *Sparrowhawk* did, as also the Indiamen, of which the anchorage was full. The rain inland was furious, and the soil being red, as the water poured over the precipices and out of the mouths of the river, the sea was soon red also, till it enveloped those vessels that were nearer the shore. First a schooner weighed, got becalmed and in the doldrums cast the wrong way, went on shore and to pieces

232

in no time. This set off a large American brig, that also, after
floundering about for a time, went on shore. The *Sparrowhawk*
then cut away and I unshackled, got a slip rope to give the brig a
cast and followed suit ; the slip rope carried away and we were within
an ace foul of an Indiaman in crossing her bows. I should have done
so, had she not cleverly veered a little out of our way. And here I
was at sea, blowing a gale of wind for a whole fortnight. Had I known
in the first instance that we should have been so long detained, it
would have been a question of starting off at once, but as it continued
from day to day we could do nothing better than hold on. One day
it moderated and I bore up for Madeira again, but as we got in
shore it thickened and became as bad as ever ; all this time I kept
in sight of the *Sparrowhawk*, till it moderated sufficiently to part
company, when I bore up and picked up my buoy and thought all
right ; but after heaving a strain that brought the tar out of the
rope, it parted and we let go another anchor. The cable must
have hitched over a rock or another anchor ; as for the buoy of
the anchor, the Madeira boats had walked off with it, being copper.
Looking round, I saw the *Sparrowhawk* pick up her buoy and went
on board her, taking with me her purser, who had been left behind.
When I got alongside she was going astern at a great rate, and I
found she was off the bank and had let go another anchor, the chain
running out rapidly, its coils cutting into their launch on the booms.
To her captain I said : ' You are off the bank ! ' ' Oh ! no, sir,
the master says no, and that she will bring up directly.' There was
he with the lead in his hands looking for soundings ; by this time she
had run out two whole cables and so I left her. She never got
an inch of the cables in, and, therefore, lost two anchors and nearly
three cables, and did not get in again till the evening of the second
day, just as I was starting on my way.

We passed through the Teneriffe Islands, sighted St Antonio,
off the Cape de Verdes, crossed the Equator, long. 31 W., and made
the coast of Brazil about Cape Scarah. While in sight of this, we
came across a curious and wonderful piece of naval architecture—a
sort of catamaran, a raft (nothing more) of seven or eight cocoa trees
with a short mast and lateen sail. We got to windward of her, and
gave her a tow rope and bought two fine large fishes ; we pointed to
the land and asked if it was not Scarah. After a time—' Si, senor,
Scarāh, Scarāh.' The crew consisted of five and a boy, no shelter
whatever, merely two or three sticks on which were hung their nets.

While running alongside to the westward, I chanced to look on
deck, and to my surprise found ourselves closer in than I expected.

233

' What water have we ? ' to the quarter-master. ' I can see the bottom, sir.' Down with the helm, turn the hands up, down studding sails and brace up ; the wind was moderate and the sea smooth ; leadsmen in the chains called half-five, five, half-four, four, half-three, three. ' 'Bout ship ! ' and when in four fathoms round again, the same soundings as before, till mark three, when round once more ; we had evidently run into a sort of creek. When in shore again in half-three, I once more tacked and stood out till three fathoms ; when just about to go round, the call was half-three, then four and into clear water. Here I must notice the conduct of the senior mid., Mr Smith, who repeated my orders, but never shewed the least interest in what was going on, shewing a determined sullen manner that must have been noticed by all ; he was a very unbending severe disciplinarian, and although I tried hard to keep with him, yet I never punished men half to his satisfaction. He was mate of the lower deck of the *Rochfort*, 80, in the Mediterranean, and had shot rolled at him by the men. I never could get over his conduct on that, to me, most trying time, and the reason I found out afterwards was that I had asked one of the other mids. to dine with me twice to his once ! After this scrape I could look round. It was a sandy shore at the mouth of a small stream ; there was a clump of trees covering eight or ten acres of ground all dead, and had been so apparently for years ; white skeletons, a most dreary melancholy sight. There were no birds, no living thing that we could discern. In following the Admiralty's sailing directions, we came upon an island, and steered N.W. from it, till about the distance of ten or twelve miles, then kept direct west outside and to clear the Crown Shoals, which we were careful to avoid, and here, while feeling our way with the lead, we sounded with twelve fathoms on one side and six on the other. I doubted the leadsmen and tried myself with the same result ; we, therefore, stood out more off the coast, and in the end made the only safe headland, Mount Itacolumi, a remarkable sugarloaf hill, for which we ran and, at the estimated distance of twelve miles, bore up south for Maranham, trying the deep sea lead till we struck eighteen fathoms, then very gradually sixteen, fifteen, fourteen, ten, nine and five fathoms, let go the anchor ; sending a boat sounding, we found ourselves on the borders of the shoal, middle ground ; so up anchor and dropt into eight fathoms ; but here was the puzzle, to get our anchors : we put a great strain on and at last up came the anchor, minus one fluke. I tried the lead myself ; directly it touched the bottom it took quite a tug to pull it out again ; evidently a species of sucking quicksand. There we remained till the next morning, when I made signal for a pilot, with a gun, and attempted to weigh, gathering the cable with the pressing stopper at the main hatchway. As the brig rose to the sea, the cable cut through the combings of the hatch to the beams of the lower deck, besides injuring the capstan, and four of the men at it, one seriously, a quarter-master, one of the best men in the brig. Well, I ceased all attempts, till the brig swung broadside on to the swell, and then with runners and tackles to assist, got a strong purchase, when—' Heave and away ! ' and up came the anchor with the loss of both flukes. Here was a pretty go, only the stream anchor left ; we lashed the stream to the broken small bower, and having got our pilot, ran into Maranham, where we anchored close off the city in smooth water, a perfect mill-pond. The consul, captain of the port, and a captain of a Brazilian man-of-war came on board to pay their respects, and I followed the consul, Mr Hesketh, on shore, to wait on the governor.

I consider our passage from Portsmouth to Maranham—thirty-six days—a very tolerable one. We had a first-rate chronometer, its daily loss being six-tenths of a second, and this rate it bore till we returned it into store at Portsmouth.

Mr Hesketh, when he shewed me a bedroom, said, ' Now, *captain*, here is your room, which I hope you will occupy all the time you are here. It is something to get a man-of-war in our harbour, and we must make the most of it ' ; so here I was for a whole month. In the garden there was a flag-staff, and I had a few flags sent to make signals, which the black servants were too happy in bending on for me. I passed a most agreeable time, dinner parties continued among the merchants in a very hospitable way. I could make little return for all Mr Hesketh's outlay, excepting asking if he had a few empty bottles, which I got him to send off, and I fillèd six dozen of them with very prime madeira. While at that island I ordered a month's supply of wine for the *Onyx*, the consul saying if I did not mind a little difference in the charge he would send two small casks off for myself. It was a chance I should not get in a hurry, and the wine was most excellent.

I landed the dilapidated capstan at the dockyard, and our armourer put it completely to rights. I also purchased two bower anchors there, not quite as heavy as our own, but very good substitutes. I was able to go through a regular outfit of the brig low and aloft.

For a length of time I was looked on with great suspicion. There was a beautiful slaver at anchor, a schooner, full rigged, and of very doubtful appearance. It was thought I was looking after her, and a constant guard was kept on the watch to prevent any sudden attack on my side. In the harbour she was safe enough, but outside it would be very different.

Of the society at Maranham, beyond the English, I can say nothing. I was only within the doors of three natives. One old lady I was introduced to thought I was over young to be in command, was very inquisitive, asked if I were married, said I must take a Brazilian wife away. At one house I was in, the *lady* was seated at the end of the room, and a row of ladies on either side the length of the room, and each gentleman on coming in had to walk through them, make his salaam, and back astern the best way he might. We in general were late in bed, about midnight. I used to go into the gallery and crow, and was directly answered by every cock in the city. One morning on turning out, I saw an ants' covered way, constructed in the night through the floor, right up the side of the room in the attic above, and on naming it to Mr Hesketh was informed it was a sure sign of the approach of the rainy season. He told me it would be useless to destroy this covered way, it would be rebuilt as fast as cut down. The negroes seemed to be in a contented humour, if one could judge by the laughing humorous songs made at my expense by the gangs of ten or twelve labouring with the weight of a large cask of wine, one singing, the rest joining in chorus.

One day, walking with F. Birch on the south side of the harbour, we came upon a very large snake. I fortunately had my gun and shot at it as it reared its head, to have a look at us, I suppose. It bounded off the ground, lashed about furiously for some time, and then was quiet. I reloaded before approaching him, but he had had enough. The beast measured ten feet, and was as thick as the calf of my leg. We brought him on board, skinned and stuffed the creature with cotton wool, and hung him in the rigging to dry. A large bird, a man-of-war bird, or boatswain, early one morning made a dash at him, and would have carried him off had he been less securely hung.

Occasionally we were left with a long sweep of mud, and one morning I was surprised at the sight of a whole regiment of the flamingo, or scarlet ibis, marching on the mud. We wounded one, and after an exciting chase brought him on board. He gradually pined away and died. I brought it home and saw it afterwards well set up at Sir Robert Stopford's.

I gave one dinner party on board ; the consul and six others, as many as we could contrive to sit. Tinned meats were then in their infancy. I astonished them with a six-pound piece of salmon to begin with, and then with a fillet of veal. They wondered how I became possessed of such a fish, as also of the first-rate joint of veal. The fact was that my old friend Dr Griffiths sent me two hampers of good things from Fortnum and Mason's before starting, and these were a part of the lot.

I must not omit saying, that expecting to meet Captain Foster, and knowing how greatly he would appreciate whatever I brought from England, I had got a keg of tripe, a keg of tongues and sounds, some tinned meats, and a sack of potatoes for him. Finding, at the end of three weeks, there was no appearance, I thought to use the tripe and tongues, but they had run to oil, and were totally un-eatable. As these recollections come across me I note them.

All the houses are shut up during the day; every care taken to exclude the sun; the same with the theatres; and I observed that one side of the house was comparatively empty,—the side that had the rays of the sun on it.

The main square of the city, that was merely dry sand, began to turn green, the rains coming on, and my month was up. I got a pilot, who was, however, taken away for the *Nova de Janeiro*, a schooner packet for Para. I put myself under the charge of a fine spanking merchant ship, but on finding him with the main topsail shivering, I headed him. I made sail and overtook the Brazilian. Hailed her, saying that—' I had no pilot, and should keep close to him.' I found that on most points I had the heels of him. Fol-lowing not far astern, I noticed he was running right into an Indian village, if I could judge by the number of lights; I burned a blue light to warn him, and, just in time, they hauled off. We soon came to the Gallera de Samba, about six miles from the pilot station, a snug spot, where we made signal for a pilot. One fire, a pilot would come off; two fires, a pilot must be sent for; and three fires, no pilot to be had. One fire was shown. I went on board my friend, and had some sweetmeats with him. About three A.M., a pilot came off, and I up anchor at once, and waited for my friend, who was screaming at me not to leave him in the lurch; when off we both started, crossed the bar of the river. There was a tremendous surf, and we stood up the Para, a branch of the great Amazon; till we were above forty or fifty miles up, we could not distinguish the opposite shore, when the river suddenly contracted by a large island being in the way. My friend here had the better of me; before the wind, studding sails, and smooth water, what cared he! he was all right. It was setting in for the evening. Far up the river, there was a black bank of heavy clouds right across us. Heavy thunder and lightning playing in various parts of the dark mass,—evidently the commencement of the rainy season. The schooner went recklessly on. I thought she would catch it, and she did, with a vengeance. All was adrift ; she was on her beam ends, her jib caught the squall, filled, burst out of the bolt rope, and flew away into the black region. I sheered inshore, waited till the squall nearly met us, tearing up the water, then ' shorten sail,' and everything was snug in a trice. ' Let go the anchor ' ; and in an instant we were in a foam, wind and very heavy rain, which lasted about an hour, bringing all sorts of flying insects on board, small birds, the gigantic Brazilian moth (the size of my hand), butterflies, large green crickets, locusts in fact, lantern and fire flies innumerable. A quartermaster and I were the only ones left on deck, the men all below out of the way of the extraordinary heavy rain, which, however, did not last.

At Madeira I was presented with a coati-mundi, a great pet of mine ; a most affectionate creature. While running down the trades, and I sitting on the poop, with my back resting against the main boom, the creature nestling at my feet, coiled up almost in a ball, would not permit anyone near me ; first a shrill whistle, and then a dash at an approaching foot, with its sharp teeth. This creature was a friend indeed with the large *oily* and *juicy* locust ; he caught them with great dexterity with his two paws, then into his mouth,—it seemed one motion only. These were its natural food, of which he had been long debarred. The end was, his stomach was blown out like a football. The next day, when some stray ones were pointed out to him, it was absolutely ridiculous to see his face, shewing utter loathing, cocking his long nose, shewing his teeth, holding his head aside, and looking askance at the insects.

In a way I kept no table, but occasionally there was a plum-pudding, which came to the share of the mids. One day, by chance, Jocko got the remains, and as he left the cabin with the pudding in his mouth, I heard an exclamation, ' Hang it ! That's too bad ! ' and instant chase was given. Jocko took to the rigging, and in the main top began his feast, but he was stormed, and the chase resumed, till poor Jocko dropped the dainty, which was squashed on the deck.

Well, the following day we pursued our voyage, and let go the anchor off the city of Para, an ancient city, lies about 100 miles up a branch of the Amazon, the bank wooded down to the water,—in fact, for many miles the trees grew into the water, and all being evergreens of various shades, you may fancy how pleasing to the
238

eyes the scene is. I sent an officer to the governor, stating our object of looking for the *Chanticleer*, and waiting at Para some three or four days ; and that I should salute the Brazilian flag, provided my salute was returned ; which was done. After paying my respects to the governor, I went on board the schooner, and was told by the second officer, that the captain, after knocking down one of the crew with a handspike, shook his fist at me, saying—' Look at that English captain laughing at me, with all his sails set, look at him, look at him ! there he goes, takes all his sails in, laughing at us.' He told me the man was like a wild beast. Well, the merchants came off with the consul, no *Chanticleer* had been heard of. The consul took me for a ride round the city ; the road was a splendid one, but with scarcely room for wheels, the dense mass of rich foliage creeping into the way ; when about three miles out, we cut into a footway at right angles and came across three copper-coloured Indians, very slightly clad, and armed with bows and arrows ; seeing a large blackbird in a tree, I held out a half-dollar, pointing at it ; one fellow smiled, up with his bow and very long arrow, I suppose six or seven feet long, and brought the bird down, at least he killed it, but it hung in the branches. The consul told me they were very expert with their archery.

The next day I and two of my officers had a second breakfast with the governor, who was very civil and chatty, the consul acting as interpreter. He had received notice of our arrival from Maranham. I had another pleasant ride the same afternoon. Para was a very large town, three or four churches and a cathedral. The third day, before starting, I dined with the merchants, a large *noisy* party ; a man shouted out—' John Boteler, John Harvey I mean, I know you and your uncle, the admiral, I knew you all at Barbadoes in sixteen, seventeen and eighteen ' ; and here he shut up, I made nothing out of him further. Coming off late at night, my boat at the end of a long low sort of jetty, the coxswain said he believed a rat was in the boat. ' Well,' I said, ' take care he does not get into the brig,' and when I came alongside I had a lantern in the boat to hunt for him, not a vestige could be seen of him. The gig was hoisted up ; in the middle of the night, I was disturbed by a shout : the rat was seen to run in by the boat's davits and get on board. The beast was seen two or three times in the course of a few days ; at last, happy thought ! Jocko was put upon the scent ; away the creature went quite elated, and in a short time appeared with the rat in his jaws ; he quite laughed at the spree, and being chased, took to the rigging and enjoyed his feast.

I could get a pilot, but no boat, so was obliged to start, run over the bars and then work back to the pilot station and land the pilot ; a pull of six or seven miles, and then off for Trinidad. Nothing particular on the way ; we amused ourselves with the tricks of a marmoset monkey, he weighed but five ounces ; the little creature would hide itself in my uniform cap, and would strut about with a straw for a stick like a little wrinkled old man.

About thirty miles to the eastward of Trinidad is a large rock, or small island, right in our track, and which I passed very near ; and here I was in some doubt as to going into the Gulf of Paria by the Serpent's Mouth, instead of the Dragon's Mouth, but my courage failed me and I stood on for the latter, cutting along with a strong sea breeze. I tried the Egg Mouth but got becalmed, was obliged to out boats and tow the brig back into the breeze and try another opening further from the land, where I went in, but could not fetch further than Napareen shore, in the neighbourhood of the Pitch Lake, where we anchored for the night. At daylight, up anchor and beat up for Porto Spain, shewed our number and were answered by the *Mersey*, Captain Courtenay ; and here it was that I was hailed as Tom Best, one of her lieutenants, who, a short time before, was invalided and supposed to be sent back by the authorities. I was thought so like him, and when in the *Albion*, at Lisbon, we were pitted against each other.

I went on shore with Captain Courtenay to the governor, General Grant, and met with a most flattering reception, dining there every day, and on the third morning taking up my quarters at Government House, and remaining there all the time I was at Trinidad, till I became uneasy ; the general then wrote a letter to me to delay my sailing till the 10th January, that the merchants might be able to reply to their letters by the packet. I sent the brig down to Shagaramus Bay to complete water ; we had a succession of invites to a maroon party, a dinner at the attorney-general's, Mr Fuller, where I met two bishops, of Barbadoes and of Olympus ; and there it was, ' William,' to his black servant, ' a glass of wine with the bishop ; no, no, my lord bishop on the right.' Calling on Mrs Fuller the next day I noticed the marks of the ants on one of the chairs and named it. ' You are mistaken, Mr Boteler, we are clear of that pest, thank goodness·! ' but I gave the chair a wrench and it tumbled all to powder. There was a great commotion, for on examination one-half of the chairs were found infected. Another day I rode on a little Spanish jennet to a review of the 2nd West Indian Regiment and had luncheon with the officers. Then a ball

at Government House, to which we supplied flags, &c., for decorating
the rooms. After dancing awhile I went into the cardroom on the
invitation of Major ——, R.A., the governor's secretary. I won a
bumper rubber and was paid eight dollars and a quarter doubloon ;
I never dreamed of such high stakes, but having won the first rubber
I could not deny a second, and again got a full rubber of twelve
dollars. Two more after this, losing and winning. Captain Courtenay also asked me to dine with him ; altogether I had a real good
time. The governor seemed to have a charmed life, the first down
in the morning, though never in bed till much after midnight. I
shall not forget starting up in a fright one morning, he with his
finger and thumb holding my nose gently. I thought I was stifling.
' Eh, Mr Boteler, it is time to be up.'

The last day was a party and the Romanist bishop volunteered
to take me to my boat in his curricle. I saw that he was going
wrong and named it. ' All right, sir, just to cool my horses,' instead
of which we drove up to a stately gateway, with two large stone
balls on the pillars, his house ; where I had to alight and have a
parting glass with him ; he was a most cheerful, genial character.
After this to my boat. I called alongside of an English merchant
ship for Lieutenant Claxton and his black servant, ' Peter,' to whom
I was to give a passage to Barbadoes. He, the merchant captain,
and the governor all told me it was useless to attempt passing
through the Dragon's Mouth at night, but I persevered, up anchor,
and ran through with ease, catching a strong sea breeze, and lay
well up for Barbadoes. I must digress to tell of my senior mate,
Mr Smith,[1] who came to me one day, saying that he had seen his
name in the paper as being promoted. I wished him joy on the
occasion and thought no more about it, though it seemed to me he
expected something more ; my only notion was that the others
might be included. As I have just said, we lay up well, weathered
Grenada, Tobago, right away for Barbadoes and were off Carlisle
Bay on the 15th. I could have got in the same night, but thought
it more prudent to wait till daylight. I then pushed in and was
boarded by the officer of the guard, Harry Sturt, of the *Hyacinth*.
I had known him at Lisbon. When he found I was beating in,
inside of all the merchantmen, he left and I continued, till close in
to Martindale's Wharf to complete our water, and anchored where
I saw a clear spot of sand. Two or three canoes followed me ; in
one I saw Poll Smashum, bumboat woman of the *Orontes* in 1814,
and of the *Antelope* in '16, '17 and '18, and, in another, Black Rose,

---

[1] Henry Sidney Smith, Lieutenant, November 20th, 1829.

my washerwoman. I did not shew myself till the gig was manned, knowing well the outcry, and here it was: 'Goody God ! Massa John, how you do, sar, who eber tink of seeing you here ? How Massa Henry, Mr Harby, and de admiral ? ' Their delight was great. I desired them to be admitted and recommended Black Rose for washing. I waited upon the captain of the *Hyacinth*, and then went on shore to Mr Cavan's, *en route* for the governor, Sir James Lyon. 'Why,' said Cavan, 'here he comes,' and a tall, gentlemanly man, dressed entirely in white, came to the door and was introduced to me as Sir Charles Smith, and on my staring, they laughed, and said he was acting governor so long, that they still called him so. I had a letter for Sir Charles which I gave him. 'Oh,' said he, 'it is from my friend, Major ——. He says you owe him a little money and that I am to take it out of you at whist. I must see the old hen at home first, I then will name a day.' I left them and Cavan sent me on to Government House, where I was kindly received and asked to dine on the second day, the first I was engaged to Cavan. I then, after securing a bed at Betsy Austin's, called alongside the *Hyacinth*, and was agreeably surprised at receiving my commission as commander. The long-coveted rank.

On returning to the brig I was met by Mr Smith, who, in his eagerness to tell me, obstructed my going over the gangway. ' I am a lieutenant, sir. Here is " Murray's List " [1] with my name in it ; you will believe it now, sir.' 'I am very glad indeed, I did not doubt it at Trinidad.' ' Of course, sir, you will relieve me now of all duty ? ' ' You take me by surprise, sir ; I think not.' ' Then, sir, you are the only officer in the service that would treat me so ; I shall go into the doctor's list, sir.' ' No you won't, you will go to your cabin and consider yourself under close arrest,' and I called on the assistant-surgeon and Mr Birch as witnesses. Strange that he should so take it ; he had done duty clearly as first lieutenant from the time he joined, and if *all*, as I had expected, had been promoted at the same time, where should I have been had each objected in the same way ! I went on shore, dined with Mr Cavan, and slept at Betsy Austin's. Returning to the boat I was hailed—' How are you, Mr Boteler ? Glad to see you here again.' Looking round, I saw Captain Cook, the captain of the port. ' I knew you by your *gait*, sir.' After a chat, I went on board, saw that the watering had gone off well, and that we should be complete the next day. And as to Mr Smith, I was told he was in such a way, and his behaviour was so extraordinary all night, that Harris had sat up with him,

---

[1] The official Navy List, then published by John Murray.

they feared he would destroy himself. I was walking the deck, mooning over the affair, when up stalked Poll Smashum, her arm on my back. 'Soly John, what um matter wid you? Keep up your spirits, all will be well.' 'Poll, be quiet!' What a guy I must have been in the eyes of the crew! the woman behaving with such familiarity to their commander on the quarter deck. That day I dined with the governor; Abraham, the monkey, in the adjoining room, with a chain round his waist and a pole with a house at the top, for him to retire to. Captain D'Urban, *aide-de-camp*, asked if Abraham was to be loosened. 'By all means,' said Sir James. We were at dessert and the monkey was admitted; with a bound it was on the table, one paw was in the guava jelly, another into the sour sop, and then on to the top of a large bookcase; then after grimacing and licking his chops, he made another assault on the table, jumping over me and digging his paws, as before, in two different plates, and his mouth in another, winking and blinking at the company, as only monkeys can, setting us all laughing. Jocko was then secured again to his pole, Sir James laughing heartily. But what a mess Abraham made! I was very cosy with D'Urban, his brother John being with me in the *Albion*. Sir James asked me to his table again, but I was engaged, so down to Betsy Austin, where I again slept.

The following day on board again. While sitting in my cabin, a knock at the door and in came Mr Smith. I started from my seat in surprise, and could not help shewing it. He said—'I have come to apologise to you, sir, for my intemperance. I could not help it. I thought, having been a midshipman for so many years, I was entitled to more consideration.' 'But,' I replied, 'you gave no time for consideration; supposing the others had been promoted at the same time, all might have expected the like consideration as you term it. Your length in the service must have taught you that no officer can quit his berth till superseded. I was in a ship where the captain had his flag rank and the first lieutenant was made commander: both continued their duty till superseded. In my own case I am now commander. Why do I not strike?' 'Oh, in your case there is a vast difference!' 'None whatever, and why should I be subjected to the loss of your support? Had you been behind the door when I was speaking of you to Sir Robert Stopford, you would never have acted in this way; were I to state the whole case to the Admiralty, your commission would be a dead letter. However, I do not wish to kick one who is down. You will return to your duty; I release you from arrest.' In a short time after this I

followed him on deck and there told him he was relieved from all
further duties, that he might go below, that I never wished to see
his face again on deck.   That day, Birch, Stopford and I dined at
Shot Hall with Sir C. Smith ; we had a pleasant evening, and when
cards were produced I affected ignorance, thinking of high stakes,
when they proved moderate, quarter dollar points and one dollar on
the rub ; I was content and won two rubbers.   On the third day
Stopford and I dined with the Comptroller of Customs, Mr Stockland,
who sent us a canoe full of oranges, fruit and a dozen of claret.

I lifted the anchor that evening and dropped further out, and
the following day took my leave of Barbadoes and made sail for
England.   It was somewhat a chapter of accidents, but we left
Maranham, Para, Trinidad and Barbadoes on a Wednesday, and
we arrived at all those places on Sunday, as we termed it, our lucky
day.   I must not leave out our very handsome macaw, with gorgeous
plumage and a most powerful beak ; it was against my orders for
any garment to be left on the hammock nettings.   I noticed the
jacket of one of the mids. there, and that it caught the eye of the
bird, who directly made towards it ; I knew the result but *awaited*
it !   The bird, with great deliberation, took off nearly every button
by the shank, much to the disgust of the owner, who was up too
late to disturb the operation.   One word more of Mr Smith ; he
was fool enough to get entangled with and marry the barmaid of
the Lamb and Flag, at Portsmouth.   Two or three days after we
were ordered to sea, and I started him off when outside, in a fisherman's boat, so that I was not unmindful of him, and I made him
a present on the occasion of his marriage.

We had rather a buffeting passage the first part of our way
home, partly attributable to my attempting a straight cut ; however, we encountered a strong breeze, almost, I may call it, a gale,
from the N.W., and for five or six days bowled along at the rate of
207, 213, 208, 220 and 196 ; our quarter-boats were nearly washed
away ; I had it, at one time, in contemplation of heaving to, the
following sea was so heavy, and seemed likely to poop us.   I had
the greatest confidence in our splendid chronometer, although I was
somewhat startled by a wrong longitude being given me by a Yankee
merchant ship.   We made no land, seeing none till Friday, 18th
March, when we were close upon the Needles, after which we hurried
along, taking the time to brush up, to the Motherbank, and to get
into Portsmouth Harbour.   At the Motherbank the quarantine
officer acquainted me with my brother Tom's decease.   A sad
blow indeed to me ; he was a manly and fine fellow, and struggled
244

with unwonted perseverance to the last ; but I had too much in
hand to dwell on it as much as I should otherwise have done.

I went on shore to the admiral, of course, and was received
with his usual kindness and consideration ; I had soon, letters from
' your affectionate friends,' at the Navy Office, inquiring as to the
defects of the anchors, as also impressing me with £1. 17s. 6d.,
charged on the supply of bread by the consul at Maranham. Nearly
twenty years from this time, when at Plymouth, seeing my boy
William off for sea, the boatswain of the dockyard (little Cable)
shewed a ' few links of our chain ' hung up in the blacksmith's
shop as a curiosity, shewing the goodness of the iron ; three of the
links being absolutely flattened in the hawse hole, with the strain
put on in endeavouring to weigh the anchor, before they, the anchors,
gave way. I dined with the admiral and commissioner, Sir Michael
Seymour, and on the day following, after giving up all my mess traps,
pots, kettles and pans, to Lieutenant Dawson, of the Royal College,
I gave up also the *Onyx* to him, after having the command of her
eighteen months, certainly, I may justly say, the happiest time
of my sea life. Two little pigs were brought on board as part of
my sea stock on leaving Portsmouth, in a sack by my steward.
They grew and thrived rapidly ; pigs do on board ship. One I
killed on nearing the coast of Brazil, and I intended slaughtering
the other on our passage home, but here I was at fault, he had
become the pet of the crew, and I had a deputation begging his life.
' You see, sir, he is just one of us ; he knows us all and takes his grog
daily like any Christian.' It was laughable to see him playing with
the men. Well, I could do no less than give in.

I set off for London, called on Dr Griffiths at Rochester, and on
to my mother at Dover. Very soon after this the *Cornelia*, schooner,
arrived. She was the vessel my brother Thomas purchased from
Captain Owen in Africa for a tender, and for which the Admiralty
put an impress on him for £130, besides putting an embargo on his
wages to the amount of as much more. I had, in conjunction with
my brother William, a long correspondence with the Admiralty,
with the view of taking off the impress. They took the schooner
and we got off from the impress. Had my brother survived I have
no doubt but he would have retained the schooner. As it was she
was an unlucky vessel ; she put into the Azores, the midshipman
in charge went mad, and the consul there put a mate of a merchant
ship in charge, to bring her and my brother's *wreck* of property
home, and it took me some considerable time to arrange his affairs.
I then went down in a steamer to Weymouth, on my way to Lyme,

with my sisters, servant and baggage ; the weather was such that
the captain would not guarantee our landing at Lyme. While at
Lyme another break in the family, the sudden death of my brother
Edward, eleven months younger than Thomas. He had the living of
St Clement's, Sandwich, but only for about eighteen months. I was
off to administer to his effects.

While in Kent I went to London, called at the Admiralty and
shewed myself to Sir James Graham and Sir Thomas Hardy, who
received me most kindly, said he had nothing to offer me, that Sir
James Graham took all the patronage, but added ' How would you
like to command a steamer ? '   ' I should much like it, Sir Thomas,
and if I may say it to you, depend upon it, in case of a future war,
steam will take a prominent part.' ' How would you arm them ? ' · 'A
big gun forward and aft and a couple of broadside ones in case of
getting to close quarters.'   ' Just my idea ; it is a hobby of mine ; I
make no promise, but I put your name down third on my list.'   I was
all cock-a-hoop, went down to Dover, and on board the steam packet,
and had one trip across to Boulogne by way of mastering steam.

In a short time the papers named three steamers being launched,
two given away. I went to London and saw Sir Thomas Hardy.
While talking to me a messenger looked in, saying the first lord
wished to see him.   I had no time to speak of the steamer, and soon
after she was given to another officer. My brother Henry told me
Sir Thomas at the club asked after me, saying I had not been near
them. My own diffidence kept me away ; but there it was. Captain
William Ramsay afterwards told me that on calling at the Admiralty
Sir Thomas said to him, ' I can get no application for a steamer ;
you call them smoke-jacks,' &c. Ramsay declined the imputation,
and was directly offered and accepted the command of the *Terrible*.[1]
All these three officers were promoted at the end of three years, and
I was left in the lurch ; my own doing, I must confess.

In London I fell in with my old captain, Sir Jahleel Brenton,
then Lieutenant-Governor of Greenwich Hospital, and was asked
to dine. At the table was the governor, Sir Richard Keats, and
Lady Keats, and a large party.   In the middle of dinner Lady Keats
said to Sir Jahleel, ' Pray do you know a Captain Boteler of the
navy ? '   ' Who, ma'am ? ' and she began to spell my name.   ' The
gentleman half-way down the table.'   There was a momentary pause,
then all began to talk, rather confusing to me. Captain Brenton,
who sat next to me, said, ' Hallo, is that you ? '   I said yes, that I

---

[1] *Terrible* should be *Dee* (see the notice of Captain William Ramsay in O'Byrne's
Naval Biographical Dictionary, which possibly Boteler misread).

was about to be connected with her ladyship, and I supposed she was enquiring my character. ' Hang it, man, ask her to take wine—— you have no tact.' Sir Jahleel told me she was dreadfully put out, and that he, by way of comforting her, said at a party he was talking to Lady R——, when another lady came up with, ' Pray, Sir Jahleel, can you tell me who Lady R—— was ? ' ' You had better ask Lady R—— herself.' Now this was somewhat worse, for there was a screw loose with Lady R——. When dinner was over, in the drawing-room Lady Keats came to me and asked after Mr West.[1] I cannot let slip all my naval friends yet. While at the Spring Garden Coffee House I heard the unmistakable voice of Captain William Ramsay saying, ' Which is his room ? I will wake him up.' The chambermaid pointed out my room and in came long Ramsay. ' Well, Boteler, how are you ? ' and we had a long chat. Ramsay breakfasted with me ; he had just arrived home from the coast of Africa, promoted for his gallant capture of a noted slaver, a large brig of eight guns and sixty men, Ramsay commanding the *Black Joke* schooner, two guns and thirty men. I had difficulty in getting anything out of Ramsay till going up Regent Street, when he told me the whole business, swinging his arms about, and in a loud Scotch voice. ' You see, Boteler, I had the *Black Joke*, the commodore's tender, and I got scent of this slaver about to leave the old Cameroons, and she heard of me and made light of my schooner. " Everyone fights the *Black Joke*, you see." So in a day or so I saw him coming out ; he did not seem to notice me, but kept his way with all sail set, studding sails low and aloft, and he contrived to cross me, and was apparently getting clear, when the wind dropped nearly to a calm, when I out sweeps and so managed to come up with him, and so you see, Boteler, I felt it incumbent to make a speech, and I called the men aft and said, " Now, my men, we will fire the gun, give three cheers and all board, that will do," and we dashed to her quarters with such force that the schooner bounded off, leaving me and six or seven men fighting like mad ' (and here Ramsay was swinging his long arms about to the amuse- ment of two gentlemen who were near us), ' when young Haines (do you mind young Haines ?) called the men to the other side and with a few strokes of the sweeps brought the schooner to again, and the rest boarded and we carried her, and I shackled the captain and crew to the chain cable, and put a man with an axe at the cat- head, saying, " Now, if you dare to move I will cut away and drag

---

[1] On August 15th, 1832, Commander Boteler married Helen Agnes, fifth daughter of Mr James West of Bryanston Square, London.

you all overboard " ' (and this part he told with a loud voice). She
had 250 slaves on board.

I must still hanker about the navy. I had made a compact with
my wife that I would not apply for appointment, but if one was
offered I would not refuse it. This was at the time my uncle, Sir
Thomas Harvey, was appointed commander-in-chief on the West
Indian and Halifax station.[1] He, as I heard, said, ' John Boteler
seems comfortable enough with his wife ; I will not disturb him, and
he does not seem anxious to go.'

Years after I tried for the coastguard, when Sir Thomas
Troubridge said, ' You were at Barham Down election and had
the largest Tory cockade of your party.' I said, ' That is true, a
lady made it ; it covered the side of my hat and I wore it.' ' You
were in that row at Canterbury, when so many heads were broken.'
I said, ' It's true, I was, but I had not even a switch.' ' Never mind,
sir, your colours encouraged it.' I was as flat as a lizard in a shop
door-way as the crowd passed. He also said, ' Your mother gives
all her votes on one side and your father was a high Tory.' I said,
' If you come to the dead I am off.' All this he repeated laughing ;
a laugh to him, but death to me. He added, by the way, ' If we
have an appointment to dispose of, and A is for us, and B against
us, we give it to A.' So after this it turned out : I made another
application for the coastguard and was refused on the plea of the
mark being out of my mouth (too old), and in six weeks the appointment was given to my brother Henry, the only Whig of the family,
and he was my senior by more than a year.[2]

As an effectual close to my sea life, on the 15th August, 1832,
I married, and we celebrated our golden wedding at Taplow, in 1882,
at the residence of my eldest son, William John Casberd Boteler.[3]

In concluding these recollections, I may here say that I wrote
them off-hand without any idea of publication, and only for the
perusal of my immediate family, so that I may fairly beg their
indulgence for all loosely worded stories.

[1] In March 1839 Vice Admiral Sir Thomas Harvey was appointed Commander-
in-Chief, West Indies, Halifax and Newfoundland, with his flag in the *Winchester*
(Captain John Parker). His Flag Lieutenant was his eldest son, Thomas Harvey ;
upon whose promotion, Henry Harvey, another son and one of the *Winchester's*
lieutenants, succeeded. The Commander of the *Winchester* (which post Commander
Boteler might have been offered) was William W. P. Johnson, who, in 1830, married
Elizabeth, eldest daughter of the Admiral.

[2] Captain Sir E. Thomas Troubridge was from 1835 to 1841 a member of the
Board of Admiralty and M.P. for Sandwich. Commander Henry Boteler was (says
O'Byrne's *Naval Biographical Dictionary*) employed for three years, 1833-6, in the
Coast Guard ; as Superintendent of the Packet Service at Dover, 1837-41 ; and
from 1841 till 1846 as Inspecting Commander in the Coastguard.

[3] Commander W. J. Casberd Boteler, R.N., died May 15th, 1907.

INDEX

S

NAVY RECORDS SOCIETY

LIST OF MEMBERS

1942

PATRON :

H.R.H. THE DUKE OF KENT, K.G., K.T., G.C.M.G., G.C.V.O.

Aberdeen, University of.
Adelaide, South Australia, Public Library of.
Admiralty Library, London, S.W. 1.
Aldershot, Prince Consort's Library.
Allenby, R. F. H., The Beacon, Shanklin, Isle of Wight.
Ampthill, Commander Lord, R.N., Marlborough Club, Pall Mall, S.W. 1.
Anderson, R. C., Litt.D., F.S.A., F.R.Hist.S., Nunney Court, Frome, Somerset.
Antiquaries, Society of, Burlington House, Piccadilly, W. 1.
Archdale, Lieut.-Commander H., R.N., Riverside, Ballinamallard, Co. Fermanagh.
Arrowsmith, H. C., " Moorings," Grove Road, Southlands, Stone, Staffs.
Athenæum, The, Pall Mall, S.W. 1.
*Atkinson, C. T., 16 Chadlington Road, Oxford.
Augustin-Normand, Augustin, 81 Boulevard François 1ᵉʳ, Le Havre.
Australia, Commonwealth National Library, Canberra.
Australia, Naval Board.

Baddeley, Sir Vincent W., K.C.B., Dyars Close, Cookham Dean, Berks.
†Baker, Lieutenant A. A. W., R.N.
†Balfour, Lieut. Ian M., R.N.
Baltimore, U.S.A., The Enoch Pratt Free Library.
Baltimore, U.S.A., The Johns Hopkins University Library.
Barnes, George R., 3 Albert Terrace, N.W. 1.
Barnes, Sir J. Sidney, K.B.E., C.B., Admiralty, S.W. 1.
Bath, Victoria Art Gallery and Municipal Library.
Beadon, Colonel R. H., C.B.E., Gotton House, Taunton, Somerset.

* Original Members (1893).
† Addresses of Officers serving in His Majesty's ships have been omitted.

†Beattie, Lieut.-Commander S. H., R.N.
Beer, E. S. de, F.R.Hist.S., 11 Sussex Place, N.W. 1.
Belfast, Linen Hall Library.
Bell, Commander L. H., R.N., O.B.E., Admiralty, S.W. 1.
†Bennett, Lieut.-Commander G. M., R.N.
Bennett, Lieut.-Commander T. G., R.N., 55 Gurney Court Road, St. Albans, Herts.
Bentinck, Admiral Sir Rudolf W., K.C.B., K.C.M.G., Winklebury Hill, Basingstoke, Hants.
Bergne, Paymaster-Lieutenant D. A'Court, R.N., Shotley Gate, Ipswich, Suffolk.
Binney, Vice-Admiral Sir T. Hugh, K.C.B., D.S.O.
Birmingham Public Libraries.
Birmingham University Library, Edmund Street, Birmingham, 3.
†Blackham, Lieut.-Commander J. L., R.N.
Blake, Admiral Sir Geoffrey, K.C.B., D.S.O., Lady Cross Lodge, Brockenhurst, Hants.
Blake, Lieutenant T. M., R.N., Monckton House, Alverstoke, Hants.
Blencowe, O. J., Orleton, Filey Road, Scarborough.
†Blundell, Lieut.-Commander G. C., R.N.
Bolton, Central Reference Library.
Bonner-Smith, D., F.R.Hist.S., The Library, Admiralty, S.W. 1.
Boston, Massachusetts, U.S.A., The Athenæum.
Boston, Massachusetts, U.S.A., Public Library of.
Boultbee, Lieut.-Colonel W. R. P., R.M., 38 Priestfields, Rochester.
Boulton, Lieut.-Colonel O., M.A., T.D., Kenward, Yalding.
Boyd, Rear-Admiral Denis, D.S.C., 21 Lexham Gardens, W. 8.
Boyle, Captain H. L., C.B.E., R.N., 4 East Crescent, Whitby, Yorks.
Bradley, P. Brendon, M.A., D.Litt., " Stepaside," 4 Greystone Gardens, Northwick Circle, Kenton, Middlx.
Brasier-Creagh, Lieut.-Commander B. R., R.N., Guards Club, Brook Street, W. 1.
Brindley, Harold H., F.S.A., 25 Madingley Road, Cambridge.
Bristol, The University Library.
British Museum (*copies presented*).
Brock, Commander P. W., R.N., Kingston, Effingham, Surrey.
Brocklebank, Captain Henry C. Royds, C.B.E., R.N., Charlton House, Shaftesbury, Dorset.
Brooke, Mrs. Cecil, Hampton Court Palace, Middlx.
Brown, Thomas W. F., D.Sc., Craig Holme, Jesmond Park West, Newcastle-upon-Tyne.
Brown University Library, Providence, Rhode Island, U.S.A.
Browning, Admiral Sir Montague E., G.C.B., G.C.M.G., G.C.V.O., Sleepers Hill House, Winchester.
†Bruce, Lieutenant E., R.N.
Bullocke, J. G., 5 Dartmouth Grove, Greenwich, S.E. 10.
Burgersdijk & Niermans, Nieuwsteeg, 1, Leiden, Holland.
Burn, Dugald S., C.I.E., 14 The Park, Golder's Hill, N.W. 11.

† Addresses of Officers serving in His Majesty's ships have been omitted.

†Burrough, Rear-Admiral H. M., C.B.
†Burton, Commander E. A., R.N.
Butler-Bowdon, Lieut.-Commander M. E., R.N., Southgate House, Clown,
near Chesterfield, Derbyshire.

Calcutta, Imperial Library, Government of India.
Caldecote, The Right Hon. Viscount, P.C., C.B.E., K.C., LL.D., 10 Eaton
Square, S.W. 1.
California, U.S.A., University of.
Callender, Professor Sir Geoffrey A. R., F.S.A., F.R.Hist.S., A.I.N.A.,
9 Rawlinson Road, Oxford.
Cambridge, Seeley Historical Library, The Old Schools, Bene't Street.
Cambridge, University Library (*copies presented*).
Canada, Department of National Defence, Ottawa.
Cardiff, The Public Libraries.
Carter, Sir Archibald, K.C.B., K.C.I.E.
†Carter, Captain Thomas G., O.B.E., R.N.
Cartwright, Captain Montague G., R.N., The Anchorage, Shortheath,
Farnham, Surrey.
†Casement, Lieut.-Commander J. J., R.N.
†Cazalet, Commander P. G. L., R.N.
†Chandler, Lieut.-Commander R. B., R.N.
Chatfield, Admiral of the Fleet Lord, G.C.B., O.M., K.C.M.G., C.V.O.,
D.C.L., The Small House, Farnham Common.
Chicago, U.S.A., Newberry Library.
Chicago, U.S.A., University of.
Chichester, Lieutenant M. G., R.N., Emwell, Warminster, Wilts.
Chilton, Vice-Admiral F. G. G., C.B., Hamel's Mead, Buntingford, Herts.
Chirnside, Russell M., " Mornmoot," Whittlesea, Victoria, Australia.
†Churchill, Lieut.-Commander C. F. H., R.N.
Churchill, The Right Hon. Winston L. Spencer, C.H., M.P., Chartwell
Manor, Westerham.
Cincinnati, Public Library of, Ohio, U.S.A.
Cincinnati University Library, Cincinnati, Ohio, U.S.A.
Cleveland-Stevens, W., K.C., 17 Old Buildings, Lincoln's Inn, W.C. 2.
†Cole, Paymaster-Lieutenant J. H. M.
Columbia University Library, New York, U.S.A.
Congress, U.S.A., Library of.
Connelly, Peter J., 81 The Drive, Ilford, Essex.
Conservative Club, St. James's Street, S.W.
Constitutional Club, Northumberland Avenue, W.C. 2.
Copenhagen, The Royal Library.
Copley, Peter, 10 Hampstead Square, N.W. 3.
Corderoy, G., 15 Warwick Square, S.W. 1
Cornell University, U.S.A.
Costeker, Miss E. P., 15 Marlborough Road, Bournemouth West.

† Addresses of Officers serving in His Majesty's ships have been omitted.

*Cottesloe, Lord, C.B., The Old House, Swanbourne, Bletchley, Bucks.
Cotton, G. F., C.B., M.V.O., O.B.E., Empire Hotel, Bath.
Creswell, Commander J., R.N., Bubspool House, East Coker, Yeovil.
Crick, The Venerable Archdeacon T., C.B.E., Chaplain of the Fleet.
Croydon, Free Public Library.
Cruising Association, The, Chiltern Court, Baker Street, N.W. 1.
†Cunliffe, Captain R. L. B., R.N.
Cunninghame-Graham, Captain A. B., R.N., Ardoch, Cardross, Dumbartonshire, Scotland.
Curtis, Vice-Admiral B., C.B., C.M.G., D.S.O., "Falklands," Beach Road, Emsworth, Hants.

Danckwerts, Rear-Admiral V. H., C.M.G., Merton Lodge, Emsworth, Hants.
Dartmouth College Library, Hanover, New Hampshire, U.S.A.
Dasent, Captain W., R.N.
Davidson, Viscount, P.C., G.C.V.O., C.H., C.B., Norcott Court, Berkhamstead, Herts.
Davies, General Sir Francis J., K.C.B., K.C.M.G., K.C.V.O., Elmley Castle, Pershore, Worcs.
Deare, Commander N. B., R.N., Royal Thames Yacht Club, 60 Knightsbridge, S.W. 1.
Derby, The Earl of, K.G., G.C.V.O., C.B., Knowsley, Prescot, Lancs.
Dewar, Captain Alfred C., O.B.E., B.Litt., F.R.Hist.S., R.N. (Hon. Secretary), c/o The Library, Admiralty, S.W. 1.
†Dick, Captain R. M., D.S.C., R.N.
*Digby, Captain The Hon. Gerald F., R.N., Lewcombe Manor, Dorchester.
Donovan, Lieut.-Commander J., R.A.N., Flinders Naval Depot, Victoria, Australia.
Dorling, Captain H. Taprell, D.S.O., F.R.Hist.S., R.N., 97 Rivermead Court, Hurlingham, S.W. 6.
Douin, Capitaine de Corvette G., Suez Canal Company, Ismailia, Egypt.
Draper, S., Feversham House, Welham Road, Norton, Malton, Yorks.
Dreyer, Admiral Sir Frederic C., G.B.E., K.C.B., Forest Brow, Liss Forest, Hampshire.
†Driscoll, Rev. W. J., R.N.
Dublin, Trinity College Library (*copies presented*).
Duke University Library, Durham, North Carolina.
†Dumas, Lieutenant D. B. G., R.N.

Eason, Paymaster-Captain V., O.B.E., D.S.C., R.N., H.M.S. *Raleigh*, Tor Point, E. Cornwall.
Eastwick, Miss C., The Mill House, Iffley, Oxford.
Edinburgh Public Libraries.
Edinburgh, Signet Library.

* Original Members (1893).
† Addresses of Officers serving in His Majesty's ships have been omitted.

Edinburgh, University of.
Edwards, Francis, 83 High Street, Marylebone, W. 1.
†Egerton, Rear-Admiral Brian.
Eldridge, Cecil H., 20 Ormonde Road, Branksome Park, Bournemouth.
†Elliot, Lieut.-Commander W., R.N.
Ellis, Commander C., R.N.
Elphinstone, Kenneth V., Artillery Mansions, S.W. 1.
Excellent, H.M.S., The Officers' Library, Portsmouth.

Fardell, Commander K. M., R.N., Nidderdale, Sunwine Place, Exmouth.
Fayle, C. E., O.B.E., 10 Hornsey Lane, N. 6.
Foreign Office Library.
Foster, R. Lionel, Egton Manor, Egton Bridge, Yorks.
†Franks, Lieut.-Commander R. D., O.B.E., R.N.
Fremantle, Admiral Sir Sydney R., G.C.B., M.V.O., 30 Bullingham
    Mansions, Church Street, W. 8.
French, Admiral Sir Wilfred, K.C.B., C.M.G., c/o Westminster Bank Ltd.,
    26 Haymarket, S.W. 1.
Fuller, Admiral Sir Cyril T. M., K.C.B., C.M.G., D.S.O., Douthwaite
    Dale, Hutton-le-Hole, Yorks.

Galpin, Commander W. S., R.N., The Moorings, Meads, Eastbourne.
†Gascoigne, Instructor-Lieutenant J. C., B.Sc., R.N.
Glasgow, Institute of Accountants and Actuaries in, 142 St. Vincent
    Street, Glasgow, C.2.
Glasgow, Mitchell Library.
Glasgow, University of.
Godfrey, Rear-Admiral J. H., C.B.
Goodenough, Commander M. G., R.N., 16 Wilton Street, S.W. 1.
*Greene, Sir W. Graham, K.C.B. (Hon. Treasurer), Hanover Court,
    Hanover Square, W. 1.
Gretton, Colonel the Right Hon. John, C.B.E., M.P., Stapleford Park,
    Melton Mowbray.
Guildhall Library, The, E.C.
Gurner, Vice-Admiral Victor G., 178 St. James's Court, Buckingham
    Gate, S.W. 1.

Hague, The, Department of Defence, Holland.
Hall, Instructor Rear-Admiral A. E., C.B., C.B.E., A.R.C.S., R.N.,
    10 Liskeard Gardens, Blackheath, S.E. 3.

* Original Members (1893).
† Addresses of Officers serving in His Majesty's ships have been omitted.

Hall, Admiral Sir W. Reginald, K.C.M.G., C.B., D.C.L., The Ropeway, Beaulieu, Hants.
Hamilton, Rear-Admiral Louis H. K., D.S.O.
Hamilton, Vice-Admiral R. C., Thursley Corner, Thursley, Surrey.
Hardie, R. P., 13 Palmerston Road, Edinburgh.
Harries, L. H., Highmeads, 69 Upland Road, Sutton, Surrey.
Harvard College Library, Cambridge, Mass.
†Haslehurst, Paymaster-Commander E., R.N.
Hawkins, Commander G. A. B., M.V.O., D.S.C., R.N., 31 Norfolk Crescent, W. 2.
Haworth, Lieutenant M. G., R.N., Lower Peover Hall, near Knutsford, Cheshire.
Hensman, Captain M., D.S.O., R.N., Coney Weston Hall, Bury St. Edmunds.
†Henwood, Paymaster-Lieut.-Commander A. E., R.N.
†Hilken, Commander T. J. N., R.N.
†Hinton, Commander E. P., M.V.O., R.N.
Hodges, H. W., F.R.Hist.S., Windmill House, Wingrave, Aylesbury.
Holck, Orlogskaptajn P., R.D.N., Helsebakken 7, Hellerup, Denmark.
Hood, The Hon. Lady, 20 Upper Brook Street, S.W. 1.
Hope, Admiral Sir George P. W., K.C.B., K.C.M.G., Common House, Plaistow, Billingshurst, Sussex.
Horne, Lieutenant J. B. R., R.N.
†Horton, Commander C. Ivan, R.N.
*Hudleston, Rear-Admiral Ralph, Hutton John, Penrith.
Hull Public Libraries.
Humphreys, Lieut.-Commander L. A., R.N.
Hunt, Ernest W., Phoenix House, 127 Featherston Street, Wellington, C. 1, New Zealand.
Hunter, B. R., 4 Pembridge Villas, W. 11.
Huntington Library and Art Gallery, San Marino, California.
Hussey, Lieut.-Commander W. F. E., D.S.C., R.N., 1 Queen's Gate, Southsea, Hants.

Illinois, University Library, Urbana, U.S.A.
India Office, The.
Indiana University Library, Bloomington, Ind., U.S.A.
Inglesby, Paymaster-Lieutenant E. V., R.N.
Ingram, Captain Bruce S., O.B.E., M.C., Commonwealth House, 1 New Oxford Street, W.C. 1.
Iowa, Library of State University of, Library Annex, Iowa City, Iowa, U.S.A.
Ireland, National Library of, Dublin.
Iveagh, Captain The Earl of, C.B., C.M.G., R.N.V.R., 11 St. James's Square, S.W.

*Jackson, Admiral Sir Thomas, K.B.E., C.B., M.V.O., Wolley, Uplyme, Dorset.

Jackson, Rear-Admiral W. L., D.S.O., R.N., Northwood House, Fareham, Hants.

†Jacomb, Captain H. B., R.N.

James, W. Ashton (Hon. Auditor), South Muskham Prebend, Southwell, Notts.

James, Admiral Sir William James, K.C.B., The Road Farm, Churt, Surrey.

Jones, Commander L. T. Peyton, R.N., Sunnyside, Monument Green, Weybridge.

Karlskrona, Kungl. Orlogsmannasällskapet, Sweden.

Keate, Miss E. M., M.B.E., 16c Cresswell Gardens, Old Brompton Road, S.W. 5.

†Kennedy-Purvis, Admiral Sir Charles, K.C.B.

Kenyon, Sir Frederic G., G.B.E., K.C.B., D.Litt., LL.D., F.B.A., F.S.A., Kirkstead, Godstone, Surrey (President).

Keyes, Admiral of the Fleet Sir Roger J. B., Bart., G.C.B., K.C.V.O., C.M.G., D.S.O., LL.D., D.C.L., M.P., Tingewick House, Tingewick, Bucks.

Kinahan, Captain H. R. G., R.N., Suncourt, Lee-on-Solent.

Kipling, Lieutenant R. F., R.N., Millerground, Windermere.

Kirk, Captain A. G., U.S.N., Navy Department, Washington, D.C., U.S.A.

Kitson, Vice-Admiral Sir Henry K., K.B.E., C.B., Monk's Hill, Tilford, Farnham, Surrey.

Knox, Captain Dudley W., U.S.N., Navy Department, Washington, D.C.

Lambe, Air Vice-Marshal Sir Charles L., K.C.B., C.M.G., D.S.O., Grove House, Semley, Shaftesbury.

Lambert, D. G., Av. Rodrigues Alves 303/331, Rio de Janeiro, Brazil.

Langdon, Miss A., 2D Grand Parade, Old Portsmouth.

Laughton, L. G. Carr, 8A Arnison Road, E. Molesey, Surrey.

†Lawder, Paymaster-Lieutenant M.C., R.N.

Le Marchant, Admiral E. R., D.S.O., Danehurst, Hordle, Hants.

Lee of Fareham, The Right Hon. Viscount, P.C., G.C.B., G.C.S.I., G.B.E., LL.D., Avening, Glos.

Leeds Library, The, Commercial Street, Leeds.

Leeds, The University of.

Lewis, Professor Michael A., F.R.Hist.S., Royal Naval College, Greenwich, S.E. 10.

Linlithgow, His Excellency The Most Hon. the Marquess of, K.T., P.C., G.M.S.I., G.M.I.E., D.L., T.D., Viceroy's House, New Delhi, India.

---

* Original Members (1893).

† Addresses of Officers serving in His Majesty's ships have been omitted.

Little, Admiral Sir Charles J. Colebrook, K.C.B., Martins, Thakeham, Sussex.
Liverpool, Public Libraries.
Liverpool, The University of.
†Livesey, Lieutenant J. L., R.N.
London Library, The, St. James's Square, S.W. 1.
London, The Institute of Historical Research, Malet Street, W.C. 1.
London Library, The University of, The Goldsmiths' Librarian, Senate House, W.C. 1.
Longhurst, C., C.B., Committee of Imperial Defence, Whitehall, S.W. 1.
Longsdon, Commander E. H., R.N., United Service Club, Pall Mall, S.W. 1.
Lords, House of, Library.
Lowther, L. W. H., Club Union, Concordia, Entre Rios, Argentine.
Lund, Sweden, University of.
Lyon, Vice-Admiral Sir George H. D'Oyly, C.B., Strangeways, Limpsfield, Surrey.

McArthur, Instructor-Commander G. K., R.N., Beaumont College, Old Windsor, Bucks.
McCall, J. Home, Thimble Cottage, 27 Rosemont Road, Richmond, Surrey.
McClintock, Lieutenant-Commander J. L. E., Brakey Hill, South Godstone, Surrey.
McCormick-Goodhart, Commander L., O.B.E., R.N.V.R., Langley Park, Silver Spring, Maryland, U.S.A.
†McDougall, Lieut.-Commander A. R., R.N.V.R.
McGill University Library, Montreal.
McMurtrie, F. E., Mandeville, Hoddesdon, Herts.
Malcolm, Lieut.-Commander C. J. O., R.N., Sheet House, Petersfield, Hants.
Malta Public Library, Valetta.
Manchester, Public Libraries, St. Peter's Square, Manchester, 2.
Manchester, The John Rylands Library, Deansgate.
Manchester, The University of.
Markham, Sir Henry V., K.C.B., M.C.
Mason, C. C., O.B.E., Beverley, Bentley Road, Cambridge.
Mason, F. van Wyck, 630 Fifth Avenue, New York, U.S.A.
Massachusetts Historical Society, 1154 Boylston Street, Boston, Mass.
†Mathers, Lieutenant P. D. G., R.N.
Matheson, Lieut.-Commander A. F., R.N., Little Scatwell, Strathpeffer, Ross-shire.
May, Captain Arthur De K. L., C.B.E., R.N., Langaller, Catisfield, Fareham, Hants.
Melbourne Public Library.
Melbourne, University of.

† Addresses of Officers serving in His Majesty's ships have been omitted.

Merriman, Commander R. D., D.S.C., R.I.N., "Tremadoc," Smoke Lane, Reigate, Surrey.
Michell, Engineer-Commander R. A. C., R.N., Westwood, Wootton Bridge, Isle of Wight.
Michigan, University of, Ann Arbor, U.S.A.
†Miles, Lieut.-Commander G. R., R.C.N.
Miller, Lieut.-Commander W. Davis, U.S.N.R., " Deepwell," Wakefield, Rhode Island.
Minnesota, University Library, Minneapolis, Minn., U.S.A.
Missouri University Library, Columbia, Mo., U.S.A.
Monsell, Commander the Right Hon. Viscount, G.B.E., R.N., Dumbleton Hall, Evesham, Warwick.
Montgomery, Lieut.-Commander J. R. C., R.N., Hurstmead, Haywards Heath, Sussex.
Moore, Sir Alan, Bart., Hancox, Battle, Sussex.
Moore, Sub-Lieutenant H. D. L., R.N.V.R., Little Hollow, Stoke Bishop, Bristol.
†Moore, Vice-Admiral H. R., C.B., C.V.O., D.S.O.
Morgan, Lieut.-Commander E. V. St. J., R.N.
Morrell, Paymaster-Captain A. W., R.N., 1 Keswick House, Raymond Road, Wimbledon, S.W. 19.
Morris, S. Grave, 83 Belsize Park Gardens, N.W. 3.
Morse, Captain J. A. V., C.B., D.S.O., R.N., Chute Collis, near Andover, Wilts.
†Moss, Rev. W. H. O., R.N.
Mountbatten, Vice-Admiral the Lord Louis, G.C.V.O., Brook House, Upper Brook Street, W. 1.
Moxham, Captain J. H., R.M., 144 St. Margaret's Road, Edgware, Middlx.
Murray, C. W., Couldoran, Kishorn, Strathcarron.

Naish, George P. B., National Maritime Museum, Greenwich, S.E. 10.
National Maritime Museum, Greenwich.
National Portrait Gallery.
Naval and Military Club, 94 Piccadilly, W. 1.
Nebraska, University of, Lincoln, Nebraska, U.S.A.
Nederlandsch Historisch Scheepvaart Museum, Amsterdam.
Newcastle-upon-Tyne, Public Library.
New South Wales, Public Library of, Sydney.
New York, Public Library.
New York, State Library.
New York University, Washington Square Library, 100 Washington Square East, New York.
New York Yacht Club, 37 West 44th Street, New York, U.S.A.
New Zealand, The Chief Librarian, General Assembly Library, Wellington.

† Addresses of Officers serving in His Majesty's ships have been omitted.

New Zealand, Alexander Turnbull Library, Wellington, C. 1, N.Z.
Nijhoff, Martinus, F.R.Hist.S., Lange Voorhout 9, The Hague.
Norway, Admiralstaben Bibliotek, Festningen, Oslo.
Nottingham, Central Public Library.
*Nugent, Vice-Admiral Raymond A., C.M.G., Dean House, Lee-on-
 Solent.

†O'Hara, Paymaster-Lieutenant J., R.N.
†Oliver, Captain R. D., D.S.C., R.N.
Ommanney, John L. N., Midshipman, R.N.
Ottawa, Canada, Library of Parliament.
Ottawa, Public Archives of, Canada.
Overton, E. M., 30 Westfield Road, Edgbaston, Birmingham, 15.
Owen, C. V., F.R.Hist.S., F.S.S.
Owen, Commander J. H., F.R.Hist.S., R.N., Broadwater House, Steven-
 age, Herts.
Oxford, All Souls College.
Oxford, Bodleian Library (*copies presented*).
Oxford, Exeter College.
Oxford, Rhodes House Library.
Oxford, Trinity College.

†Packer, Captain H. A., R.N.
Pares, Richard, 6 Oriel Street, Oxford.
Paris, Bibliothèque Nationale.
Parkinson, C. N., F.R.Hist.S., Ph.D., Emmanuel College, Cambridge.
Parminter, Paymaster-Lieutenant Geoffrey de C., R.N.
Patterson, C. D., Gulladuff, Craigavad, Co. Down.
Pearson, Paymaster-Lieutenant A. L., R.N., 3 Abbotsway, Muncaster,
 York.
Pegram, Rear-Admiral F. H., R.N.
Pelling, John L., Hackins Hey, Liverpool, 2.
Penn, C. D., F.R.Hist.S., c/o Marlborough College, Wilts.
Pennsylvania, U.S.A., Historical Society of.
Pennsylvania, University of, Philadelphia.
Petree, J. Foster, 27 Downside Road, Sutton, Surrey.
†Petrie-Hay, Paymaster-Lieutenant A. J., R.N.
†Phibbs, Lieut.-Commander K. H. J. L., R.N.
Philadelphia, U.S.A., Library Company of.
Phillimore, Captain Valentine E. B., C.B.E., D.S.O., R.N., United Service
 Club, Pall Mall, S.W. 1.
Pinsent, Commander Clive, R.N., Edinglassie Lodge, near Huntly,
 Aberdeenshire, N.B.
†Pitcairn-Jones, Commander C. G., R.N.

* Original Members (1893).
† Addresses of Officers serving in His Majesty's ships have been omitted.

Plunkett-Ernle-Erle-Drax, Admiral the Hon. Sir Reginald, K.C.B., D.S.O., Charborough Park, Wareham, Dorset.
Plymouth, Central Public Library.
Pool, Bernard, Contract Department, Admiralty.
Pooll, Captain W. S. Batten, Rode Manor, Bath.
Portsmouth, Central Public Library.
Portsmouth, H.M. Navigation School.
†Pound, Admiral of the Fleet Sir A. Dudley, G.C.B., G.C.V.O.
Powell, Rev. J. R., St. Barnabas Vicarage, High Street, Homerton, E. 9.
Prendergast, Admiral Sir Robert, K.C.B., Meads House, Meads, Eastbourne.
Previté-Orton, C. W., Litt.D., F.B.A., F.R.Hist.S., St. John's College, Cambridge.
Price, Sub-Lieutenant G. D. A., R.N.V.R.
Princeton University, New Jersey, U.S.A.
Pring, Paymaster Lieut.-Commander L. W., R.N., R.N. Air Station, Lee-on-Solent, Hants.
†Prophit, Paymaster-Commander W. J. G., R.N.
Public Record Office, The.

Queensland, University of.

Raikes, Vice-Admiral R. H. T., C.B., C.V.O., D.S.O., Fort Blockhouse, Gosport, Hants.
Ramsay, Admiral The Hon. Sir Alexander, G.C.V.O., K.C.B., D.S.O.
Reading, Free Public Libraries.
Reading, The University Library.
Reform Club, Pall Mall, S.W.
*Richmond, Admiral Sir Herbert W., K.C.B., D.C.L., Master's Lodge, Downing College, Cambridge.
Ringrose, Captain C. H., R.N., Skelton Castle, Skelton-in-Cleveland, Yorks.
Robertson, G.M., Bryanston School, Blandford, Dorset.
Rodney, The Hon. Simon, K6, The Albany, Piccadilly, W. 1.
Roper, Lieut.-Commander E. G., R.N., "Broombank," Seascale, Cumberland.
Rouse, W. H. D., Litt.D., F.R.G.S., M.R.A.S., Histon Manor, Cambs.
Rowbotham, Commander W. B., R.N.
Royal Australian Naval College.
Royal Cruising Club, 1 New Square, Lincoln's Inn, W.C. 2.
Royal Empire Society, Northumberland Avenue, W.C. 2.
Royal Engineers' Institute, Chatham.
Royal Historical Society, 96 Cheyne Walk, Chelsea, S.W. 10.
Royal Institution, 21 Albemarle Street, W. 1.

* Original Members (1893).
† Addresses of Officers serving in His Majesty's ships have been omitted.

Royal Marine Barracks, Officers' Library, Eastney, Portsmouth.
Royal Marine Barracks, Officers' Library, Plymouth.
Royal Naval Barracks, Chatham.
Royal Naval Barracks, Devonport.
Royal Naval Club, Portsmouth.
Royal Naval College, Dartmouth.
Royal Naval College, Greenwich.
Royal Naval Engineering College, Devonport.
Royal Naval Port Library, Devonport.
Royal Naval Port Library, Portsmouth.
Royal Naval Staff College, Greenwich (2 *copies*).
Royal Thames Yacht Club, 60 Knightsbridge, S.W. 1.
Royal United Service Institution, Whitehall, S.W. 1.
*Runciman, The Right Hon. Viscount, D.C.L., LL.D., J.P., Doxford, Chathill, Northumberland.
Rutherford, Miss G., 2 Phillimore Place, W. 8.
Rutter, Owen, The Croft, Wargrave, Berks.

Sandwich, The Right Hon. The Earl of, Hinchingbrooke, Huntingdon.
San Francisco, U.S.A., Free Library.
Sarell, Lieut.-Commander R. I. A., R.N., Braeside, Ashurst Road, near East Grinstead, Sussex.
Saunders, Lieut.-Commander R., D.S.O., R.N.V.R., 6 Douglas Mansions, Quex Road, N.W. 6.
Scotland, National Library of, Edinburgh (*copies presented*).
Scott, A., c/o Royal Bank of Scotland, Edinburgh.
Scurfield, Commander B. G., A.M., R.N., Hinnies, Yelverton, Devon.
Sheffield, University of.
Shelley, Captain R., R.N., The Pickeridge, Stoke Poges, Bucks.
†Sherley-Price, Rev. L., M.A., R.N.
Sinclair, Major Robert, R.M., Royal Marine Barracks, Plymouth.
Skinner, Paymaster Lieut.-Commander R. M. P., R.N., Mountsfield, Rye, Sussex.
Smith, Admiral Sir Aubrey C., K.B.E., C.B., M.V.O., 71 Gloucester Place, W. 1.
Smith, Commander T. M., R.N., " Rozel," 15 St. Ronan's Road, Southsea, Hants.
†Sommerville, Lieutenant I. F., R.N.
Southborough, The Right Hon. Lord, G.C.B., G.C.M.G., G.C.V.O., K.C.S.I., 17 Airlie Gardens, Campden Hill, W. 8.
Spicer, Captain Stewart D., R.N., Salt Mill House, Fishbourne, Chichester.
†Spooner, Rear-Admiral E. J., D.S.O., R.N.
Stanhope, The Right Hon. Earl, K.G., D.S.O., M.C., D.L., Chevening, Sevenoaks.
Stephens, Captain W. D., R.N., The Old Vicarage, Easebourne, Midhurst, Sussex.

Stewart, Commander A. T., O.B.E , R.N., Langness, Bush Hill, Winchmore Hill, N 21
Stewart, Captain R. R., R.N , Old Mill Cottage, Droxford, Hants.
Stockholm, Royal Library.
Stokoe, W F. (Hon. Auditor), Admiralty, S.W. 1
Strafford, The Right Hon. The Earl of, D L., 5 St. James's Square, S.W. 1.
Stubbs, E R., 44 Fernwood Avenue, Streatham, S.W. 16.
Sutherland, Paymaster-Lieutenant D. M., R N V R., 6 Northmoor Road, Oxford.
Swan, Captain E. W , O.B.E., V.D , D L., R N.V.R., Newbrough Park, Fourstones, Northumberland.
Swinson, B H., c/o The Caribbean Petroleum Co , Maracaibo, Venezuela.
†Symes, Lieutenant E D , R N

Talbot, Admiral Sir Cecil P., K B E , C.B , D.S.O , Orchard Mains, Wych Hill, Woking, Surrey.
Taylor, Rear-Admiral A Hugh, O.B E , The Manor House, Diss, Norfolk.
Taylor, Commander N B. D., D.S.C , R N.
†Thistleton-Smith, Lieut.-Commander G , R.N.
Thursfield, Rear-Admiral H. G., Little Park House, Farnham, Surrey.
Toronto, Legislative Library, Parliament Buildings.
Toronto, Public Library, College and St. George Streets
Townsend-Green, Lieut -Commander A., R.N , Green Bank, Field Place, Weybridge, Surrey
Travellers Club, 106 Pall Mall, S W. 1.
†Trentham, Lieut.-Commander D P., R N
Trevelyan, Professor G M., O M , C.B E., Litt D , LL D., F R.Hist S., Garden Corner, West Road, Cambridge
Triggs, Major Bernard, R.E., F.R I B A., 40 Dover Street, W. 1.
Trinity House, Corporation of, Tower Hill, E C. 3.
Troubridge, Captain T. H., R.N., Middle Oakshott, Hawkley, Liss, Hants.
†Turnbull, Lieut -Commander G F., R N.

United Service Club, Pall Mall, S.W. 1.
U.S Naval Academy, Annapolis, Md., U S A
U.S. Navy Department, Washington, D C , U.S.A.
United University Club, 1 Suffolk Street, S W. 1.

Vandervell, Commander H., R.N V R , 15 Wedderburn Road, Hampstead, N.W. 3.
Van Stockum, W P , & Son, Buitenhof 36, The Hague, Holland.
Vaughan, Paymaster-Commander H. R. H , R.N., Nantymwyn, Rhandirmwyn, Llandovery, Carmarthenshire
Vernon, H.M S , Mess Secretary, Ward Room Mess, Portsmouth.
Verwijnen, Commander G J , Royal Netherland Navy, Juliana van Stolbergplein No 18A, The Hague, Netherlands.

† Addresses of Officers serving in His Majesty's ships have been omitted

Wales, National Library of (*copies presented*).
Walling, R. V., " Caradon," Lackford Road, Chipstead, Surrey.
Warnsinck, Captain J. C. M., Royal Netherland Navy, Van Alkemade-
laan 332, The Hague, Netherlands.
Washington University Library.
†Waters, Lieutenant D. W., R.N.
Watson, Vice-Admiral B. C., C.B., D.S.O., Court House, Hambledon,
Hants.
*Webb, Admiral Sir Richard, K.C.M.G., C.B., Elbridge, Windlesham,
Surrey.
Weir, The Right Hon. Viscount, G.C.B., LL.D., D.L., Holm Foundry,
Cathcart, Glasgow.
Westminster Public Library, Buckingham Palace Road, S.W. 1.
White, L. R. B., Gavarnie, Ersham Road, Hailsham, Sussex.
Whiting, Professor C. E., D.D., B.C.L., F.S.A., F.R.Hist.S., St. Chad's
College, Durham.
†Whiting, Instructor-Commander R. O., R.N.
Wiggins, H. P., Hans Cottage, Henley-on-Thames, Oxon.
†Wilkinson, Lieutenant J. V., R.N.
Willett, Commander B. R., D.S.C., R.N., The Old Mill House, Bedhamp-
ton, Hants.
Willis, H. C., H.M.S. *Vernon*, Portsmouth.
Winchester College, The Librarian.
Wisconsin, U.S.A., State Historical Society of.
†Woodward, S. M.

Yale University, New Haven, Conn., U.S.A.
Yeates, Engineer-Commander F. E., R.N., Radland, St. Dominick,
Cornwall.

The Hon. Secretary (c/o The Library, Admiralty, S.W. 1) will be obliged if members will communicate any change of address.

* Original Members (1893).
† Addresses of Officers serving in His Majesty's ships have been omitted.

Printed in England at THE BALLANTYNE PRESS
SPOTTISWOODE, BALLANTYNE & CO. LTD.
Colchester, London & Eton